Advanced English Practice

Second Edition

B. D. GRAVER

Advanced English Practice

Second Edition

With Key

Oxford University Press

Oxford University Press, Walton Street, Oxford OX2 6DP

OXFORD LONDON GLASGOW
NEW YORK TORONTO MELBOURNE WELLINGTON
KUALA LUMPUR SINGAPORE JAKARTA HONG KONG TOKYO
DELHI BOMBAY CALCUTTA MADRAS KARACHI
IBADAN NAIROBI DAR ES SALAAM CAPE TOWN

ISBN 0 19 432190 8

© *Oxford University Press 1963, 1971*
First edition published 1963
Second edition 1971
Ninth impression 1979

The author and publisher are grateful to the Times
Newspapers Limited, Her Majesty's Stationery Office
and the University of Cambridge Local Examinations
Syndicate for permission to reproduce short extracts
which appear in the exercises in Section One.

Printed in Great Britain by
Richard Clay (The Chaucer Press) Ltd
Bungay, Suffolk

Contents

SECTION THREE: VOCABULARY WORK

SECTION FOUR: COMPOSITION WORK

General Introduction

The aim of this new edition of *Advanced English Practice* remains the same as that of the original edition: to provide a variety of language material for foreign students at advanced level, either preparing for the Cambridge Certificate of Proficiency or working at equivalent levels in universities and colleges.

While it has been assumed that students will already have completed a course of basic instruction up to Cambridge First Certificate level, the book provides ample material for consolidating the student's grasp of fundamentals and for revising those structures that students constantly have difficulty in mastering, before proceeding to a more mature examination of structure and vocabulary.

At the same time, an attempt has been made to go beyond the simpler 'space-filling' type of language drill and, wherever possible, to place the responsibility for construction squarely on the student's shoulders. There is, therefore, some emphasis on exercises in 'free completion', where the student is asked to supply not just one word (relative pronoun, gerund, preposition, etc.), but a phrase or clause incorporating the word. The student thus creates sentences of his own within a given setting, which enables him to practise different skills as naturally as possible and, in addition, gives him a more positive appreciation of the structures he is practising. Exercises of a more familiar type have, however, been included to help give a sense of continuity to students when first embarking on a Proficiency course.

Exercises of the 'free completion' type can perhaps be practised most profitably through written exercises, but there is much to be said for more written work in class at this stage in the student's language learning, and it will be found that, in this way, each student makes a greater contribution to the collective progress of the class. One other practical advantage afforded is that such exercises may more easily be repeated at intervals for revision, the growing mastery and maturity of the student being reflected in the quality of the sentences he produces. The instruction *Rewrite* is, however, sometimes used simply for convenience, and does not necessarily mean that an exercise cannot or should not be done orally.

The preparation of this new edition has made possible the

addition of new exercise material on modal auxiliary verbs and the various verb tenses, as well as the revision, re-grading, and expansion of existing material (especially in Section One—*The Fundamentals of Grammar*). It is hoped that the book will now be not only more generally useful but also easier to use. At the same time, I have been able to make provision for the needs of students who may be working alone, and also for those of both the student and the non-English teacher who may not have ready access to reference books. Section One is now liberally annotated, incorporating both new material and also notes that were formerly given separately in appendices. The Appendix *Notes on Clauses* has been retained in a revised form, and may be found useful for the work in Section Two of the book. A list of reference books is given on pages xvii–xviii. A key has been provided in this edition, though the book is also available without.

I should like to thank Professor F. R. Palmer for reading the manuscript of this edition and for his helpful comments towards its improvement.

Notes for the Teacher

The more general aims of the book have been set out above, but teachers may find useful a few more specific observations on the arrangement of material and some suggestions on how it may best be used.

Sections One, Three, and Four may be used simultaneously, the composition work serving both as a reflector of the student's progress in his mastery of syntax and grasp of vocabulary, and also as an indicator of what aspects of the language need further study. The material in Section Two should be left until later in the course, and in any case until a good deal of the work in Section One has been completed.

Section One

The material has been arranged under subject-headings, and the teacher should feel free to start on any of these subjects, according to the current needs of his students. The exercises on each particular subject are, however, graded, and it is inadvisable to work uninterruptedly through all of them; at the beginning of the student's course, only the first few under each subject-heading should be used; students may later go on to the more searching exercises in each subject, while the most difficult ones of all should be attempted only towards the end of their course. It is assumed that no teacher would, in any case, work through all the exercises on, for example, modal auxiliary verbs simply because they are grouped together for convenience.

Teachers will, moreover, find that grammatical points dealt with in one exercise may also be embodied in another under a different subject-heading. A knowledge of inversion techniques or of the gerund, for instance, will be required in the later exercises in the use of the passive, as it would be unnecessarily artificial, especially in the more advanced exercises in any one subject, rigorously to exclude structures that have a natural place in the practice material.

This section is liberally provided with notes, and is intended to serve as a reference book as well as a source of practice material. The contents of this section are listed in detail on pages v–viii, so that teachers and students can refer to any item that currently needs practice, and find both explanation and exercises. The notes precede the relevant exercises, but this does not mean that the teacher should either read the notes in class, or give the explanations, before doing the exercises. (It is, however, advisable for the teacher or the student working alone to read them for himself, since the exercises follow closely the approach adopted in the notes.)

Whenever dealing with a structure that is characteristic of spoken English, the teacher should devise a suitable oral presentation of his own, so that structures can be presented situationally. Some of the exercises are presented through question and answer and may themselves suggest further suitable lines of approach. Teachers will find many useful ideas in the four volumes of A. S. Hornby's *The Teaching of Structural Words and Sentence Patterns* (Oxford University Press).

Explanation (and discussion) has its place, however, especially with advanced students. It can be an aid to motivation with students who need to be given the opportunity to use their capacity and inclination for theoretical understanding, and it reassures some students if they can grasp a linguistic feature intellectually. The notes try to deal with some difficult theoretical problems, minor as well as major ones, and attempt to answer some of the awkward questions that advanced students are apt to ask. Of course, teachers will know, and students should bear in mind, that there is no substitute for practice itself.

Students at advanced level should, in any case, be encouraged to develop a healthy scepticism of 'rules' until they have had an opportunity to measure them against the facts of English as they find it. Research projects are a valuable aid in developing the student's critical awareness of what English is really like. Provided the teacher gives the necessary framework for investigation, students can be asked to examine modern written English of various registers and styles, with a view to finding out, say, how often the passive is used and whether or not the 'agent' is expressed; or how relative clauses are used, what pattern of choice emerges between the various pronouns, when pronouns are expressed and when omitted, etc. Given the necessary help, students can discover and build up their own grammar of English, in however limited a way.

Section Two

The material in this section, unlike that in Sections One and

Three, should be used systematically throughout. The exercises in synthesis (or controlled composition) have been given a place for two reasons: not only is a knowledge of the technique required by some examiners, but, what is more important, students need guidance in what they will inevitably attempt: the expression of connected ideas in complex sentences. Students should always, of course, be encouraged to write within their limitations, but the cult of writing in short sentences doesn't always lead to the most natural mode of expression, and students should be shown that a complex sentence isn't necessarily a complicated one. An attempt has been made to add interest to the exercises by incorporating some facts about England and the English.

Section Three

The material may be used in a variety of ways. Many of the exercises will be found more effective if they are first given as homework and then discussed in class. Some may be used to form the basis of regular sessions in class in the use of an English dictionary. Others will be found suitable for oral practice. The teacher is left a free hand in using the material in a way that best answers the needs of his students.

Students should be encouraged to read English newspapers and to listen to the radio or to watch television as an adjunct to the work they do in school, and wherever possible one or two hours of class time should be set aside each week for newspaper study. Though this may present a difficulty for students studying abroad, it is particularly valuable for them, since they lack the advantage of an English environment as an aid to their studies. It will also be found especially useful by the foreign teacher of English, who can in this way broaden the scope of lessons and introduce students to more colloquial forms of the language. Teachers will find the annual publication *Britain—An Official Handbook* (HMSO) useful as a reference book on many aspects of British life and institutions, and students may be referred to this book where the relevant material under the subject-heading 'General Knowledge' is unfamiliar to them.

Section Four

It is, finally, through composition work that teachers can best measure the overall achievement of a student at any particular stage in his language learning. (This is not intended to be a claim for composition as a means of objective testing.) While it has been left to the teacher to instruct students in essay-writing techniques (since this lies outside the scope of this book), some exercises leading up to the full-scale essay are included at the beginning of this section. Many students find composition work unfamiliar or difficult, and the earlier exercises should help, partly in that they are limited in scope, and partly in that they demand a simple descriptive technique.

The exercises in arguments 'for' and 'against' should provide a link between the simple descriptive paragraphs and the full-scale essay. Class discussion of essay subjects can do much, under the guidance of the teacher, to prompt a wider view of the topics to be treated. The first set of composition subjects consists of those making fewer demands on the students in regard to both subject and length. The subjects in the second set should provide the basis of composition work for students in the later part of a Proficiency course.

Select Lists of Books for Reference and Further Study

It is difficult to make a fair selection from the ever-increasing wealth of material available to both teachers and students. The following selection necessarily represents a personal choice, but one which I hope may be useful to teachers who lack the facilities for examining a large range of books at first hand.

Many of the books have been published or reprinted in recent years, and should be fairly readily obtainable. Publishers will, in any case, always welcome enquiries from teachers, and send up-to-date catalogues on request. Books marked with an asterisk are suitable for study or reference by advanced students. One book that all advanced students would do well to possess is an English dictionary designed for foreign students.

List A (Grammar and Usage, and Dictionaries)

*BALL, W. J. *A Practical Guide to Colloquial Idiom* (Longman)

*CLOSE, R. A. *English as a Foreign Language* (Allen & Unwin)

*CLOSE, R. A. *A Reference Grammar for Students of English* (Longman)

*COWIE, A. P. and MACKIN, R. *Oxford Dictionary of Current Idiomatic English*, Vol. I (Oxford)

*HORNBY, A. S. *Guide to Patterns and Usage in English* (Oxford)

*HORNBY, A. S. *Oxford Advanced Learner's Dictionary of Current English* (Oxford)

HORNBY, A. S. *Oxford Student's Dictionary of Current English* (Oxford)

JOOS, M. *The English Verb—Form and Meanings* (University of Wisconsin Press)

*LEECH, G. and SVARTVIK, J. *A Communicative Grammar of English* (Longman)

Longman Dictionary of Contemporary English (Longman)

PALMER, F. R. *The English Verb* (Longman)

QUIRK, R., GREENBAUM, S., LEECH, G., and SVARTVIK, J. *A Grammar of Contemporary English* (Longman)

*QUIRK, R. and GREENBAUM, S. *A University Grammar of English* (Longman)

SCHEUERWEGHS, G. *Present-day English Syntax* (Longman)

STRANG, B. M. H. *Modern English Structure* (Arnold)

*THOMSON, A. J. and MARTINET, A. V. *A Practical English Grammar* (Oxford)

TWADDELL, W. F. *The English Verb Auxiliaries* (Brown University Press)
*WOOD, F. T. *Current English Usage* (Macmillan)

List B (Teaching problems and procedures)

ABERCROMBIE, D. *Problems and Principles in Language Study* (Longman)
HALLIDAY, M. A. K., MCINTOSH, A., and STREVENS, P. D. *The Linguistic Sciences and Language Teaching* (Longman)
HILL, L. A. *Selected Articles on the Teaching of English as a Foreign Language* (Oxford)
HORNBY, A. S. *The Teaching of Structural Words and Sentence Patterns*, Stages 1–4 (Oxford)
LEE, W. R. (Ed.) *English Language Teaching Journal*[1] (published quarterly by Oxford University Press in association with the British Council)
LEE, W. R. (Ed.) *ELT Selections 1* and *ELT Selections 2* (Oxford)
MACKEY, W. F. *Language Teaching Analysis* (Longman)
QUIRK, R. and SMITH, A. H. (Ed.) *The Teaching of English* (Oxford)
STREVENS, Peter *New Orientations in the Teaching of English* (Oxford)

List C (General; and background reading)

Britain—An Official Handbook (published annually by Her Majesty's Stationery Office)
*BROMHEAD, P. *Life in Modern Britain* (Longman)
GIMSON, A. C. *An Introduction to the Pronunciation of English* (Arnold)
LEECH, Geoffrey *Semantics* (Penguin)
O'CONNOR, J. D. *Better English Pronunciation* (Cambridge)
O'CONNOR, J. D. *Phonetics* (Penguin)
PALMER, Frank *Grammar* (Penguin)
*POTTER, S. *Our Language* (Penguin)
*QUIRK, R. *The Use of English* (Longman)
ROBINS, R. H. *General Linguistics—An Introductory Survey* (Longman)
*STREVENS, Peter *British and American English* (Collier-Macmillan)

---

[1] Teachers will find this publication especially useful: it keeps one up to date on current linguistic theory, presents the results of recent research on grammatical and other features of English, discusses a variety of classroom problems and procedures, and reviews a selection of recently published books.

SECTION ONE
THE FUNDAMENTALS OF GRAMMAR

General review of tenses and verb forms[1]

1 Write out the sentences, using the most logical tense or form of the verbs in brackets. The words in italics should be put in their correct position in relation to the verb.

1 Hello! I (try) to telephone you all week. Where you (be)?
2 'I don't think we (meet) before?' 'Well, I (see) you once at a party, but we *not* (be) introduced then.'
3 It (look) as if this light (burn) all night. I must (forget) (switch) it off before I (go) to bed last night.
4 Come in now. I'm sorry (keep) you (wait) so long.
5 I (buy) the book, but when I (hear) the opinion of the critics, I (change) my mind.
6 At last you're here! I (wait) here for more than half an hour. I might (know) you (be) late!
7 My father (work) in Canada for the last year, so by the time he (return) the month after next I *not* (see) him for fourteen months.
8 When you (see) him again you (be struck) by the way his health (improve) since he (go) to Switzerland.
9 If you (tell) me you *already* (buy) the book, I *not* (give) it to you as a birthday present, but now it (be) too late.
10 I (ring) the bell once more, but as he *not* (answer) yet, I think he must (go) out. I *not* (bother) (come) all this way if I (know).
11 It's just as well we (bring) a guide-book with us. If we *not* (have), we (be) completely lost.
12 You can't (remember) (tell) him how to get here. If you (have), he (arrive) long before now.

2 Instructions as above

1 By the time the firemen (arrive), the house (be) ablaze from top to bottom, but it (be) clear that if someone (give) the alarm

[1] These exercises may be used as a preliminary test of the student's grasp of the language. They incorporate many points of grammar that are dealt with more fully in later exercises.

1

earlier, they might (stand) a chance of (save) the building.

2 I wish you (tell) me last week that you (come) to London. If I (know) in time, you *not* (have to) stay in a hotel.

3 Why you *not* (tell) me you (can) lend me the money? I *not* (need) (borrow) it from the bank.

4 The driver said he *not* (can) (understand) why the car (break down) during the race. It (undergo) thorough testing before (be) entered in the competition.

5 It's time we (go). If we *not* (leave) now, we (miss) the last train.

6 (Be) you cut off while I (talk) to you just now? You (be)? I think something must (go) wrong with the telephone.

7 The manager (talk) to an important customer at the moment but he (be) free (see) you presently. (Like) you (take) a seat for a few minutes?

8 I know I ought (write) to you before, but I (be) so busy recently that I *not* (have) time for (write) letters. I (telephone) you instead, but I (forget) your number.

9 When I last (see) him, he (live) in London. He (tell) me then that he (think) of (emigrate) to Australia, and he may *well* (do) so by now.

10 I (be) very excited at the prospect of (go) (ski). It (be) the first time I (try). I think there's nothing like (ski) for (make) a holiday enjoyable.

11 I wish you (let) me (know) you *not* (be able) to come to dinner. I *certainly not* (go) to all this trouble if I (know).

12 He said he *not* (want) (see) the film as he (hear) that it (be) not as good as the critics (suggest).

3 Instructions as above.

1 It's a great pity you *not* (come) to Brighton with us last Saturday. As you *never* (see) the sea before, it (be) a new experience for you.

2 By the time I (complete) my studies next month, I (live) in London for nearly a year. I *not* (think) I (stay) any longer after that.

3 It's odd that you (mention) his name. I *just* (think) about him and (wonder) what (become) of him.

4 I *not* (call) on him just yet if I (be) you, as I don't think he (get) home from work.

5 He said he (wish) he (be able) (see) you before he (leave). He

(like) (say) goodbye personally. He (hope) you (accept) his apologies.

6 (Be) you sure there (be) no one in the room next door? I (can swear) I heard someone (talk) in there.

7 'Mr Smith *not* (work) here for four years. (Be) you sure you (get) the right name?' 'Quite sure. He (ring) me only yesterday, and I *certainly not* (come) here if he *not* (ask) me to.'

8 Not until we (arrive) at his house we (discover) that he (be) on holiday, and that we (waste) our time in (call) on him.

9 It *not* (take) very long (get) here after all. We *not* (need) (take) a taxi. We could (save) the money we (spend) and (have) dinner on the train.

10 It's high time you (make) up your mind about (choose) a career. If you *not* (decide) soon, you *never* (settle) down to anything.

11 The blackmailer *not* (realize) that the police (be informed) of his activities, and that his victim (be asked) (go on) (talk) to him while the call (be traced).

12 You *hardly* (believe) it, but that (be) the third time tonight someone (telephone) me and then (apologize) for (get) the wrong number. The next time the phone (ring) I *not* (answer).

Modal auxiliary verbs

Introductory notes

There are only twelve modal auxiliary verbs, but they are used with very great frequency and in a wide range of meanings. They express concepts or attitudes relating to recommendation, obligation, necessity, and prohibition; permission and refusal; possibility, expectation, probability and certainty; promise and intention; ability and willingness.

The set of twelve verbs consists of four paired forms—*can, could*; *may, might*; *shall, should*; *will, would*; and four single forms —*must, ought, need, dare*. There are no other forms, and all modals are therefore, to varying degrees, 'defective' verbs. The two verbs *need* and *dare* present special problems: *dare* can follow the grammatical patterns of either modal auxiliaries or lexical, 'regular' verbs, while *need* contrasts grammatically with the regular verb *to need*.

The grammatical (or 'formal') contrast between modals and regular verbs is perhaps best illustrated and summarized in sentences with question tags:

– – – –	*can* *may* *need* *dare*	NOT	go,	*can* *may* *need* *dare*
	ought		to go,	*ought*
doesN'T	*want* *like* *need* *dare*	—	to go,	*does*

He ———————————————————————————— he?

The principal distinctive formal features of modal verbs are, explicitly:

a. negative sentences are formed by adding *not* after the modal verb;[1]

b. interrogative sentences are formed by inverting the subject and the modal verb;[1]

c. there is no -*s* ending in the third person singular in the present tense, as there is with regular verbs (*he* wants, likes, etc.);

d. the modal verbs are followed by the infinitive of a verb without *to* (except in the case of *ought*).

All these features contribute to the distinction between the two grammatical patterns of *dare*, and between the modal verb *need* and the regular verb *to need*:

Regular	*Modal*
He dares / needs to go.	—
He *doesn't* dare / need to go	He dare / need *not* go.
Does he dare / need to go?	*Dare / Need* he go?

Note that the modal verb *need*, and *dare* in its modal pattern, are used only in negative and interrogative sentences.

[1] This feature is, of course, common to *all* auxiliary verbs.

The modal verbs (including *dare* and *need* as modals) have no infinitive form, and no participle forms. Hence the need on occasion for a number of more or less synonymous expressions having a fuller range of forms—*be able to*, or *have to*, for example. It would not be possible to use *can* or *must* in the following:

I'd like *to be able* to speak English fluently. (infinitive)
No one *has been able* to solve the problem. (present perfect)
I'*m having to* read this very carefully. (present continuous)

The modal verbs are also limited in their range of time reference. When used with the 'present' infinitive of the main verb, they generally have a present or future time reference:

He
can *or* could
may *or* might
will *or* would help you e.g. immediately, later
shall *or* should
　　must
　　ought to

The use of the alternatives *could, might, would, should,* suggests a more tentative attitude on the part of the speaker. In requests, it represents what is commonly called the 'polite' form: 'Would (*or* Could) you help me?' This particular use of *could, might, would, should,* is consistent with their appearance in either of two forms of conditional sentences (though there may, of course, be slight differences in meaning between the two versions):

I think he
could
might
would help you if you
should

tell
told him your problem.

It is misleading to regard *could* as the equivalent in past *time* of *can*, *might* as the equivalent of *may*, etc. Of the four past tense forms (*could, might, would, should*), only the first three are used to refer to past *time* when followed by a present infinitive, and then only within a restricted range of meanings:[1]

He *could* speak several languages by the time he was ten.
He was very independent, and *would* never ask for help.
Try as he *might*, he *couldn't* get the car to start.

[1] See tables I and II on page 7.

5

The use of the four past tense forms is, however, automatic in sequence of tenses in reported speech:[1]

‘He
| can *or* could |
| may *or* might |
| will *or* would |
| shall *or* should |
tell me.’ = I said he
| could |
| might |
| would |
| should |
tell me.

The four single forms *must, ought to, dare, need*, may be left un-changed in reported speech:

‘He oughtn’t to tell anyone.’ = I said he oughtn’t to tell
| mustn't |
| daren't |
| needn't |
| mustn't |
| daren't | anyone |
| needn't |

We cannot, of course, use *must, needn't* or *ought to* with a present infinitive to refer to a time earlier than the time of speaking.[2] It is impossible to say:

*I
| must |
| needn't |
| ought to |
do it yesterday.

However, in the reported speech examples given above, these verbs do *not* refer to a time earlier than the time of speaking. In the statement ‘You mustn't tell anyone’, the obligation (not to tell any-one) exists from the time when it is expressed, i.e. from now on-wards. Similarly, in the report *I said he mustn't tell anyone*, the obligation (not to tell anyone) existed from the time when it was expressed, i.e. from then onwards, and not at some earlier time.

At this point, it is important to recognize a distinction between two uses of modal verbs, as illustrated in tables I and II below. In table I, the modal verbs are all used to assert various degrees of likelihood regarding the truth of the statement (It's certain,

[1] It is important to understand that the term ‘past tense’ is essentially only a convenient label for a particular form of a verb. *Tense* and *time* are not always synonymous terms in English, and although a past tense often refers to the chronological past, it does not *necessarily* do so. The past tenses of both modal and other verbs are frequently used with a present or future time reference, especially in ‘tentative’ or ‘unreal’ conditional sentences:

I *could* come tomorrow, if that's convenient. (future)
If you *came* at ten tomorrow, you'd probably find him in. (future)
If I *knew* how it *worked*, I *could* tell him what to do. (present)

[2] *Dare* is perhaps unique, in that we can say:

I didn't dare (to)
or I daren't   mention it to him yesterday.
or I dared not

probable, possible, etc., that this is true), whereas in table II, the modal verbs are used to refer to ability, duty, willingness, permission, etc., in relation to the subject:

	must		*logical conclusion*
	can't/couldn't		*logical conclusion*
I. He	will/would	be there already.	*belief*
	may/might		*possibility*
	could		*possibility*
	should/ought to		*probability*

	must		*obligation*
	needn't		*absence of obligation*
	should/ought to		*recommendation*
II. He	shall	go immediately.	*promise*
	will		*willingness*
	may		*permission*
	can		*ability or permission*

We can extend the range of time reference of the modal verbs as used in table I and refer to past time by using the 'perfect' infinitive of the main verb, as in table Ia:

	must	
	can't/couldn't	
Ia. He	will/would	have been there yesterday.
	may/might	
	could	
	should/ought to	

The use of the perfect infinitive in such cases generally refers to 'real' past: it does not usually affect the truth of the statement, and in only a limited number of contexts can it indicate 'unreal' past (i.e. contrary to past fact). Note also that it is possible to use the present tenses *can, will, may,* with the perfect infinitive, to refer to past time.

If we wish to refer to 'real' past time with the modal verbs as used in table II, we either use the past tense of the modal verbs, if appropriate (and if available), or we use a synonymous verb phrase (*had to, didn't need to, was able to, was permitted to,* etc.). If the modal verbs as used in table II are followed by a perfect infinitive, they always indicate 'unreal' past:

7

```
                 needn't
                 should/ought to
He would                          have gone yesterday.
                 might
                 could
```

At this stage, however, the problem of usage and meaning becomes more complex, and this will be discussed and practised, together with other aspects of the contextual use (i.e. the 'meaning') of modal verbs in general, in the notes and exercises that follow. The modal verbs in their various applications are assigned to use I or use II as illustrated above.

Ability or potential (II): can, could, be able to

Can is used to indicate (1) the possession of ability in general, or (2) being in a position, in particular circumstances, to perform the activity denoted by the main verb:

 1 He can speak German fluently.
 2 I can (*or* could[1]) give him an answer, e.g. now, later, tomorrow.

In sentence *1*, *can* forms part of a statement having general current validity, whereas in *2*, it refers to an ability existing in certain circumstances at the present or future time indicated. It is important to recognize this distinction between ability in general, and ability in specific circumstances. It is also important to note that both sentences refer to a *potential* performance of the action mentioned (speaking, giving), not to an *actual* performance.

 1a He could speak German fluently, e.g. when he was younger.

This sentence represents a situation in the chronological past parallel to that in sentence *1*. It refers to the possession of the ability to speak German, not to an actual performance of speaking.

 2a I could have given him an answer, e.g. yesterday.

[1] *Could* functions here as the 'tentative' form of *can*, and may relate to a conditional idea:
    I could give him an answer tomorrow e.g. if he wants (*or* wanted) one.
In tentative or conditional statements, *could* + present infinitive always refers to present or future time. See Exercise 6.

8

This is the exact parallel in past time of sentence *2*, and means 'I was in a position to give him an answer' (ability in specific circumstances at a specific time). Again, it does *not* refer to an actual performance; indeed, it implies that I did not give him an answer. Such sentences suggest a conditional idea:

I could have given him an answer e.g. if he had asked me.

If we wish to refer to an *actual* performance, we use a form of *be able to*, as in sentence *2b* below:

2b I was able to give him an answer, e.g. yesterday.

3 I $\frac{\text{can see}}{\text{could hear}}$ quite clearly what you $\frac{\text{are doing}}{\text{were saying}}$.

Verbs like *see*, *hear*, *understand*, etc., come into a special category. The ability to see and the performance of seeing are inseparable (I can see = *I am seeing, I could see = *I was seeing)[1], and in this case the use of *could* is possible when referring to an actual performance in past time.

The negative form *couldn't* necessarily implies non-performance of an action, and may always be used to refer to past time:

4 He can't speak German fluently.
4a He couldn't speak German fluently, e.g. when I knew him.
5 I can't give him an answer, e.g. right now.
5a I couldn't give him an answer, e.g. yesterday.

In all the examples so far, we could substitute a form of *be able to* for *can* or *could*, but we tend to use the latter (shorter) forms where possible.

4 Rewrite the sentences, using the adverbs suggested, so that they refer to a parallel situation in past time (i.e. potential, not actual, performance). Any words in italics should be omitted in your answers.

a. He can speak German fluently. (when he was younger)
He could speak German fluently when he was younger.
b. I can give him an answer. (last week)
I could have given him an answer last week.

[1] We do not, of course, normally use these verbs in the continuous form.

1 He can drive a car. (when he was eighteen)
2 I find I can understand English better than I can speak it. (when I first arrived in England)
3 I can let you have the money *tomorrow*. (yesterday)
4 You can persuade him to come, if anyone can. (last week)
5 My daughter can play the piano beautifully. (at one time)
6 You can see that he is bored to death. (at the party last night)
7 I can't get into the house. (because I had forgotten my key)
8 We can overhear every word our neighbours say. (in the hotel we stayed at)
9 The doctor can see you *later today*. (yesterday)
10 (When they asked my advice) I can suggest only one way of solving the problem.
11 I can well understand how you feel about the situation. (at the time)
12 I can't get the letter translated immediately, but I could get it done *by tomorrow morning*. (by the following morning)

As we have seen, *can* may be used with a future time reference ('I can see you tomorrow'), but in this case the ability is more or less taken for granted now and is not really in question. In cases where ability will exist only eventually, or where it is dependent on some other event in the future, we use *be able* with *will* ('*ll*) or *shall*:[1]

> By the time he finishes his course, he'*ll be able to* speak English well.

We also use *be able* when we wish to indicate that an action was in fact performed in the past:

> After looking at his notes again, he *was able to* complete the exercise.

Since *can* and *could* lack infinitive and participle forms, we use *be able* where an infinitive or a 'perfect' form is required (*be able* is not used in the continuous form):

> Ask that policeman over there. He should (*or* ought to) *be able to* help you.
> This is all the information I'*ve been able to* get so far.

[1] Compare this with the notes on *must*, page 34.

5 Replace the words in italics with a suitable form of *be able to*. (NB *not to be able to = to be unable to*)

1 If we don't book seats soon, *it won't be possible for us to* get into the theatre.
2 In two months' time, we *shall be in a position to* give you the examination results.
3 The main road was under repair, but *it was possible for us to* take an alternative route.
4 By pretending to be ignorant of the rules, he *managed to* escape being punished.
5 Luckily, we retraced our steps and *succeeded in finding* our way again.
6 *It has been impossible for me to* get to the bank yet, so I haven't any money.
7 May I borrow this piece of material? I'd like *to have the opportunity of showing* it to my wife.
8 He took a 'crash' course in Spanish—he wanted *to be in a position to* speak it when he went on business to S. America.
9 They bought their first house last year: previously, *it had been impossible for them to* get a loan.
10 They went to see their MP, taking with them a petition for which they *had managed to* get 25,000 signatures.

When *could* (+ *present infinitive*) is used as the tentative form of *can*, it has a present or future time reference (see footnote on page 8):

a. I could do it for you now if you like.
b. I can't do it immediately, but I could do it tomorrow morning.

The reported version of sentence *b* is:

> I told him I couldn't do it immediately, but that I could do it the following morning.

In conditional sentences, *could* very often represents the 'unreal' present:

> If I knew how it worked, I could tell him what to do. (= but I don't know, so I can't tell him)

The equivalent form of *be able* in this case is *would be able* (not, of course, *was able*).

11

In a conditional sentence, *could* + *perfect infinitive* expresses unreal past:

> If I had known how it worked, I could have told him what to do. (= but I didn't know, so I couldn't tell him)

6 Complete the sentences, using *could* + *present* or *perfect infinitive*.

1 If the teacher spoke a little more slowly, . . .
2 If the roads weren't so icy, . . .
3 If you didn't live so far away, . . .
4 . . . if I weren't so busy.
5 If the traffic hadn't been so heavy, . . .
6 . . . if you had let me know earlier.
7 If we had a bit more time, . . .
8 . . . if we had had a bit more time.
9 If we had the right materials for the job, . . .
10 . . . if we had had the right materials for the job.

7 When you have checked your answers to the last exercise, re-write your answers, replacing *could* by a suitable form of *be able*.

General characteristics (II): can, could

Can and *could* are also used to refer to a general characteristic or quality that may show itself from time to time:

> A house in London can cost a lot of money.
> He could be very unpleasant when he was angry.

Neither of these sentences refers to an actual occurrence of the phenomena referred to, and *be able* is not used as a substitute for *can* or *could* in such sentences.

8 Replace the words in italics, using *can* or *could* together with the words given in brackets, e.g.
> Learning a foreign language *isn't always easy*. (sometimes difficult)
> Learning a foreign language *can sometimes be difficult*.

1 She *doesn't always remember everything*. (quite forgetful)
2 Holidays abroad *aren't necessarily expensive*. (quite cheap)
3 Racial harmony *isn't always easy* to achieve. (difficult)

4 When I was at school, discipline *wasn't generally lax.* (very strict)
5 He *wasn't miserable all the time.* (occasionally, quite gay)
6 September *isn't by any means a bad* month for taking a holiday in England. (wonderful)
7 Students at university *don't always approve* of the way their courses are run. (very critical)
8 The English method of numbering houses *isn't always as clear as it might be* for a stranger. (very confusing)
9 She *doesn't always* look *so plain.* (quite pretty at times)
10 English cooking *isn't necessarily bad.* (in fact, excellent)

Possibility (I) and permission (II): can, could, may, might

Note: At this point, we meet one of the features of modal verbs that often causes difficulty: many modal verbs have more than one meaning or use, and in some cases two different modal verbs have some meanings or uses in common, but are not completely interchangeable. The situation may be compared to that of two countries with a common frontier: at the meeting point of the two countries, two different languages may be equally acceptable or valid; but as one travels away from the frontier in one direction or the other, only one language or another will be usable.

For practical purposes, students need learn only the more important distinctions. A fuller description may be found in the reference books listed at the beginning of this book.

1 A fuller description can/may be found in the reference books listed at the beginning of this book.

In this sentence, *can* and *may* are fully interchangeable, *may* being a little more formal.

2 Agreement between management and unions *may* be reached tomorrow.

Assuming we wish to state a possibility rather than a fact, only *may* is appropriate in this sentence, which means 'It is possible that agreement will be reached'. The distinction between sentences *1* and *2* may be paraphrased as:

(1) It is possible for this to be done at any time (= statement of present *fact*)

13

(2) It is possible that this will be done (= statement of future *possibility*)

Might represents the tentative form of *may* as used in sentence 2:

>   may
> 3a I might be wrong, of course. (present)
>   could

>   may
> 3b The two parties might reach agreement tomorrow. (future)
>   could

Could (often stressed) is quite commonly used as an alternative to tentative *might*, as in *3a* and *3b*.

Could is not used in this way, however, in affirmative negative sentences:

> 4a They *may* (or *might*) not reach agreement tomorrow.
> 4b They *could* not reach agreement tomorrow.

These sentences have quite different meanings, and the reason for this lies in the way the negative particle *not* operates. In affirmative sentences with *may* or *might* (in the sense of possibility), *not* goes with the main verb:

> They may/might *not reach* agreement tomorrow
> = It *is possible* that they *will NOT reach* agreement.

With *could*, however, *not* goes with the modal (unless we use a very special stress and intonation pattern):

> They *could not* reach agreement tomorrow.
> = It is NOT *possible* that they *will reach* agreement.

In this sentence, moreover, *could* operates in a conditional context: 'They could not reach agreement tomorrow, e.g. even if they sat talking all day.'

9 Replace the words in italics with a clause using *may*, *might*, or *could*, as in sentences *3* and *4a* above. (Note that all the sentences refer to present or future possibility.)

1 *Perhaps* you *will find* you have made a mistake.
2 *It is just conceivable that* we *shall* get an answer tomorrow.

3 Accept his offer now. *It is just possible that* he *will* change his mind later.

4 Owing to the strike, trains *will possibly* be subject to delays.

5 *It is possible that* parents *will* find that they cannot understand the new teaching methods being introduced in primary schools.

6 We *shall possibly* find we can't get accommodation, as we haven't booked rooms.

7 Ask your bank manager. He *will perhaps* be able to advise you better than I can.

8 Let's not wait any longer. *It's possible that* he *won't* turn up at all.

9 *It is not impossible that* the Government's policy *will* prove to be little short of disastrous.

10 *It is quite possible that* getting the two sides to agree *will* not be as easy as some people imagine.

In the last exercise, *might* and *could* represented the tentative form corresponding to *may*. They did not refer to past time, but to present or future. To refer to past time, we use *may*, *might*, or *could* with a perfect infinitive:

> No statement was issued after yesterday's talks, but it is thought that the two parties *may have reached* agreement. (= It is possible that they reached agreement)

Might and *could* suggest that the possibility is a little more remote:

> The two parties *might/could* have reached agreement.

This sentence, however, is potentially ambiguous, and only the context or situation will make clear which of the following meanings is intended:

a. It is just possible that the two parties reached agreement. (but we don't actually know whether they did or not)

or, in a conditional context:

b. The two parties might/could have reached agreement, e.g. if they had been prepared to be more flexible. (but we know they didn't in fact reach agreement)

10 Respond to the statements or questions with a sentence suggesting a possible explanation, using *may*, *might*, or *could* + the *perfect infinitive* of the verbs given, e.g.

Why isn't he here? (may, miss)
He may have missed the train.

1 No one is waiting at the bus stop. (may, miss)
2 He didn't come to the party last night. (might, not want)
3 No one has answered the door. (might, go out)
4 How on earth did the thief get in? (could, break)
5 Why didn't the teacher explain? (may, not know)
6 How did they know about our plans? (could, guess)
7 He didn't seem surprised when I told him. (may, already know)
8 They should have been here long before now. (may, lose)
9 I haven't seen my neighbours for over a week. (may, go)
10 Why hasn't she written to me? (could, forget)
11 I can't understand why he didn't look me up while he was down here. (may, not have)
12 It's strange that he hasn't said any more about his plans to emigrate. (might, change)

Giving permission, we use *can* or *may*, though the latter is generally considered more formal:

    1 You can/may speak to the patient for just a few minutes e.g. now, later, tomorrow.

Asking for permission, we use *can* or *may*; asking tentatively ('politely'), we use *could* or *might*:

    2 Can/May   Could/Might   I speak to you for a moment?

In the reported version of sentence *1*, we use *could* or *might*:

    3 The nurse said we could/might speak to the patient for just a few minutes.

We do not, however, use *could* or *might* + *present infinitive* to refer to permission given in past time. We are obliged to use a paraphrase:

    4 We had (*or* were given) permission to speak to the patient.

Since we were given permission, we presumably acted on it and spoke to the patient. *Could* and *might* + *perfect infinitive* suggest that permission existed but wasn't acted on, perhaps because of ignorance on the part of the subject:

    5 You could/might have come yesterday e.g. if you had wanted to.

16

11 Rewrite the statements and questions in reported speech.

1 'You may leave work early this evening if you want to,' the manager told me.
2 'You can put off making a decision for a week, but no longer,' his interviewer told him.
3 'Could I see your passports, please?' the Customs officer asked us.
4 'May I ask you a rather personal question?' the teacher asked the student.
5 'You can borrow my notes provided you take care of them,' I told my friend.
6 'Might I see that photograph you're holding?' the police inspector asked his colleague.
7 'Cars may be parked at the rear of the building,' the notice stated.
8 'Might I interrupt you for a moment?' the chairman asked the speaker politely.
9 'May I join you?' he asked his friend.
10 'The travel allowance may not be used for any form of capital expenditure or investment outside the Sterling Area,' the regulations stated.

Other uses of 'may' and 'might'

May is often used in clauses with a concessive meaning (I):

Your job may be very demanding, *but* at least it isn't boring.
= *Although* (I am prepared to admit that) your job is very demanding, at least it isn't boring.

May + perfect infinitive is used for referring to past time:

The work may have been difficult, but at least it was interesting.

12 Rewrite the sentences, using *may* as in the examples above.

1 Although the restaurant is expensive, the cuisine is excellent.
2 Although the method is crude, it's certainly effective.
3 Although he is badly paid, his work is very rewarding.
4 Although the book is long, you could hardly call it boring.
5 Although he is old, he isn't by any means senile.
6 Although the climb was exhausting, the view from the top made it well worth while.

17

7 Although I was rude to him, I feel he had given me every justification.
8 Although he acted unwisely, he was at least trying to do something constructive.
9 Although his work has improved, it still isn't good enough.
10 Although old-age pensions have risen considerably, they haven't kept pace with the cost of living.

Might is sometimes used as a tentative way of making a request, suggestion or recommendation (II):

> You might send me a postcard while you're on holiday.

In some contexts, *might* suggests sarcasm or annoyance on the part of the speaker:

> You might look where you're going!
> You might have told me you weren't coming!

13 Rewrite the sentences, using *might* as in the above examples, and beginning with the word in italics.

1 Perhaps *you* would let me know tomorrow.
2 I wish *he* would be a little more tactful!
3 I think perhaps *you* should ask him if it is convenient before you call on him.
4 Perhaps *you* would post this letter for me while you're out shopping.
5 I'm annoyed that *you* didn't warn me that the car was nearly out of petrol.
6 I think *you* should at least have apologized for what you said.
7 I'm irritated that *he* didn't try to look at the problem from my point of view.
8 I'm annoyed that *she* doesn't keep her room reasonably tidy.

Expectation or probability (I): should, ought to

Should and *ought to* are often used to indicate what is regarded as probable or what may reasonably be expected.

> The introduction of new machinery should contribute greatly to better profits next year.

Should and *ought to* + *perfect infinitive* refer to expectations in past time, and may indicate that expectations were not realized or fulfilled:

> He should have passed the examination easily.

This sentence will yield two interpretations:

a. Perhaps he has passed—this, at least, is what I expected. (said, probably, before the examination results are known)
b. He didn't pass—this is not what I expected (said, probably, after the results are known)

14 Rewrite the sentences, using *should* or *ought to* as in the examples above.

1 The Conservatives are expected to win the next election.
2 There will probably be a lot of people at the meeting.
3 The weather forecast says it will probably be fine tomorrow.
4 Our visitors were expected to arrive long before now.
5 It probably won't be too difficult to get over the problem.
6 The meeting was expected to have finished by now.
7 The Cabinet will probably be meeting tomorrow to discuss the economic situation.
8 We didn't expect that it would take so long to get there. (It . . .)
9 The new regulations probably won't affect foreigners already living in this country.
10 We expect to be able to move into our new house at the end of the month.

See also 'Advice and recommendation' (II) (page 29)

Inference and logical conclusion (I): must, can't

We use *must* to assert what we infer or conclude to be the most likely interpretation of a situation or events:

> He must be at least sixty.

We don't know for a fact that this is true, but taking everything into account, we think that it is almost certainly so. The opposite of *must* in this sense is *can't*:

> John: He must be at least sixty.
> Peter: Oh no! He can't be anything like as old as that.

John is almost certain that 'He' is sixty, and Peter is equally certain that 'He' is not. In reported speech, this dialogue becomes:

> John said he must be at least sixty, but Peter thought he couldn't be anything like as old as that.

To refer to past time, we use *must* and *can't* (or *couldn't*) with the perfect infinitive:

> It must have been a great shock to him. (It was a great shock, I feel sure)
>
> You can't (*or* couldn't) have understood what he said. (It seems clear that you didn't understand)

15 Complete the responses to the statements, using *must* or *can't*, to suggest what seems to be the most likely explanation.

1 His fiancée writes to him every day. She must . . .
2 I don't seem to have my key with me. I must have . . .
3 He drives a Rolls-Royce and his wife a Mercedes. They must . . .
4 No one thought he would be offered the job, but he was. The person who interviewed him must have . . .
5 He has no idea what the book is about. He can't have . . .
6 He talks about going to the moon next year. He must . . .
7 She didn't reply to his letter. She can't have . . .
8 He wears glasses all the time. His eyesight can't . . .
9 They haven't been on speaking terms recently. They must have . . .
10 He said he would ring, but he hasn't. He must have . . .
11 The last bus has already gone. It must . . . than I thought.
12 I'm amazed that she married him so soon. She can't have . . .

Belief and conjecture (I): will, would

Will and *would* are used to express belief or conjecture. Although they lack the assertive force of *must* and *can't* (in the sense of inference or logical conclusion), they do not necessarily indicate any less certainty on the part of the speaker. Indeed, the truth of what is asserted is more or less taken for granted.

Used with the present infinitive, *will* and *would* refer to present time:

> You will already be familiar with this subject.

This is not a statement relating to future time, but means 'You are, I feel sure, already familiar with this subject.'

Would is used as the tentative form of *will*, and is more commonly used than *will* in questions (which necessarily indicate some lack of certainty):

> He wouldn't be a friend of yours, I suppose?
> Would your name be Smith, by any chance?

To refer to past time, we use *will* and *would* with the perfect infinitive:

> John: I met a charming girl at your party last night.
> Peter: Ah, yes! That will/would have been my cousin Sarah.

16 Rewrite the sentences, using *will* or *would* with the appropriate infinitive form, and omitting any words in brackets.

1 This is (probably) what we're looking for.
2 Ah! It's half-past eight. That is the postman at the door, (I should think).
3 You appreciate (I am sure) that this puts me in a very difficult position.
4 As you have no doubt heard, he's getting married soon.
5 You (probably) haven't seen this morning's headlines, I suppose?
6 I met Mr Jones at the interview. He was the manager's personal assistant, I assume.
7 You (almost certainly) don't know my name, of course, but I was a friend of your father's.
8 You haven't (by any chance) seen my gloves anywhere, I suppose?
9 Don't call on them just now. The family (almost certainly) haven't finished their evening meal yet.
10 Unless you explained it very carefully, he (almost certainly) didn't understand properly.

Characteristic behaviour (II): will, would

Will may be used to refer to a characteristic or persistent pattern of behaviour or of events:

> *1* When he has a problem to solve, he will work at it until he finds an answer.

This isn't a prediction about a future event, but a statement having general current validity. *Would* is used to refer to a similar situation in past time:

2 When he had a problem to solve, he would work at it until he found an answer.

In these sentences, we could use the simple present tense instead of *will* and the simple past tense (or *used to*) instead of *would*, with little change except for a loss of emphasis:

1a When he has a problem to solve, he works at it until he finds an answer.

2a When he had a problem to solve, he worked (*or* used to work[1]) at it until he found an answer.

If *will* and *would* are stressed, it indicates that the speaker finds a persistent pattern of behaviour annoying:

3 (The one thing I dislike about him is that) he *will* borrow my things without asking.

4 (The one thing I disliked about him was that) he *would* borrow my things without asking.

In these sentences, a substitution of the simple present or past for *will* or *would* is possible only if we express the clauses in brackets, but such a substitution in any case weakens the force of the original considerably.

17 Replace the words in italics by *will* or *would* + *present infinitive*. If the statements appear to indicate the speaker's annoyance, underline the modal verb to indicate that it is stressed.

1 My children love watching television. They *sit* for hours without saying a word.
2 He's very absent-minded. He often *buys* things and then *leaves* the shop without paying.
3 My wife *persistently leaves* things where other people can fall over them!
4 When we lived in the north, the water pipes *used to freeze* every winter, and we *had* to call in a plumber.
5 The chairman's main fault was that he *persistently interrupted* the speakers before they had finished.
6 I tried to refuse his invitation, but he *repeatedly insisted* on my coming.

---

[1] 'Used to work' carries an added implication of contrast between past and present, suggesting 'this once happened habitually but doesn't now.'

7 Why *do you persist in being* so difficult?
8 My headmaster had great authority. Whenever he spoke, everyone *used to listen* attentively.
9 No wonder the house is cold! You *always go out* and leave the
doors open!
10 In the nineteenth century, people *used to go* to church on Sunday
as a matter of course.

Inherent capacity (II): will, would

Will for present time and *would* for past time may refer to the
possession of an inherent quality or a capacity in relation to things
(as opposed to people):

> 1 The pound in your pocket will buy far less today than it
> would ten years ago.

Such sentences are half statement of fact and half prediction, and
they often suggest that the fact or prediction can be put to the test
and verified.
The use of *will* and *would* may even suggest that an object is
capable of co-operation or willingness (or their absence):

> 2 This suitcase will hold everything.
> 3 The car wouldn't start. (Compare: The car refused to start)

Used in this latter sense, *will* or *would* may appear in the 'if'
clause of a conditional sentence:[1]

> 4 If one suitcase will hold everything, we shan't have so much
> luggage to carry.

18 Complete each short dialogue, using *will* together with one of the
verbs in the list. The negative form will be needed in some cases.

seat   bear   do   fit   hold   reach   suit   work

1 'Is your car very fast?' 'Oh, yes! It . . . over a 100 miles an hour.'
2 'Is that jug big enough?' 'Oh, yes! It . . . at least a gallon.'
3 'What's wrong with that machine?' 'I don't know. It simply . . .
4 'Why haven't you opened the door?' 'This key . . . the lock.'

[1] *Will* and *would* are not, however, used with the verb *be* in a conditional
clause: we do not say *'If this suitcase *will be* big enough for everything, . . .'
See also *Conditional Sentences*, p. 91.

5 'How big is the Royal Festival Hall?' 'Oh! It . . . up to 3,000 people.'
6 'Is that ladder long enough?' 'Oh, yes! It . . . up to the roof.'
7 'Shall we say 7.30?' 'Yes, that time . . . me perfectly.'
8 'Is it safe to walk on the ice?' 'Oh, yes! It . . . your weight easily.'

Prediction: shall, will

There are many ways of referring to future events in English, and the use of *shall* and *will* is among the many means at our disposal (see notes on page 55). We have already seen that all modal verbs can refer to future time. They do, however, carry some additional implication (e.g. ability, permission, possibility). *Shall* and *will*, similarly, often carry an additional implication (e.g. promise, refusal, determination), and their use in a purely predictive function, i.e. simply to state what lies in store in the future, is only one of their several uses.

In the restricted use of 'pure' future, *shall* is used only after *I* or *we*, and is often replaced by *will* or *'ll*, especially in speech.[1] When used with other pronouns, *shall* does not have a purely predictive meaning, and is not interchangeable with *will*.[2]

       shall
 1 I will be on holiday next week.
       'll

In this sentence, *shall*, *will*, and the short form *'ll* are all used simply to state what the future holds. The pronouns *I* and *we* naturally occur more commonly in the spoken language than in the written, and the use of the short form *'ll* is therefore extremely common in speech.[3]

[1] It might be truer to say that in spoken English the choice lies between *I shall* (ai ʃəl) and *I'll* (ail), or between *we shall* (wi: ʃəl) and *we'll* (wi:l).
[2] The forms 'You shall know tomorrow' (the speaker promises) and 'He shall do it again' (the speaker promises to enforce action) are still occasionally heard in spoken English, but the use of *shall* in this sense appears to be common only with a relatively small number of verbs, e.g. *have*: 'You/he shall have it as soon as I've finished with it.' It is not sufficiently current in general to justify further comment or practice, although it is quite commonly found in highly formal or legalistic written English.
[3] In more formal situations (e.g. broadcasts, speeches, lectures) and when the spoken language is written down (e.g. in letters, printed talks), the full forms *shall* and *will* are normally used.

This is where difficulties arise for the foreign learner: since *'ll* obscures the formal distinction between *shall* and *will*, students are in doubt as to the interpretation of *'ll* in contexts where a choice between *shall* and *will* may represent a choice between two meanings:

> shall
> *2* I think I will finish the work tonight.
> 'll

This sentence illustrates the problem, where in the case of *will* and *'ll* the precise meaning of the speaker would be made clear only by the context, situation, or intonation:

a. I think I shall finish the work tonight. ('pure' future)
b. I think I will finish the work tonight. ('pure' future or intention?)
c. I think I'll finish the work tonight. (*a* or *b*?)

Will and *'ll* as substitutes for *shall* after *I/we* are ambiguous only in a sentence like *2*, where the context will support the idea of promise, willingness, or intention. In any case, such an ambiguity would hardly lead to a fatal misunderstanding!

In negative sentences, we use *shan't* and *won't*, and the short form *'ll not* is not often used. As far as meaning is concerned, the same considerations apply as for *shall* and *will*.

The interrogative *shall/I we?* used with an active verb form does not generally occur with a 'pure' future meaning, since we rarely ask other people about what our own future actions will be. It may, however, be used in a 'pure' future sense with verbs denoting actions or events which do not depend on the speaker for their performance:

> *3* Shall
> Will I hear from you soon?

Shall I? is also used in a 'pure' future sense with passive verbs, since the speaker is not in this case asking about his own future activities:

> *4* Shall
> Will I be told what to do?

In most cases, however, *shall I?* used with an active verb form represents a request on the part of the speaker to know the wishes or opinion of the person being addressed, and in this sense it is never replaced by *will*:

> 5 Shall I order a taxi for you?

What does this mean for the foreign learner? Students will probably find that they use *'ll* quite frequently in their own speech, thus obviating the need to choose between *shall* and *will* after *I/we*. Where a choice is necessary, e.g. in negative sentences and in the written language, it is advisable to use *shall* (or *shan't*) if there is any need to avoid ambiguity.

Two further points may be mentioned here:

(1) In contexts where only a 'pure' future interpretation would be acceptable, *shall* appears to be a more likely choice than *will*:

> I shall be able to tell you tomorrow.
> I shall have to do it tomorrow.

Of course, *'ll* is a perfectly possible alternative here.

(2) On the other hand, statements such as 'I shall kill myself' (threat?) and 'I shall die' ('pure' future), make an interesting comparison: it would seem that *shall* takes its 'colour' in any particular sentence from the main verb or the total context (as is true of many modal verbs). Certainly, *shall* does not always express 'pure' future.

Perhaps the most important thing is that students should understand that *shall* and *will* have several distinctly different uses, and it should not be assumed that these two words simply function as part of what is called 'the future tense'.

Reported Speech

> 6 'I shall be able to come.'
> 6a I said I would (*or* should) be able to come.
> 6b You said you would be able to come.
> 6c He said he would be able to come.

For reporting *I shall*, a choice between *should* and *would* arises only when the speaker reports his own words, as in *6a*. In fact, we tend increasingly to use only *would*,[1] possibly because of the potential ambiguity of *should* in some contexts: *I said I should be able to come* could be interpreted as the reported version of 'I

---

[1] Students must remember that these remarks are not in any way applicable to *should* as a modal verb synonymous with *ought to*.

26

should be able to come' = This is what I may reasonably expect to be able to do.

If the report is made by a person other than the original speaker, only *would* is used, as in *6b* and *6c*. These remarks also apply when we report 'pure' future questions beginning *Shall I?*:

> 7 'Shall I hear from you soon?'
> 7a I asked if I would (*or* should) hear from him soon.
> 7b You asked if you would hear from him soon.
> 7c He asked if he would hear from him soon.

19 Rewrite the sentences in direct speech, using *shall*, and omitting the words in brackets, e.g.

> (I said) I wouldn't be easy in my mind till the question was properly settled.
> 'I shan't be easy in my mind till the question is properly settled.'

1 (He said) he could manage for the time being, but he would need some help later.
2 (The chairman pointed out that) when the new wage agreement came into force, they would be obliged to raise prices to offset the cost.
3 (The speaker said that) he would have more to say about that problem later.
4 (I told him) I would be writing to him again within a day or two to let him know the precise arrangements.
5 (He told his wife that) he would be working late at the office that evening.
6 (He asked if) I thought we would need to take maps with us.
7 (I said that) I wouldn't be sorry to see the end of the bad weather.
8 He assumed he would be given all the necessary information.
9 (It was my opinion that) we would never get there, at the rate we were going.
10 (He reminded me that) we would be making an early start the following morning, so we mustn't be late to bed.

After the pronouns *you*, *he* (*she*, *it*) and *they*, only *will* is used in a purely predictive sense. It should be noted, however, that in many cases *will* may carry an additional implication, particularly after the pronoun *you*. In statements, *you will* may represent an instruction rather than a prediction:

'You will arrive punctually in future,' the manager told him.

In questions, *will you?* may represent either (a) a request for information, or (b) a request for action:

a. 'Will you know the result soon?'
b. 'Will (*or* would) you go and see the manager, please?'

In some cases, the meaning of a sentence may be ambiguous:

'Will you tell him what I said?'
= *a* 'Are you going to tell him what I said?'
or *b* 'Will you tell him what I said, (please)?'

Such problems of meaning are often only theoretical, since the speaker can (and generally does) put the question in a way that makes his meaning clear: he will probably say either *a* or *b* (or 'Would you tell him, please?'—clearly a request).

The predictive function of *will* is most obviously illustrated and most commonly seen after *he* (*she*, *it*) *they*, and after nouns generally:

The astronauts will splash down at 6 p.m. our time tomorrow.

The uses of *will* as described above are not a source of difficulty, in the sense that they do not involve a choice between *will* and *shall*. But students should be sensitive to the nuances of meaning expressed by *will*, both those indicated above and those practised in earlier exercises, and should not always assume that *will* is functioning in a 'pure' future sense, or necessarily in a future sense at all.[1]

20 Explain what meaning lies behind the use of *will* ('*ll*) in the following sentences.

1 It's no good phoning him at his office. He'*ll* be on his way home now.
2 Why *will* you ask such stupid questions?
3 *Will* you clear away the dinner things?
4 If you'*ll* clear away the dinner things, I'*ll* make the coffee.
5 The luggage boot *will* never take all those cases!
6 You'*ll* do as you're told.
7 The meeting *will* begin at 6.30.

[1] See also *Conditional Sentences*, page 91.

8 He can be quite obstinate, but he'*ll* generally see sense in the end.
9 The Queen *will* not be present at the opening of Parliament this year.
10 Don't worry! I'*ll* let you know by tomorrow, without fail.
11 Ah! Here we are! This *will* be the restaurant they recommended to us.
12 This table's too small for a dinner party. It'*ll* only seat four in comfort.

Advice and recommendation (II): shall, should, ought to, had better

Shall I?[1] generally represents a request on the part of the speaker to know the wishes or opinion of the person being addressed:

> Shall I try this number again?

Only in limited circumstances is it used in a 'pure' future sense (see page 25). *Shall I?* is, of course, much stronger than *Should I?*, and calls for a firm response such as *Yes, please do* rather than *Yes, you should*. Nevertheless, *shall I?* and *should I?* are clearly related.

In the reported speech versions of such questions, *shall* always becomes *should* (never *would*):

> I   I
> You asked if you should try his number again.
> He   he

Should and *ought to* express advice or recommendation. The advice or recommendation may relate to everyday or practical matters, or to what is morally desirable:

> You should/ought to read that book. You'd enjoy it.
> You should/ought to see a doctor if you're still feeling ill tomorrow.
> You shouldn't/ought not to tell lies.

All these sentences have a present or future time reference.

The question is sometimes raised 'Which is the stronger—*should* or *ought to?*' There is no absolute answer to this question,

---

[1] *Shall you?* is outdated and may be disregarded. A question such as 'Shall my wife make you some tea?' (again, asking about the wishes of the person addressed) is very formal, and an alternative is far more likely, viz., 'Would you like my wife to make you some tea?'

29

but it is worth noting that *should* has a strong and a weak form phonetically (ʃud, ʃəd), whereas *ought to* has only the strong form (ɔːt tu), and may thus appear to be more emphatic when contrasted with /ʃəd/.

Had better (*'d better*) is used to suggest the wisest course of action in a particular situation:

> You'd better see a doctor if you're still feeling ill tomorrow.

The short form *'d better* is usual in affirmative positive sentences. In affirmative negative sentences, the negative particle *not* comes after the complete phrase:

> You'd better *not* make a mistake next time.

In interrogative negative sentences, however, *n't* comes after *had*:

> Hadn't you better see who that is at the door?

Had better is used almost exclusively with the present infinitive, and refers to present or future time. *Should* and *ought to* are used with the perfect infinitive to refer to past time, and in this case the sentences always imply that the opposite was in fact true:

> He should/ought to have been a little more tactful. (i.e. but he wasn't tactful)

21 Respond to the statements by giving advice or making a recommendation, using *should*, *ought to*, or *'d better*, with a suitable infinitive form, e.g.

> I've got toothache.—You'd better go to the dentist.
> He failed his exam.—He should have worked harder.

1 John's terribly overweight.
2 You're always late for work!
3 Our train leaves in a few minutes.
4 Peter was involved in an accident with his car.
5 Someone's stolen my wallet!
6 The rain is coming through the roof.
7 Our tent was always getting blown down when we were on holiday.
8 Mary got terribly sunburnt yesterday.
9 We're spending our holidays in Spain next summer.
10 This suit of mine is just about done for!

11 I've been feeling rather off colour recently.
12 We ran out of wine half way through the party.
13 John's always complaining about being underpaid.
14 We all got soaked in yesterday's downpour.
15 Let's face it. We're hopelessly lost!

Other uses of 'should'[1]

Should may be used in a conditional clause, and has the effect of making it seem less likely that the condition will be fulfilled:

> If he should come while I'm at lunch, tell him I'll be back at two.

This use of should is practised in Exercise 74, in the section on conditional sentences.

Should is often used in a 'that' clause, after verbs like suggest, recommend, require, decide, etc.:

> I suggested (that) he should take legal advice.
> The law requires that all motor cars should be tested regularly for safety and efficiency.

Should is sometimes omitted in such sentences, leaving only the infinitive without to:

> I suggested (that) he take legal advice.

The verb form is then sometimes 'regularized' to give the 'normal' sequence of tenses:

> I suggested (that) he took legal advice.

22 Rewrite the sentences, incorporating a clause introduced by that, following the verbs suggested in brackets, e.g.

> I wanted him to take legal advice. (suggest)
> I suggested that he should take legal advice.

1 The Government wanted the housing programme to be speeded up. (recommend)
2 The judge wanted the court to adjourn for lunch. (order)
3 The Speaker wanted the MP to withdraw his remark. (rule)
4 The Colonel wanted his troops to attack at dawn. (decide)
5 The chairman wanted the minutes to be taken as read. (propose)
6 Teachers wanted more nursery schools to be set up. (advocate)

[1] Ought to is not used in any of these cases.

7 The magistrate wanted the man to be released. (direct)

8 The police wanted members of the public not to approach the two men but to report to the nearest police station. (give instructions)

9 Shareholders wanted the Board to give more detailed information about profits. (demand)

10 The employers wanted the men to return to work so that negotiations could begin. (urge)

Should is sometimes used in adverbial clauses of purpose, after the conjunctions *so that, in order that, lest, in case*, etc.:

I have put everything in writing so that you should know exactly how things stand.

23 Join the pairs of sentences, using the conjunctions given in brackets, e.g.

I have put everything in writing. I want you to know exactly how things stand. (so that)
I have put everything in writing so that you should know exactly how things stand.

1 He left the letter on the hall table. He wanted me to be sure of seeing it when I came in. (so that)

2 The two students talked in undertones. They didn't want the teacher to overhear what they were saying. (so that)

3 The police issued a warning. They wanted the public to be aware of the danger. (in order that)

4 I'm taking an umbrella. It may rain. (in case)

5 He keeps his wife's jewels in the bank. He fears the house may be burgled. (lest)

6 I don't want you to think I'm not telling the truth. I have brought two witnesses with me. (lest)

7 He sent his son to university. He wanted him to have the best possible chance of a good career. (so that)

8 I asked you to come here. I wanted you to have an opportunity to explain things yourself. (so that)

9 Loudspeakers were fixed in an adjoining hall. Everyone would have an opportunity to hear the speech. (so that)

10 I'll give you my telephone number. You may want to get in touch with me again. (in case)

Should is also used in a 'that' clause after adjectives expressing pleasure, surprise, shock, or disapproval, in sentences of the pattern:

S × to be × adjective × that clause
I'm horrified that he should have told anyone.

This use of *should* is particularly common when the subject is *it*:

It's odd that you should mention his name.

A similar pattern is found after adjectives like *important, essential, vital*:

It's vital that you should be there to meet him.

24 Rewrite the sentences, beginning with *it*, as in the example:

How odd! Both our wives have the same name.
It's odd that both our wives should have the same name.

1 Quite naturally, you're upset about what's happened.
2 It's incredible! We've been living in the same street for two years and have never got to know each other.
3 You missed the one talk that was worth hearing. What a pity!
4 That's curious! He asked you to come rather than me.
5 It's typical of him. He expects everyone else to do all the work.
6 Isn't it odd! They're getting married, after all they've said about marriage.
7 You have to pay so much tax. It's crazy!
8 Look over the agreement before you sign it. This is essential.
9 Read the instructions carefully before you start answering the questions. This is important.
10 How splendid! You'll be coming to live near us.
11 You've bought the house we once thought of buying ourselves How interesting!
12 Emergency supplies must reach the area quickly. This is vital.

Obligation and necessity(II): must, mustn't, have to

1 Candidates must attempt all the questions.
2 I simply must tell you what happened.
3 We must make an early start tomorrow.
4 You must see the film if you get a chance.

As we can see from these sentences, *must* varies in meaning from the expression of an instruction or of what is obligatory (as in *1*), to the expression of a sense of inner compulsion (*2*), and then to the expression of what is necessary or inevitable in the speaker's opinion (*3*). In sentence *4*, *must* expresses little more than pressing advice, and represents a 'stronger' form of *should*.

In every sentence, however, *must* expresses the authority of the speaker, or a decision or firm opinion on the speaker's part. If obligation or necessity is imposed by a person other than the speaker, or by force of circumstance, we use *have to*:

1a You have to answer all the questions. (The teacher explains to students the requirements of the examiners)

2a I have to tell you what happened. (Those are the instructions I've been given)

3a We have to make an early start tomorrow. (Circumstances or arrangements make it necessary)

4a You'll have to see the film tomorrow if you don't want to miss it. (It won't be showing any longer)

Must can be used with adverbs having a present or future time reference:

We must discuss that question e.g. now, later, next week.

However, the obligation or necessity is felt by the speaker to exist *now*, and it is the activity denoted by the main verb (*discuss*) that lies in the future. In cases where the obligation or necessity will exist only eventually, or where it is dependent on some other event, we use *have to* with *will* (*'ll*) or *shall*:[1]

5 If we miss the last bus, we shall have to walk.

We use the simple present tense of *have to* to indicate (*6*) what is habitual, or (*7*) what is already planned or arranged for the future:

6 I have to get up at seven every morning.

7 We have to be there at ten tomorrow.

An alternative form, *have got to*, is commonly used in sentences like *7*, and reinforces the idea of external authority:

We've got to be there at ten tomorrow.

[1] Compare this with the notes on *can* (page 10).

The interrogative form in the present tense is generally formed with *do*:

6a What time do you have to get up?
    (rather than: What time have you to get up)
7a What time do we have to be there?
    (rather than: What time have we to be there?)
    or What time have we got to be there?

Must can be left unchanged in reported speech (see page 6):

'You must tell me how to do it.'
I said he must tell me how to do it.

Must cannot, however, be used to refer to obligation or necessity existing before the time of speaking. Instead, we use *had to*:

I had to shout to make myself heard above the noise.
(I tell you this *now*)

We also use forms of *have to* in the many situations where *must* lacks the necessary verb forms:

I'm having to read this very carefully. (present continuous)
I've had to give up the idea. (present perfect)
I told him *I'd had to* give up the idea. (past perfect)
We may *have to* change our plans. (infinitive without *to*)
It's a pity *to have to* give up the idea. (infinitive)
No one likes *having to* pay taxes. (gerund)
You'*d have to* do it if he insisted. (conditional)
You'*d have had to* do it if he'd insisted. (conditional perfect)

In view of the fact that forms of *have to* are sometimes the only ones available, it is hardly surprising that a distinction in meaning between *must* and *have to* is not always rigidly maintained in those cases where both verbs are possible grammatically. As often as not, however, students will find that English usage bears out the distinction mentioned earlier, and that the choice of one form rather than another reflects a difference in attitude on the part of the speaker.

One other verb phrase needs to be considered here: *am/is/are to*. This sometimes expresses a command or instruction issuing from the speaker, or imposed on the speaker by external authority:

You are to give this letter to the manager. (Those are the instructions I'm giving you, or the instructions I'm passing on from some other authority.)

We are to be there by ten o'clock. (Those are the instructions we have received.)

Such sentences always have a future time reference, and the form *will be to* is never used. In reported speech, and to refer to past time, we use *was/were to*:

I told him he was to give the letter to the manager.
We left at eight o'clock—we were to be there by ten.

Was/were to + *perfect infinitive* generally implies that instructions were not carried out:

You were to have given the letter to the manager. (implying *but you didn't*)

If *must* is followed by a perfect infinitive, it nearly always indicates an inference on the part of the speaker (see page 19):

It must have been a great shock to him. (= It was a great shock, I feel sure)

Students will, however, find occasional examples where *must* + *perfect infinitive* is equivalent in meaning to 'It is essential that this should already have been done':

To be eligible for a full pension, an employee must have contributed to the fund for at least twenty years.

In all the examples so far, *must*, *have to*, etc., express the necessity for positive action on the part of the subject. To express the necessity for non-action, we use *mustn't* or *am/is/are not to*:

You mustn't say anything about it.
(= You must say nothing about it.)
You are not to say anything about it.
(= You are to say nothing about it.)

Students should note, therefore, that *must* (and *am/is/are to*) always expresses obligation, whether for positive or negative action. Although the negative particle *not* is often attached to *must* in the form *n't* (= *mustn't*), it does not cancel the obligation, but instead relates to the main verb:

You must
TELL him.
NOT TELL him.

25 Complete the sentences with *must*, *mustn't*, or a suitable form of *have to*.

1 We . . . hurry, or we'll be late.
2 'Application forms . . . be returned to this office within 15 days.'
3 You . . . visit us again some time.
4 I can never remember people's phone numbers. I always . . . look
them up.
5 The car broke down, and we . . . have it towed to a garage.
6 The situation has now become intolerable, and something . . . be
done about it immediately.
7 I realize how difficult the situation is, but you . . . try not to let it
get you down.
8 'Visas where required . . . be obtained in advance of travel to the
countries concerned.'
9 I'm sorry to . . . tell you this, but you leave me no alternative.
10 It's not fair! I always . . . do the dirty work!
11 You really . . . try to be a little more tactful.
12 No one likes . . . work at the weekend.
13 Whichever party forms the next government . . . probably reintroduce some sort of prices and incomes policy.
14 'Candidates . . . write in ink, and . . . write on one side of the
paper only.'
15 The verdict of a jury . . . be unanimous: if its members are unable
to reach agreement, the case . . . be retried before a new jury.
16 We have made quite a lot of progress, but we . . . forget that
several other problems still . . . cleared up before we can say that
agreement is in sight.
17 Fortunately, the crowd dispersed peaceably. If they hadn't, the
police might . . . use force.
18 We . . . make the job sound too difficult, or he won't take it on.
19 He suddenly took a turn for the worse, and I . . . call the doctor in
the middle of the night.
20 If a similar problem crops up again, you . . . report it to me at
once.
21 It's a very difficult choice to . . . make.

26 When you have checked your answers to the last exercise, write
the sentences in reported speech, using the sentence openings
suggested below.

1 I pointed out that . . .
2 The advertisement stipulated that . . .
3 I told him . . .

4 He said . . .
5 We explained that . . .
6 The tenants stated that . . .
7 I told him . . .
8 The regulations laid down that . . .
9 I said . . .
10 He complained that . . .
11 He told me . . .
12 I agreed that . . .
13 The editorial argued that . . .
14 The instructions stated that . . .
15 According to the book I was reading, the verdict . . .
16 At the end of the meeting, the union leader said . . .
17 The newspaper reported that . . .
18 I warned the others that . . .
19 She told her neighbour that her husband . . .
20 I made it clear to him that if . . .
21 He felt . . .

Absence of obligation or necessity (II): needn't, not need to, not have to

1 You needn't come if you don't want to.
2 You don't need to see a doctor. You're perfectly healthy.
3 I don't have to[1] work on Saturdays.

The use of the three forms illustrated above has several parallels with the use of *must* and *have to*, namely:

a. *needn't* generally expresses the authority of the speaker, while the other two verbs denote that external authority, or circumstances, remove the obligation or necessity for action;
b. *needn't + present infinitive* has only a present or future time reference, although it can be left unchanged in reported speech:

4 I told him he needn't come if he didn't want to.

If the absence of obligation or necessity will exist only eventually or is dependent on some other event, we use one of the other two verbs, with *will* and *shall*:

[1] The negative form *don't have to* is used throughout the examples in preference to the alternative form *haven't to*.

38

5 When you get an assistant, perhaps you won't have to work quite so hard yourself.

The simple present tenses *don't have to* and *don't need to* express (6) what is habitual, or (7) what is already planned or arranged for the future:

6 I don't need to get up till eight to get to work on time.
7 We don't have to be there till ten tomorrow.
   or We haven't got to be there till ten tomorrow.

c. We use negative forms of *have to* and *need to* in the many situations where *needn't* lacks the necessary verb forms.
d. In view of the fact that the 'deficiencies' of *needn't* are supplied by the other verbs, distinctions in meaning between the three verbs are not always maintained.

We can, in fact, sometimes make distinctions in meaning, which students will find more clearly expressed in some contexts than in others. Sentence *1* above, for example, is coloured by the permissive attitude of the speaker ('You can please yourself what you do'), whereas sentence *2* is a statement of objective fact ('It isn't necessary'). The difference between *don't need to* and *don't have to* in sentences *2* and *3* may be paraphrased as:

2a It isn't necessary for you to see a doctor.
3a I am not obliged to work on Saturdays.

'It isn't necessary for me to work on Saturdays' does, of course, amount to the same thing, though it presents the situation in a slightly different way.

A more important distinction is the grammatical one between *don't need to* and *needn't*. *Don't need to* is part of the regular verb *to need*. Negative and interrogative sentences are formed using *do*, as with other regular verbs, and there is a full range of verb tenses. *To need* may be followed by (8) a noun, or (9) an infinitive or gerund:

8 He $\begin{array}{l}\text{needs/needed}\\\text{doesn't need/didn't need}\end{array}$ your help.

$\begin{array}{l}\text{Does}\\\text{Did}\end{array}$ he need your help?

9 I $\begin{array}{l}\text{need/needed}\\\text{don't need/didn't need}\end{array}$ to see him immediately.

39

A gerund after *to need* is the equivalent of a passive infinitive:

9a My pen needs filling. = My pen needs to be filled.

The modal auxiliary verb *need* is always used in negative and interrogative sentences, which, as with other auxiliary verbs, are made by adding *not* (*n't*) to the auxiliary verb, and by inversion of the subject and auxiliary verb:

He needn't come. Need he come?[1]

The positive form *need* is, however, found in sentences that already contain a negative verb or adverb:

I don't think that need worry us unduly.
You need study only the first two chapters.

The above sentences also illustrate the fact that the auxiliary verb *need*, like other auxiliary verbs, is followed by the infinitive without *to*, and that there is no *-s* ending after 'third person' subjects.

Needn't is followed by a perfect infinitive to indicate the absence of necessity or obligation in the past:

He needn't have come.

This sentence may be compared with others containing similar verb forms (auxiliary verb + perfect infinitive), which often suggest the idea 'contrary to fact':[2]

You shouldn't have come. (but you came)
You could have come. (but you didn't come)
He needn't have come. (but he came)

Needn't + *perfect infinitive* always expresses *unreal* past, and contrasts with *didn't need to*, which nearly always expresses *real* past:

I needn't have gone. (but I went)
I didn't need to go. (so presumably I didn't go)

27 Rewrite the clauses in italics, using *needn't* or a suitable negative form of *have to* or *need to*. For the purpose of this exercise,

[1] The interrogative forms *must I?* and *need I?* are more or less synonymous, although *need I?* often suggests that the speaker hopes for a negative answer. The positive answer to both *must I?* and *need I?* is 'Yes, you must' (never *'Yes, you need'), and the negative answer is 'No, you needn't'.

[2] See notes on pages 6–8.

assume that 'obligation' is expressed with a form of *have to*, and that 'necessity' is expressed with *needn't* or a form of *need to*.

1 *It isn't necessary for us to leave* so soon. The show doesn't start till eight.
2 *You're not obliged to come* just to please me.
3 I don't think *it's necessary for us to take* his threats too seriously.
4 The advantage of hire purchase is that *you're not obliged to pay* for the goods in a lump sum.
5 *It isn't necessary for you to decide* immediately. You can let me know tomorrow.
6 It's a bank holiday tomorrow, so *you're not obliged to go* to work.
7 *You're not obliged to take* my word for it. You can go and see for yourself.
8 If we get everything ready now, *we shan't be obliged to rush* around doing everything at the last minute.
9 If you listened more carefully, *it wouldn't be necessary for me* to keep repeating things just for your benefit.
10 He doesn't know what work is. *He's never been obliged to earn* his own living.
11 *You're not obliged to do* everything he tells you, *are* you?
12 *It's hardly necessary for me to say* how grateful I am for all you've done.
13 *It was quite unnecessary for you to have told* John anything. It was none of his business.
14 I shan't be able to come tomorrow, but *it's unnecessary for this to make* any difference to your plans.
15 He was completely at a loss. *He had never been obliged to deal* with such a situation before.
16 The house had just been decorated, so *it wasn't necessary for us to do* anything before we moved in.
17 They offered him the job on the strength of his letter. *He wasn't even required to have* an interview.
18 You were disappointed, I realize, but *there was no need for you to have made* such a fuss in public.
19 Unless you choose to tell him yourself, *it is unnecessary for him ever to discover* what happened.
20 *It's unnecessary for you to be* alarmed.
21 Nothing new came up at the meeting. I don't think *it was necessary for me to have gone*.

28 When you have checked your answers to the last exercise, write the sentences in reported speech, using the sentence openings suggested below.

1 I felt we . . .
2 He made it clear that I . . .
3 I didn't think we . . .
4 I pointed out to him the advantage of hire purchase: you . . .
5 He told me . . .
6 He reminded me that . . .
7 He obviously didn't believe me, so I said he . . .
8 My idea was that . . .
9 The teacher told the student that . . .
10 I couldn't help saying that . . .
11 I pointed out to my friend that . . .
12 He felt he . . .
13 He thought I had been very indiscreet, and said . . .
14 I told them all that . . .
15 It was obvious to me that . . .
16 They told their friend that, when they moved in, . . .
17 I thought he had been very lucky—they . . .
18 He realized I . . . disappointed, but felt that . . .
19 As you pointed out to me, quite rightly, unless . . .
20 I assured him that . . .
21 He said that . . .

The verb forms of English

Introductory notes

The notes and exercises that follow are mainly concerned with establishing how the different forms of English verbs are used to express the *aspect* ('simple', 'continuous', or 'perfect') of an action or event, and only secondarily with problems of tense or time (present, past, or future).[1] Problems in learning the use of these forms may arise because either the student's native language does not make the same distinctions as English or, if and when it does, it makes the distinctions in a different way.

[1] Students should note, in any case, that the terms 'tense' and 'time' are not to be regarded as synonymous in English. The term 'tense' is used to refer to a verb *form*, not to chronological time. See note on page 6.

The choice of verb form (simple, continuous, perfect) made by an English speaker depends on many factors, and not on a rigid set of grammatical rules. Students may have learned not to say e.g. *I have seen the film yesterday*, following a 'rule' that we cannot make a specific reference to the time of a past event when we use the present perfect tense. But this is a negative way of looking at the problem: it gives no indication (except, perhaps, by implication) of what the use of the present perfect tense *means* to an English speaker, or of the considerations that determine the choice of the present perfect rather than, say, the past simple in situations where the use of either form seems theoretically possible.

The choice of one verb form rather than another may be determined by the nature of the action or event itself, and the circumstances in which it occurs:

a. I *read* all his books. (present simple)
b. I'*ve read* all his books.
c. When our visitor *arrived*, my wife *made* tea.
d. When our visitor *arrived*, my wife *was making* tea.

Assuming 'he' is a writer (and not simply a friend with a large library), sentence *a* states that I read his books as they are published, and implies that 'he' is still an active writer whose books I shall continue to read if any more are published. Sentence *b* states that I have read all the books 'he' has written so far. 'He' *may* still be an active writer, but he may equally well have ceased writing (or may, indeed, be dead). In *c*, our visitor arrived and then my wife made tea, whereas in *d*, tea-making was already in progress when our visitor arrived. In these examples, the 'meaning' of the situation determines the verb form chosen in order to express that meaning.

The choice of verb form may, however, depend entirely on the speaker's viewpoint. The speaker may wish to take a 'synoptic' view, a view of an action or series of actions *as a whole*, in which case he chooses the 'simple' verb form. In describing a scientific experiment, a demonstrator is more likely to take this view—he is interested in his acts, or in phenomena, as items in a chain of events:

I *place* a bell jar over the candle, and after a few moments the water gradually *rises*.

43

If the speaker is more concerned with drawing attention to the fact that an activity is in progress and is in a state of incompletion, he chooses the continuous verb form:

> I'*m placing* a bell jar over the candle. There! Can you see what'*s happening*? The water *is* gradually *rising*.

In each case, the actions or phenomena are the same, but the speaker looks at them differently.

In other cases, the choice of verb form may be restricted by limitations in the *meaning* of the verb. A verb like *contain*, for example, refers to a state or condition, where an essential element in the meaning of the verb is that of duration or permanence. It is extremely unlikely that a speaker would use such a verb in the continuous form:

> The book *contains* a lot of useless information.

The three sets of notes and exercises that follow deal with each aspect in turn, (simple, continuous, perfect), discussing each in greater detail, and with further examples.

The 'simple' forms: present and past

Present simple

> *1* Water *boils* at 100° C.
> *2* He *works* in a bank.
> *3* I (always) *take* sugar in coffee.

The present simple form is used to refer to the existence of a situation or state of affairs which either *is* permanent (sentence *1*), or is *regarded* as permanent (*2*), or to refer to repeated or habitual actions (*3*).

The verb in *1* is in fact completely timeless: it predicates what is true for all time; while in *2*, the verb refers to a constant and unchanging feature of the current situation, a situation that is regarded as permanent. The present simple used in these ways is particularly characteristic of scientific and technical English, and of expository writing generally.

The verb in *3* refers to one of 'my' habits, which presumably existed before now, and which may be assumed to continue to exist in the future. Someone who knows me would say, when offering coffee, whether yesterday, today, or tomorrow, 'Ah, yes. You *take* sugar, don't you?'

The name 'neutral' present is sometimes given to the verb as used in *1* and *2*, and the name 'iterative' present to the verb as used in *3*.

29 Complete these sentences so that they represent a universal truth or a situation that may be regarded as permanent, using the present simple ('neutral') of the verbs in the list. Add any other words that may be needed to complete the sentences, e.g., *a, the, at, on*, etc.

| believe | exist | float | flow | generate | indicate | lie |
| make | rise | sell | set | stand | treat | work |

1 The sun . . . east, and . . . west.
2 A tobacconist . . . cigarettes.
3 The Thames . . . London.
4 Deep snow . . . summit of Mont Blanc.
5 London . . . Thames
6 Water . . . moon. (negative)
7 Jet aircraft . . . lot of noise.
8 Combustion . . . heat.
9 Hospitals . . . sick.
10 A drop in barometric pressure . . . change in the weather.
11 Computers . . . great speed.
12 Oil . . . water
13 An atheist . . . God. (negative)

30 The following passage explains the workings of an automatic ticket barrier on the London Underground Railway system. Complete the passage, using the present simple tense of the verbs in the list. Use each verb once only.

| be | buy | leave | let | record |
| release | scan | show | suck | take |

When you . . . a ticket you . . . it to a machine which . . . it in, . . . it, . . . it, and . . . a barrier for you—in about a third of a second. And when you . . . a station a similar gate . . . your ticket from you (always assuming you've got the correct ticket) and . . . you out, returning your ticket if it . . . a season.

31 The following passage comes from a commentary accompanying a chart. The chart compares the tax paid by executives in Britain, France, Germany, the Netherlands, Australia, and the U.S.A. Complete the passage with the present simple tense of the verbs in the list.

apply	be	face	have	illustrate	leave
make	move	pay	reach	receive	

Already, at £5,000 a year, the British executive . . . a higher tax rate than in the United States, Germany, or France. Then, from £5,000 to £10,000, he . . . the sharpest rise in marginal tax rates in any of the countries. At £10,000 a year the Briton . . . a marginal rate of some 70p in the pound. As he . . . from £10,000 to £20,000, the British executive . . . a tax burden which . . . far heavier than that in any of the other five industrial countries.

Cash figures probably best . . . the point. In improving his salary from £10,000 to £15,000 a year the British executive . . . (*passive*) with about £1,100 after tax. His American and French opposite numbers . . . (*passive*) with more than £3,000, the German with over £2,500 and the Dutch and Australian with between £1,500 and £2,000. By the time he . . . £20,000 the British director is paying an average tax rate of 60p in the pound, compared with 40p in Germany, 30p in the United States and 25p in France.

The high tax rates in Britain . . . two important and undesirable effects. First, the British executive . . . a relatively small reward for extra work and responsibility. With marginal tax rates at 75p or above (which . . . at about £10,000 a year) it . . . perfectly sound financial sense for a British executive to prefer leisure to extra work or responsibility. Secondly, and of great possible long-term importance, there . . . little financial incentive for the British executive to take risks.

32 Answer the questions, using the present simple ('iterative') of a verb, together with the adverb suggested. *Note:* Adverbs like *sometimes, often, hardly ever,* etc., are frequently associated with the use of the present simple iterative: their meaning and use are, of course, fully consistent with the 'meaning' of this verb form. These adverbs generally come before the simple verb form.

1 When do you get up? (generally)
2 What do you do on Saturday mornings? (often)

3 Where do you spend your summer holidays? (occasionally)
4 What sort of radio programmes do you not listen to? (never)
5 How do you travel to work or school? (always)
6 What sort of books do you rarely read? (hardly ever)
7 What sort of films do you enjoy? (nearly always)
8 What punctuation does one find at the end of a printed sentence? (usually)
9 What do your parents ask you to do for them? (sometimes)
10 What do you keep in your pockets or your handbag? (usually)
11 What do you take if you have a headache? (generally)
12 Where do you meet your friends? (frequently)

33 Write sentences using each of these verbs in the present simple, describing the activities or characteristics or appearance of some of your relatives, neighbours, friends, colleagues at work, or fellow-students. You may include the following adverbs (if appropriate) in your sentences: *always, often, usually, generally, occasionally, rarely, seldom, hardly ever*.

1 catch 2 drink 3 go 4 live 5 play 6 smoke 7 take
8 walk 9 wear 10 work

34 Write a short paragraph of about 80 words on one of the following, using the present simple tense.

1 Describe how you spend a typical morning, afternoon, or evening on any weekday.
2 Describe the day-to-day activities of your place of work or your school.
3 Describe what happens in your country at Christmas, or on some other important day in your national calendar.

If we wish to refer to the 'actual' present, we generally use a continuous form (but see examples *4, 5a*, and *5b* below). We may thus compare *boil* and *work* as used in examples *1* and *2* (page 44) with the continuous as used in sentences *1a* and *2a*:

 1 Water *boils* at 100° C.
 1a You can make the tea. The water*'s boiling*.
 2 He *works* in a bank.
 2a My husband*'s working* in the garden. (at the moment)

47

There are, however, some verbs in English that are not normally used in a continuous form because their meaning is incompatible with the characteristic 'meaning' of the continuous, i.e. uncompleted action or series of actions, and limited duration (see notes on 'continuous' forms, pages 56 ff.). Two such verbs appear in the following sentence, and in this case they refer to the 'actual' present:

4 I *know* what you *mean*.

Examples *1–4* represent the commonest uses of the present simple, but it is also used in the following ways:

i   in (a) descriptions accompanying demonstrations or experiments, or in (b) commentaries on radio or television:[1]

5a We *make* sure that the current *is* switched off, and then *remove* the cover plate.

5b Smith *hits* that one off the back foot, and the ball *goes* straight to the boundary.

In the case of commentaries, the speaker may also use the present continuous. The choice will depend either on the duration of the action, or on the speaker's point of view.

ii   in (a) announcements (this use is similar to example *2* above), and in (b) headlines:

6a This park *opens* half an hour after sunrise and *closes* half an hour before sunset.

6b America *puts forward* peace plan.

iii as (a) the 'historic'[2] or 'dramatic' present, which is used to give immediacy to past events (real or fictitious), and in (b) stage directions:

7a I *rush* to the station, and *find* I've just missed the train! (real event, colloquial usage)

When Hamlet *meets* his father's ghost, he *learns* the truth about his uncle Claudius. (fictitious event)

7b (Petkoff *goes* beside Sergius; *looks* curiously over his left shoulder as he *signs*; and *says* with childlike envy):

[1] These are, of course, two further examples of the present simple indicating 'actual' present. In any comprehensive view of the use of the present simple, therefore, it is important to note that this tense can represent both 'habitual' and 'actual' present. Similarly, it is important to note that the present continuous may be used for 'habitual' as well as 'actual' present (see pages 56 and 69).

[2] The 'historic' present is not, however, used for narrating historical events in history books, although it *is* used when historical facts are presented in note form.

35 The following is a recipe for making iced coffee mousse. Imagine that you are giving a demonstration to a cookery class, and change the verbs in italics from the imperative form into the present simple, using the subject *I* or *we*. The words in brackets do not appear in the original text, but are needed in the spoken demonstration. You should also supply other essential words where there are spaces in the text. Begin your 'demonstration' as suggested at the end of the text.

ICED COFFEE MOUSSE Serves 6
3 eggs
½ pint strong black coffee
½ oz. (or 1 level tablespoon) powdered gelatine
3 oz. caster sugar.
½ pint double cream

Measure the coffee into a small saucepan, *sprinkle* in the gelatine and *leave* . . . to soak for five minutes. (Next) *Crack* the egg yolks and whites into separate basins. (Now) *Add* the sugar to the egg yolks; (then) *place* the basin over a saucepan of hot water and *whisk* until . . . mixture is thick and light in colour. (That's ready now, so) *Remove* . . . from the heat and gradually *whisk* in the dissolved gelatine. *Continue* beating until . . . cooled a little. (Next) *Beat* the egg whites stiffly; (and then) *beat* the cream lightly. (Now) *Use* a metal spoon, and *fold* . . . egg whites and cream into the egg yolk mixture. *Pour* . . . into a serving dish, and *chill* . . . until . . . set firm.
('Now here is a recipe for iced coffee mousse for six persons. We need three eggs, . . .')

36 Complete the headlines with the present simple tense of the verbs in the list, putting the verb in its correct position. Do not add any other words.

continue	crash	demand	fear	find
forecast	hit	launch	retain	survive

1 MP URGENT INQUIRY
2 INJURIES ENGLISH TEAM
3 CONSUMER BOOM
4 BRITISH RAILWAYS LOWER LOSSES
5 PLANE IN FOG

6 AMERICA MOON ROCKET
7 BOYS GOLD COIN HOARD
8 WINDOWS SONIC BANGS
9 DOCTORS FLU EPIDEMIC
10 CHAMPION TITLE

Past simple

   8 He *worked* in a bank all his life.
   9 When I was in England, I *drank* tea with breakfast.
  10 I *knew* what he *meant*.
  11 I *made* sure the current *was switched off*, and then *removed* the cover plate.

The past simple is used to refer to actions or events completed in past time, and the examples above are analogous to sentences *2*, *3*, *4*, and *5* in the present simple (pages 44 and 48). There is no analogous use of the past tense as in sentence *1* (page 44), since universal truths are independent of time.

In *8*, his working in a bank was a constant and unchanging feature of his past life (either he is now dead, or he has retired), and this use of the verb form could be classified as past 'neutral'. In *9*, the verb expresses an habitual action in the past (past 'iterative'). In *10*, the verbs belong to the special group not normally used in a continuous form, and they refer to the past 'actual'. Sentence *11* could be either the description in retrospect of a demonstration or experiment; or it could be simply the narration of past events—one of the commonest uses of the past simple (past 'narrative').[1]

37 Complete the sentences, using the present simple or past simple of the verbs suggested. (NB. These verbs are not normally used in a continuous form.)

1 I understood exactly what . . . (mean)
2 . . . everything he tells me. (not believe)
3 Listen! . . . there's someone at the door. (think)
4 Five plus five . . . (make)
5 . . . his suit. (not match)
6 John . . . when he was young. (resemble)

---

[1] It is unnecessary for students to learn the different names used here for the different 'meanings', but it is useful to note that such distinctions in meaning can be made.

7 Who . . . to? (belong)
8 The . . . ten gallons. (hold)
9 How . . . where I lived? (know)
10 Do you think the winner . . .? (deserve)
11 . . . what I see? (see)
12 The book . . . (include)
13 This wine . . . (taste)
14 How do I look in this dress? . . . me? (suit)
15 . . . better than he speaks. (understand)
16 What exactly . . . of? (consist)

38 Complete the following biographical note with the past simple tense ('narrative') of the verbs in the list.

accompany	appear	join	leave
make	produce	prove	be

GARRICK, David (1717–79), . . . S. Johnson's pupil at Edial, and . . . him when he . . . Lichfield for London. He first . . . as an actor at Ipswich in 1741, and in the same year . . . his reputation in the part of Richard III. He subsequently . . . his versatility by many triumphs in both tragic and comic parts. In 1747 he . . . Lacy in the management of Drury Lane Theatre, where he . . . a large number of Shakespeare's dramas. He . . . his last appearance in 1776.

39 Answer the questions, using the past simple tense of the verbs in italics, together with any adverbs suggested. (NB. If this exercise is done in class, students may themselves ask each other the questions.)

1 Where did you *spend* your holiday last year?
2 Why did you *choose* this place for a holiday?
3 At what time of year did you *go*?
4 How did you *travel*?
5 Who did you *go* with?
6 What sort of luggage did you *take*?
7 Where did you *live*?
8 How did you *pay* for your accommodation—in cash or by cheque?
9 What other people did you *meet*?

10 How did you *spend* your time?
11 What sort of food did you *eat*?
12 What did you *drink* with dinner? (usually)
13 What sort of weather did you *have*?
14 How many hours did you *sleep* each night? (generally)
15 At what time did you *wake* up each day? (generally)
16 At what time did you *get* up? (usually)
17 Who did you *send* postcards to?
18 What did you *bring* home as souvenirs?
19 How much did the holiday *cost* altogether?
20 How did you *feel* when you got back home?

40 Give a step-by-step description of your activities from the moment you got up this morning.

41 Re-tell the story or plot of one of the following:

1 A book you have read recently.
2 A film or play you have seen recently at the cinema or theatre or on television

Present simple with adverbs having future time reference

12 The examination *begins* at 9.0 a.m. *tomorrow morning*.

The present simple can be used with adverbs having a future time reference when the action or event is regarded as part of a fixed timetable. This differs a little in meaning from the present continuous used with such adverbs (see page 62), in that the present continuous implies an element of *personal* agreement, planning, or intention on the part of the subject, whereas the present simple does not.

Verbs commonly used in this way are those associated with announcements about timetables, schedules, organized events, etc., for example, *begin, end, stop, leave, depart, arrive, come, go, open, close*. There is an analogous use of the past simple:

13 He set his alarm for seven o'clock: the examination *began* at 9.0 the following morning.

There are also some verbs that are *not* used in this way, viz., those verbs not normally used in a continuous form—verbs referring to

52

activities of the mind or senses (*know, understand, realize*, etc.), and those referring to a state or condition (*contain, resemble, equal*, etc.). We do not make statements such as:

> *I know the answer tomorrow.
> *He resembles his father in a few years' time.

42 Rewrite the sentences, using the present simple tense of the verbs in italics, and omitting any words that may then be unnecessary.

1 The exhibition is due to *close* on Friday next week.
2 Clearance of the site for the new concert hall is scheduled to *begin* next month.
3 I haven't time to discuss it now. My plane is due to *leave* in twenty minutes.
4 It has been fixed that the new regulations should *come* into force from the beginning of the new year.
5 What time is the concert due to *end* this evening?
6 The arrangements are that the Commonwealth Games should *open* at Crystal Palace next Monday.
7 The ship is scheduled to *make* her maiden voyage next month.
8 Next year, the winter term is due to *finish* on 28th March, and the spring term to *start* on 7th April.
9 When has it been arranged for you to *take up* your new appointment?
10 The new motorway is due to *open* to traffic tomorrow.

Present simple in adverbial clauses of time referring to future

> *14* He won't be satisfied until he *gets* an apology.

In adverbial clauses of time referring to future, we use one of the present tenses. We do not use *shall* or *will* in a predictive sense in such clauses. The conjunctions commonly used to introduce time clauses are: *when, as soon as, before, after, until, once, by the time* (*that*), *the moment* (*that*). To this list we can also add the conditional conjunction *if*.

There are two points to note, however:

(i) *When* may introduce a noun clause, in which case the restriction does not apply. We can compare two sentences:

a. He will tell you (e.g. what you want to know) *when he has the necessary information.*

The clause in italics says *when* he will tell you, and is an adverbial clause of time. We therefore use the present simple tense.

b. He will tell you *when he will have the necessary information.*

Here, the clause in italics says *what* he will tell you (i.e. it is a noun clause), and is the grammatical equivalent of 'what you want to know' in sentence *a*. In sentence *b*, moreover, we could add an adverb of time:

> *Tomorrow* he will tell you when he will have the necessary information.

(ii) *Will* is often used in a modal sense, expressing willingness or agreement on the part of the subject. Used in this sense, it may appear in a time clause or a conditional clause:

c. You'll have to pay him before he *will do* anything.
d. Everything will be all right if you *will* all *do* as you're told.

43 Complete the sentences with the present simple tense or a future form of the verbs in brackets.

1 Thousands of vending machines (have) to be converted before decimalization (take) place.
2 The employers (start) negotiations as soon as the men (return) to work.
3 The Government (have) to decide what to do about these naval bases before the present treaty (expire).
4 What he (do) when he (leave) school?
5 As soon as there (be) even a temporary break in the weather, the climbers (renew) their attempts to reach the summit.
6 After the monsoon (set) in, no further attempts (be) possible.
7 Many familiar faces (be) absent from Parliament when the new session (open) next Thursday.
8 If we (not leave) soon, the party (be) over by the time we (get) there.
9 If you (wait) much longer before you (make) up your mind, it (be) too late.
10 When Concorde (come) into service, the journey from New York to London (take) only 3 hours 20 minutes.

11 How popular supersonic travel (become) once Concorde (be) in service?
12 We (interrupt) our programmes the moment we (have) any further news of the situation.
13 If you (not tell) him everything now, he simply (keep on) pestering you until you (do).
14 As soon as we (hear) from the suppliers, we (let) you know when the goods (be) in stock.

A note on the 'future'

We have already seen that the *present simple* can be used with adverbs having a future time reference:

> The Olympic Games *begin* in two week's time.

The *present continuous* can also be used in this way, but introduces an additional element of personal planning, intention or agreement on the part of the subject:

> I *am meeting* him at six-thirty tomorrow evening.

The form *going to* × *infinitive* is very commonly used to express intention on the part of the subject, or to express what appears likely or inevitable:

> I *am going to tell* him what has happened.
> It's *going to be* difficult to persuade him to change his mind.

The forms *will/shall* × *infinitive* may be used in a purely predictive way:

> I *shall be* forty-five next Saturday.
> The astronauts *will splash down* at 6 p.m. our time tomorrow.

However, *shall* and *will* often function as modal verbs, carrying an attitudinal implication (promise, threat, determination, probability, etc.), and as there are so many other ways of referring to future time, it can be misleading to speak of a 'future tense', as if it were something as formally distinct as, say, the present or past tense. Any references made in these notes (for convenience) to 'future' should be considered in this context.

The 'Continuous' Forms

Present continuous

1a Do be quiet! I'*m trying* to hear what the man'*s saying*.
1b Do you think I look any thinner? I'*m slimming*.
1c We'*re eating* in the kitchen during this cold weather.

The continuous forms represent actions or events, or series of actions or events, viewed at some point between their beginning and end. They imply that an action or series of actions has already begun but is not yet completed. At the same time, they indicate that the duration of the action or series of actions is limited.

In sentence *1a*, the continuous form indicates an activity in progress at the very moment of speaking; while in *1b*, it indicates a temporary activity over a more extended period of time. Sentence *1c* refers to a *series* of actions of limited duration: the repeated act of eating, whenever it occurs, occurs in the kitchen, but this is viewed as a temporary arrangement ('during this cold weather'). *1c* is, in other words, concerned with *habitual* activity, but habitual activity over a limited period of time.

It should be clear from the above examples and comments that the continuous forms do not *necessarily* indicate that an action is being performed at the very moment of speaking. This *is* so in *1a*, where we could say 'I'm trying at this very moment to listen to what the man is saying (at this very moment)'. But we would not say **'I'm slimming at this very moment'* in *1b*; and in *1c*, it is very possible that we are *not* engaged in eating in the kitchen at the very moment of speaking.

The one feature that is common to all three sentences, however, is that the action or series of actions is regarded as incomplete or temporary (of limited duration). We can contrast the meaning and use of the simple and continuous forms in sentences like the following:

a. They spend a lot of money on improving their house.
b. They're spending a lot of money on improving their house.

Sentence *a* is a general observation on a more or less permanent state of affairs, whereas *b* implies that their spending money on their house is a temporary phenomenon. There is a difference in the facts of the situation, and this determines the choice of verb form.

In other cases, however, the choice of verb form may depend entirely on the speaker's viewpoint, as explained on page 43:

c. I place a bell jar over the candle, and after a few seconds the water gradually rises.

d. I'm placing a bell jar over the candle. There! Can you see what's happening? The water's gradually rising.

Here the facts of the situation are the same in both cases, but the speaker looks at those facts differently.

44 Complete the sentences with the present continuous tense of the verbs in the list, putting the adverbs in italics in their correct position. Use the short form of auxiliary verbs where possible.

act	be	begin	boil	brush	come
die	drive	get on	give	go	happen
jump	kill	read	take	try	

1 Do be quiet, will you? I . . . to concentrate.
2 The tea won't be long. The kettle *nearly* . . .
3 Don't take the newspaper away! I *still* . . . it.
4 Let's sit down for a while. My feet . . . me.
5 Do tell me what happened! I . . . to hear.
6 I'll be ready in a minute. I *just* . . . my hair.
7 I won't have another drink, thanks. I . . .
8 I . . . to work by bus this week—my car . . . trouble.
9 Peter . . . very strangely these days. What's come over him?
10 Just listen to that noise! What on earth . . . out there?
11 How you . . . in your new job?
12 He should have arrived by now. I . . . to think he *not* . . .
13 You *rather* . . . to conclusions?
14 Why you *not* . . . the medicine the doctor prescribed?
15 Don't you think you . . . rather foolish?

45 Reconstruct the sentences, using the present continuous tense of the verbs related to the nouns in capitals, and beginning your sentences with the words in italics. It may be necessary to omit some words, and some adjectives need to be changed into adverbs. All the sentences illustrate the use of the present continuous to denote a temporary activity over an extended period of time, e.g.

There is a vigorous EXERCISE of their powers under the new Act on the part of *Customs authorities*.

Customs authorities *are vigorously exercising* their powers under the new Act.

1 There is a gradual CHANGE-OVER in *industry* to the metric system.
2 One effect of *the present credit squeeze* is a severe REDUCTION in the ability of the average citizen to save a greater proportion of his income.
3 There is an EXPANSION of *the Company's activities abroad.*
4 There is a significant RISE in *living standards* in most European countries.
5 The INVESTIGATION of the crime is in the hands of *the police.*
6 The RESULT of *the strike* at London Airport is heavy delays to passengers.
7 There is a steady IMPROVEMENT in *passenger services* on suburban lines.
8 There is a FIGHT among *domestic appliance manufacturers* to maintain their position in a stagnant market.
9 In many factories, there is now a REPLACEMENT of *old-style canteens* by modern vending machines. There is a steady GAIN in favour among workers of *these new methods.*
10 One result of *the re-equipment programmes* of the road haulage industry is the CREATION of a tremendous domestic demand for commercial vehicles.
11 With *one big motor manufacturer*, there is the EXTENSION of the use of semi-automatic gearboxes to more and more vehicles.
12 There is also a RECOGNITION among *British exporters* of the efficiency of door-to-door road haulage as a method of delivering goods, and one result is the EMERGENCE of *a new race* of bilingual lorry drivers. There is, in fact, a constant CHANGE in *the European transport scene.*

Past continuous

2a I asked them to be quiet. I *was trying* to hear what the man *was saying.*
2b I thought she looked thinner. Apparently, she *was slimming.*
2c We had moved the dining-table into the kitchen—we *were eating* there during the cold weather.

These three sentences describe situations in past time parallel to the present situations in sentences *1a–1c* (page 56). In sentence *2a*, the continuous indicates an activity in progress at that very moment of past time. In *2b*, it indicates an activity of limited duration over a longer (unspecified) period of past time; while in *2c*, it refers to a series of actions limited in duration to the period mentioned ('during the cold weather').

In *2a*, the actual time at which the activity was in progress is suggested by the context (i.e. at the time when I asked them to be quiet), but in such sentences, the time is often specified by an adverbial:

> At 11 o'clock,
> When the storm broke, I was working in the garden.

We can contrast the use of the past continuous and the past simple in the main clause:

a. When our visitor arrived, my wife was making tea.
b. When our visitor arrived, my wife made tea.

In *a*, tea-making was in progress when our visitor arrived, whereas in *b*, tea-making took place after (and probably as a result of) our visitor's arrival.

The past continuous is also used to draw attention to continuous activity during a specified period in the past:

3a I was working all day last Saturday.
3b I was giving a lesson between two o'clock and three.

In many such sentences, however, there may be very little difference between the past simple and the past continuous:

> We watched television all evening.
> We were watching television all evening.

The phrase *all evening* itself expresses the idea of duration, and the continuous form simply reinforces that idea. This is yet another example where the choice of one form rather than the other represents little more than a difference in attitude or emphasis on the part of the speaker.

46 Complete the sentences with the past simple or the past continuous of the verbs in brackets. In Nos. 7 and 9, you will need to use either the simple or continuous form of the infinitive. The adverbs in italics should be put in their correct position.

1 Who was that girl you (talk) to when I (pass) you in the street?
2 He (sleep) soundly when he (awaken—*passive*) by a noise. He (go) downstairs to find out what (happen). He (know) something must be wrong because the dog (bark) furiously.
3 He (not take) my remarks seriously. In fact, he (think) I (joke).
4 A storm (break) while the golfers (approach) the half way stage in the competition. They (take) shelter in the clubhouse, and play (restart) as soon as the rain (stop).
5 The men (drink) together when an argument (break out). The men *soon* (come) to blows, and the publican (call) the police. The situation *just* (begin) to get out of hand, when the police (arrive) and (take) the two men to the police station. While they (get) out of the police car, one man (make) a break for it, and (succeed) in getting away. They *still* (look) for the man two hours later.
6 One of the airliner's tyres (burst) as it (taxi) along the runway. Fortunately, no one (injure—*passive*).
7 What (go on) in your house when I (call) on you last night? I (ring) the bell three times, but you (not answer) the door. Judging by the noise that (come) from the sitting room, I (think) you must (have) a party.
8 I (look) for you in the theatre all evening. Where you (sit)?
9 When I (leave) the airport, John and his wife *still* (talk) to the customs official. They (seem) (have) some difficulty over their passports.
10 It's odd you should mention seeing him last night. I *just* (wonder) what had become of him. I suppose you (not ask) where he (live) these days?

47 The American spacecraft Apollo 13 was about 205,000 miles from earth on its journey to the moon, when an explosion occurred. What follows is part of the conversation that took place between the spacecraft and mission control at Houston, Texas. All the verbs in brackets were used in the present simple or present continuous, or the past simple or past continuous. Put the verbs in the most suitable of these forms, using the short forms of the auxiliary verbs where appropriate.

At 04.04, British Summer Time, Captain Lovell (report): 'Hey! We've got a problem here.'

Twenty-one minutes later he (tell) mission control: 'It (look) to me, looking out the hatch, like we (vent) something into space. It (be) gas of some kind.'

Mission control (ask): 'Can you tell us anything about the venting? Where it (come) from; what window you (see) it at?'

Spacecraft: 'It (come) out of window one right now Jack. Something (give) us a breach, Jack, both in pitch and roll so I (suspect) that maybe it (be) whatever it (be) that (spin) back there.'

Later, during the first critical hours when mission control (work) desperately but calmly towards a solution that would give the three astronauts a chance of survival, (come) this agitated message from the spacecraft: 'I (transmit). I (not have) any current now. Hey, it (be) off. It (be) dead.'

For three hours, one of the three fuel-cells (keep—*passive*) working on the command module. But at 05.40, B.S.T., Fred Haise (report) that cabin oxygen pressure (fall). Mission control (order) the emergency batteries to be activated.

The spacecraft (report): 'Jack it (look) like o_2 pressure (be) just a hair over 200.'

MC: 'We (confirm) that here and the temperature also (confirm) it.'

SC: 'Okay. It (look) like it still (go) down?'

MC: 'It slowly (go) down to zero and we (start) to think about the LM (lunar module) lifeboat.'

SC: 'Yes, that (be) something we (think) about too.'

48 Complete the sentences with the present simple or present continuous, the simple or continuous infinitive, or the present participle form of the verbs in brackets. (NB. The infinitive particle 'to' is supplied where necessary.)

1 Caravanning (appear) to (gain) in popularity in Britain.
2 Why you (sit) there (watch) television when you (know) you ought to (get) on with your work?
3 Is there anything I can (get on) with while I (wait)?
4 I (think) I (hear) someone (talk) in the next room.
5 Perhaps you should (leave) now? Your friend may (wait) for you outside.
6 I wouldn't (call) on them just now. They'll probably (have) their dinner.
7 He (say) he (know) someone who'll (do) the job. I (wonder) who he can (think) of?
8 If I were at home now, I'd (sit) down (do) nothing.

9 His appearance (seem) to (improve) now that he (have) a steady girl friend.
10 I can (smell) something (burn). Can *you*?
11 We must (travel) at a snail's pace. All the other cars (overtake) us.
12 Can we (accept) what he (say) at its face value? He may or may not (tell) the truth.

Continuous forms with adverbs referring to future time

4a I'*m meeting* John at six-thirty tomorrow.
4b I left home at six: I *was meeting* John at six-thirty.

When used with an adverb referring to future time, the present continuous indicates that the action or event is pre-arranged. We could paraphrase sentence *4a*:

I have arranged to meet John at six-thirty tomorrow.

(This is not to say that the two sentences are exactly the same: in *4a*, the focus of interest is on the meeting, whereas in the paraphrase our attention is directed towards the arrangement.)

Sentence *4b* represents a situation in past time parallel to the situation in *4a* in present/future time: my meeting John at six-thirty was part of a pre-arranged plan that existed at the time I left home.

The past continuous sometimes refers to plans that do not or did not materialize:

5a I was coming to see you tomorrow, but now I find I can't.

More frequently, we find the form *going to* instead (this form would not be used in *5a* for stylistic reasons—we would not say *'I was going to come to see you'):

5b I was going to tell you myself (i.e. but I find you already know).

49 Replace the words in italics by the present continuous or past continuous of the verbs in capitals.

1 *The plan is that* Union leaders *should* MEET the Minister of Labour tomorrow to discuss the strike situation.
2 I *have arranged to* TAKE a week's holiday starting next Monday.
3 *Do* you *intend to* VISIT the exhibition before it closes?

4 I can't see you this evening because I *plan to* GO out.
5 Some friends of ours *have arranged to* COME to stay with us. We *have agreed to* MEET them at the airport this evening.
6 You needn't have told him, because I *had arranged to* SEE him myself later in the week.
7 The Prime Minister said *arrangements had been made for him to* HOLD a press conference the following day.
8 When *does* Sviatoslav Richter *plan to* COME to London again? That is the question on the lips of many concert-goers.
9 The chairman of the bank said that they *planned to* OPEN three new branches in the town the following month.
10 *The plan is that* they TAKE the show on a provincial tour after its initial run in London.

Future continuous [1]

> *6a* This time tomorrow, we'*ll be crossing* the Atlantic.
> *6b* We'd better move the dining-table into the kitchen. We'*ll be eating* there during the winter.

The continuous form in sentence *6a*, as in examples *1a* and *2a*, indicates an activity in progress at a specific time, in this case in the future. In *6b*, it indicates that the speaker views the series of future actions (eating in the kitchen) as a temporary arrangement.

The use of the continuous form of the infinitive after *will* (and other auxiliary verbs) may be compared with the simple infinitive, and also with the present continuous referring to future:

> *7a* I'*ll see* him about it tomorrow.
> *7b* I'*m seeing* him about it tomorrow.
> *7c* I'*ll be seeing* him about it tomorrow.

In *7a*, the speaker is making a promise or announcing a decision about his future actions, whereas in *7b*, the speaker implies that plans have already been made. The difference between sentences like *7b* and *7c* is sometimes negligible, but the use of the continuous infinitive often suggests that the action or event will occur as part of the normal pattern of events, and not necessarily as part of a pre-arranged plan.

In a question, the use of the continuous infinitive may

---

[1] The term 'future' is used here for convenience to indicate chronological future, and not to represent 'the future continuous tense'.

represent the prelude to a request or suggestion for some further action in the event of an affirmative answer:

Will you be seeing him tomorrow?

If the answer to the question is 'Yes', the speaker might go on to make a request: 'Well, in that case, could you tell him I got his letter?'

There can, however, be a more significant difference between the present continuous referring to future, and the future continuous as illustrated in sentences *6a* and *6b*: the present continuous refers to the time at which a future event is planned to take place, whereas the future continuous can indicate that the action or event will already be in progress at some future time:

a. I'm giving a lesson at two o'clock tomorrow. (This is the time when the lesson will begin.)
b. I shall be giving a lesson at two o'clock tomorrow. (The lesson may already be in progress at that time.)

50 Complete the sentences with the simple or continuous infinitive form of the verbs in brackets.

1 Will you (come) to the concert this evening? If so, we'll (meet) you there.
2 I'd rather you didn't call tomorrow afternoon. I shall (entertain) visitors.
3 What do you think you'll (do) at this time next year?
4 'Listeners who missed any of these talks may (like) to know that we shall (repeat) the whole series during the next four weeks.'
5 I'll (see) him next week, so I will (mention) it to him then.
6 I shall (work) late at the office this evening, so I won't (get) home till about ten.
7 You'll (disappoint) her if you don't go. Now that you've promised, she'll (expect) you.
8 'Do you think they'll still (wait) for us when we get there?' 'Oh, yes! They won't (go) till we arrive.'
9 We can't (make) any definitive plans for October, because we may (move) house then.
10 When you arrive at the airport, an escort will (wait) for you. You'll (recognize) him very easily. He'll (wear) a dark green suit and a yellow tie.

Perfect continuous

8a Go out and get some fresh air! You've *been sitting* there reading all morning.

8b Look at the mess my paper's in! Who's *been reading* it?

9a I thought he needed some fresh air. He'd *been sitting* there reading all morning.

9b When I saw the mess my paper was in, it was obvious that someone *had been reading* it.

10 By next Christmas, I *shall have been living* in London for two years.

In examples *1a–1c* and *2a–2c* (pages 56 and 58), the continuous forms indicate actions or series of actions viewed at some point between their beginning and end. Although these forms imply that the action began at some earlier time and ended at some later time, they draw our attention only to the situation at the particular time indicated by the context.

The perfect continuous forms, in common with other continuous forms, draw attention to the duration of an action and indicate that the duration of the action is limited. But they differ from other continuous forms in that they indicate *explicitly* that the action or series of actions began at some point earlier in time (before *now*, before a time in the *past*, or before a *future* time).

In sentences *8a*, *9a*, and *10*, the action is in progress up to and including the time indicated by the context. This is not an essential feature of the perfect continuous forms, as we can see in *8b* and *9b*—no one is actually reading the paper at the time the question is asked.

In every case, however, the action is relevant to the current situation: in *8a* and *9a*, 'you' need some fresh air at the time referred to because of your earlier activity; in *8b* and *9b*, 'my' paper is in a mess because of someone's earlier reading of it; while in *10*, a period of two years will be complete when next Christmas comes. (See notes on the 'perfect' forms, page 69.)

51 Complete the sentences with the present perfect continuous or past perfect continuous of the verbs in the list.

ask	expect	fly	give	learn	listen	look
operate	point out	say	see	wait	work	

1 At last you're here! I . . . for you for over twenty minutes.
2 He knows quite a lot of English. He . . . it for six years.
3 She finally said 'Yes'. He . . . her to marry him for years.
4 I think I need a break. I . . . solidly for the last three hours.
5 You . . . to a word I . . ., have you?
6 For some time now, T.U.C. leaders . . . the necessity for Trade Union reform.
7 The police, who . . . trouble during the civil rights demonstration, were surprised by the eventual absence of violence.
8 The manager went down with pneumonia. He . . . unwell for several days.
9 The chairman said that the Board of Directors . . . serious thought to the possibility of entering the American market.
10 At the inquiry into the plane crash, the pilot said in evidence that he . . . this type of aircraft for ten years.
11 I know why you're having nightmares. You . . . too many horror films recently.
12 The new one-way scheme . . . for just over twelve months, and traffic has improved considerably as a result.

Verbs not normally used in continuous forms

We have seen that the distinctive characteristic of continuous forms is that they refer to actions or series of actions viewed at some point between their beginning and end, and that they indicate limited duration. There is a number of verbs whose inherent meaning is not easily compatible with the use of the continuous:

a. verbs referring to activities of the mind, the emotions or the senses, e.g. think, believe, understand, remember, forget, wish, want, like, love, hate, notice, recognize, hear, see, feel, smell, etc.;
b. verbs referring to a state or condition, where an essential element in the meaning of the verbs is that of permanence, e.g. contain, equal, resemble, belong, own, have (= possess), include, comprise, etc.

These two sets of verbs are rarely used in a continuous form for the reason given above—the meaning of the verbs is not easily compatible with the 'meaning' of the continuous forms.

Some of the verbs may, however, occur in the continuous form in certain circumstances:

(1) The verbs may have more than one meaning or use, and one of these meanings may be compatible with the use of a continuous form:

11a What *do* you *think* I should do? (= what is your opinion?)
11b What *are* you *thinking* about? (= what is going on in your mind at the present moment?)
12a I *see* you've got a new car. (= I perceive)[1]
12b I'*m seeing* him later this evening. (= I've planned to meet him)

(2) We may use the continuous form if we wish to stress the idea that something is happening by degrees, but in this case, the sentence nearly always contains a specific reference to the idea 'by degrees' or 'gradually':

13 Now that my eyes are getting used to the dark, I'*m seeing* things a bit more clearly.

(3) Some of the verbs of sensation have both a transitive and an intransitive use, and it is possible to use a continuous form when the verb is used transitively:

14a This sauce *tastes* superb. Did you make it yourself?
14b I'*m tasting* the sauce to see if there's enough spice in it.

The verb 'taste' in *14a* refers to a 'state' ('superb'), which is regarded as a permanent quality of this sauce; whereas in *14b*, the verb refers to an activity taking place at the moment of speaking and limited in duration.

---

[1] We can also compare verbs like *see* and *hear* (referring to normal human functions, which we cannot start or stop at will) with the prepositional verbs *look at* and *listen to* (referring to actions which we can choose either to do or not to do). In a classroom, a teacher might ask his students:

Can you *see* the blackboard?
Are you *looking* at the blackboard?
Can you *hear* what I'm saying?
Are you *listening* to what I'm saying?

Part of a conversation might run as follows:

Did you *hear* what I said?
Well, I *heard* you say something, but I *wasn't listening*.

52 Answer the questions to describe this book, using the present simple tense.

1 How much does it weigh?
2 How big is it? (use the verb 'measure')
3 How much does it cost in your country?
4 How many copies do you have?
5 How many exercises does it contain?
6 Does the cover feel smooth or rough?
7 Does the cover look shiny or dull?
8 Where do the exercises on phrasal verbs come?
9 What type of exercise do you like best?
10 What does the book lack in your opinion?

53 Complete the sentences with the present simple or present continuous tense of the verbs in brackets. The adverbs in italics should be put in their correct position.

1 I (think) you *already* (know) my views on the matter.
2 I'm tired of working in an office. I (think) of changing my job.
3 I *just* (smell) your roses. They (not smell) wonderful?
4 I *gradually* (forget) all the French I ever learnt at school.
5 You (see) that house over there? No, not there! You (not look) where my finger (point).
6 I (not hear) anything. You *just* (imagine) things.
7 The court (hear) this particular part of the evidence in private.
8 I *just* (taste) the cocktail to see if there's enough gin in it. Here! How it (taste) to you?
9 I (think) my daughter (see) too much of that young man these days, and I (not approve) of it.
10 Don't take his remarks too seriously. He's so upset that I (not think) he *really* (know) what he (say).
11 The monument (stand) on a hill overlooking the town.
12 You (realize) that you (stand) on my toe?
13 The town (have) a population of 50,000.
14 The resort (have) a big influx of foreign visitors this year.

Note: We do not normally use adverbs such as *often*, *generally*, *sometimes*, etc., with verbs in the continuous form: the ideas *often* and *for the time being* do not, on the whole, go easily together. Nor do we use the continuous form with adverbials denoting a certain number of occasions. We can say:

I *have been ringing* the doorbell *for several minutes*, but no one has answered.

But we do not say:

*I *have been ringing* the doorbell *six times*, but no one has answered.

We do, however, use *always* (constantly, perpetually, continually, forever) with a continuous form:

He's *always asking* me for money.[1]

The continuous form with *always* (or synonymous expressions) suggests that the action or event is a persistently recurrent (and often irritating) feature of the situation at the time referred to. This use of the continuous form to represent habitually repeated but sporadic activity is very common.

The 'perfect' forms

Present

1 John: I've *read* the book.
  Peter: What's it like? *Is* it worth reading?
2 John: What on earth *have you been doing*? Your clothes *are covered* in paint.
  Peter: I've *been decorating* the room upstairs. Come and see it. It *looks* marvellous.

Past

3 John: When I *got* there, everyone *had gone* home.
  Peter: So you *didn't meet* them?
  John: No, of course not.
4 When I *looked* at the state my room *was* in, I *could see* it *hadn't been cleaned*.

---

[1] 'He always asks me for money' says simply that whenever he needs money, or whenever he sees me, he asks me for money. It says *nothing* about the *frequency* of his requests, which may not in fact occur very often: he may not often need money, or he may not see me very often.

Future

5 We *shall have finished* the repairs to your car by tomorrow morning. It *will be* ready for you at 11 o'clock.

The perfect forms imply two ideas:

i that an action or event occurred *before* the time indicated by the context or situation: it *has* happened before *now*, it *had* happened before a certain time in the *past*, or it *will have happened* before a certain time in the *future*; and

ii that this action or event *has* produced, *had* produced, or *will have* produced a result or a state of affairs that *is* relevant to the present situation, *was* relevant to the past situation, or *will be* relevant to the future situation.

An important characteristic of perfect forms is, therefore, that they explicitly link an earlier action or event with the current situation. In examples *1* and *2*, we understand that *reading*, *doing*, and *decorating* all occurred before now, and that each of these past actions or events has a direct relevance to the current situation (present): Peter asks what the book *is* like, Peter's clothes *are covered* in paint (the room, fortunately, *looks* marvellous!)

In *3*, everyone's going home occurred before John *got* there, with the result that he *didn't meet* anyone (past); while in *4*, the non-occurrence of cleaning earlier in the past meant that the earlier state of affairs remained unchanged at the time of my looking at the room (past). In *5*, the garage will finish the work at some time *before* 11 o'clock tomorrow, by which time the repairs to my car *will be* in a state of completion (future).

In each case, the *time* of the action or event is irrelevant, or is at least disregarded. The important elements are the occurrence of the action itself and the current results or state of affairs produced by it.

If we wish to direct attention specifically to the state of affairs brought about by an earlier action without drawing attention to the activity that has produced this state, we can use the auxiliary verb 'be' together with an adjective (or passive participle):

6a The floor *is* clean.
6b The chair *is broken*.

While there is little ultimate difference in meaning between these sentences and:

7a The floor *has been cleaned.*
7b The chair *has been broken.*

our attention in *6* is directed to the present result, the past action being only implied; while in *7*, our attention is directed first to the past action, the present result then being implied.

Difficulties for foreign learners arise either from the fact that their own language hasn't led them to look at events in this way, or from the fact that their language contains a verb form that *looks* similar to the English form but *operates* differently.

English speakers frequently switch their specific focus of interest from one aspect of events to another:

> John: I'm getting married soon.
> Peter: So I*'ve heard.*
> John: Oh! When *did* you *hear* about it?
> Peter: Your father *told* me *yesterday.*

Peter's first reply is tantamount to his saying 'I *know*'. John's interest then focuses specifically on the time of the past event— *when* Peter *heard.* But we could not, even in the interests of economy, condense both Peter's replies into:

> *I've heard yesterday.

In other words, we cannot combine a *specific reference* to the *time* of a past event with a verb form that implies a *specific reference* to its *current relevance.* This does not, however, mean that the use of the past simple necessarily excludes the possibility of current relevance (though it often does):

> I know what your boss is like. I worked for him two years ago.

If we omit the phrase *two years ago*, the present perfect could (and probably would) be used, representing the 'indefinite' past:

> I know what your boss is like. I've worked for him.

54 In each of the following sentences, the words in italics indicate the state of affairs existing at a particular time. Rewrite the sentences, using a perfect tense of the verbs in brackets, to indicate that an earlier action or event *has* produced, *had* produced, or *will have* produced the current result or state, e.g.

When we arrived at the stadium, the match *was already in progress*. (start)

When we arrived at the stadium, the match *had already started*.

1 We *are in unanimous agreement* on what should be done. (agree)
2 By the time the doctor arrived, the man *was already dead*. (die)
3 By the end of 1970, our current housing programme *will be in a state of completion*. (complete—*passive*)
4 If we don't hurry, the meeting *will already be in progress* by the time we get there. (start)
5 When we got to the airport, we found that all flights *were off* because of the fog. (cancel—*passive*)
6 Do you think he *will already be at* the house when we arrive? (reach)
7 When she got home, she found that her parents *were already in* bed. (go)
8 By the end of next week, he *will be out of* hospital. (leave)
9 Our plans *are different*: we're not going after all. (change)
10 *The name of the book escapes me.* (forget)
11 They missed their plane. When they reached the airport, it *was already airborne*. (take off)
12 They *are husband and wife* at last. (get married)

55 Complete the sentences, using a perfect tense of the verbs in brackets, to suggest what *has* occurred, *had* occurred, or *will have* occurred to produce the situations described, e.g.

He knows France very well. He . . . (spend)
He has spent a lot of time there.

1 I don't know your friend Smith. I . . . (never meet)
2 Don't ask me what spinach tastes like. I . . . (not try)
3 When he first arrived, he couldn't speak a word of English. He . . . (never study before)
4 He went to see a doctor. He . . . for some time. (feel ill)
5 If you keep forgetting to water the plants, there won't be any by the end of the week. They . . . (all die)
6 He woke up feeling tired because he . . . (not sleep)
7 There isn't any more typing paper. It . . . (all use up—*passive*)
8 A: How's your son getting on at School? B: I don't really know. I . . . teachers for some time. (not speak)

9 We got home to find the whole house turned upside down. Thieves obviously . . . (break in and ransack)

10 A: Don't you know what the book is about? B: No, I . . . (not yet read)

11 A: Why didn't you come to the meeting? B: I . . . (not tell—*passive*)

12 I couldn't telephone you—I . . . (forget)

13 Don't worry about the telegram. It . . . (already send—*passive*)

14 You can stop looking for my gloves. I . . . (just find)

56 Respond to the statements and questions, using the present perfect or past perfect simple or continuous tense. (NB. The passive form may be found suitable in some cases.)

1 A: Your hands are filthy. B: Yes, I . . .

2 A: What's this book doing here? B: I . . .

3 A: Where do all these empty bottles come from? B: We . . .

4 A: These letters are still unopened. B: Yes, I . . .

5 A: All the pavements are wet. B: Yes, didn't you know? It . . .

6 A: There's an ambulance at the house next door. B: I expect someone . . .

7 A: Why aren't you at work today? B: I . . .

8 A: You've got a lovely tan. B: Yes, I . . .

9 A: You didn't come to the meeting. B: No, I thought it . . .

10 A: I hear you're leaving the firm. B: Yes, I . . .

57 The following passage is taken from a review of Britain's economic situation during the year 1965–66, as seen at the end of 1966. Complete the passage with the present perfect tense of the verbs in the list. Use each verb once only.

be   continue   grow   lead   leave   resume   rise

The most far-reaching problem . . . to be the balance of payments. Periodic balance of payments crises . . . to sharp checks to economic expansion and productive investment; these in turn . . . the country vulnerable to further foreign exchange difficulties when expansion . . . (*passive*). Britain's exports . . . at only an average rate of about 3 per cent per annum in volume over the past decade; the corresponding increase in the volume of imports of manufactures . . . particularly sharply. The average current surplus on visible and invisible trade together . . .

(*negative*) sufficient, therefore, to finance Britain's overseas expenditure.

58 The following paragraph is a summary of Britain's economic progress during the decade 1960–69 as seen at the end of 1969. Complete the paragraph with the present perfect tense of the verbs in the list. Use each verb once only.

be   improve   maintain   make   progress

Viewed as a whole the British economy . . . considerable progress over the past decade. Its rate of growth, if not so fast as that of some other industrial countries, . . . higher than in any earlier period over the past 50 years. At the same time relatively full employment . . . (*passive*) and consumption and living standards . . . steadily. Moreover, modernization of productive industry and the distributive system . . . despite persistent balance of payments difficulties.

59 In each example, one sentence (or clause) relates to an uncompleted action or series of actions in an extended period of present time, and the other relates to an action or series of actions that have occurred at some time before the present and having relevance to the current situation. Rewrite the sentences, using the present continuous tense in one sentence (or clause) of each example, and the present perfect in the other. The adverbs in italics should be put in their correct position.

1 He (write) a history of England in six volumes. Two volumes *already* (publish—*passive*)
2 The housing programme *now* (go ahead) quickly. Three new blocks of flats *already* (complete—*passive*)
3 The talks *rapidly* (approach) an end. Agreement *already* (reach—*passive*) on most points.
4 We *at present* (take) vigorous steps to modernize our factories. Much of our obsolete plant *already* (scrap—*passive*).
5 There is nothing new in what I (say). Indeed, it *often* (say—*passive*) before.
6 The Gallery *currently* (try) to build up its collection of *19th* century British paintings. Two important works by Millais (acquire—*passive*) over the last three months.

7 The Chancellor *constantly* (receive) suggestions for simplifying the tax system. These *on occasion* (be) quite sensible.

8 The Company (push ahead) with its plans for the establishment of new supermarkets. Five new stores (open—*passive*) during the past twelve months.

9 The Government *apparently* (manage) to keep wage demands in check. Only two pay increases (sanction—*passive*) during the last six months.

10 Troops *still* (have to) deal with sporadic outbreaks of violence, although the situation *now* (quieten down) considerably.

60 Answer the questions, using the present perfect tense.

1 What films have you seen this month?
2 What new places have you visited this year?
3 What new buildings have been completed in your town during the year?
4 How many cigarettes have you smoked today?
5 How much money have you spent this week?
6 What different types of lesson have you had today?
7 How many phone calls have you made since the beginning of this week?
8 What has your weather been like this month?
9 How many holidays have you spent abroad over the past six years?
10 Which of your friends haven't you seen for some time?
11 How long have you lived in your present house?
12 What articles have you lost during the past year?
13 How long have you been learning English?
14 How many questions have you answered so far?
15 How many questions have been answered correctly by your class as a whole?
16 How long has it taken to complete this exercise?

For and since

The perfect tenses are used with *for*, together with a phrase denoting a *period* of time, to indicate the duration or continuance of an action or state of affairs up to the time specified by the context or situation:

> *8a* I*'ve lived* (or I*'ve been living*) in London for twelve years. (up to the present time—say, 1970)

8b By the end of 1960, I'*d lived* (or I'*d been living*) in London for two years.

8c By the end of 1975, I *shall have lived* (or I *shall have been living*) in London for seventeen years.

The present perfect and past perfect tenses are used with *since*, together with a phrase or clause denoting the *beginning* of an action or state of affairs, to indicate the continuance of that action or state of affairs from the time specified until the present time, or until the time specified in the past:

9a I'*ve lived* in London since I was 21.

9b At the age of 40, he decided to move to the north of England. He *had* (up to that time) *lived* in London since he was 21, and had some misgivings about moving.

Since is also used as in *9a* and *9b* after the construction: *It's ×period of time*:

a. It's a long time since I met him.

However, the present perfect is also occasionally found after *since* in such sentences:

b. It's a long time since I've met him.

While there is little, if any, difference between these two sentences, we could perhaps make a distinction in emphasis (or focus of interest) by means of a paraphrase:

a. I last met him a long time ago. (the speaker is thinking primarily of the time of the last meeting)

b. I haven't met him for a long time. (the speaker is thinking of the length of time that has elapsed)

The use of perfect tenses appears to create special difficulties for foreign learners in sentences like the following:

10a He has never met you before. (during the whole of past time and up to the present)

10b That's the second time someone has interrupted me this evening. (during the whole of this evening and up to now)

10c This is the first cigarette I've smoked today. (during the whole of today and up to now)

11a I first spoke to him last Friday. I had never met him before. (during the whole of previous time and up to then—last Friday)

11b There was a knock at the door. It was the second time someone had interrupted me that evening. (during the whole of
that evening and up to then—the time of the knock at the
door)

11c I lit up at seven yesterday evening. It was the first cigarette
I had smoked that day. (during the whole of that day and
up to then—seven o'clock)

The *present* perfect in sentences 10*a*–10*c* automatically implies
'until now', while in *11a*–*11c* the *past* perfect indicates 'until
then', the time of 'then' being specified by the context or situation.

61 Rewrite the sentences, using the past simple tense for one of the
verbs in each example, and the present perfect tense for the
remaining verbs. The adverbs in italics should be put in their
correct position.

1 More people (take) holidays abroad since the foreign allowance
to tourists. (raise—*passive*).

2 The export performance of many companies (show) a striking
improvement since devaluation *first* (announce—*passive*).

3 Since British Railways (introduce) its new inter-city expresses,
many businessmen (take) to travelling by train.

4 Since I (make) my report last year, there (be) a steady improvement in the Company's trading position. The performance of
our overseas branch, which *now* (establish—*passive*) for five years,
(be) particularly encouraging.

5 Since the Government report *first* (publish—*passive*) conditions
(change) considerably.

6 Since the new laws (introduce—*passive*), the flow of immigrants
into Britain (reduce—*passive*) to a trickle.

7 The number of unofficial strikes in the factory (go down) drama-
tically since the new system of incentives (institute—*passive*).

8 The railways in Britain (be) under State control since they
(nationalize—*passive*) in 1948.

9 The new manager (have) many problems to solve since he (take
over) six months ago.

10 Output of vehicles (rise) to 1½ million in 1967, since when it
(remain) fairly static.

62 Rewrite the sentences, using the present perfect tense with *since* or *for*, as appropriate, e.g.

   a. He was last in touch with me three weeks ago.
      He hasn't been in touch with me for three weeks.
   b. The President last visited Britain in 1967.
      The President hasn't visited Britain since 1967.

1 I last went to the dentist two months ago.
2 He last spoke to me about his plans a year ago.
3 When I last met him he was 15 years old.
4 He last wrote to me when I was in America.
5 It last rained three weeks ago.
6 The side last won a home game two months ago.
7 I last had a cold last winter.
8 I last set eyes on him when he borrowed some money from me.
9 The Company last made a profit in 1968.
10 I last went on holiday six months ago.
11 The last time we saw a batsman of his calibre was in the days of Bradman.
12 I last mentioned it to him when we met a month ago.

63 Rewrite the sentences, using *since* as in the example, e.g.

      He was last in touch with me three weeks ago.
      It's three weeks since he was in touch with me.

1 I last went to the dentist two months ago.
2 He last spoke to me about his plans a year ago.
3 It last rained three weeks ago.
4 The side last won a home game two months ago.
5 I last went on holiday six months ago.
6 I last smoked a cigarette four days ago.
7 They wrote ten days ago, saying they had sent the goods.
8 We were last living all under one roof a long time ago.
9 I last read the book such a long time ago that I've forgotten what it's about.
10 He last visited us it seems ages ago.

Simple and continuous perfect forms (see also page 65)

12a Go out and get some fresh air! You've been sitting there reading all morning.
12b Look at the mess my paper's in! Who's been reading it?

In *12a*, the activity of sitting began at some earlier time and is still in progress at the time when the remark is made, whereas in *12b*, the verb draws attention to the duration of an activity that occurred before the time of speaking and which is not now taking place. In both cases, however, the action is relevant to the current situation: 'you' need some fresh air now because of your sitting reading all morning; 'my' paper is in a mess because of someone's earlier reading of it.

There are three points to note here:

(1) In sentences like *12a*, it would be possible to use the simple perfect form, because the phrase *all morning* itself expresses the idea of duration:

> Go out and get some fresh air! You've sat there reading all morning.

The use of the continuous form in this sentence is largely a matter of emphasis—it focuses attention on the duration of the activity. (See page 59 on the continuous forms.)

(2) Where such considerations do not apply, the choice is determined by either the nature of the action (*13a*, *13b*) or the meaning of the verb (*14*):

13a Joan: Ouch!
     John: What've you done?
     Joan: I've just cut my finger.

Joan would not reply 'I've been cutting my finger'—the accident is the work of a moment. We can compare this with:

13b John: Why are you crying?
     Joan: I've been cutting up onions for the last ten minutes.

On the other hand, the meaning of some verbs expresses the idea of duration, and the choice between simple and continuous may be an open one:[1]

14 I've $\genfrac{}{}{0pt}{}{\text{lived}}{\text{been living}}$ in London for five years.

(3) In other cases, the choice may depend on the contrast between completed and uncompleted action:

[1] Students should bear in mind that there are some verbs that are not normally used in any of the continuous forms. See page 66.

Who's been reading my paper?

Although the activity of reading has now finished, the speaker does not suggest that someone has read the whole paper, but simply that someone has been engaged in the process of reading it for a limited period in earlier time.

64 Complete the sentences with the simple or continuous form of the present perfect tense of the verbs in brackets. Use the short forms of the auxiliary verb where appropriate. The adverbs in italics should be put in their correct position.

1 I (write) the letter, so perhaps you would post it for me.
2 For the last two years, he (write) a history of the Civil War.
3 A: What you (do) for the last half hour? B: I (sit) here working at this problem.
4 We *always* (live) in a bungalow, so it will seem strange when we move into a house.
5 How you (keep)? Well, I hope.
6 You look very upset. What (happen)?
7 He shouldn't drive this evening. He (drink).
8 I'd better not drive. I *already* (drink) quite a lot.
9 The meat must be nearly ready. It (cook) for nearly an hour.
10 You (not finish) that book yet? You (read) it for more than a week.
11 I wonder if John (forget) my number. I (expect) him to call for the past two hours.
12 I'm sorry we're late. You (wait) long?
13 A: How long (know) you the truth? B: I *only just* (find out), but I (find out) a lot of other things just recently.
14 If he (ask) me that question once, he (ask) me a dozen times.

Present perfect in adverbial clauses of time referring to future

15 You can go when you've finished your work.

In adverbial clauses of time referring to future, we use one of the present tenses (see page 53). We do not use *shall* or *will* in a predictive sense in such clauses. The conjunctions commonly used to introduce time clauses are: *when, as soon as, before, after, until, once, by the time* (*that*), *the moment* (*that*).

In some sentences, there may be little difference in meaning between the present simple and the present perfect in the time clause:

16 I shall leave as soon as the meeting ends.
     I shall leave as soon as the meeting has ended.

In other cases, however, there are two factors that appear to operate in determining an English speaker's choice:

(1) The perfect forms indicate that an action or event occurs *before* the time indicated by the context. We can, therefore, distinguish between:

17a Come over and see us when our guests leave.
17b Come over and see us when our guests have left.

Sentence *17a* might suggest that the arrival of one set of visitors will coincide with the leaving of the other, whereas *17b* clearly indicates that 'our guests' will no longer be with us when our other visitors come.

A great deal depends on the meaning of the verb involved; either the present perfect or the present simple is appropriate in *16* above, while only the present perfect makes good sense in *18*:

18 We can go out as soon as we've had dinner.
     (not * We can go out as soon as we have dinner)

(2) The perfect forms also indicate that an action or event has produced a result or state of affairs that is relevant to the current situation, and there is often a causal connection between the time clause and the main clause:

19 You'll feel a lot better after you've had a rest.

The conjunction *after* itself clearly establishes the time relationship between the two activities or events, and the present perfect is used here to establish the causal connection between these events rather than to establish a time difference between them.

65 Rewrite the sentences, using the imperative or a future form in one clause, and the present perfect in the other.

1 I (let) you know as soon as I (finish).
2 (Not start) on Section 2 until you (complete) all the questions in Section 1.

3 (Not make up) your mind until you (have) a chance to give the matter some thought.
4 I (be) ready for some lunch by the time I (finish) digging the garden.
5 Where man (go) in space after he (conquer) the moon?
6 You (get) used to our methods when you (work) here a bit longer. And once you (get) used to our methods, you (find) the job a lot easier.
7 The builders (start) work as soon as the plans (approve—*passive*) by the Local Authority.
8 He (make) a very fine tennis player when he (have) a little more competitive experience.
9 As soon as we (thrash out) this problem we (be able) to go ahead.
10 Please (not smoke) until after the plane (take off).

66 When you have checked your answers to the above exercise, rewrite the sentences in reported speech, beginning as suggested.

1 I promised to . . .
2 The examinees were instructed not . . .
3 I told him not . . .
4 He told his wife that . . .
5 The editorial asked where . . .
6 The manager assured the trainee that . . .
7 The architect told his client that . . .
8 His coach was of the opinion that . . .
9 The chairman agreed that . . .
10 The air hostess asked the passengers not . . .

Much of what was said about the choice between the present simple and the present perfect in future time clauses (pages 80–81) also applies to the choice between the past simple and past perfect in past time clauses. In some sentences, there may be little difference in meaning between the two verb forms:

20 I left as soon as the meeting ended.
   I left as soon as the meeting had ended.

If, however, we need to make a time distinction between two past events, we use the past perfect for the earlier of the two events:

21a We went out as soon as we'd had dinner.
21b When I got there, everyone had gone home.

We also use the past perfect if we wish to establish a causal connection between two clauses, even when a time distinction between two events is already made clear by a conjunction:

22   After he had given the police his name and address, he was allowed to go.

We could paraphrase the time clause in 22 in either of two ways:

a. When the police *were in possession* of the necessary information, . . . (this expresses the current relevance of his having given his name and address)
b. *Because* the police were in possession of the necessary information, . . . (this expresses the causal connection)

If we wish to list a number of past events *simply as a sequence,* and if the time distinction between these events is made clear by words like *after, before, first, next, later,* etc., we can use a succession of past simple forms:

> We *had* a very busy evening. First the Smiths *came* for cocktails, and we *were* later *joined* for dinner by the Joneses. Shortly after the Joneses *arrived,* we *got* a phone call from the Robinsons to say they *couldn't come.* We *ate* an enormous meal, and then *looked* at some slides of our holiday in Majorca. At 11.30 the Joneses *left* in a hurry to catch the last bus, and half an hour later the Smiths *called* a taxi to take them home.

In noun clauses, following the past tense of verbs like *realize, know, think,* etc., the past perfect contrasts in meaning with the past simple:

> realized
> 23a I knew   *he had acted stupidly.*
> thought

> realized
> 23b I knew   *he* (sometimes) *acted stupidly.*
> thought

In 23a, the noun clause (in italics) refers to something already done before the act of realizing, knowing or thinking, whereas in 23b, it refers to what was a recurrent feature of the situation at that time in the past.

In adjectival (relative) clauses, a similar distinction applies:

24a He apologized for any trouble *he had caused.*
24b He (generally) apologized for any trouble *he caused.*

The past perfect is, of course, used quite regularly in all three types of clause mentioned (adverbial, noun, and adjectival) when associated with *for* and *since*:

25a He dropped out of the race after *he had been running* for only five minutes.
   We hardly recognized each other, *because we hadn't met* since we were quite young.
   We immediately recognized each other, *although we hadn't met* for years.
25b We all knew *he had been drinking heavily* since his wife died.
25c The divers came across a wreck *that had lain on the sea bed* for over 200 years.

The past perfect (like other perfect tenses) is also frequently used in association with the adverbs *already, just, yet, still,* and *before*:

26a When I got there, the meeting had $\genfrac{}{}{0pt}{}{\text{already}}{\text{just}}$ started.

26b When I last spoke to him, he $\genfrac{}{}{0pt}{}{\text{hadn't yet}}{\text{still hadn't}}$ heard the result.

26c He particularly wanted to visit London because he had never been there before.

67 Rewrite the sentences, using the past simple or past perfect of the verbs in brackets, as appropriate. The adverbs in italics should be put in their correct position.

1 We (get down) to business as soon as we (introduce—*passive*) to each other.
2 When Queen Victoria (die) in 1901, she (reign) for over 60 years.
3 Once they (settle) the agenda, the committee (circulate) it to all members of the society.
4 Nothing (move—*passive*) in the room until after the police (take) photographs.
5 He (refuse) to sign the agreement until after certain points (clear up—*passive*).
6 We all (realize) what a lucky escape we (have).

7 A friend of mine (return) to his house after a holiday to find it (break into—*passive*).

8 None of his teachers (understand) how he (manage) to fail the examination.

9 I (write) to the suppliers asking why the goods (not arrive) *yet*. They (reply) to say that they *already* (send—*passive*).

10 I (call) at the manager's office, but (discover) I *just* (miss) him. He (go out) for lunch.

11 A search party (set out) to look for the two climbers, who (leave) their hotel early that morning and who *still* (not return).

12 The troops (have) great difficulty in breaking through the defences, which (strengthen—*passive*) considerably during the preceding month.

13 The scientist suddenly (see) the answer to the problem that (occupy) his mind for the last two months.

14 The team (win) the game against a side that *previously* (not beat—*passive*) at home that season.

15 The Company (decide) to continue with a design that (stand) the test of time.

68 Rewrite the sentences, using the past simple tense for *one* verb in each example, and the past perfect for the remaining verb or verbs. Any adverbs in italics should be placed in their correct position.

1 The results last term (be) better than anyone (expect).

2 What (happen) next was just what everyone (fear).

3 We eventually (arrive) at a solution, but not the one we (envisage).

4 Not one person (agree) with him. This was something he (not anticipate).

5 Ten o'clock, and the climbers (be) *already* near the summit. They (make) better progress than they *ever* (dare) to hope for.

6 No one (seem) to know exactly what arrangements (make—*passive*) for accommodation.

7 The stop-watch (say) three minutes, fifty-eight seconds—he (break) the world record. He (succeed) in doing what *previously* (think—*passive*) impossible.

8 Now (begin) the exploration of a territory that no European *ever* (set) foot on before.

9 The motorist (discover) to his relief that he (not take) the wrong road after all.

10 The Government (find) itself forced to adopt policies it *earlier* (reject).

69 Complete the passage with the past perfect tense of the verbs in the list. Use each verb once only.

open   start   invite   fix   publish

It is planned that 1,000 miles of motorways should be completed by the early 1970s. At the end of May 1969 in England and Wales, 570 miles . . . (*passive*) for traffic and construction . . . or tenders . . . (*passive*) for a further 294 miles. The lines of an additional 221 miles . . . (*passive*) and draft schemes . . . (*passive*) for 96 miles.

70 Replace the non-finite clauses in italics with finite clauses,[1] using the past perfect tense. Suitable conjunctions have been suggested where necessary. (NB. *Since* is used to introduce a clause of *reason* in these examples, *not* a clause of time.)

1 He gave up hope of passing the examination, *having already failed it twice.* (since)
2 *Having made quite sure* that everything was ready for an emergency blast-off, the astronauts stepped out of the lunar module and on to the moon's surface. (when)
3 The two parties decided to break off negotiations, *having come no nearer to a solution* during three days of continuous discussion. (since)
4 Mr Smith retired at the age of 70, *having spent nearly 40 years with the Company.* (after)
5 I was amazed when he accepted a drink, *having always assumed* that he was a teetotaller. (since)
6 He lost interest in his job, *having failed to obtain promotion.* (since)
7 The MP resigned through ill health, after *having represented his constituency for over 25 years.*
8 I had to get a new passport, *my old one having expired.* (since)
9 The newspaper finally ceased publication, *its circulation having dropped steadily* over a period of years. (since)

---

[1] For an explanation of these terms, see the Appendix, pages 293–294.

10 The coin was something of a rarity, *only a small number having ever been put into circulation.* (as)

71 The following is a report of part of a speech made by the Minister of Technology in a Parliamentary debate on January 23rd, 1969. Rewrite the passage in direct speech, paying special attention to your rendering of the verbs which appear in the past perfect tense. Begin at the second paragraph.

MR BENN, Minister of Technology (Bristol, South-East, Lab.) moved the second reading of the Shipbuilding Industry Bill.

He said it raised from £200m. to £400m. the statutory ceiling on the guarantees he could give to facilitate the financing of orders for ships placed by British owners with British shipyards.

In 1966 British shipbuilders had booked orders for only 380,000 gross tons which was 2·1 per cent of the world merchant ship orders. In 1967 figures were 1,040,000 tons which represented 4·7 per cent of world orders and in 1968 new orders amounted to 2,560,000 gross tons representing 10 per cent of world orders. This was a remarkable growth. This pressure had meant that British yards had been taking both home and export orders for delivery further ahead than seemed possible in the winter of 1966–67.

Net home orders which had amounted to just over 250,000 tons in 1966 reached nearly 1m. tons in 1967 and 1,500,000 in 1968.

It had never been intended that the guarantee scheme should mean feather-bedding the industry; nor had there been any belief that mergers by themselves would guarantee the efficiency of the industry.

The board was taking a new initiative with the industry to provide help that was not limited to the provision of grants and loans. They had formed a committee of shipbuilding finance directors who were examining accounting methods. They had promised or made grants totalling nearly £6m. and loans totalling over £14m., and other applications were coming up for consideration.

The Q.E.2[1] was by far the largest project on which the industry was engaged. The Government had not in any way intervened

[1] 'Queen Elizabeth II' was built for Cunard Shipping Company, and made her maiden voyage to New York on 2nd May, 1969.

in its design, construction, or in the choice of equipment installed. The ship was an extremely fine one as Government technical experts were able to confirm. He had discussed the recent misfortunes with both the chairmen of Cunard and of Upper Clyde Shipbuilders Ltd. He had also consulted Sir William Swallow who had been looking into the possible effects on the shipbuilding industry.

The present position on completion of the accommodation and engine failures had been widely reported in the press, and there was nothing more that he could add.

For use of the past perfect in unreal conditions, see exercises 81-85.

Conditional sentences

Introductory notes

0 If you *heat* ice, it *melts*.
1 If we *catch* the 10 o'clock train, we *shall* (can, may, etc.) *get* there by lunch-time.
2 If we *caught* the 10 o'clock train, we *would* (could, might, etc.) *get* there by lunch-time.
3 If we *had caught* the 10 o'clock train, we *would* (could, might, etc.) *have got* there by lunch-time.

There are many possible sequences of tense in conditional sentences, but the examples above represent perhaps the four commonest and the most useful ones to learn initially. Each of the sentences may be divided into two parts:

0a If you heat ice
 b it melts
1a If we catch the 10 o'clock train
 b we shall get there by lunch-time
2a If we caught the 10 o'clock train
 b we would get there by lunch-time
3a If we had caught the 10 o'clock train
 b we would have got there by lunch-time

Part *a* of each sentence (introduced by *if*) is called a *conditional clause*. It states the condition that must be satisfied before part *b* may be true. Part *b* of each sentence is called the *main* (principal) *clause*. The two parts of each sentence may be written in reverse order with no change in meaning, though the conditional clause tends to become less emphatic when placed second:

0 Ice melts if you heat it.
1 We shall get there by lunch-time if we catch the 10 o'clock train.
2 We would get there by lunch-time if we caught the 10 o'clock train.
3 We would have got there by lunch-time if we had caught the 10 o'clock train.

It is worth noting that in these four sentences *the conditional clause does not contain a conditional verb form.*

Type O-cause and effect

a. If you *heat* ice, it *melts.*
b. If I *make* a promise, I *keep* it.

These sentences are statements of universal truth or general validity, and in this type of sentence, *if* corresponds closely in meaning to *when(ever)*. Statements in this form commonly appear in factual discussions or explanatory (particularly scientific and technical) material. The tenses in both the conditional and the main clause are the same. Sentence *b* may be written in the past tense with a similar correspondence between the verb forms in the two clauses:

c. If I *made* a promise, I *kept* it.

72 Answer the questions with conditional sentences like *a* or *b*, e.g.

What happens if you heat ice?
If you heat ice, it melts.

Note: In this example, *you* is equivalent to *one*. In the reply, therefore, we also use *you*, (not *I*).

1 What happens if flowers don't get any water?
2 What must a motorist do if the traffic lights are at red?
3 What materials do you need if you want to write a letter? (*you = one*)

89

4 What do you like to drink if you're very thirsty? (*you = you*)
5 Who do businessmen go to see if they want to borrow money?
6 What do you expect a teacher to do if you make a mistake?
7 What must one have if one wants to visit a foreign country?
8 Who do people go to see if they feel ill?
9 What happens if there is a power failure?
10 How do people dress in your country if they work in an office?

Type 1—basic forms

a. If we *catch* the 10 o'clock train, we *shall* (can, may, etc.) *get* there by lunch-time.
b. If you *wake up* before me, *give* me a call.

In these sentences, the conditional clauses represent OPEN conditions; that is, conditions that may or may not be fulfilled. We make such statements when the action or event mentioned in the conditional clause is being actively considered, or is under discussion, or appears likely to happen. Such statements can even be comments on decisions already taken.

Conditions of this sort are sometimes labelled 'probable', but it is important to note that the probability of the condition being fulfilled often exists only in the mind of the speaker. If, for example, it seems likely that someone is going to do something foolish or dangerous, we give a warning:

If you *touch* that plate, you*'ll burn* your hand.

Only a fool would fulfil the condition in these circumstances.
The commonest sequence of tenses in this type of sentence is:

(If) present tense, (Main) Future (or Modal verb) *or* Imperative

Note that *will* and *shall* are not used in a predictive sense in the conditional clause, even though it is the future that is referred to.

73 Write conditional sentences like *a* or *b* above, using the given fact in your conditional clause, and adding a suitable completion, e.g.

He's thinking of going to England.
If he *goes* to England, he *will have to* learn English.

1 It looks as if those shoes in the window are my size.
2 Don't drop that vase!
3 It looks like being fine tomorrow.
4 My father has suggested that I change my job.
5 It seems that we'll be late for the theatre.
6 Don't lose my library book!
7 You may meet some friends of mine in London.
8 He expects to pass his exam.
9 They're hoping it will be a baby boy.
10 I anticipate getting a rise in salary next year.

Type 1—variations

a. If we *should miss* the 10 o'clock train, we *shan't get* there till after lunch.

The introduction of *should* (sometimes stressed) in the *conditional clause* has the effect of making it seem less likely that the condition will be fulfilled. It is possible to substitute *by any chance* for *should*, without changing the meaning:

> If *by any chance* we *miss* the 10 o'clock train, we *shan't get* there till after lunch.

We may call this a *condition of remote possibility*, and this variation may be applied to *any* conditional clause of this first type. Note that only *should* (never 'would') is used in this way.

b. If you *will reserve* seats, we *shall be* sure of a comfortable journey.

We saw earlier that *will* is not used in a predictive sense in the conditional clause in conditionals of Type 1, even though the sentence has a future time reference. In the above sentence, *will* in the conditional clause is not an auxiliary indicating future; it is a modal verb, and introduces the idea of 'your' agreeing, or being willing, to do what is suggested.[1] We cannot use this construction in the following sentence:

> If he *gets* my letter in time, he'*ll be able* to change his plans.

We cannot say *'If he will get my letter in time', since 'he' can hardly exercise any willingness or unwillingness to get it. Students

[1] It is possible to use the tentative or 'polite' form *would* in the conditional clause, the rest of the sentence being unchanged: If you *would* reserve seats, we shall be sure of a comfortable journey. See also page 23 and page 98.

must, therefore, be careful to use *will* in this way only where the context will support the idea of co-operation, agreement, or willingness on the part of the subject.

74 Rewrite the sentences, substituting for the words in italics a verb form as in *a* above (Nos. 1–5) or as in *b* (Nos. 6–10).

a. If *by any chance* you *die* before retiring age, your widow will receive your pension for a period of 7 years after your death.

If you *should die* before retiring age, your widow will receive your pension for a period of 7 years after your death. (Nos. 1–5)

b. If the unions *are prepared to accept* new productivity agreements, the employers will meet their wage demands.

If the unions *will accept* new productivity agreements, the employers will meet their wage demands. (Nos. 6–10)

1 If *by any chance* your car *needs* any attention during the first twelve months, take it to an authorized dealer.

2 If *by any chance* I *am* a little late coming home, don't wait up for me.

3 If the baby *wakes up* (*though I doubt he will*), give him some warm milk.

4 If *by some unlucky chance* the talks *break down*, it will be a black day for industry.

5 If *by some remote chance* he *dares* to show his face again, I shall give him a piece of my mind!

6 If he *is willing to accept* the nomination, a lot of electors will vote for him.

7 If you *are prepared to take* the trouble to read his letter carefully, you will see what he means.

8 If you *are agreeable to waiting* a few more minutes, the doctor will see you without your making an appointment.

9 If my father *is willing to give* me permission, I shall spend a few months abroad.

10 What will you do if he *refuses to give* you permission?

Type 1—alternative forms

a. *Set* your alarm clock, and you *won't oversleep*.

b. *Set* your alarm clock, or (else) you*'ll oversleep*.

In these sentences, the imperative construction is equivalent to an 'if' clause. We can rewrite the sentences, using *if*:

a. If you *set* your alarm clock, you *won't oversleep*.
b. If you *don't set* your alarm clock, you'll oversleep.

Note that the conjunction 'and' implies a verb form in the conditional clause of the same sign (positive or negative) as the imperative; whereas 'or (else)' implies a verb form of the opposite sign. Thus in *a.* '*Set . . . and . . .*' becomes 'If you *set . . .*'; whereas in *b.* '*Set . . . or . . .*' becomes 'If you *don't set . . .*'

Type 1—summary of forms

(If) present tense, (Main) future *or* imperative

> If we *catch* the early train, we'*ll get* there by lunch-time.
> If you *wake up* before me, *give* me a call.

(If) should × infinitive, (Main) future *or* imperative

> If we *should miss* the early train, we *shan't get* there till after lunch. (*should = by any chance*)
> If anyone *should call* while I'm out, *tell* them I'll be back at two.

(If) will × infinitive, (Main) future *or* imperative

> If you'*ll cook* the dinner, I'*ll do* the washing up afterwards.
> If he *will do* the work quickly, *give* him the contract.
> (*will = be willing*)

Imperative, (Main) and *or* or × future

> *Set* your alarm clock, *and* you *won't oversleep*.
> *Set* your alarm clock, *or* (else) you'*ll oversleep*.

75 Complete the sentences, following one of the patterns for conditionals of Type 1.

1 We'll just manage to catch the train if . . .
2 If I see him again, I . . .
3 I will accept your explanation only if . . .
4 Tell me the truth or you . . .
5 If my bank manager will lend me the money, . . .

6 What will happen if . . .?
7 If you don't hear from me by next Friday, . . .
8 If the Government continues to antagonize the Trade Unions in this way, . . .
9 If your work continues to improve, . . .
10 . . . only if you will promise not to tell anyone else.
11 Look up the answer in the key only if . . .
12 What will he say if . . .?
13 If the worst should come to the worst, . . .
14 Give me time and . . .

Type 2—basic forms

a. If we *caught* the 10 o'clock train, we *would* (could, might, etc.) *get* there by lunch-time.
b. If I *came into* a fortune, I *would give up* working.
c. If I *knew* how it worked, I *could tell* you what to do.

In these sentences, the conditional clauses represent what is *a* possible, *b* hypothetical/imaginary, or *c* contrary to present fact. The verb form in the conditional clause represents the attitude of the speaker towards the condition; it *does not represent time*, which is indicated (if at all) by other elements in the context or situation.

Sentence *a* is analogous to Type 1 ('If we catch . . ., we shall get . . .'), but it is more suppositional. The speaker either regards catching that train as improbable, or he wishes to put forward in a more tentative or 'polite' way the suggestion of catching it. It does not *necessarily* follow that the condition is *in fact* unlikely to be fulfilled.

Sentence *b*, on the other hand, is much more hypothetical: it is a form of day-dreaming in which we all indulge at times. Sentence *c* presents us with a totally imaginary (or unreal) situation with reference to the time of speaking: it implies that I *don't*, in fact, *know* how it works, so I *can't* tell you what to do. Note that the *past* tense is used here to indicate *present* unreality.

The three sentences are formally identical: they all have the same sequence of tenses:

> (If) past tense, (Main) conditional

However, contextually (i.e. in their meaning and use) they are rather different. They represent three points on a scale of de-

94

creasing probability, from *a* suppositional or tentative but possible, to *b* hypothetical but not impossible, to *c* contrary to present fact, and hence unreal. Note that the conditional tense is not used in the conditional clause.

Note: It is, of course, possible to use *should* as well as *would* after *I/we* (see examples *a* and *b* above), but *would* (or *'d*) is commoner. Moreover, since *should* also functions as a modal verb synonymous with *ought to*, its use could occasionally lead to ambiguity:

1 If you *asked* me tomorrow, I would be able to give you the answer.
2 If you *asked* me tomorrow, I should be able to give you the answer.
3 If you *ask* me tomorrow, I should be able to give you the answer.

Sentences *1* and *2* can have the same meaning—my ability to give you the answer would be *the certain result* of your asking me tomorrow; but sentence *2* may also mean that my ability to give you the answer is *the result that could reasonably be expected* from your asking me tomorrow.

The meanings would be quite distinct in spoken English, since *should* is unstressed in the first case ($\int$əd) and stressed in the second ($\int$ud).

There is no ambiguity in the following sentence, where only one interpretation makes good sense:

If I followed his advice, I would/should be a fool (= the certain result.)

Sentence *3* above illustrates *should* used unequivocally in the sense of expectation.

76 Complete the sentences, following the pattern of Type 2 conditionals. You should find that many of your sentences can be interpreted as 'tentative' suggestions.

1 If you explained the situation to your solicitor, he . . .
2 Perhaps he . . ., if you spoke to him yourself.
3 If you changed your job, you . . .
4 If you went to see a doctor, he . . .
5 If we bought a house in the country, we . . .

6 If they came to see us in London, we . . .
7 I'm sure he would take the job on if . . .
8 If you took the shoes back to the shop, they . . .
9 If you read the book a second time, you . . .
10 If we all pooled our resources, we . . .

77 Answer the questions with conditional statements of Type 2.

1 What cities or other places of interest would you visit if you went to America? (Russia? Brazil? Australia? etc.)
2 What would you do (or not do) if you could live your life over again.
3 What would you say or do if someone called you a fool?
4 What first name would you choose for yourself if you were able to change now?
5 What famous person would you like to meet if you had the chance?
6 Which country would you choose if you decided to live abroad?
7 What changes would you make in your house, assuming you had the money?
8 What would you do if you saw a house on fire?
9 What would you do if you had something stolen?
10 Which books or gramophone records would you take with you if you went to live on a desert island?

78 Write sentences like example *c* above (page 94), based on the given facts, e.g.

> The soup *isn't* hot, so it *isn't* very enjoyable.
> If the soup *were* hot, it *would be* very enjoyable.

1 Since she doesn't love him, she won't marry him.
2 Our teacher explains things clearly, so we understand his lessons.
3 As I haven't a watch, I can't tell you the time.
4 Britain doesn't export enough, so she has a constant balance of payments problem.
5 Since I know the meaning of the word, I don't have to look it up.
6 This exercise is easy, so everyone will get the correct answers.
7 I know the answer so I can tell you.
8 We haven't any matches so we can't light the fire.

As we saw in example *c* above (page 94), the idea of something contrary to *present* fact is conveyed by the use of the *past* tense in the conditional clause. We also use the past tense to refer to present unreality after the verb *wish* ('if only' also expresses the wish of the speaker), and after expressions like *I'd rather* and *It's time:*

a. I wish (that) I *were* rich! (If only I *were* rich!)
b. I'd rather you *told* me frankly what you think.
c. It's time (It's about time, It's high time) we *left*.

We never use the present tense or a future form after *wish*. We use either the past tense as illustrated above, or we can use *would* (not 'will') to indicate that people or events frustrate our desires:

> I wish you would hurry up!
> I wish it would stop raining! (If only it would stop raining!)
> Cp. I *hope* it *will* stop raining soon.

Note: The subjunctive hardly survives as a distinctive form nowadays, except in the past tense of *to be* in conditional clauses, when *were* is used for all Persons: *If* I/you/he/she/it/we/they *were*.

79 Write out the sentences, using the verbs in brackets in the correct tense. Then write a conditional sentence based on each answer, e.g.

> I wish I (earn) more money.
> I wish I *earned* more money. Why? Because if I *earned* more money, I'd *be able* to buy a bigger car.

1 I wish I (can) speak several languages.
2 I wish I (have) a car.
3 She wishes her parents (approve) of her boy friend.
4 I wish I (be) older (*or* younger).
5 I wish you (like) 'pop' music.

Type 2—variations

a. If were *were to miss* the 10 o'clock train, we *wouldn't get* there till after lunch.

The use of *were to* in the conditional clause sometimes has the effect of emphasizing the suppositional nature of the condition, and is in some ways analogous to the use of *should* in conditional clauses in Type 1: we can often substitute *by any chance* without changing the meaning:

> If *by any chance* we *missed* the 10 o'clock train, we *wouldn't get* there till after lunch.

Were to is used for all Persons, and this variation may be applied to *any* conditional clause of this second type.[1]

b. If you *would reserve* seats, we *would be* sure of a comfortable journey.

In this sentence, *would* is not part of a conditional tense; it is a modal verb, and represents a more tentative (or 'polite') form of *will* as used in conditional clauses of Type 1 (see p. 91). It introduces the idea of 'your' agreeing, or being willing, to do what is suggested. We cannot use this construction in the following sentence:

> If he *got* my letter in time, he *would be able* to change his plans.

We cannot say **'If he *would get* my letter in time', since 'he' can hardly exercise any willingness or unwillingness to get it. Students must, therefore, be careful to use *would* in this way only where the context will support the idea of co-operation, agreement, or willingness on the part of the subject.

Type 2—summary of forms

(If) past tense, (Main) conditional

> If we *caught* the early train, we'*d get* there by lunch-time.

(If) were to × infinitive, (Main) conditional

> If we *were to miss* the early train, we *wouldn't get* there till after lunch.

[1] It is important to distinguish between *were to* used as part of a conditional construction, and the different forms *am/is/are to* and *was/were to*, used to indicate obligation. The difference is illustrated in the following pair of sentences:

1 If he were to get in touch with me, I could explain.
= Supposing he got in touch with me, . . .
2 If he was to get in touch with me, why hasn't he done so?
= If the arrangement was that he should get in touch with me, why . . .

(If) would × infinitive, (Main) conditional

> If you'*d cook* the dinner, I'*d do* the washing up afterwards.

80 Complete the sentences, following one of the patterns for conditionals of Type 2.

1 What . . . if you were in my shoes?
2 If . . ., I wouldn't think of changing my job.
3 If my father were to say such a thing to me, . . .
4 How would you react if . . .?
5 If only you would read more carefully, . . .
6 If you were to stay in England just a few months longer, . . .
7 Do you think I would be telling you this if . . .?
8 I wouldn't buy the picture even if . . .
9 It might only add to our difficulties if . . .
10 Even if he knew the truth, what . . .?
11 If only he would admit he was wrong, . . .
12 I'd much rather you . . .

Type 3—basic forms, and variation

a. If we *had caught* the 10 o'clock train, we *would* (could, might, etc.) *have got* there by lunch-time.

This sentence is completely hypothetical, and represents what is contrary to past fact. In this case, the *past perfect* tense is used to indicate *past* unreality—we *didn't catch* the 10 o'clock train, so we *didn't get* there by lunch-time.

This is analogous to the use of the past tense to indicate present unreality in Type 2c, and tense usage after the verb *wish* follows the same pattern: we use the past perfect to refer to something wished-for in the past:

> I wish you *had told* me before. (but you *didn't*)

Variations on sentence *a* are not very common, though sentences like the following are occasionally met with:

b. If you *were to have asked* me, I *would have been* only too willing to help.

81 Write sentences like *a* above, based on the given facts, e.g.

> As you *didn't explain* your problem to me, I *wasn't* able to help you.

If you *had explained* your problem to me, I *would have been* able to help you.

1 He didn't give me his number, so I couldn't telephone him.
2 As the sun was in the right direction, the photographs came out very well.
3 The shop didn't pack the goods properly, so they got damaged.
4 The Government raised taxes, so they were very unpopular.
5 He wasn't able to answer all the questions, so he didn't pass the examination.

82 Write sentences like *a* above, basing your *conditional* clause on the given fact, and adding a suitable main clause, e.g.

She didn't take the medicine.
If she *had taken* the medicine, she *would have felt* much better.

1 He passed his examination.
2 We didn't get there on time.
3 She didn't read the book.
4 We understood what he was saying.
5 The rocket didn't go into orbit.

83 Repeat the above exercise, basing your *main clause* on the given fact, and adding a suitable conditional clause, e.g.

She didn't take the medicine.
She *would have taken* the medicine if it *hadn't tasted* so awful.

It is possible for each of the two clauses in a conditional sentence to have a different time reference, and in this case we get a 'mixed' type of sentence:

If we *had brought* a map with us, we *would know* which road to take.

The conditional clause represents a situation contrary to a *past* fact (we *didn't bring* a map), and the main clause represents a situation contrary to a *present* fact (we *don't know* which road to take).

84 Write sentences like the example above, based on the given facts.

1 He failed his examination last year, so he is taking it again in June.
2 The Government made so many mistakes when it first came to office that it won't win the next election.
3 We missed the train, so we're waiting on this cold platform.
4 There was a very sharp frost last night, so we're able to go skating today.
5 Since you didn't take my advice, you're in a difficult position now.

85 Complete the sentences, following one of the patterns for conditionals of Type 3.

1 I would have enjoyed the party much more if . . .
2 It . . . if the sea hadn't been so rough.
3 Would you have been able to come next Tuesday if . . .?
4 If you had taken my advice, . . .
5 If I had realized that you were really serious in what you said, . . .
6 If it hadn't been for the fact that his father has influence, . . .
7 If he were to have told me the truth in the first place, . . .
8 Would you have lent him the money if . . .?
9 What difference would it have made, even if . . .?
10 If the fire brigade had arrived but a quarter of an hour earlier, . . .
11 I'm sure she wouldn't have married him if . . .
12 If . . ., we would have left without them.

Inversion

An inversion of subject and verb may be used instead of *if* in the conditional clause of some types of sentences:

1 *Should you need* my help again, just give me a ring.
= If you should need my help again, . . .
2 *Were the Government to go back* on this election pledge, there would be a revolt among back-benchers.
= If the Government were to go back . . .
3 *Had I known* you were ill, I would have visited you.
= If I had known you were ill, . . .

The first and third types of inversion occur in both the written language and (though less commonly) the spoken. The second type, however, is generally confined to the written language. All occur most commonly when 'it' is the subject and 'be' is the verb in the conditional clause.

86 Rewrite the sentences, making an inversion in the conditional clauses, as in the examples above.

1 If you should need to consult me again, you can contact me at this number.
2 The talks will continue throughout the night if the need should arise.
3 If you should be late once again, you'll lose your job.
4 If it were not for the fact that his father is on the board of directors, he would never have got the job.
5 If such a merger were ever to be proposed, it would undoubtedly be referred to the Monopolies Commission.
6 If it were not for the expense involved, I would go there by air.
7 If it hadn't been for your laziness, you could have finished the work by now.
8 If he had taken a little more time to think, he might have acted more sensibly.
9 If the attempted assassination had succeeded, there would almost certainly have been civil and political chaos.
10 If purchase tax on cars had been raised yet again, there would have been an outcry from the motor manufacturers.

Conjunctions introducing conditional clauses

The conditional clauses in all the examples so far have begun with *if*. In type *0*, *if* is closely related in meaning to *when(ever)*:

> If I make a promise, I keep it.

In some cases, *if* corresponds closely to *as*, *since*, or *because*:

> If (as you say) you haven't done the homework, you won't be able to follow this lesson.

If can also introduce a concessive-type clause:

> If *you* know the answer, nobody else does.
> =Although you may know the answer, nobody else does.

Other conjunctions commonly used to introduce 'true' conditional clauses are illustrated in the following sentences:

Suppose (or *supposing*) you told him the truth, what could
he do about it?

You can borrow my notes *on condition* (or *provided*) that you
give them back to me tomorrow.

You can come with us, *so long as* (or *as long as*) you don't
make a nuisance of yourself.

For a negative condition, we can use *unless*, which in many
cases has the same meaning as *if . . . not*,[1] though it is more
emphatic:

He wouldn't have come *unless* you *had* invited him.
= He wouldn't have come *if* you *hadn't* invited him.

Unless is especially useful for introducing clauses that contain
other negative elements, and we could not substitute *if . . . not*
in the following sentence:

Don't ask me to explain unless you really don't understand.

In case poses a rather special problem. It introduces a con-
tingency or possibility against which a precaution is needed in
advance. The difference between *in case* and *if* is illustrated in
the following two sentences:

a. I'm taking an umbrella in case it rains later on.
b. I'll take an umbrella if it rains later on.

In *a*, I am taking an umbrella *now*, whatever the weather and
even if it's fine now, so as to be prepared for the later possibility
of its raining. In *b*, my decision whether or not to take an umbrella (later on) will depend on whether or not it is raining at the
time.

87 Complete the sentences, following any correct sequence of
tenses.

1 If only . . ., you wouldn't now be in such a difficult position.
2 If . . ., tell him I'm out.
3 I can't understand why . . ., unless he thinks we are all fools.
4 If you are to succeed in your career, . . .
5 So long as . . ., swimming in this river is fairly safe.
6 If you were to explain the situation to him, I'm sure . . .

[1] Teachers will realize that this does not account for all occurrences of *unless*.
For an interesting consideration of the problem, see *English Language
Teaching*, Vol. XXIV, No. 2, p. 154.

7 Is there any point in your coming with us if . . .?
8 How . . ., if you didn't know my address?
9 Should Mr Smith ring up while I'm at lunch, . . .
10 The electors can't possibly form an opinion unless . . .
11 If . . ., I shall blame you for it.
12 If you knew the answer, why . . .?
13 My neighbour said I could borrow his lawn-mower provided that . . .
14 If anything has occurred to make you change your mind, . . .
15 When . . ., supposing we left immediately?
16 Had it been anyone but you that spoke to me in such a way, . . .
17 How I wish . . .
18 Should the Government be defeated on this vital issue, the Prime Minister . . .
19 If you . . ., you have only to say so.
20 If you really have been studying English for so long, it's about time you . . .

88 Describe the town where you live, or your place of work, or your school, incorporating (a) comments on its disadvantages or shortcomings ('If they had installed a lift in the building, we wouldn't have to walk up so many stairs'; 'If there were more cinemas in the town, it would be a livelier place'); (b) suggestions for future projects ('If the authorities improved the road system, we wouldn't get so many traffic jams'); and (c) comments on the possible outcome of ideas or plans already under discussion ('They're talking of widening the main street. If they do, a lot of houses and shops will have to come down.')

Conditionals in reported speech

1 'If we catch the early train, we'll get there by lunch-time.' In reported speech this becomes:

> I thought that if we caught the early train, we'd get there by lunch-time.

It can be seen that Type 1 of the conditional sentences becomes Type 2 in reported speech.

2a 'If we caught the early train, we'd get there by lunch-time.'

This type of conditional sentence represents a supposition or a tentative suggestion of what *could* happen at some time in the future. The tenses do not change in reported speech, since the meaning would change if we reported:

> I thought that if we had caught the early train, we'd have got there by lunch-time.

This reported version gives the impression that we didn't, in fact, catch the early train, and that we didn't get there by lunch-time. We can say only:

> I suggested that if we caught the early train, we'd get there by lunch-time.
> *or* I suggested that if we were to catch the early train, we'd get there by lunch-time.

2b 'If I came into a fortune, I'd give up working.'

Again, the sentence is concerned with what could conceivably happen at some time in the future, and the tenses would remain unchanged in reported speech:

> He said that if he came into a fortune he'd give up working.

2c 'If I knew how it worked, I could tell you what to do.'

As we have already seen, this sentence differs from 2a and 2b in that it represents present unreality, (page 94), and in this case the tenses may change in reported speech:

> I said that if I'd known how it worked, I could have told him what to do.

Such changes are not essential, however, and in some cases would be incorrect:

> 'If I knew the answer to all your questions, I'd be a genius.'

Although this sentence, like 2c, presents us with an imaginary (or unreal) situation, the situation in this case is conceived in general terms (i.e. without reference to a particular moment). Ideas of this nature cannot be expressed in any other form than that given, whether reported or not.

3 'If we'd caught the early train, we'd have got there by lunch-time.'

In this type of sentence, the tenses necessarily remain the same in reported speech.

Note:
> 'Are you willing to help me do this job?'

105

This is a simple question, and should not be confused with a conditional sentence when, in reported speech, it is introduced by *if* (= *whether*):

I asked him if he *was* willing to help me do the job.

The subjunctive 'if he *were* willing' is not required, and would be incorrect if used here.

89 When you have checked your answers to Exercise 75[1], rewrite the sentences in reported speech, using the sentence openings suggested below.

1 I pointed out that we . . .
2 I promised that if . . .
3 I made it clear that I . . .
4 I advised him to . . .
5 I knew that if . . .
6 I wondered what . . .
7 He said that if I . . .
8 It was the editor's opinion that if . . .
9 His teacher thought that if . . .
10 He said he . . . only if I . . .
11 The students were told to . . .
12 I wanted to have some idea of what . . .
13 I reassured him, saying that if . . .
14 I asked him to . . .

90 When you have checked your answers to Exercise 76[1], rewrite the sentences in reported speech, using the sentence openings suggested below.

1 He felt that if I . . .
2 It was suggested that perhaps he . . . if I . . .
3 He thought that if I . . .
4 He said that if I . . .
5 I pointed out that if we . . .
6 We promised that if they . . .
7 I was sure he . . .
8 His advice was that if I . . .

[1] Students may, if they wish, work from the suggested answers given in the key.

106

9 My opinion was that if . . .
10 He suggested that if . . .

The passive voice

Introductory Notes

The passive is frequently used in English to express ideas that require a reflexive or impersonal construction in other languages, and in many cases is also used where other languages use the active. The exercises that follow are aimed at giving the student practice in a number of applications of the passive that may be new to him.

It is assumed that students will already know how to construct the passive of the finite verb forms, but the non-finite forms may be less familiar:

	Active	*Passive*
Infinitive	to choose	to be chosen
Perfect Infinitive	to have chosen	to have been chosen
Participle and Gerund	choosing	being chosen
Perfect Participle and Gerund	having chosen	having been chosen

Bearing in mind that the passive is far commoner in English than in some other languages, students must know *when* to use it: converting active into passive (and vice versa) may be useful for practice purposes, but the process is essentially an artificial one. The following observations may serve as a general guide:

1. When the active form would involve the use of an indefinite or vague pronoun or noun as subject, we generally prefer to use the passive (the agent with 'by' is not expressed):

a. I've been robbed! (Someone has robbed me!)
b. The building had to be demolished. (They had to demolish the building.)
c. It is assumed that the Government will do something to relieve the situation. (People assume that the Government will do something to relieve the situation.)

Note that in *c* the construction with the impersonal *it* as subject is preferable to the active form introduced by the vague pronoun *people.*

2. The passive provides a means of avoiding an awkward change of subject in the middle of a sentence:

> The Prime Minister arrived back in London last night, and was immediately besieged by reporters. (The Prime Minister arrived back in London last night, and reporters immediately besieged him.)

3. The passive may be used when we wish to make a statement sound impersonal (perhaps out of modesty, or when we have some unpleasant statement to make). The management of a company might be quite happy to announce:

> The new working methods we have introduced will result in higher earnings for all workers.

They might well prefer, however, to use the passive in giving the following information, in order to avoid drawing attention to the fact that they themselves are responsible:

> The new working methods that are to be introduced may result in some redundancies.

Similarly, we may express more impersonally, and thus more forcibly, the order given in *a* below, by using the passive as in *b*:

a. You must tidy up this room.
b. This room must be tidied up.

4. The passive is not, therefore, simply an equivalent alternative to the active. While both forms of expressing an idea may be syntactically possible, we tend to choose the passive for one of the reasons described above, or if we are interested in what *happened* to 'X' rather than in what 'Y' *did*:

a. The escaped convict was arrested two days later.
(The police arrested the escaped convict two days later.)
b. Several trees were struck by lightning in last night's storm.
(Lightning struck several trees in last night's storm.)

In *a*, the passive is used because we are interested in what *happened* to the escaped convict; and the agent is omitted, not, as in earlier examples, because it is a vague or indefinite noun, but because it is self-evident from the context.

In *b*, the passive form is to be preferred to the active, even though the agent is neither vague nor self-evident, again because we are more interested in what *happened* to the trees than in what the lightning *did*. In this particular case, moreover, we would hesitate to imply volition on the part of the lightning by making it the subject of a sentence in the active.

5. Some ideas, however, may be expressed naturally and effectively in either the active or the passive form:

a. France beat England in yesterday's rugby international.
b. England was beaten by France in yesterday's rugby international.

In such cases, our choice will depend on what we regard as the 'focus of interest' in the sentence.

91 Rewrite the sentences in the passive, omitting the words in brackets. The numbers in brackets at the end of the sentence indicate the number of passives to be used if there are more than one.

1 (Everyone) knows this fact very well.
2 (They) opened the theatre only last month.
3 (People) will soon forget it.
4 (You) must write the answers in ink.
5 (Someone) has taken two of my books.
6 (We) have already filled the vacancy.
7 What should (one) do in such cases?
8 Did (they) say anything interesting?
9 Did (no one) ever make it clear how (one) operated the machine? (2)
10 (One) should sow new lawns in September.
11 I don't think (anyone) can do it.
12 (They) would undoubtedly have sent him to prison if (they) had found him guilty. (2)
13 (You) must finish the work by seven o'clock.
14 (They) are now manufacturing this type of transistor radio in Japan.
15 (No one) could possibly have known the secret.
16 Has (someone) made all the necessary arrangements?
17 Fortunately, (no one) had said anything about it.
18 (We) will execute all orders promptly.
19 (The police) kept the man in custody.
20 Does (someone) clean all the rooms regularly?

92 Complete the sentences with a passive construction, using the verbs given and in the form suggested. (NB. The term 'infinitive' includes the infinitive without 'to'.)

1 Much of London (destroy) by fire in the seventeenth century. (Past Simple)
2 The man who (bite) by a snake was given a serum. (Past Perfect)
3 A leader should be a man who can (respect). (Infinitive)
4 Many slums (demolish) to make way for new buildings. (Present Continuous)
5 The police (instruct) to take firm action against hooligans. (Present Perfect)
6 He (save) from bankruptcy by the kindness of a friend. (Past Simple)
7 A cease-fire (expect) (declare) later this week. (Present Simple, Infinitive)
8 A great deal of research (do) into the possible causes of cancer. (Present Perfect)
9 The worker claimed that he (victimize) by his employers. (Past Continuous)
10 The tenant (evict) for not paying his rent. (Past Simple)
11 It (think) that the Government would do something to help. (Past Perfect)
12 Three hundred new houses (build) by the end of next year. (Future Perfect)
13 Because of a strike, work on the building had to (discontinue). (Infinitive)
14 The witness strongly objected to (cross-examine). (Gerund)
15 (Threaten) by a blackmailer, he immediately informed the police. (Perfect Participle)
16 I'm not accustomed to (treat) in that way. (Gerund)
17 The passengers ought (inform) that the train (withdraw) from service. (Perfect Infinitive, Past Perfect)
18 Customers (ask) to ensure that they (give) the correct change before leaving the shop, as mistakes cannot afterwards (rectify). (Present Simple, Present Perfect, Infinitive)
19 Was he very upset at (not offer) the job? (Gerund)
20 The man was sent to prison for six months, (find) guilty of fraud. (Perfect Participle)

Students will have seen, from examples in the previous exercises, that sentences in the passive form frequently contain no reference to the 'agent'. The verb in the passive may, however, like active verb forms, be followed by a variety of prepositional constructions. The following exercise will give practice in using different prepositions after verbs in the passive.

93 Complete the sentences with a passive construction, using the verbs given and in the form suggested, and adding a suitable preposition, e.g.

> The new proposals (discuss) ... our next meeting. (Future)
> The new proposals will be discussed *at* our next meeting.

1 A surcharge of 10 per cent (add) ... patrons' bills to cover gratuities to hotel staff. (Present Simple)
2 Surplus grain (send) ... the stricken area and (distribute) ... the starving population. (Past Simple)
3 These recordings (make) ... the rehearsals immediately preceding the concert. (Past Simple)
4 A meeting (arrange) ... the Commonwealth Prime Ministers. (Present Perfect)
5 A member of the Opposition pointed out that very few new hospitals (build) ... the end of the war. (Past Perfect)
6 He wanted nothing except (leave) ... peace. (Infinitive)
7 Don't you think a solicitor should (consult) ... this question? (Perfect Infinitive)
8 These tablets should (keep) ... of the reach of children. (Infinitive)
9 America (discover) ... the end of the fifteenth century. (Past Simple)
10 The full impact of the strike (not feel) ... next week, by which time present stocks (exhaust). (Future, Future Perfect)
11 The two cottages now (convert) ... one house. (Present Perfect)
12 All new models of this car (equip) ... safety belts. (Future)
13 The results of the examination (not know) ... two months. (Future)
14 No one had supposed that the motion would (defeat) ... such a large majority. (Infinitive)
15 The bridge has had (close) ... repairs. (Infinitive)
16 Did you know that this case (investigate) ... a member of the C.I.D.? (Present Continuous)
17 All lights must (switch off) ... 11 p.m. (Infinitive)

18 Nothing (hear) . . . him since he left the country six weeks ago. (Present Perfect)
19 The goods should (handle) . . . greater care. (Perfect Infinitive)
20 You (meet) . . . the airport. (Future)

Some common verbs may be used in combination with adverbs to form 'phrasal verbs' with idiomatic meanings: e.g. *put off* = *postpone*. Students should take care to retain the particle with such verbs in a passive construction:

a. They will have *to put off* the meeting till later in the week. (Active)
b. The meeting will have *to be put off* till later in the week. (Passive)

Similar care should be taken with those verbs that are followed by a preposition:

a. We *insist on* punctuality in this office. (Active)
b. Punctuality *is insisted on* in this office. (Passive)

94 Answer the questions, using a passive form of the verbs in brackets, together with a suitable adverbial particle (off, on, in, out, up, down, etc.), e.g.

What generally happens to houses that are unfit to live in? (pull)
They *are* generally *pulled down.*

1 What must be done with a bad tooth? (pull)
2 What has to be done with dirty crockery and cutlery at the end of a meal? (wash)
3 What should happen if mistakes appear in a student's work? (point)
4 What might happen if you crossed a busy road without looking? (knock)
5 What would happen to a lighted candle if there were a sudden gust of wind? (blow)
6 What may happen to a man who has committed his first offence? (let)
7 What often happens if negotiations look like being unsuccessful? (break)
8 What happens to traffic in a traffic jam? (hold)

9 What happens to workers if they become redundant? (lay)
10 What is done with spoken evidence given to a policeman? (take)
11 What must be done if a plan or an idea proves unworkable? (give)
12 A notice has disappeared from a noticeboard. What must have happened? (take)
13 I dropped a £1 note in the street, and can't find it. What could have happened to it? (pick)
14 No one can attend a meeting on that date. What could be done to solve the problem? (put)

95 Rewrite the sentences in the passive.

1 They gave up the search after three hours.
2 They ought to have pointed that out to me at the very beginning.
3 No one brought up that question at the meeting.
4 Someone should look into the matter.
5 It was clear that the parents had brought the child up well.
6 We had to put off our visit until later.
7 I was shocked to hear that someone had broken into your house.
8 They gave me to understand that they would call on my services if they needed them. (3)
9 Don't speak until someone speaks to you.
10 He will stop showing off if people take no notice of him.
11 His bank manager turned down his request for a loan.
12 They are putting up many new buildings in London.
13 You must account for every penny you spent.
14 They pointed out that no one could deal with the matter until they knew all the facts. (3)
15 Someone hasn't stuck this stamp on very firmly.
16 Police had to break the meeting up.
17 Events will bear out the truth of what I'm saying.
18 An official held us up at the Customs for half an hour.
19 How can we bring about the desired result?
20 He hates people making fun of him. (Passive Gerund)

96 Complete the sentences with a passive construction, using the verbs given, and in a suitable form.

1 The new washing machines (turn out) at the rate of fifty a day.
2 When her husband died, she naturally assumed that she (provide for).

3 We've had to move into a hotel while the house we've just bought (do up).
4 The employee was assured of his (take on) again as soon as work was available.
5 Richard always (tell off) for careless mistakes nowadays.
6 The meanings of all new words should (look up) in the dictionary.
7 In his anxiety to reach the rendezvous on time, the driver forgot that the car still (run in).
8 The agreement had to (draw up) in the presence of two witnesses.
9 Some Heads of Government now fear that negotiations (break off) before a settlement is reached.
10 The chairman of the board of directors assured shareholders that the matter of the deficiency (look into) by the time the next meeting was held.
11 He felt he (let down) badly by his best friend.
12 The search party had little idea where to start looking, the climber's tracks (blot out) by a recent snowstorm.

There is one particular construction in the passive that may appear strange to students. In a sentence like the following, there are two objects, one direct and one indirect:

> The crowd gave *the King a great reception*.

If this is expressed in the passive, we generally make the indirect object the subject, especially as the indirect object in this type of sentence is, more often than not, personal, and we tend to be more interested in persons than things. Furthermore, the person will generally be more particularized than the thing, and may, in the subject position, help to establish the context of the sentence more readily:

> *The King* was given a great reception by the crowd.

There are occasions, however, when we wish to make the direct object the subject (or, we might say, the 'focus of interest') of the passive construction. In such cases, we would be implying a greater interest in *what is done* than in *to whom it is done*:

a. We shall offer *a high salary* to a *really suitable applicant*. (Active)
b. *A high salary* will be offered to a really suitable applicant. (Passive)

97 Rewrite the sentences in the passive, making the words in italics the subject of the sentence or clause in which they appear.

1 They gave *the oldest councillor* the freedom of the city.
2 They denied *access to the secret documents* to all but a few.
3 Someone showed *the child* how to use the telephone.
4 They declared *him* 'persona non grata' and allowed him only forty-eight hours to leave the country. (2)
5 They gave *him* artificial respiration.
6 Why didn't they offer *him* the job?
7 Didn't they promise *you* a rise in salary at the beginning of the year?
8 Someone left *him* a legacy of £10,000.
9 When he looked at the stamps, he found they had sold *him* forgeries.
10 What did they pay *you* for doing the job?
11 Someone should tell *him* never to do that again.
12 They asked *you* to meet me here at 11 o'clock, not half-past.
13 Will someone send *me* the details?
14 We shall send you *the goods* as soon as they are available.
15 Someone must teach *that boy* a lesson!
16 We must give *slum-clearance* priority over the building of new properties.

98 Answer the questions, using a passive construction, e.g.

> What might a man be recommended if he became ill through overwork?
> He might be recommended a long holiday.

1 What should someone be given when he's hysterical?
2 Wages or a salary—which is a schoolmaster paid?
3 In a cross-examination, who is asked what by whom?
4 What must an immigration officer be shown before one is permitted to enter a foreign country?
5 Who is sent what at Christmas?
6 If you wrote to a school for information, what might you be sent?
7 What is a patient given before an operation?
8 What would you most resent being told?
9 What opportunity would you like to be offered?
10 How much is a Member of Parliament paid in your country? (a nurse? a secretary? a bus driver? etc.)

11 What might a man's friends be left in his will?
12 In a totalitarian state, what are the people denied?
13 What would you need to be lent if you were hard up?
14 What foreign languages were you taught at school?

Another type of sentence that has two possible forms in the passive is that consisting of *Subject* × *Verb* (say, think, feel, expect, etc.) × *Noun Clause Object*:

a. They say that he knows some very influential people.
b. People felt that the social workers were doing valuable work.
c. Everyone thought that the Government had shown scant regard for public opinion.

The ideas expressed in these sentences would, for reasons of style, generally be presented in the passive. One possible construction is that where the sentence is introduced by the impersonal *it*:

a. It is said that he knows some very influential people.
b. It was felt that the social workers were doing valuable work.
c. It was thought that the Government had shown scant regard for public opinion.

The use of this impersonal construction in the passive is preferable to the use of a vague or indefinite pronoun as subject in the active. But in many cases a third construction is possible: the subject of the noun clause may be made the subject of the whole sentence in the passive. A special characteristic of this construction is that the verb in the noun clause takes the infinitive form:

a. He is said *to know* some very influential people.
b. The social workers were felt *to be doing* valuable work.
c. The Government was thought *to have shown* scant regard for public opinion.

Note: Sentences *b* and *c* can, of course, be directly related to corresponding sentences in the active, using the infinitive:

b. People felt the social workers to be doing valuable work.
c. Everyone thought the Government to have shown scant regard for public opinion.

There are two points to note here, however:

(1) In the active sentences, a construction with a 'that' clause is commoner than the infinitive, whereas in the passive the infinitive is preferred where it is structurally possible.

116

(2) The infinitive construction in the passive does not necessarily represent a transformation of a corresponding infinitive in the active. We do not say *'They say him to know some influential people', because this construction is not available to the verb *say*.[1]

The form of the infinitive depends on whether or not the time reference of the verb in the noun clause is the same as that of the verb in the introductory (main) clause. If the time reference is the same, use the 'present' infinitive:

> It *is said* that he *knows*
> = He is said *to know* some very influential people.
> It *was said* that he *knew*
> = He was said *to know*

If the verb in the noun clause has a time reference anterior to that of the verb in the main clause, use the 'perfect' infinitive:

> It *is thought* that he *acted*
> = He is thought *to have acted* very foolishly.
> It *was thought* that he *had acted*
> = He was thought *to have acted*

99 Rewrite the sentences in an alternative passive form, beginning your sentences with the words in italics.

1 It is said that *he* is an honest, hard-working man.
2 It is considered that *this surgeon* is a brilliant practitioner.
3 It is now thought that *some redundancy in the Midlands* is inevitable.
4 It was proved that *the statements he had made* were false.
5 It was understood that *Mr Smith* was willing to meet the British Prime Minister.
6 It is believed that *the Chancellor* is thinking of imposing special taxes to raise extra revenue.
7 It is expected that *the electricity supply industry* will be running into surplus capacity by next year.
8 It is reported that *several American motor manufacturers* are planning to set up assembly plants overseas.
9 It is expected that *the brewers* will raise the price of beer in the near future.

[1] See -*Ing forms, Infinitives, and 'that' Clauses*, p. 173 ff.

10 It was claimed that *the drug* produced no undesirable side-effects.
11 It is said that *the police* acted with great restraint, despite provocation.
12 It was alleged that *the Prime Minister* had misled the House.
13 It is believed that *the Government* has had second thoughts on this problem.
14 It was believed that *the explosion* had been caused by a mine.
15 It is presumed that *the ship's radio equipment* was put out of action during the fire.
16 It was later admitted that *the information* had been obtained from unreliable sources.

Advanced exercises in conversion

100 Rewrite in the passive the sentences or clauses containing a verb in italics.

1 The fact that the new scheme *raised* such a storm of disapproval means that no one can *have explained* it properly to the public.
2 His father *warned* him not to let others *lead* him astray.
3 The chairman of the committee complained that they *were taking up* too much time in discussing trivialities.
4 People *put down* the boy's rudeness to his parents' *having spoiled* him.
5 The British *don't accept* Fascism, any more than they *do* Communism.
6 Couldn't we *ask* someone to do the work privately without anyone *knowing*?
7 They *didn't discover* until later that someone *had stolen* the picture. ('Not until later . . .')
8 They *had* never before *sent* anyone to prison for that particular crime. ('Never before . . .')
9 They could *make* the law effective only in this way. ('Only in this way . . .')
10 They *debated* this question fully in Parliament on very few occasions. ('On very few occasions . . .')

101 Instructions as above.

1 People *said* that no one could *reach* any agreement on this question.
2 The army *put down* the rebellion and *declared* martial law.

3 He wanted them *to treat* the information as confidential.

4 They *will dispose* of his property and *share* the proceeds among his family.

5 If they *had told* me that someone was *to bring up* the subject of finance at the next meeting, I wouldn't have mentioned it. ('Had I . . .')

6 He dislikes his fellow-workers *thinking* him a fool.

7 The public *having ignored* him for many years, the writer suddenly became famous. ('After . . .')

8 If someone should *prove* beyond doubt that an accident *caused* the fire, the police *will*, naturally, *release* the man they *are* at present *holding* on suspicion of arson. ('Should it . . .')

9 On their *informing* him that the police *wanted* him, the man realized that his accomplice *had betrayed* him.

10 When the police finally *discovered* the stolen car, they *found* that someone *had stripped* it of most of its fittings and *had let* the air out of its tyres.

102 Rewrite in the active the sentences or clauses containing a verb in italics. Where the agent is not stated, a suitable subject for the sentence or clause should be inferred from the context.

1 A speech to the nation was *to have been made* by the Prime Minister, but it had *to be cancelled* at the last minute because of a Cabinet crisis.

2 The fire *was* finally *got* under control, but not before extensive damage *had been caused*.

3 The car thief *was arrested* after *having been chased* for more than an hour.

4 Don't let yourself *be depressed* by your failure.

5 In view of the widespread concern that *is felt* by the community at the plan for a main road *to be built* through the village, it *has been decided* by the local Council that a special inquiry *should be held*.

6 Patrons *are* respectfully *informed* that the right *is reserved* for admission *to be refused* to anyone, without any reason *being given*.

7 The house *had been broken into*, and two thousand pounds' worth of jewellery *had been stolen*.

8 Only after it *had been subjected* to searching laboratory tests by the scientists *was* the new vaccine *put* on the market by the Company.

9 It *was stated* by Macaulay that Byron *had been hounded* out of

Britain by the British public in one of its periodic fits of morality.

10 The plan *hadn't been* at all *well thought out* by the leader.

11 It ought *to have been made* quite clear to the shareholders before the annual meeting *was held* that they *would not be allowed* to vote for a new Board by proxy.

12 Your lawyer's advice *should have been obtained* before any decision *was made* by you for the matter *to be taken* further.

13 He needn't *have been caused* so much distress by *being told* by the army authorities that his brother had died in action, as it *was* later *discovered* that a mistake *had been made* as to the missing man's identity.

14 Information about the source from which the startling news *had been obtained was withheld* by the reporter.

15 A majestic performance of Beethoven's ninth symphony *was given* by the Minneapolis Symphony Orchestra at a Festival Hall concert.

Relative clauses

Defining relative clauses

If you look up the words *conductor* or *doctor* or *liar* in *The Advanced Learner's Dictionary*, you will find the following explanations (the words in parenthesis are not given in the dictionary, nor are italics used):

(A) conductor (is a) person *who collects fares on a bus or tram.*
(A) doctor (is a) person *who has been trained in medical science.*
(A) liar (is a) person *who habitually tells lies.*

If we omit the words in italics, we learn only that a conductor is a person, a doctor is a person, and a liar is a person. We would clearly regard such explanations as unsatisfactory, even though as sentences they are grammatically complete. The 'persons' are defined, or distinguished from each other (and from any others one could think of), by the *relative clauses* in italics: the relative clauses are *defining*.

The definition of *conductor* is no longer simply 'a person', but 'a person who collects fares on a bus or tram'. The relative clause is an essential part of the whole definition, and cannot be omitted if the sentence as a whole is to make useful sense. Similarly, it would be impossible to answer the following question without the defining relative clause in italics:

What do we call a person *who habitually tells lies*?

The answer is, of course:

A person *who habitually tells lies* is called a liar.

Again, the answer would be incomplete without the defining relative clause in italics. The subject of the sentence is no longer simply 'a person', but 'a person who habitually tells lies'.

All these examples show that the defining relative clauses provide an indispensable definition of the word 'person' (called the *antecedent*—the word to which the relative clause relates). They are not separated from the antecedent by commas in writing, nor by a pause in speech. This is a basic feature of all *defining* relative clauses.

103 Give your own explanations of the following words, using the same structure as in the example.

A liar is a person who habitually tells lies.

an atheist	a barber	a spokesman	a stockbroker
an actor	a newsagent	an eyewitness	a greengrocer
a journalist	an MP	a solicitor	a teetotaller

104 Answer the questions, using the same structure as in the example.

A person who has been trained in medical science is called a doctor.

What do we call—

a person who steals things?
a person who makes beer?
a person who makes clothes?
a person who prepares technical plans and drawings?
a person who sets examinations?
a person who owns shares in a company?
a person who is skilled in foreign languages?
a person who goes to the theatre regularly?

a person who manages a public house?
a person who rides a bicycle?
a person who is nominated for an office or position?
a person who receives treatment in a hospital?
a person who writes plays?
a person who has the right to sit in the House of Lords?
a person who writes about plays, films, concerts, etc., for a
newspaper?

The relative pronoun *that* is used only in *defining* clauses,[1] and
can refer to persons or things. *Who* (for persons) and *which* (for
things) may, of course, be used instead:

> I dislike women *THAT chatter incessantly*.
> I dislike women *WHO chatter incessantly*.
> Old age is a problem *THAT should concern us all*.
> Old age is a problem *WHICH should concern us all*.

All the relative clauses here are defining: there are no commas
between the antecedents and the relative pronouns (and no pauses
in speech). Students will find it instructive to note examples of
usage in modern written English, in order to see what pattern of
choice emerges in such clauses (i.e. *that* or *who*, *that* or *which*?).

With regard to the choice of *that* or *who*, both are equally
appropriate if the antecedent is a vague or generalized noun or
pronoun:

> He's the sort of man *that/who will do anything to help people
> in trouble*.
> I need someone *that/who can do the work quickly*.

If, however, the antecedent is more definite or particularized, *who*
is a far more likely choice:

> The aunt *who came to see us last week* is my father's sister.

With antecedents denoting *things*, the choice of *that* or *which*
seems more a matter of individual taste; but there are a few cases
where *that* is preferred to *which* (introducing, of course, defining
relative clauses):

[1] It is advisable that students should treat this as a 'rule', although they will
sometimes find *that* used in non-defining clauses in modern written English.

a. When the antecedent is an indefinite pronoun:

The Government has promised to do ALL *that* lies in its power to alleviate the hardships of those made homeless by the floods.

b. When the antecedent is qualified by a superlative:

This is the FUNNIEST film *that* has ever come from Ealing Studios.

c. When the antecedent is qualified by an ordinal number:

The FIRST statement *that* was issued by the press attaché at the Palace gave very few details.

d. When the antecedent is the complement of 'to be':

It's a book *that* will be very popular.

The problem of choosing the appropriate relative pronoun in defining relative clauses very often doesn't arise:

The library didn't have the book (that *or* which) I wanted.

This sentence consists of two clauses:

1 The library didn't have the book (Main clause)
2 (that *or* which) I wanted (Relative clause)

The relative clause tells us which book the library didn't have; it defines the antecedent *book*; it is a defining relative clause. We may analyse the relative clause thus:

that *or* which (object) I (subject) wanted (verb)

It is a distinctive characteristic of *defining* relative clauses that the relative pronoun may be omitted, without any change of meaning in the sentence as a whole, when it is *not* the *subject* of the relative clause. It not only *may* be omitted, it very often *is*, particularly in spoken English:

The library didn't have the book *I wanted*.

The same is true of *whom*[1] in a *defining* relative clause—it is very often omitted:

Was the man *you spoke to just now* a friend of yours?

[1] If the pronoun is expressed in speech, *who* is often used instead of *whom* in such relative clauses, except when preceded by a preposition.

Such clauses are called 'contact clauses', and are very common in both speech and writing, as students will soon realize if they examine the constructions (that!) they themselves use. Here are a few more sentences where the relative pronoun is omitted (the relative clauses are in italics):

> You ought to have seen the look *she gave him.*
> The play *we saw last night* was disappointing.
> Did you know the girl *he married*?

Students will, in fact, have very little difficulty in using relative pronouns correctly in speech. Non-defining clauses (see page 128) hardly ever occur in the spoken language; they tend to sound formal and unnatural. The meaning of *a* below would, in speech, probably be expressed as in *b*:

a. That oak chair, which is now rather worm-eaten, belonged to my great-grandfather.
b. 'That oak chair belonged to my great-grandfather, you know. It's rather worm-eaten now, I'm afraid.'

When relative clauses occur in the spoken language, they are nearly all *defining* clauses (but see Exercise 118). Furthermore, as already shown, a large number of defining clauses are of the type where the relative pronoun may be omitted.

105 Join the sentences by changing the second sentence of each pair into a defining relative clause. Use contact clauses (i.e. omit the relative pronoun) if the relative pronoun is not the subject of its clause. The antecedents are printed in italics, e.g.

> The *aims* are very laudable. The society is pursuing these aims.
> The aims *the society is pursuing* are very laudable.

1 The *pipeline* has been severed. It carries the town's water supplies.
2 The *exhibition* was not very interesting. My friend took me to see it.
3 One of the chief *things* is to save money, manpower, and time. A computer can do this thing.
4 Trade Union legislation is one major *problem*. The Government has yet to tackle this problem.
5 Immigration is an *issue*. This issue raises strong emotions.

124

6 There is still a great deal of *work*. This work has to be done before the building is ready for occupation.

7 Paintings by Renoir realized record prices in the *sale*. The sale took place at Sotheby's in London yesterday.

8 There is evidence that many *men* were in fact willing to accept the Company's revised pay offer. These men went on strike.

9 The pools winner used a *system*. This system, he said, had won him several small amounts over the years.

10 The *gales* caused widespread damage. They swept across southern England last night.

11 British shipyards are now quoting *prices*. These prices compare favourably with foreign competitors.

12 Is the *offer* still open? You made the offer last week.

13 The number of *people* will place a heavy strain on airport facilities. These people will be travelling by air in the 1980's.

14 Only by exporting enough can we pay for the *goods*. We buy these goods from abroad.

15 Members of the local sub-aqua club came across a *wreck*. It had lain on the sea-bed for over 200 years.

16 The problem today is to build houses at a *price*. Young couples can afford to pay this price.

17 I know the very *person*. He will do the job quickly.

18 The problem in New Towns is that it takes three generations to create the closely-knit *community life*. This community life gives older towns their homeliness and character.

19 There is no doubt, however, that the New Towns have transformed the lives of many *people*. These people might otherwise still be living in overcrowded towns.

20 In some areas of Britain, unemployment is a *fact of life*. People have grown accustomed to facing this fact.

106 Add relative clauses defining the words in italics, using contact clauses where appropriate.

a. The Council has decided to ask every *tenant* to move to a smaller house or a flat.
The Council has decided to ask every tenant *who has a house bigger than he needs* to move to a smaller house or a flat.

b. He's the sort of *person*.
He's the sort of person *that must always be doing something new.*

c. There was *nothing*.
There was nothing *I could do* to help. (Contact clause)

1 Any *man* should be sent to prison.
2 The *suit* is identical to one my brother bought.
3 In London every *Englishman* carries a rolled umbrella and wears a bowler hat.
4 *Laws* should be repealed.
5 The *yacht* arrived first.
6 The *house* has been demolished.
7 The *car* was driven by the world champion.
8 Would you like to see the *photographs*?
9 He's the most intelligent *man*.
10 He will do *anything*.
11 The *man* was her uncle.
12 That's the third *telephone call*.
13 *Nothing* is ever a success.
14 He enjoys talking to *anyone*.
15 I always feel confidence in *someone*.

107 Instructions as above.

1 Students generally like a *teacher*.
2 Teachers generally like *students*.
3 He lends money only to *people*.
4 Is that all the *work*?
5 The sort of *food* is not the same as Continental food.
6 Children like *aunts and uncles*.
7 Men dislike *women*.
8 Women dislike *men*.
9 The *excuse* was unacceptable.
10 The stretch of *water* is called the English Channel.
11 I will pay for the *damage*.
12 I am sure there isn't *anyone* among the audience here tonight.
13 My father is a *man*.
14 I detest *people*.
15 Switzerland is a *country*.

108 Complete the sentences, incorporating contact clauses.

a. The equipment the climbers . . .
The equipment *the climbers took with them* proved unsuitable.
b. . . . the tennis club my friend . . .
I'd like to join the tennis club *my friend belongs to*.

Note that this exercise requires the completion of both the main clause and the relative clause.

1 The shoes you . . .
2 The speech the Prime Minister . . .
3 . . . the book you . . .
4 Every letter he . . .
5 The holiday we . . .
6 Some singers I . . .
7 The teacher the students . . .
8 Every meal my wife . . .
9 The house my friends . . .
10 . . . the clothes the English . . .?
11 . . . every word the speaker . . .
12 One problem the Government . . .
13 . . . the medicine the doctor . . .
14 The rockets the Americans . . .
15 . . . the information the policeman . . .?

109 Instructions as above.

1 . . . every school he . . .
2 The question the student . . .
3 The situation the Company . . .
4 . . . the advice your lawyer . . .?
5 All the money my grandfather . . .
6 The finest performance the orchestra . . .
7 The three men the police . . .
8 Some sermons the vicar . . .
9 The goods the customer . . .
10 . . . anything I . . .?
11 . . . the plans the architect . . .
12 . . . the Mr Smith you . . .?
13 . . . the girl my brother . . .
14 The plan we . . .
15 . . . the London I . . .

Non-defining relative clauses

The Victoria Line, *which was opened in March 1969,* was London's first complete new tube for 60 years.

If we omit the relative clause (in italics), we are left with the statement 'The Victoria Line was London's first complete new tube for 60 years'. The relative clause gives additional information about the antecedent (*Victoria Line*), but does not define it: the 'Line' in question is already sufficiently defined by 'Victoria'.

The relative clause is in this case called *non-defining* (or *parenthetical*), and is enclosed by commas. Whether we include the clause or not, the meaning of the main clause remains exactly the same. In fact, the main clause and relative clause could (though with less economy) be presented as two separate statements:

The Victoria Line was London's first complete new tube for 60 years. It was opened in March 1969.

The relative clause could even be represented by an independent clause in parenthesis. In this case, it is clearly seen as incidental information, mentioned 'by the way':

The Victoria Line (it was opened in March 1969) was London's first complete new tube for 60 years.

The omission or insertion of commas may represent a difference in meaning between two otherwise identical sentences:

a. He has a sister who works at the United Nations headquarters in Geneva. (Defining)
b. He has a sister, who works at the United Nations headquarters in Geneva. (Non-defining)

The absence of a comma after *sister* in *a* implies that 'he' has more than one sister; that one of them in particular is being referred to —the one who works in Geneva. The necessity for definition is shown more clearly in a sentence like the following:

He has a sister who works at the United Nations headquarters in Geneva, and another who works as a typist in a London bank.

The presence of a comma in *b* implies that 'he' has only one sister (it is, therefore, impossible to define which one), and the relative clause simply gives more information about her.

A further point of contrast between defining and non-defining clauses is that the relative pronoun *cannot* be omitted in non-defining clauses, even if it is not the subject of its clause:

a. The Victoria Line, *which* was opened in 1969, was London's first complete new tube for 60 years. (*which* = subject)
b. The Victoria Line, *which* the Queen opened in 1969, was London's first complete new tube for 60 years. (*which* = object)

Students will find many examples in modern written English where commas are omitted before non-defining relative clauses. The writer's meaning may be perfectly unambiguous without the use of commas, or there may be stylistic reasons for omitting them. Nevertheless, students are advised to follow the 'rules' of punctuation illustrated in the above examples, since observation of these patterns is less likely to lead to confusion.

In these notes, the distinction between defining and non-defining relative clauses has been illustrated by omitting the relative clause from a sentence, examining the main clause that remains, and deciding whether or not it makes satisfactory sense without the relative clause. Certainly, if we omit a defining relative clause, we may be left with a sentence that is obviously incomplete, or perhaps even absurd:

My father is a man *who believes in discipline.*

One should bear in mind, however, that the examples have been chosen and presented so as to provide as 'dramatic' a contrast as possible between the two types of clause. All the examples are, moreover, isolated sentences. In practice, the context or situation determines whether we need a defining clause or not. As an opening statement, the following sentence needs its defining relative clause:

The new houses *they're building in our road* are just like little square boxes.

Without the defining relative clause, we wouldn't know which new houses were being referred to. If, however, the 'new houses' are already defined by a preceding statement, no further definition is necessary:

A lot of the big old Victorian houses in our road have been

pulled down to make way for a modern development. I can't say I like it—the new houses are just like little square boxes.

110 Join the sentences, using *which* or *who* in non-defining relative clauses, and inserting the appropriate punctuation, e.g.

His latest play has been a great success. It was well reviewed by the critics.
His latest play, which was well reviewed by the critics, has been a great success.

1 This industrial dispute has now been settled. It disrupted production at six Midlands factories while it lasted.
2 The Prime Minister's reshuffle means that the Cabinet will be reduced to twenty. It now has twenty-two members.
3 Some London policemen were sent to America on a goodwill visit. They are well known for their politeness and helpfulness.
4 Three acres of land go with this estate. The estate is situated in one of the most beautiful parts of rural England.
5 The Chancellor of the Exchequer later issued a statement to the press. He had earlier refused to speak to reporters.
6 Covent Garden's latest production of *Don Giovanni* looks like being a huge success. It opened at the Royal Opera House last night.
7 The new official guide to London contains a wealth of information for visitors. It will appear in the bookshops next week.
8 His first speech was better than his second. The first speech was broadcast. He gave the second before an audience.
9 Foreign visitors often find that English weather is not so bad as they had supposed. They often associate it with fog and rain. It sometimes makes them dread coming to England.
10 Queen Elizabeth II is a descendant of the Saxon king, Egbert. He united all England in the year 829.
11 The Houses of Parliament were begun in 1840 and completed in 1857. They cost £3,000,000 to build.
12 The British Broadcasting Corporation launched the world's first public television service in 1936. As the British Broadcasting Company, it had begun sound broadcasting in 1922.
13 The Independent Television Authority provides a commercial television service, with advertising. It was set up in 1954.

14 Imports in January fell below December's figure. December's figure was artificially inflated by a sharp rise in imports following the end of the dock strike.

Non-defining clauses sometimes have an explanatory function: they may suggest an adverbial idea, implying the reason or cause of the facts presented in the main clause:

> The manufacturers soon stopped marketing the drug, which was found to have serious side-effects. (i.e. *because* it was found to have serious side-effects)

111 Rewrite the sentences, substituting a non-defining relative clause for the adverbial clauses in italics, e.g.

> In 1930 the Company moved from its home in West Street, *since this was now too small for its ever-increasing volume of business.*
> In 1930 the Company moved from its home in West Street, which was now too small for its ever-increasing volume of business.

1 Few people could follow the speaker, *since he spoke extremely quickly.*
2 His doctor advised him to change to an outdoor job, *as this would be much better for his health.*
3 Many teachers are enthusiastic about overhead projectors, *since they are more flexible in use than the traditional blackboard.*
4 The airline has grounded all planes of this type, *since they have been the subject of several recent accidents and near-accidents.*
5 The MP for Oxbridge was expelled from membership of his party, *having failed to support the Conservatives in Parliament on numerous occasions.*
6 When our car needs servicing, I always take it to our local garage, *because it gives better and quicker service than some of the larger garages in town.*
7 We didn't like his manner, *since to our way of thinking it was rather offhand.*
8 This new car will be very popular with family motorists, *since it seats five people in comfort and takes a mountain of luggage.*
9 More and more information is now being stored on microfilm,

131

since this is one of the most effective means of compressing a large amount of information into a small space.

10 The shop readily agreed to exchange the goods, *since they were obviously substandard.*

112 Add non-defining clauses relating to the words in italics, using *which*, *who*, or *whom*. Insert the appropriate punctuation, e.g.

> The *Foreign Secretary* held a short press conference at the airport.
>
> The Foreign Secretary, *who was besieged by reporters* when his plane landed, held a short press conference at the airport.

1 His latest *book* is about his adventures in Africa.
2 The *Royal Shakespeare Theatre Company* is world famous.
3 British Leyland's latest sports *car* should boost British exports to America.
4 His *father* has offered him a partnership.
5 The use of *asbestos* will make the building much safer.
6 The new highway *code* should make for greater safety for all road-users.
7 The subject of his *talk* was 'Gardening for Pleasure'.
8 The missing woman's *bicycle* has been found in the river.
9 The Company didn't reply to his *letter of application.*
10 *The Boat Race* takes place annually from Putney to Mortlake on the Thames.
11 *North Sea Gas* is now used by many British housewives.
12 Last night's *meeting* broke up in disorder.
13 The Council has decided to replace the old Victorian gaslighting in the streets by new sodium *lighting.*
14 *Trams* are still used in several European cities.
15 Spring *flowers* are a delight to the eye.

113 Instructions as above.

1 We hope to attract investors to our new savings *scheme.*
2 The *cliffs of Dover* are a startling white.
3 The winning *horse* was trained in Ireland.
4 I was amazed to learn that my *grandfather* was a keen cyclist.
5 *Joseph Conrad* wrote all his books in English.

6 *British Railways* are being modernized.

7 The *University of Cambridge* comprises more than twenty colleges.

8 The defending *lawyer* made a great impression on the jury.

9 Scientists assume that *water* does not exist on the moon.

10 *George Bernard Shaw* died in 1950.

11 *Fleet Street* is situated in the heart of London.

12 While in Edinburgh we went to the *Festival of Arts and Music*.

13 Last year's spring *tides* caused much damage to property.

14 Foreigners often take some time to get used to the English *breakfast*.

15 This year's *harvest* has been disappointing.

Whose

Whose is the only possessive form of relative pronoun in English, and is used to refer to both persons and things. It is nearly always preferred to the prepositional construction *of whom* (when, of course, this indicates possession), and is also often preferred to *of which* (again, when this indicates possession):

a. The man *whose coat had been stolen* immediately reported the theft. (Defining)
(Not 'The man the coat of whom had been stolen . . .')

b. The damaged ship, *whose crew has now been taken off*, was listing dangerously when last seen. (Non-defining)
(Rather than 'The damaged ship, the crew of which has now been taken off, . . .')

114 Join the sentences by changing the second sentence of each pair into a defining or non-defining relative clause. The structure of your relative clause should reflect the structure of the original sentence.

a. The headmaster spoke to the boys. Their work was below standard.
The headmaster spoke to the boys *whose* work was below standard. (Defining)

b. The new motor-caravan should prove an attraction at the motor show. *Its* interior height can be increased by raising the roof.
The new motor-caravan, *whose* interior height can be increased by raising the roof, should prove an attraction at the motor show. (Non-defining)

c. The new motor-caravan should prove an attraction at the motor show. *The interior height of the caravan* can be increased by raising the roof.

The new motor-caravan, *the interior height of which* can be increased by raising the roof, should prove an attraction at the motor show.

1 London looks forward to the visit of Sviatoslav Richter. His virtuosity is now a byword among concert-goers.

2 The Prime Minister may be forced to resign. His support in the party has seriously declined.

3 Bertrand Russell died in 1970. His philosophical writings made a profound impact on philosophers all over the world.

4 The Government's new Pensions Bill will be debated in Parliament next week. Its provisions are a matter of considerable controversy.

5 The U.S. President is unlikely to seek a second term of office. His administration has been under constant fire during the last eighteen months.

6 Very few people understood his lecture. The subject of his lecture was very obscure.

7 The car driver was sent to prison for six months. The entire blame for the accident rested on his shoulders.

8 Lord Nelson was famous for his naval exploits. A column was erected in his memory in Trafalgar Square in London.

9 'I have pleasure in introducing to you the man. Without his generosity your society would cease to exist.'

10 'Sir—Mr Jack Smith should check his facts more carefully. His letter was published in your columns yesterday.'

11 The fire started on the first floor of the hospital. Many of its patients are elderly and infirm.

12 The latest model of this car gives much more passenger room. Its exterior dimensions remain unchanged.

13 We would not advise buying shares in this Company. Its results last year were worse even than forecast, and its long-term recovery must remain a matter of doubt.

14 I interviewed several of the men. Their contracts had been terminated by the Company at short notice.

15 Many back-benchers are finding it difficult to support the Government. They have considerable misgivings over some of the Government's policies.

Prepositional relative clauses

1. Defining clauses.

When the relative pronoun (expressed or understood) is the object of a preposition in a *defining* relative clause, the preposition if often placed at the end of the clause. A preposition cannot, in any case, be placed before the relative pronoun *that*:

a. Is this the book (that/which) *you asked me for*? (for which you asked me?)
b. This is the person (that/whom[1]) *I was telling you about*. (about whom I was telling you)
c. The police learned that the man (that/whom[1]) *they were looking for* had been seen boarding a train at Euston. (the man for whom they were looking)

It is very unlikely that the alternative forms (in brackets) would be used in sentences *a* and *b*. The sentences would sound forced and unnatural. The alternative form is, however, possible in *c*, though it results in greater formality of style.

Two of the factors determining the placing of prepositions are:

i Is the sentence spoken or written? If *spoken*, the preposition is much more likely to come at the end of its clause. At the same time, this makes it possible to omit the relative pronoun (see *a* and *b* above).

ii Is the style formal or informal? If *informal*, the preposition is likely to come at the end of its clause, even in written English (see example *c* above).

There are, however, two other considerations, which concern the way in which the preposition functions:

iii Verb + preposition combinations such as *take after* (= resemble) and *put up with* (= tolerate) represent new 'words' whose meanings are independent of their constituent elements. The two elements (or three) are then inseparable, and the preposition must always follow the verb:

The person (that/whom[1]) *he takes after* is his mother.
This is something (that/which) *I refuse to put up with*.

[1] See footnote on page 123.

iv The preposition may, on the other hand, represent part of a prepositional noun phrase, and be entirely independent of the verb in its clause. In this case, the preposition always precedes the relative pronoun:

He signed an agreement. *Under this agreement* he would be entitled to a commission on sales.
= He signed an agreement *under which* he would be entitled to a commission on sales.

2. Non-defining clauses

In a non-defining relative clause, it is almost a general rule for the preposition to come before the relative pronoun:

The new hospital, *in which* the Queen has taken a great personal interest, will be officially opened in March.
The headmaster, *with whom* the parents had discussed their son's future, advised the boy to take up engineering.

One important exception is the verb + preposition combinations mentioned above:

No one puts any faith in the Government's promises, *which* they have frequently *gone back on* in the past.

115 Join the sentences by changing the second sentence of each pair into a *defining* relative clause.

a. Is this the book? You asked me for it.
Is this the book *you asked me for*?
b. If you die before the policy matures, your wife receives the benefits. You yourself would have been entitled to these benefits.
If you die before the policy matures, your wife receives the benefits *to which you yourself would have been entitled.*

1 I don't find the person a very congenial companion. I'm sharing a flat with him.
2 Here's the address. You should write to this address.
3 I can assure you that David is a man. You can absolutely depend on him.
4 I can't remember the name of the person. I gave the money to him.

5 This is a job. You can take your time over it, because I'm not in any particular hurry.

6 The teacher said that two of the pupils had suddenly disappeared. He was responsible for them.

7 Some foreign businessmen thought that British exports should increase after devaluation. I spoke to these businessmen recently.

8 The language teachers' association provides a medium. Through this medium ideas can be shared and discussed.

9 The men's decision to return to work provides a breathing space. Both men and management can think again during this breathing space.

10 The steel chassis gives it great strength. The car is built around the steel chassis.

11 The Minister formulated a basis. The talks could start on this basis.

12 The two sides have agreed to have further talks on a pay and productivity structure. Under this pay and productivity structure the men would be paid at an hourly rate.

13 The scientist produced a working model. Reliable tests could be conducted on this model.

14 Coronary thrombosis is a disease. High sugar consumption is believed to play a part in this disease.

15 Many planners believe that towns should be compact places. Everybody lives near his neighbour in these places.

116 Complete the sentences, incorporating contact clauses with an end-preposition. Some sentences require the completion of both the relative clause and the main clause, e.g.

The place we . . . has a terrible train service.
The place *we've just moved to* has a terrible train service.

1 . . . the cupboard the wine glasses . . .?
2 . . . the material the curtains . . .
3 . . . the book this quotation . . .?
4 . . . the cup this saucer . . .
5 . . . the name of the programme we're . . .?
6 . . . is a subject I . . .
7 These aren't the books I . . .
8 Is there nobody here I . . .?
9 . . . the house her daughter . . .
10 . . . the name of the school you . . .?

11 ... the safe the money ...
12 The situation we ... was very dangerous.

117 Join the sentences, using non-defining clauses with a prepositional construction, e.g.

> The new tunnel under the Thames will divert a great deal of
> traffic from the worst congested crossing-points. *The line
> of this tunnel* has yet to be finally determined.
>
> The new tunnel under the Thames, *the line of which has yet
> to be finally determined*, will divert a great deal of traffic
> from the worst congested crossing-points.

1 The eighty-nine passengers all escaped without serious injury.
Four of the passengers were British.
2 The country now has 300 power stations. All of them are part of a
national network.
3 The speaker posed four highly important questions. The answers
to these questions proved very illuminating.
4 The U.N. proposed the establishment of an international peace-
keeping force. The composition and power of this force would be
a matter for agreement among U.N. members.
5 The plans for the new by-pass have now been approved by the
Local Authority. By means of this by-pass, heavy congestion in
the city centre will be considerably relieved.
6 The Bill for the abolition of resale price maintenance was eventually passed by Parliament. Mr Heath had staked his political
reputation on it.
7 This new project could earn a great deal of much-needed foreign
currency for Britain. The Government has given financial support to this project.
8 The Labour Party's latest manifesto contains many new proposals.
The most far-reaching of these proposals are concerned with
secondary education.
9 'I should like to pay tribute to our loyal and hard-working staff.
Without their unremitting support it would not have been
possible to produce last year's spectacular rise in profits.'
10 The Government intends to introduce a new Bill on taxation.
The study of its provisions will be the work of experts on both
sides of the House.
11 From the beginning of 1970, the oil company intends using
250,000 ton tankers. It already has ten of these on order.

12 Our advertising agency has twenty branch offices in Europe. Two of them are in London.

13 In 1969, the British housewife spent 8½d each week on baked beans. We are the world's top consumers of baked beans.

14 The Campaign for Nuclear Disarmament attracted some very influential supporters. Bertrand Russell, the eminent philosopher, was among these supporters.

15 For electoral purposes, the United Kingdom is divided into constituencies. Each of them returns one member to Parliament.

Co-ordinate relative clauses

As we have already seen (page 128), it is possible for non-defining clauses to be represented by separate sentences, though often with less economy or neatness of style. Non-defining clauses often have a more obvious co-ordinating function when they follow, rather than interrupt, the main clause—some of the relative clauses in the last exercise could well be written as separate sentences. The co-ordinating function of non-defining clauses can be seen most clearly in sentences like the following:

a. He's not on the telephone, which makes it difficult to get in touch with him.

b. The policeman said I wasn't allowed to park my car outside my house, which I considered most unreasonable.

c. As I had lost John's new address, I wrote to his father, who will, presumably, let me know where John is now living.

In all these sentences, we could replace *which* or *who* by *and this* or *and he*. In sentences *a* and *b*, moreover, *which* does not relate to a noun antecedent, but refers back to the whole of the preceding clause. This use of non-defining clauses is common in both the spoken language and the written. Where a prepositional construction is used, however, the effect produced is one of formality, which is more appropriate to the written language:

> He invested his money in several different companies, by which means (= and by this means) he hoped to reduce the natural hazards of investment.

118 Join the sentences by changing the second sentence of each pair into a co-ordinate relative clause, e.g.

At £2,000 this car is a little expensive. *This* is bound to affect its sales in Britain.

At £2,000 this car is a little expensive, *which* is bound to affect its sales in Britain.

1 He decided not to complete his university course. This was a great disappointment to his parents.
2 We've just installed central heating. This should make a tremendous difference to the house next winter.
3 John was ill in bed. This explains why he didn't turn up last night.
4 The Company needed to diversify. This they could do quickly only by a series of take-overs.
5 The new Chairman promised to double the company's turnover within five years. This is precisely what he managed to do.
6 He blamed me for everything. I thought this very unfair.
7 I gave the message to your secretary. She was supposed to pass it on to you.
8 Few people attended last night's meeting. This was a pity, since several important matters were decided on.
9 My car's got to go in for repair. This means I'll have to take the train to work for the next few days.
10 He showed the contract to his solicitor. His solicitor advised him not to sign it in its present form.
11 The retail price of tea to the U.K. consumer has remained unchanged for more than a decade. This is remarkable in this age of inflation.
12 Critics of the new measures say that the Government has not gone far enough. This may well prove to be true.
13 Several people thought the speaker had dealt with the subject very thoroughly. This was hardly the impression I got.
14 He has given in his resignation. This was the best thing he could do in the circumstances.

119 Join the sentences by changing the second sentence of each pair into a co-ordinate relative clause, using a prepositional construction, e.g.

The police told the man loitering near the jeweller's shop to move on. At this, the man became abusive.

The police told the man loitering near the jeweller's shop to move on, at which the man became abusive.

1 The miser's eyes gleamed with greedy satisfaction as he placed the pile of banknotes in his safe. He then carefully locked the door of the safe before leaving the room.

2 The Borough Council felt that tall blocks of flats would cost too much compared with ordinary houses. In addition to this, they would look out of place among existing buildings.

3 She announced that she felt deeply hurt by her host's attitude. Having said this, she burst into tears, to the acute embarrassment of everyone else at the party.

4 Ten minutes later, Joan rang up her fiancée and apologized. To apologize required a great effort on her part.

5 Mid-April is the time for taking cuttings. In the subsequent planting of these cuttings, the greatest possible care must be taken not to bruise the stems.

6 The singer returned to give yet another encore. The audience burst into even wilder applause at this.

7 One cannot keep a horse unless one has a paddock. This fact must be borne in mind by would-be horse owners.

8 He lost two games early in the tournament. Despite this, however, he managed to carry off the championship.

9 The Company's newly-acquired subsidiaries will begin to contribute significantly to profits next year. Some allowance for this must be made when considering the long-term prospects.

10 Last year (1969) Britons spent about £6,500m. on food. Well over half of this was on packaged commodities.

11 We need a definite policy for controlling the size, density and distribution of towns. The unfortunate neglect of this in the past has been responsible for many of the worst features of present-day life in large and densely-populated cities.

12 The police discovered the thieves' hide-out two days later. By this time, however, the thieves had disappeared.

Where, when, why, and as

1. *Where* and *when* may function as relative adverbs, introducing defining or non-defining relative clauses in the same way as *which* and *who*:

a. I should like to retire to the town *where* (= in which) *I spent my youth.* (Defining)

Wine-producers say they can't remember a time *when* (= at which) *the grape harvest was worse than this year's.* (Defining) *b.* The tourists visited the Royal Mint, *where* (= in which place) *English coin is produced.* (Non-defining)

People are still talking about the historic events of last week, *when* (at which time) *the first spacemen circled the earth.* (Non-defining)

c. He was taken to the police station, *where* (= and there) *he proceeded to make a full confession.* (Co-ordinate)

She showed no signs of emotion till she reached home, *when* (= and then) *she broke down completely.* (Co-ordinate)

2. *Why* as a relative adverb introduces only defining clauses:

You haven't given me one good reason *why* (= for which) *I should agree to help you.*

3. *As* may introduce a defining relative clause, commonly after *the same* or *such*:

They went to the same hotel *as we always stay at.*
(Cp. They went to the hotel *that* we always stay at.)
The student wasn't working hard enough, and such work *as he had done* was very poor.
(Cp. . . . and the work *that* he had done . . .)

As may also introduce a non-defining (co-ordinate) clause. Such clauses differ from all other relative clauses, however, in that they can *precede* the main clause, as well as interrupting or following it:

As he later admitted, it was a stupid thing to do.
It was, as he later admitted, a stupid thing to do.
It was a stupid thing to do, as he later admitted.

120 Replace the words in italics by *when, where, why,* or (Nos. 13–17) a construction with *as.*

1 The days *in which* you could travel without a passport are a thing of the past.
2 In 1842, Charles Dickens went to America, *in which country* he advocated international copyright and the abolition of slavery.
3 There are times *at which* everyone needs to be alone.
4 Have you ever been in a situation *in which* you know the other person is right yet you can't agree with him?
5 He remembered several occasions in the past *on which* he had experienced a similar feeling.

6 Shakespeare arrived in London about 1586, *and there*, some time later, he became a member of the Lord Chamberlain's company of players.

7 I can't think of any reason *for which* you should take all the blame for what happened.

8 The car showed its true qualities on Continental roads, *on which* it was possible to drive up to 500 miles a day without undue strain.

9 This Company has now introduced a policy *under which* premiums are related to the age of the driver.

10 The whole family wants to emigrate to a country *in which* there is more scope for individual enterprise.

11 British industry must begin to make changes long before 1975, *in which year* Britain begins to go metric.

12 The fire brigade arrived two hours after the alarm was first raised, *and then* it was too late to save much of the building.

13 If he doesn't want to join us (*and this* may well be the case) we can always ask someone else to make up a foursome.

14 John's a very lonely person, and *the particular* friends *that* he has tend to be rather odd characters.

15 Britain can solve her balance of payments problems if she tries hard enough, *which fact* has been amply proved by the trade figures of the past few months.

16 You have *exactly* the problem with your new car *that* we had when we first bought ours.

17 We had completely misjudged the situation, *which fact* we later discovered.

What

Although *what* (in one of its uses) is classified as a relative pronoun, it is unhelpful to foreign students to associate it with the relative pronouns we have used so far. The most important difference to note about the use of *what* is that it never relates back to an antecedent. It introduces a NOUN clause, not an adjectival clause, and is equivalent in meaning to *that which, the thing(s) which* or *something which*. We may compare two sentences:

a. He got *the thing which* he wanted.
b. He got   *what*   he wanted.

In *a*, the clause *which he wanted* is an adjectival clause qualifying *thing*, while in *b*, the clause *what he wanted* is a noun clause, object of the verb *got*.

121 Replace the words in italics by *what*.

1 *The thing that* the speaker said next was lost in the general uproar.
2 Why don't you explain *the idea that* you have in mind?
3 The teacher tested the students to see if they remembered *the things which* they had learned.
4 *The thing that* you're asking me to do is out of the question.
5 He's *something that*'s known as a 'bellyacher'—he's always complaining about something.
6 What a nuisance! That's just *the thing which* I didn't want to happen.
7 *The thing that* amazes me is where he gets all his energy from.
8 Would this be *the thing that* you're looking for?
9 Mind *the things that* you say to him; he's very sensitive!
10 The leader of the expedition marked out *something that* seemed to be the best route.

122 Complete the sentences with a noun clause introduced by *what*.

a. I can't imagine . . .
I can't imagine *what induced him to do such a thing*.
(Noun clause, object)
b. . . . is more important than what you say.
What you do is more important than what you say.
(Noun clause, subject)

1 No one could understand . . .
2 Were you surprised at . . .?
3 He was lucky enough to sell his car for exactly . . .
4 I'd rather you didn't say anything about . . .
5 Don't you think you ought to apologize for . . .?
6 I think he should have told me . . .
7 Will you think over . . .?
8 . . . is where he gets all his money from.
9 It's a pity you weren't at the meeting to hear . . .
10 . . . was the fact that she passed her examination despite her absence from school.

Note: Collective Nouns as Antecedents

English people as well as foreign students are often doubtful about which relative pronoun to use after words like these:

| association | body | class | club | committee |
| company | government | group | society | team |

When we use these words, we may consider them either as denoting an entity or as denoting a number of individuals, and we treat the words as singular or plural accordingly. If, for example, we are thinking of a committee as a whole, we treat it as a *thing* (singular) and use *which*; if we are thinking of it as comprising a number of people, we treat it as personal (plural) and use *who*.

The choice of pronoun depends on which particular idea is intended, the single entity or the group of individuals, but students must be careful to be consistent, and should ensure that any other pronouns that occur in the sentence are singular or plural in agreement with the relative pronoun:

a. The Prime Minister said that his Government, *which* had always expressed *its* firm belief in free enterprise, would do *its* best, while in office, to safeguard the freedom of the individual from State interference.

b. The Boat Race crew, *who* are now superbly fit, will be doing *their* best next week to revenge *themselves* for last year's defeat.

Verb patterns

with -ing forms, infinitives, and 'that' clauses

Introductory notes

Both the gerund (verb + ing) and the infinitive can function as nouns standing alone, or they can operate as verbs in non-finite noun clauses.[1]

1 The gerund and the infinitive can function as nouns. On the whole, the gerund is more readily identifiable with a noun than the infinitive is.

1.1 The gerund may stand alone as the subject of a verb:

Reading is his favourite pastime.

[1] For an explanation of this term, see page 294 in the Appendix.

The infinitive is not often used in this way (but see 2.1c).

1.2 Both may stand alone as the object of a verb:

a. I've finished *working*.
b. I want *to leave*.

1.3 Both may function as the complement of *to be*:

a. My worst vice is *smoking*.
b. Her first impulse was *to scream*.

1.4 Only the gerund, however, can be used as the object of a preposition:

> He insisted ON *coming*.

Only the gerund may be qualified by adjectives:

> This book makes GOOD LIGHT *reading*.

Only the gerund can be used with an article and can have a plural form:

> *The findings* of the court have now been made public.
> I can't keep track of his *comings* and *goings*.

2 The gerund and the infinitive can operate as verbs in non-finite noun clauses.

2.1 They may be followed by a direct or an indirect object:

a. *Closing* THE FACTORY means *putting* PEOPLE out of work. (D.O.)
b. He hates *speaking* TO STRANGERS. (I.O.)
c. *To ease* CREDIT RESTRICTIONS at this stage would be unwise. (D.O.)
d. The manager wants *to speak* TO YOU. (I.O.)

Note that in *c*, the infinitive is used in the initial position when it is followed by an object (or an adverb, or both), i.e. when it operates as a verb in a non-finite noun clause. This is fairly common in written English, but in spoken English it is much more usual to find a construction with 'anticipatory' *it*:

> *It* would do no good at all *to explain again*.
> (To explain again would do no good at all.)

2.2 They may be qualified by adverbs:

a. A teacher of English must avoid *speaking* TOO QUICKLY.
b. He wants *to leave* IMMEDIATELY.

2.3 They also have 'perfect' and passive forms:

a. The soldier was accused of *having betrayed* his country. (perfect)
b. He pretended *to have forgotten* the man's name. (perfect)
c. No one likes *being thought* a fool. (passive)
d. He doesn't want *to be told* the truth. (passive)
e. He resented *having been criticized* by the manager. (perfect passive)
f. He claimed *to have been badly treated*. (perfect passive)

3 In some of the above examples, a 'that' clause could be used after the main verb in place of the gerund or the infinitive:

a. Closing the factory means *putting* people out of work.
that people will lose their jobs.

b. He pretended *to have forgotten* the man's name.
that he had forgotten the man's name.

One of the main problems is, in fact, that of learning which form (-ing form, infinitive, or 'that' clause) should be used *after another verb*. On the whole, one can learn to associate a verb with its particular pattern (or patterns) only through practice. Verbs that are similar in meaning do not necessarily follow the same pattern:

a. I *advised* him *to see* a doctor.
b. I *suggested that* he should see a doctor.

Classification

The exercises that follow are aimed principally at giving practice in the use of the -ing forms (gerund and participle), infinitives and 'that' clauses *after another verb*, regardless of whether or not all the forms could be classified in some way as 'nouns'.[1]

Students should be encouraged to note examples they find of sentences illustrating the different verbs used in their associated

[1] Infinitives of purpose are, however, excluded.

patterns. In the course of the exercises, check-lists of verbs are given for guidance and reference. The verbs have been assigned to the following main groups:

1 verbs followed by the gerund (some may also be followed by a 'that' clause):

He *avoided* MAKING the same mistake again.
He *admitted* HAVING MADE the same mistake again.
He *admitted* (THAT) he had made the same mistake again.

2a verbs followed by an infinitive without a preceding noun (some may also be followed by a 'that' clause):

He *refused* TO GIVE me his support.
He *swore* TO HAVE his revenge.
He *swore* (THAT) he would have his revenge.

2b verbs followed by a noun + infinitive (some may also be followed by a 'that' clause):

We *invited* HER TO STAY with us.
I *reminded* HER TO COME on time.
I *reminded* HER THAT she must come on time.

2c verbs followed by an infinitive, with or without a preceding noun (some may also be followed by a 'that' clause):

I *asked* TO SEE the photograph.
I *asked* HIM TO SHOW me the photograph.
I *asked* THAT no one else should be told.

3 verbs followed by the gerund or an infinitive (some may also be followed by a 'that' clause):

He *remembered* TO GIVE her the message.
He *remembered* GIVING her the message.
He *remembered* THAT he had already given her the message.

If there are differences in meaning between such sentences, these are discussed in the notes accompanying the exercises.

4 verbs followed by a noun and a 'present' participle or (in the active) an infinitive without 'to' (some may also be followed by a 'that' clause):

I *saw* HIM DOING something very stupid.
I *saw* HIM DO something very stupid.
I *saw* THAT he was doing something very stupid.

5 verbs followed by either a 'that' clause, or by a noun + *to be* or *to have*:

I *thought* (THAT) he was a very sensible person.
I *thought* HIM TO BE a very sensible person.

There are a few verbs which appear in more than one list, but each time with a different meaning. These particular verbs have different patterns associated with the different meanings. For example, *mean* (=entail) appears in *Group 1*, and is followed by the gerund:

If we go to the evening performance, it will *mean* GETTING a baby-sitter.

Mean (=intend) appears in *Group 2c*, and is followed by an infinitive, with or without a preceding noun:

I *didn't mean* (YOU) TO TELL him till later.

Moreover, some of the verbs which are followed by a 'that' clause as an alternative to the gerund or infinitive may have a different meaning in the alternative construction:

She didn't *fancy* GOING OUT alone. (fancy = like the idea of)
I *fancy* THAT he's in for a disappointment. (fancy = imagine)

Students are advised to consult *The Advanced Learner's Dictionary* for detailed explanation and examples.

Gerunds after prepositions and phrasal verbs. The gerund is always used when a verb follows *a* a preposition, *b* a prepositional verb, or *c* a phrasal verb (verb + adverbial particle):

a. There was no hope OF *finding* any survivors from the crash.
b. I APOLOGIZED FOR *disturbing* him.
c. I GAVE UP *playing* football when I left school.

123 Complete the sentences, using gerunds, e.g.

> I wish you'd do something to help, instead of . . .
> I wish you'd do something to help, instead of *standing* there giving advice.

1 The Government was unable to make any promises about . . .
2 There are many difficulties involved in . . .
3 You must be tired of . . .
4 The boy was severely reprimanded for . . .
5 The public were warned of the dangers of . . .
6 He doesn't take any interest in . . .
7 You seem to be very fond of . . .
8 The soldier was court-martialled for . . .
9 Miners are always warned against . . .
10 Who is responsible for . . . ?
11 The answer to the housing problem seems to lie in . . .
12 You ought to think about . . ., instead of . . .
13 This new scheme goes a long way towards . . .
14 I would never think of . . .
15 They saw no reason for not . . .
16 Far from . . ., this agreement will help in . . .

124 Instructions as above

1 My doctor advised me to give up . . .
2 We had to put off . . .
3 That company specializes in . . .
4 People should be asked to refrain from . . .
5 I must apologize for . . .
6 The judge was accused of not . . .
7 He prides himself on . . .
8 I told him not to bother about . . .
9 We had to put up with . . .
10 The teacher decided against . . .
11 On . . ., he took off his hat.
12 We asked a solicitor for advice before . . .
13 By . . ., he ran the risk of . . .
14 After . . ., the customer left the shop without . . .
15 In spite of . . ., the swimmer succeeded in . . .
16 By . . ., the student improved his chances of . . .

The word *to* presents a problem: is it a 'true' preposition, or is it part of an infinitive? We can discover the function of *to* in any particular sentence by trying to put a noun after it. If a noun is possible, the gerund form of a verb must be used:

> I'm looking forward to: *my holiday*. (Noun)
> *going* on holiday. (Gerund)

It would be impossible to put a noun after *to* in the following sentence:

> I should like to: *see* you next Thursday.

This test enables us to distinguish two particularly confusing verb phrases, *used to* and *to be used to*. *Used to* + *infinitive* refers to habitual action in the past, and *used to* cannot be followed by a noun (or a gerund):

> When I was in England, I *used to eat* a big breakfast.

In the phrase *to be used to* there are three elements: the verb *to be*, a past participle functioning as an adjective, *used* (= accustomed), and a preposition *to*. The phrase is parallel in structure to, e.g., *to be interested in*, and it is possible to put a noun after *to*:

> I'm used to *his curious ways*.

If a verb follows *to be used to*, therefore, the gerund form must be used:

> I'm used to *hearing* about the odd things he does.

To be used to suggests *familiarity* through a repetition of the activity or occurrence; it does not state the existence of a habit as such. Note also that *used to* is a fixed idiom and is not used in any other tense, whereas the verbal element in *to be used to* (i.e. the verb *to be*) can be used in any appropriate tense.

125 Complete the sentences, using the gerund of a suitable verb. *To* functions as a preposition in every case. Note that the 'perfect' form is required in some sentences.

1 The Prime Minister said he was looking forward to . . . the U.S. President.
2 He should be accustomed by now to . . . English food.

3 The policeman couldn't swear to . . . the accused man at the scene of the crime.

4 Do you think your father would object to . . . me some money?

5 He said he wasn't used to . . . in public.

6 Having almost run out of money, we were reduced to . . . in a cheap hotel.

7 He tried to limit himself to . . . ten cigarettes a day.

8 Manufacturers were asked to devote all their energies to . . . exports.

9 There's one thing I dislike about him: he will never admit to . . . a mistake.

10 We shan't be going. My wife doesn't feel up to . . . so far.

11 The committee could see no alternative to . . . the plan in its original form.

12 The Government set up a Prices and Incomes Board with a view to . . . both price rises and wage demands.

126 Decide whether *to* is functioning as a preposition or as part of an infinitive, and then complete the sentences with the gerund or the infinitive of the verbs in brackets.

1 The speaker said he would confine himself to (try) to (answer) four questions.

2 By selling council houses, we are able to devote more money to (build) fresh properties.

3 Restraining home demand is the key to (increase) our exports.

4 The idea of a road pricing system—a tax on road usage—is moving rapidly nearer to (become) a reality.

5 Having suggested the scheme myself, I now feel committed to (try) to (make) it work.

6 I think that is what he said, but I can't swear to (have) heard him correctly.

7 He used to (dislike) London, but he now seems resigned to (live) there.

8 Jones came very close to (win) a gold medal for Britain in the Olympics.

9 It might be better to (try) to (discuss) it in his own language, as he isn't used to (speak) English.

10 Most educationalists agree that no teacher's duties should be limited solely to (teach).

11 Unreliable delivery dates are one of the most important obstacles to (increase) our exports.

12 Since the introduction of new services, many businessmen have taken (to) (travel) by train for journeys between 100–200 miles.

Verbs followed by the gerund

Group 1 The gerund is used after these verbs. The verbs in italics may also be followed by a clause introduced by *that*.

acknowledge[1]	fancy[1]	propose (suggest)
admit[1]	favour	recall
advocate	finish	recollect
anticipate	foresee	repent
appreciate	forgive	report
avoid	grudge	resent
celebrate	imagine[1]	resist
consider (think about)	include	resume
contemplate	involve	risk
defer	justify	stop[2]
delay	keep (persist in)	suffer
deny	mean (entail)	suggest[3]
detest	mention	tolerate
dislike	mind (object to)	understand[1]
dispute	miss	can't help (have no
doubt	necessitate	control over)
endanger	pardon	can't endure
enjoy	postpone	can't stand
entail	practise	It's no good
envisage	prevent	It's no use
escape	prohibit	It's (not) worth
excuse		

Note:

[1] Like the verbs in *Group 5*, these verbs may also be followed by a noun + *to be* or *to have*:

> The Minister acknowledged THAT the reports were substantially correct.
> The Minister acknowledged *the reports* TO BE substantially correct.

[2] The gerund after *stop* indicates the cessation of an activity:

> He stopped *smoking* on his doctor's advice.
> (i.e. He didn't smoke any more)

Stop may also be followed by an infinitive—an infinitive of purpose:

> He stopped *to smoke* a cigarette.

The infinitive indicates that he stopped (whatever he was doing) *in order to* smoke a cigarette.

³ *Suggest* raises special problems when followed by a 'that' clause. The 'full' construction is:

a. I suggest (that) he should see a specialist immediately.

However, *should* is often omitted (in any case, it simply re-inforces the idea of recommendation implied in the word *suggest*):

b. I suggest (that) he see a specialist immediately.

The dependent verb may then be 'regularized':

c. I suggest (that) he sees a specialist immediately.

Hence in the past tense we find:

a. I suggested (that) he should see a specialist immediately.
b. I suggested (that) he see a specialist immediately.
c. I suggested (that) he saw a specialist immediately.

127 Complete the sentences with the gerund of a suitable verb.

1 The newspaper's financial editor advised his readers not to buy speculative shares unless they were prepared to risk . . . their money.
2 This room will look very cheerful once you've finished . . . it.
3 I wish you wouldn't keep . . . me what I already know all too well.
4 It is difficult to see how the company can avoid . . . another loss this year.
5 The Prime Minister has stated that the Government does not intend to resume . . . supplies of arms to either side.
6 It was so ridiculous that I couldn't resist . . . outright.
7 The secretary asked if I would mind . . . for a few minutes.
8 The way to learn a language is to practise . . . it as often as possible.
9 Everyone said how much they had enjoyed . . . to the speech.
10 When you've finished the book, you can tell me if it's worth . . .
11 He was very lucky to escape . . . (*passive*) to prison.

12 The scheme was so impracticable that I refused even to consider
. . . it.
13 She was so upset that she couldn't help . . .
14 The job will entail your . . . to different parts of the country,
often at short notice.
15 The teacher said that he wouldn't tolerate my . . . late every day.
16 The question is so trivial, it hardly justifies our . . . up any more
time discussing it.

In sentences 1–13 in the above exercise, the subject of the main
verb is also the subject of the gerund. But compare these two
sentences:

a. I don't mind *saying* I was wrong.
b. I don't mind YOU (*or* YOUR?) *saying* I was wrong.

In sentence *a*, *I* is the subject of both *don't mind* and *saying*;
while in sentence *b*, there are different subjects, *I* and *you* for
the two verbs *mind* and *say* respectively. We then have to decide
which form of personal pronoun to use before the gerund, the
object form or the possessive—*YOU saying* or *YOUR saying*.[1]

We feel the necessity for a possessive form more particularly
when the gerund is the *subject* of the main verb:

YOUR *calling* on us just at this time is most inconvenient.

When the gerund is the *object* of the main verb, however, we often
use the object form of a personal pronoun, more especially in the
spoken language:

Do you mind ME *coming* as well?

The object form of a personal pronoun or other noun is always
preferred where the use of a possessive would entail an awkward
(or, in spoken English, misleading) construction:

I remember HIM and his SISTER *coming* to London.
(Not *his* and his *sister's*)

[1] In this example, and in those that follow, the gerund is operating as a verb
in a non-finite noun clause. Where the gerund has a purely noun-like function, only the possessive form is possible:
The police are to be congratulated on THEIR *handling* of the affair.
The problem of choice does not arise in analogous constructions with infinitives, where only the object form of a pronoun (or other noun) is possible:
a. I'd like to stay here.
b. I'd like YOU to stay here.

155

With other pronouns, only one form may be available:

> I don't envisage THERE *being* any real disagreement.

The possessive form also tends not to be used with common nouns (or even proper nouns) before the gerund:

> I object to the CAR *being left* there. (Not *the car's*)
> I appreciated JOHN *helping* me. (Rather than *John's*)

The use of the possessive form is, therefore, found mainly with personal pronouns, and then principally in the written language. There are, however, occasions when the possessive seems to be the preferred form in both written and spoken English, and students can become familiar with these only through practice.[1]

---

128 Replace the words in italics by a gerund construction. The object or possessive form of a pronoun or noun will be required before the gerund in some cases, e.g.

> I didn't recall *that he had said* any such thing.
> I didn't recall *him* (or *his*) *saying* (or *having said*) any such thing.

1 He didn't even acknowledge *that he had received* the invitation.
2 The witness reported *that he had seen* a dark saloon car parked outside the bank at the time of the robbery.
3 The accused admitted *that he had received* the stolen goods.
4 The headmaster suggested *that I should try* the examination again the following year.
5 I don't recollect *that I actually promised* to help you.
6 A group of MPs has advocated *that the Government should set up* a special commission of inquiry.
7 Do you anticipate *that there will be* any real problem in getting support?
8 Surely he won't deny *that he was* there on that occasion?
9 No one doubted *that he was* sincere in his beliefs.
10 I can't imagine *that he would ever agree* to such a proposition.

---

[1] For a more detailed analysis and examples of current practice in written English, students may consult Scheuerweghs: *Present-day English Syntax*, Sections 317–325.

129 Complete the sentences, using a gerund construction.

1 The public authorities should prohibit . . .
2 I strongly resent your . . .
3 It would be unwise to defer . . .
4 It's no good . . . You know how he detests . . .
5 If he mentions . . ., I shan't be able to resist . . .
6 Forgive my . . ., but don't you miss . . . now that you're living in England?
7 Fancy . . . here today!
8 Will the new job involve your . . .?
9 Why don't you stop . . . if you so dislike . . .?
10 I can't imagine his ever . . .
11 The magistrate stated that the court appreciated the man's . . .
12 My wife suggested . . . for a holiday, but I favoured . . . instead.
13 We tried to delay his . . ., our main concern being to prevent him . . .
14 I see no harm in your . . .
15 I doubt whether the landlord will insist on our . . .
16 How can we be sure of his . . .?

Verbs followed by an infinitive

It is necessary first to distinguish two important patterns:

i I offered to help. (S × V × infinitive)
ii I invited him to come. (S × V × Noun × infinitive)

We can then establish three groups of verbs:

2a those that follow only pattern *i*;
2b those that follow only pattern *ii*;
2c those that can follow either pattern *i* or pattern *ii*.

Group 2a The infinitive without a preceding noun is used after these verbs. The verbs in italics may also be followed by a clause introduced by *that*.

afford	get (reach the stage of)	*promise*
agree	*guarantee*	propose (intend)
aim	happen[1]	prove (turn out)
appear[1]	hasten	refuse
arrange	have (be obliged)	*resolve*
bother	hesitate	seek

157

care	hope	seem[1]
chance[1]	learn (how to)	strive
claim	long	swear
condescend	manage	tend
consent	offer	threaten
decide	prepare	trouble
demand	presume (take the liberty)	undertake
determine	pretend	volunteer
endeavour	proceed	vow
fail	profess	

Note:
[1] These verbs may be followed by a 'that' clause only when they have the subject *it*:

It appeared that no one had taken the problem seriously.

130 Replace the words in italics by an infinitive construction.

1 The police hope *that they will solve* the crime soon.
2 The Minister of Labour readily agreed *that he would meet* the union leaders.
3 The defeated champion swore *that he would have* his revenge.
4 The Company has decided *that it will close down* uneconomic factories.
5 He claimed *that he was* an expert in such matters.
6 The accused pretended *that he didn't understand* the lawyer's question.
7 The chairman threatened *that he would resign* if his policies were not adopted.
8 The student resolved *that he would do* better next time.
9 I vowed *that I would never follow* his advice again.
10 No teacher would profess *that he knows* all the answers.
11 The management promised *that they would look into* the workers' grievances.
12 They couldn't, however, guarantee *that they would meet* all the men's demands.

131 Complete the sentences, using an infinitive construction.

1 The question is whether anyone will volunteer . . .
2 Surely you would never consent . . .?

3 Our reporter has just telephoned to say that rescue teams will tomorrow endeavour . . .

4 Last year, miners in South Wales managed . . . Next year, they aim . . .

5 As soon as the volcano first showed signs of activity, the entire population of the village prepared . . .

6 You needn't bother . . . I've already arranged . . .

7 It's many years since I went to my home town. I'm longing . . .

8 I hesitated . . ., since I didn't know him very well.

9 It tends . . . in winter in the north of England.

10 A rather officious policeman demanded . . .

11 I'm sure you'll like him when you get . . . him better.

12 The idea proved . . . very unpopular.

132 Write sentences based on the material given. You should vary the subject of your sentences (do not use only pronouns), as well as the tense of the main verbs, e.g.

> arrange/meet/the following day
> The two sides arranged to meet for further talks the following day.

1 afford/waste/time
2 appear/understand
3 decide/work/in future
4 fail/complete/on time
5 hasten/apologize for
6 manage/avoid/accident
7 offer/repair/damage
8 refuse/listen to
9 proceed/make/long speech about
10 undertake/finish/within six months

Group 2b A noun + infinitive is used after these verbs. The verbs in italics may also be followed by a clause introduced by *that*.

accustom	entice	order[1]
aid	entitle	persuade[2]
appoint	entreat[1]	press
assist	force[4]	prompt
cause	get (= 'causative')[5]	provoke
challenge	impel	remind[2]

command[1]	implore[1]	require[1]
commission	incite	stimulate
compel[4]	induce	summon
defy	inspire	teach (how to)[3]
direct[1]	instruct[3]	tell (instruct, order)
drive	invite	tempt
empower	lead	trust[1]
enable	leave (put responsibility on)	warn[3]
encourage	oblige[4]	

Notes:

[1] No noun is found between these verbs and a 'that' clause:

> The commander ordered HIS TROOPS *to lay down* their arms.
> The commander ordered *that* his troops should lay down their arms.

Note that the use of *should* is a common feature in such clauses after these verbs. (See Exercise 22.)

[2] A noun is always found between these verbs and a 'that' clause:

> He persuaded ME *to change* my mind.
> He persuaded ME *that* his plan was preferable.

Students often confuse the patterns associated with *persuade* and *convince*. Only *persuade* can be followed by a *noun + infinitive* construction, but both verbs can be followed by a 'that' clause:

> He $\begin{smallmatrix} \text{persuaded} \\ \text{convinced} \end{smallmatrix}$ me that his plan was preferable.

The dictionary definition of *persuade* suggests that it is synonymous with *convince*, but in most contexts the two verbs do not appear to be fully interchangeable. In the above example, 'He persuaded me' tends to suggest an element of reluctance or reservation on 'my' part to accept that his plan was preferable; whereas 'He convinced me' suggests my more unreserved acceptance of the fact that his plan was preferable. It is, perhaps, mainly a matter of emphasis.

[3] A noun is optional between these verbs and a 'that' clause:

> The Chancellor warned UNIONS *not to press* for higher wages.

The Chancellor warned UNIONS *that* higher wages would mean higher prices.

The Chancellor warned *that* higher wages would mean higher prices.

⁴ *Make* is roughly synonymous with these verbs, but is followed
a. in the active, by a noun + infinitive without *to*:

He made ME *do* all the work again.

b. in the passive, by an infinitive with *to*:

I was made TO DO all the work again.

See Exercises 141, 142.

⁵ *Get* may also be followed by an object + past participle:

You should get your passport *renewed*.

'Causative' *have* is synonymous with *get*, but is followed by a noun + the infinitive without *to* (see group *4*):

Before you buy the house, you should *get* a surveyor *to look* over it.

Before you buy the house, you should *have* a surveyor *look* over it.

133 Complete the sentences with the infinitive of a suitable verb.

1 A season ticket entitles the holder . . . as many journeys as he wishes within the stated period.
2 Parents should tell their children . . . great care when crossing busy roads.
3 The Leader of the Opposition challenged the Prime Minister . . . his party's attitude on housing.
4 Having voted the chairman off the board only one week earlier, they then invited him . . . it.
5 I can't think what induced him . . . such a thing.
6 The new immigration laws require all immigrants . . . a job in England before they are allowed to enter the country.
7 The Company has commissioned a team of efficiency experts . . . organization and methods.
8 It was thought that a small group of troublemakers were inciting the workers . . .

9 The Government has now empowered local authorities . . . more council houses if they wish.

10 Bad weather prompted us . . . our holiday.

134 Rewrite the sentences in reported speech, using a *noun +
infinitive* construction with the verbs suggested in brackets.

1 'You are to appear before the magistrate at 10 a.m. on Thursday,' the letter said. (summon)

2 'Do not bathe when the red flag is flying,' the notice said. (warn)

3 His wife left him a note saying 'Don't forget to lock the door.' (remind)

4 'Passengers should check in at the airport thirty minutes before take-off,' stated a notice at the air terminal. (instruct)

5 'I do hope you'll have another drink before you go,' said my old friend. (press)

6 'Pay attention to what you're doing,' said the teacher. (tell)

7 'Please don't tell my husband,' she said to her friend. (implore)

8 'State your views openly—if you dare,' the speaker said to his opponent. (challenge)

9 'Would you like to join me for dinner?' I said to the new member. (invite)

10 'I would take a more optimistic view of the matter, if I were you,' my friend told me. (encourage)

11 'Make your way to Waterloo Station, and wait under the main clock,' the letter said. (direct)

135 Complete the sentences, using an infinitive construction.

1 What could have provoked him . . .?

2 The Government appointed a committee . . .

3 The new incentives are aimed at stimulating exporters . . .

4 Who taught you . . .?

5 Public health authorities should try harder to persuade the public . . .

6 He ordered the cab-driver . . .

7 The realities of the situation forced us . . .

8 No one could understand what led him . . .

9 Cancellation of the flight obliged many passengers . . .

10 Everyone went home immediately after the party, leaving me . . .

11 While I was filling up with petrol, I got the mechanic . . .

12 Seeing my friend's holiday brochures tempted me . . .

13 His great wealth enabled him . . .
14 The news of his failure caused the student . . .

Group 2c The infinitive, with or without a preceding noun, is
used after these verbs. The verbs in italics may also be followed
by a clause introduced by *that*.

ask[1]	*desire*[1]	*mean* (intend)[1]
beg[1]	elect	*request*[1]
choose	*expect*[1]	want
dare[2]	help[3]	*wish*[1]

Notes:
[1] No noun is found between these verbs and a 'that' clause.
[2] If no noun is used after *dare*, two patterns are possible:

a. the infinitive with *to*:

He dared *to call* me a fool to my face.

b. the infinitive without *to* (more especially in negative and
interrogative sentences). In this case, *dare* patterns like an
auxiliary verb, the negative being formed by the addition of *not*
(*n't*), and the interrogative by simple inversion of subject and
verb:

He dare*n't tell* me what happened.
Dare you mention it to him?

[3] *Help* may be followed by the infinitive with or without *to*:

Everyone helped (me) (to) clean the place up.

There is, of course, a difference between the uses of *help* in the
following sentences:

I can't help to clean the place up. (= I can't give assistance)
I can't help falling asleep. (= I can't prevent myself from
falling asleep) (See *Group 1*)

The need to make such a distinction arises only after *can't/
couldn't*.

136 Write sentences based on the given facts, beginning your answers
as suggested. Some sentences require a noun before the infinitive.

1 Young Smith will be leading the sales mission to America. The
manager thinks he's the best man for the job. (The manager has
chosen . . .)
2 I hope you didn't tell anyone. It was supposed to be a secret.
(I didn't mean . . .)

163

3 An invitation to dinner from the Robinsons? What's come over them? (I didn't expect . . .)

4 I shall never finish all this work by myself. (Will you help . . .?)

5 The manager is very firm about punctuality. (He expects . . .)

6 John is terribly inefficient these days. I doubt whether he'll keep his job much longer. (The firm will probably ask . . .)

7 I'd like some information, and you're the very person to give it to me. (I want . . .)

8 The police are interested in two particular men. An interview with them would be very helpful at this stage. (The police wish . . .)

9 The man was given two alternatives: a small fine or a term of imprisonment. He refused to pay the fine. (The man elected . . .)

10 I'm sure he didn't realize you'd be so unhappy about it. (He didn't mean . . .)

11 We really must visit your parents soon. They've asked us to go there time and again. (Your parents have been begging . . .)

12 The man was being blackmailed, but he didn't inform the police because he was afraid of any publicity. (He didn't dare . . .)

Verbs followed by the gerund or infinitive

Group 3 The gerund or infinitive may be used after these verbs. The letters *a*, *b*, and *c* indicate which infinitive pattern is possible (see pages 148 and 157). The verbs in italics may also be followed by a clause introduced by *that*.

advise b	*fear a*	omit *a*
allow[1] *b*	forbear *a*	permit[1] *b*
attempt *a*	*forbid b*	*plan a*
authorize *b*	*forget a*	*prefer c*
begin *a*	go on *a*	*recommend b*
can't bear c	hate *c*	*regret a*
cease *a*	*intend c*	*remember a*
continue *a*	like *c*	*require b*
decline *a*	loathe *c*	start *a*
deserve *a*	love *c*	try *a*
disdain *a*	need *c*	*urge b*
dread a	neglect *a*	venture *a*

Note:

[1] *Let* is roughly synonymous with these verbs, but is used only in the active, and is followed only by a noun + infinitive without *to* (never by an -ing form):

My neighbour let ME *borrow* his car.

See Exercise 141.

While all these verbs may be followed by a gerund or an infinitive this is simply an observation of what is *grammatically* possible. In some cases, the choice of form may not matter very much, while in others it may be of fundamental importance.

1. After some verbs (and after particular forms of these verbs), the choice may be determined by considerations of style rather than of meaning:

It's just starting *to rain*. (Not *starting raining*)

But the choice may also rest on the nature of the dependent verb itself. There is some correspondence between the infinitive and a 'simple' verb form, and between the gerund and a 'continuous' verb form. Some verbs are rarely used in the continuous form (see page 66), and the gerund could hardly replace the infinitive in the following sentence:

He began *to realize* that he had made a mistake.

2. With many of the verbs expressing feelings or attitudes (*like, love, prefer, hate, loathe, dread, can't bear*), the distinction between gerund and infinitive corresponds to the distinction *general* versus *particular*:

I like *looking* round antique shops.

In such sentences, the infinitive is possible, but is a less likely choice than the gerund. *Like* is very similar in this context to *enjoy* (*Group 1*).

If the verb refers to a specific action at a specific time, the infinitive is always used:

I'd like *to visit* you in your new house when you've settled in.

In this sentence, moreover, *like* corresponds more closely to the idea of desire, preference, or choice. This may help to explain why *dislike* is always followed by the gerund, while *don't like* may be followed by the gerund or an infinitive in the same way as *like*. *Dislike* is associated more exclusively with the idea of repugnance (the opposite of enjoyment):

I dislike *asking* him for favours. (i.e. I don't enjoy this)

Don't like, on the other hand, operates as the negative of *like* in both its uses:

a. I don't like *looking* round antique shops.

b. I wouldn't like *to disturb* him if he's working.
(Not 'I would dislike . . .')

Prefer raises an additional problem. The normal construction is 'to prefer one thing *to* another' (not '*than* another'):

> I prefer cigars to cigarettes.
> I prefer riding to walking.

We cannot say: I prefer to ride *to* to walk.
Nor do we say: I prefer to ride *to* walking.
When we need to complete such a construction as 'I should prefer to stay at home . . .', where it is not possible to follow with a gerund or an infinitive, we usually complete the sentence with *rather than,* as follows:

> I should prefer to stay at home rather than go out in this weather.

Alternatively, we can use the idiomatic phrase *I'd rather*:

> I'd rather stay at home than go out in this weather.[1]

3. After the verbs *remember, forget, regret,* the gerund refers to an action or event earlier in time than that of the main verb:

> He remembered *giving* (or *having given*) her the message.
> = He remembered that he had given her the message at some earlier time.

This may be compared with the use of *recall* and *recollect* in *Group 1*.

> I regret *saying* (or *having said*) that you were mistaken.
> = I regret that I said (at some earlier time) that you were mistaken.

The infinitive after these verbs refers to an action or event occurring at the same time as that of the main verb, or later:

> He remembered *to give* her the message. (He called to mind what had to be done, and *then* did it)
> Don't forget *to phone* me tomorrow! (I trust you will call to mind what is to be done, and *then* do it)
> I regret *to say* that you were mistaken. (I am sorry that I must *now* tell you that you were mistaken)

[1] Note that *'d rather* is followed by the infinitive without *to.*

4. Unlike phrasal verbs in general, *go on* may be followed by the gerund or an infinitive. The gerund after *go on* indicates that an existing state of affairs continues:

> He went on *talking*, although I had asked him to stop.

The infinitive indicates a new, or the next, activity in a chain of activities:

> Having mentioned the main problem, he went on *to talk* of other, less important matters.

5. The verb *try* is in a category of its own. If our hostess at a tea party says 'Try some of my home-made cake', she is clearly inviting us to eat some, and perhaps to give her our opinion of it; she is not inviting us to see whether or not we *can* eat it. Similarly, if we use *try + gerund*, we are not referring to the possibility or impossibility of performing the action, but to the results or experience of performing it:

> Have you ever tried *driving* in London? I have, and it's not very pleasant.

The question here is 'Have you actually had the experience of driving in London? If so, you'll know what it's like.'

Try + infinitive relates to the idea of possibility:

> You should try *to answer* all the questions. (i.e. if you can)[1]

There are many occasions when either the gerund or the infinitive makes equally good sense, but a *different* sense:

> Try *looking* at it my way. = *Look* at it my way, and see whether that makes any difference to your view.
> Try *to look* at it my way. = See if you *can* look at it from my point of view (but perhaps you lack the necessary sympathy or understanding).

To sum up: try + gerund = do something, and see what it's like;
>   try + infinitive = see whether or not you *can* do it.

---

[1] An alternative construction is *try and* + infinitive without 'to':
> Try and answer all the questions.

Note, however, that this alternative is possible only after the form *try*:
> I'll try and come early. He'll try and do it tomorrow.

But not *I/He tried and did it.

6. The gerund after *need* and *deserve* (and *want, Group 2c*) is equivalent in meaning to a passive infinitive:

> My pen needs filling (= to be filled)
> The fire wants making up (= to be made up)
> The point deserved mentioning (= to be mentioned)

137 Complete the sentences with the gerund or the infinitive of the verbs in brackets, using the correct form of any pronouns that are included.

1 If the Government's wages policy is to succeed, they must try (keep) prices in check.
2 The shareholders all think they know what should be done, but the board still needs (convince).
3 Let's invite him. I'm sure he would love (come).
4 Someone in the office had made a mistake, and the firm regretted (cause) the customer inconvenience.
5 We plan (take) our holidays abroad this year.
6 The teacher doesn't permit (smoke) during the lessons.
7 I vaguely remember (he, say) something like that.
8 Come over here! I'd like (you, see) this.
9 I always try (be) punctual, but I don't always succeed.
10 It's a tricky problem. I recommend (you, consult) an expert.
11 He'd prefer (you, go) to his place, if that's convenient.
12 A bankers' card authorizes (the holder, cash) cheques up to £30 at any branch.
13 For the second time this year, Miss Black will attempt (swim) the Channel in less than five hours.
14 A child should start (learn) a language at primary school.
15 The film was so terrifying that she could hardly bear (watch) it.
16 The new committee member did not venture (speak) at his first meeting.
17 They began (drive) at six in the morning, and were still on the road ten hours later.
18 The union leaders urged (their members, think) again before (decide) (strike).
19 He remembered (pass) on most of the information, but omitted (mention) one or two of the most important facts.
20 The reporters asked many questions which the Prime Minister declined (answer).

138 Rewrite the sentences, replacing the words in italics by a gerund or infinitive construction.

1 He preferred *that I should say* nothing about it at present.
2 She couldn't bear *that he should think* of her in that way.
3 He was surprised to find the door open. He distinctly remembered *that he had locked* it before going to bed.
4 The speaker making the radio appeal urged *that his listeners should give* generously to a deserving cause.
5 The publishers withdrew the offending passages in the book, and publicly regretted *that they had caused* anyone embarrassment.
6 The law requires *that all cars should be regularly tested* for safety and efficiency.
7 His lawyer advised him *that he should drop the case*, since it was unlikely to succeed.
8 His doctor recommended *that he should try* taking sleeping pills for a while.

139 Complete the sentences, using a gerund or an infinitive construction.

1 Do you remember . . . last night?
2 Did you remember . . . last night?
3 Our teacher didn't think we needed . . .
4 I think the piano needs . . .
5 Perhaps you would prefer not . . .
6 Does he prefer . . . to . . .?
7 I trust you won't forget . . .
8 Do your parents allow you . . .?
9 A truthful person hates . . .
10 His father has a fearsome temper. I'd hate . . .
11 Having discussed the first item on the agenda at great length, the committee went on . . .
12 I can't understand why he goes on . . ., if he hates . . .
13 You should try . . . I'm sure you'd find it much easier.
14 He may not have succeeded, but at least he tried . . .

Verbs followed by a noun + present participle

Group 4 These verbs are followed by an object and a 'present' participle or an infinitive without *to*. The verbs in italics may also be followed by a clause introduced by *that*.

feel	*notice*	*perceive*	*sense*
hear	*observe*	*see*	watch

(*Note:* When followed by a 'that' clause, several of these verbs suggest an *intellectual* awareness rather than a *physical* perception.)

These verbs are commonly called 'verbs of perception'. We can compare the use of the infinitive after these verbs with the use of a 'simple' verb form, and the present participle with a 'continuous' form:

> I saw him *enter* the shop. (I saw the whole action—he opened the door, went in, and disappeared)
> I saw him *entering* the shop. (This action was in progress when I saw him)

After these verbs in the passive, we use the infinitive with *to* or the present participle:

> The man was seen *to board* a train at Euston.
> The man was last seen *boarding* a train at Euston.

1 *Catch, spot, find, discover,* and *smell* are also associated in meaning with the above group. None, however, is followed by an infinitive. All may be followed by an object and a present participle:

> The teacher caught the pupil *cheating.*
> The search party found (spotted, discovered) the climbers *clinging* to a rock face.
> He smelt the meat *cooking.*

1.1 *Spot, find,* and *discover* may be followed by an object + past participle:

> The police found the money *hidden* in a disused garage.

They may also be followed by a 'that' clause, or by an object + *to be* or *to have.* In this case, the verbs suggest the discovery of a *fact* rather than an *act*:

> Scientists found *that* the theory was correct.
> Scientists found the theory *to be* correct.

1.2 *Smell* may also be followed by a 'that' clause:

> You could smell *that* someone had been smoking a cigar.

2 *Leave* and *keep* (someone in a certain situation or condition) share some of the characteristics of *find* and *discover.* They can be followed by an object + a present or past participle:

He left me *sitting* in the restaurant alone.
He kept me *waiting*.
He left his bicycle *propped* against a wall.
He kept the dog *chained up*.

3 'Causative' *have* shares the grammatical characteristics of many of the above verbs, though it is not related to them in meaning. It is followed by a noun and (a) the infinitive without *to*:

I'll have the electrician *check* everything while he's here.

(b) the present participle:

The doctor will soon have you *walking* again.

(c) the past participle:

We have our central heating boiler *serviced* every six months.

140 Complete the sentences, using suitable constructions from those illustrated above.

1 Did anyone see you . . .?
2 I hope your friend didn't hear you . . .
3 A huge crowd watched the firemen . . .
4 We could feel the sun . . .
5 'Don't worry!' said the doctor. 'I'll soon have you . . .'
6 You must have been very late last night. I didn't even hear you . . .
7 The pickpocket was observed . . .
8 High on the mountain, he could perceive three small figures . . .
9 I searched the desk, and discovered the letter . . .
10 The woman caught her husband . . .
11 Leave the car with me. I'll have it . . .
12 I was asked if I had noticed anyone . . .
13 When his leg was examined, it was found . . .
14 Where's my umbrella? I thought I left it . . .
15 Although the station was crowded, I soon spotted my friend . . .
16 The assistant kept the customer . . .
17 The iron's far too hot! Can't you smell the material . . .?
18 I hope they won't keep us . . .
19 They found the survivors . . .
20 We all suddenly sensed danger . . .

Make and let

These two verbs are followed by an object + infinitive without *to:*

> He made me *do* all the work again.
> My neighbour let me *borrow* his car.

141 Complete the sentences, using an infinitive construction (without *to*).

1 I've no wish to make him . . . if he doesn't want to.
2 It's no good. The car's broken down and I can't make it . . .
3 My brother refuses to let problems . . .
4 If you're not satisfied with the job, you should make the workman . . .
5 Do you think it's wise to let your children . . .?
6 Since the car was being driven erratically, the police made the driver . . .
7 We shouldn't let one small setback . . .
8 The Minister was accused of letting the situation . . .
9 Many unions seem unable to do anything to make their members . . .
10 The way the situation later developed made the Government . . .

Only *make* is used in the passive, and in this case is followed by an infinitive *with* 'to':

> I was made *to do* all the work again.

142 Answer the questions, using a passive construction with *make.*

When you were a child, what were you made to do—

1 just before going to bed?
2 as soon as you got up in the morning?
3 before you ate your meals?
4 after you had eaten your meals?
5 on Sunday mornings?
6 if you were rude to someone?
7 when you were given presents?
8 if your room was untidy?
9 whenever you felt ill?
10 if your work at school was bad?

Verbs followed by a 'that' clause

Group 5 These verbs are followed by a clause introduced by *that*. They may also be followed by an object (very often *it*) + *to be* or *to have*.

allow (admit)	feel (think)	reckon
assume	guess	recognize
believe	hear (be informed)	report
calculate	hold (maintain the	reveal
confess	opinion)	see (realize)
confirm	indicate	sense (be aware of)
consider (be of the	know	show
opinion)	learn (be informed,	state
declare	discover)	suppose
demonstrate	maintain	suspect
disclose	presume (assume)	think
estimate	prove (show	
	conclusively)	

143 Rewrite the sentences, substituting a 'that' clause for the words in italics. (NB. Students should regard their answers as the more usual construction, and the infinitive construction as a stylistic variant.)

1 The police believed *their informant to be* reliable.
2 Our correspondent reports *the situation to be* now under control.
3 The sitting member stated *it to be* unlikely that he would stand for Parliament at the next election.
4 Many British people considered *it to be* cruel to send animals in rockets into outer space.
5 Everyone assumed *what he said to be* based on fact.
6 Pressed by shareholders for further details, the chairman confessed *it to be* likely that profits would show a further fall.
7 On the other hand, he maintained *his long-term optimism to be* justified.
8 The Prime Minister clearly suspects *his party to have* little chance of winning the next election.
9 The climbers reckoned *the ascent to have taken* nearly five and a half hours.
10 The witness later disclosed *his evidence to have been* perjured.
11 Researchers have now proved *earlier theories to have been* incorrect.

12 The Government calculates *the gain in reserves to have been* somewhere in the region of £30m.

13 The man was accused of receiving goods, knowing *them to have been stolen.*

14 A group of electors declared *their candidate to be* unacceptable to them.

15 Although many MPs felt *the cost of the scheme to be* excessive, they still recognized *its implementation to be* desirable.

144 Replace the words in italics by an *object + infinitive* construction, as in the examples.

a. Our correspondent understands *that it is impossible* for tourists to enter the country at present.
Our correspondent understands *it to be* impossible for tourists to enter the country at present.

b. Members of the Government itself acknowledge *that many of their predictions* were over-optimistic.
Members of the Government itself acknowledge *many of their predictions to have been* wildly over-optimistic.

1 The Court declared *that the book was* obscene.

2 Teachers have found *that the overhead projector is* invaluable as a teaching aid.

3 The majority of critics thought *that the film was* highly original.

4 Many of the audience considered *that the speaker had overstated* his case.

5 Evidence showed *that the man's alibi was* a complete fabrication.

6 The architect's clients had assumed *that the construction of such a building was* impracticable, whereas the architect himself *believed that it was* perfectly feasible.

7 At a very early age, Paderewski revealed *that he was* a master of the keyboard.

8 Everyone knew *that he was* a man of integrity.

9 Detectives investigating the robbery discovered *that £20,000 worth of precious stones were* missing.

10 Although most people once thought *that it was* impossible, several climbers have now scaled the north face of the Eiger in winter.

Participles and gerunds

Introductory notes

1 We have seen that gerunds either (*1*) function as nouns standing alone, or (*2*) operate as verbs in non-finite noun clauses:[1]

1 Thank goodness the *hammering* has stopped!
2 *Closing the factory* means *putting people out of work.*

Participles either (*1*) function as verbal adjectives, or (*2*) operate as verbs in non-finite clauses[1] (very commonly the equivalent of adjectival or adverbial clauses):

1a Two men were trapped in the *blazing* house.
1b After last night's gales, some roads are blocked by *fallen* trees.
2a The thieves took two mail-bags *containing registered letters.* (adjectival clause—compare: 'that contained registered letters')
2b *Having received their final medical check*, the astronauts boarded their spacecraft. (adverbial clause of time—compare: 'When they had received their final medical check')
2c *Given time*, he'll make a first-class tennis player. (adverbial clause of condition—compare: 'provided he is given time')

In some cases, the participial clause is the equivalent of a co-ordinate clause:

3 Parts of an aircraft fell on to a Somerset village today, *narrowly missing a group of children.* (Compare: '. . . and narrowly missed a group of children')

Although basically there are only two participles, the 'present' participle and the 'past' participle, these two may be used in combination to make three other forms, all five forms being illustrated below:

Participles
Choosing his words with care, *the speaker* intimated that the Government was mistaken in its attitude. (Present Participle)

Gerunds
Choosing the prettiest girl in the competition proved very difficult. (Subject)

[1] For an explanation of this term, see *Notes on Clauses* in the Appendix.

Participles	Gerunds
Seen in this light, *the matter* is not as serious as people generally suppose. (Past Participle)	No equivalent form
Having picked the team to meet India in the final test match, *the selectors* now have to wait till Tuesday to discover whether or not their choice was wise. (Perfect Participle)	He regretted *having picked* Jones as captain of the team. (Object)
He wasn't asked to take on the chairmanship of the society, *being considered* insufficiently popular with all members. (Passive Present Participle)	He felt very flattered at *being considered* the best man to take on the chairmanship of the society. (Object of a preposition)
Having been told that bad weather was on the way, *the climbers* decided to put off their attempt on Eiger until the following week. (Passive Perfect Participle)	He denied *having been told* to service the engine before take-off. (Object)

2. In each of the above sentences with participles, we can see that the participle is related to a noun (the subject of the main clause), and students should avoid what is called a *misrelated* participle:

> *Standing* in the middle of the crowd, *the sense of frustration and anger* could be plainly felt.

Here, the participle is related to *the sense of frustration and anger*, which, clearly, could not be standing in the middle of the crowd. What the writer intended was:

> *Standing* in the middle of the crowd, *I* could plainly feel the sense of frustration and anger.

3. An *unrelated* participle is, however, found in the following circumstances:

a. with certain verbs, when the subject of the participle is felt to be the indefinite pronoun *one*:

Judging from recent events, the Government appears to be gaining in popularity. (= If one judges; if one may judge)

He did quite well, *taking* everything into consideration. (= When/If one takes)

b. in certain stereotyped phrases:

Strictly speaking, the Isle of Man is not part of the United Kingdom.

c. When the participle has the force of a preposition:

Regarding the question of absenteeism, a sense of responsibility seems to have been lacking in some workers. (= With regard to)

4. Sometimes the participial clause contains its own subject, in which case the construction is called *absolute*:

The holidays *being* over, we must now get down to some hard work.

England is experiencing its hardest winter for years, *some areas having lain* under six feet of snow for nearly two months.

5. Non-finite clauses, like finite clauses, may be introduced by conjunctions:

a. *While flying* over the Channel, *the pilot* saw what he thought to be a meteorite.

b. *If taken* literally, *the sentence* is nonsensical.

6. Where the non-finite clauses are adverbial (as they are in the two sentences above), the two clauses in each sentence may be reversible:

a. *The pilot* saw what he thought to be a meteorite *while flying* over the Channel.

b. *The sentence* is nonsensical *if taken* literally.

It would not be possible to reverse the order of the clauses in sentence *a* if the conjunction *while* were omitted, nor is it possible to reverse the order of the clauses in the following sentence, where the non-finite clause is adjectival:

177

The class later discussed several points *arising from the lecture*.

(*Arising from the lecture, the class later discussed several points.)

145 Replace the finite clauses in italics by non-finite clauses, using participles, and making any necessary changes in word order, e.g.

When the shop assistant discovered that he had a talent for music, he gave up his job to become a professional singer.
Discovering that he had a talent for music, *the shop assistant* gave up his job to become a professional singer.

Note: In Nos. 4 and 7, the participial clause replaces an adjectival clause, in the first case being non-defining and so used with commas, and in the second being defining and so used without commas. Participial clauses will be found a useful alternative to constructions using relative pronouns in the later exercises in synthesis. See also Exercises 173, 174 in Section Two.

1 *As he had witnessed the crime*, he was expected to give evidence in court.
2 *When the editor learned* that his newspaper had been taken over by a rival publisher, he resigned from his position.
3 I declined his offer of a loan *and said* that I didn't like owing people money.
4 The demonstrator, *who protested violently*, was led away by the police.
5 When *I visit a strange city*, I like to have a guide-book with me.
6 Although *the motion received general support from the House*, it was not carried until it had been considerably amended.
7 Motorists *who intend to take their cars with them to the Continent* are advised to make early reservations.
8 *It* strikes me *that he is an intelligent man*. ('He . . .')
9 *Now that I have heard your side of the question*, I am more inclined to agree with you.
10 *As he had been warned* that bad weather lay ahead, the ship's captain changed course.
11 *If one may judge by* what the critics say, this new play is worth seeing. (Unrelated participle)
12 *Now that spring has come*, we may perhaps look forward to better weather. (Absolute construction)

146 Join the pairs or groups of sentences, using participles, and making any necessary changes in word order, e.g.

> The employers issued an ultimatum. They threatened all workers with dismissal if they didn't return to work by the following Monday.
>
> The employers issued an ultimatum, *threatening* all workers with dismissal if they didn't return to work by the following Monday.

Note: In many of the sentences, the participial clause is the equivalent of an adverbial clause of reason, and words or phrases like *therefore* or *as a result* should be omitted. Participial clauses can, of course, have a temporal function, and in some cases both implications (causal and temporal) are intended:

> Having finished the painting, he gave a sigh of relief.
> = When he had finished the painting,
> *and* As he had finished the painting, } he gave a sigh of relief.

1 I was away at the time of the disastrous floods. I could, therefore, do nothing to help with salvage work.
2 I found I had wasted my time going to the sale. The best bargains had already been snapped up earlier in the day.
3 The rescue party decided that it would be hopeless to carry out a search while the fog persisted. They put off their rescue bid until the next day.
4 He was brought up in the belief that pleasures were sinful. As a result, he now leads an ascetic life.
5 The children had a week's holiday. The school had been closed because of an influenza epidemic.
6 One can allow for the fact that the orchestra was under-rehearsed. Even so, last night's concert was extremely disappointing.
7 He was very angry when his car broke down. He had had it serviced only a week before.
8 No one was surprised at the change in Bank Rate. It had already been confidently expected by investors.
9 The man lost interest in his work. He had been passed over in favour of an outsider when a senior position became vacant.
10 We decided not to visit Oxford. It was then the time of the summer vacation. There were few students in residence.
11 He had to put off buying a house. The bank was unable to lend him any money at that time.

179

12 The police found the small boy. He was wandering about the docks. He was, apparently, looking for somewhere to spend the night.

The sentences in the next two exercises have been designed for practice in those uses of the participle that most frequently give rise to error. The participle is not, of course, necessarily related to the *subject* of another clause. It may be related to the noun (subject or object) immediately preceding it, as in Nos. 3, 7, 9, 10, and 12 in Exercise 147, e.g.

a. The *men coming* towards us were all carrying guns.
(Related to the subject)
b. One of the disadvantages of lectures is that one doesn't generally get an opportunity of discussing with the lecturer any of the *points arising* from them. (Related to the object)

The participial clauses in these particular examples are the equivalent of adjectival clauses, each being related to an antecedent. The participle may also be used as an attributive adjective (i.e. an adjective placed immediately *before* the noun it qualifies):

John grew more and more nervous as he thought of the *approaching* interview.

As this use of the participle is not a source of error, and does in fact come naturally to students, no special practice material on it has been included.

147 Complete the sentences with participial clauses introduced by the verbs in brackets, using the form suggested and retaining the punctuation given.

a. Jones put up a good fight in the first few rounds of the contest, . . . (punch, present participle)
Jones put up a good fight in the first few rounds of the contest, punching his opponent hard and accurately.
b. . . ., the chairman assured shareholders that profits would show a distinct improvement the following year. (repeat, present participle)
Repeating what he had said earlier, the chairman assured shareholders that profits would show a distinct improvement the following year.

1 The accused was led out of the court, still firmly . . . (maintain, present participle)
2 . . ., I think my advice could be of help. (have, perfect participle)
3 They found the treasure . . . (hide, past participle)
4 While . . ., the workmen unearthed the remains of a Roman villa. (dig, present participle)
5 Motorists should take extra care when . . . (drive, present participle)
6 . . ., they decided not to spend their holiday in England. (tell, passive perfect participle)
7 I last saw him . . . (go, present participle)
8 One can now hardly see this beautiful church, high buildings . . . (erect, passive perfect participle; absolute construction)
9 The newspaper has now published an apology . . . (state, present participle)
10 The gamekeeper caught a man . . . (shoot, present participle)
11 . . ., you cannot go back on your word. (promise, perfect participle)
12 The platform was crowded with people . . . (wave, present participle)

148 Complete the sentences, retaining the punctuation given, and paying special attention to relating the correct nouns to the participles.

> *a.* Having overheard part of their conversation, . . .
> Having overheard part of their conversation, I thought it best to remain hidden until after they had left.
> *b.* . . ., being reluctant to commit himself to a long contract.
> He turned down the job he was offered, being reluctant to commit himself to a long contract.

1 Having gone into the question of how much the holiday would cost, . . .
2 Having been forbidden to read the book, . . .
3 If not treated with the respect he feels due to him, . . .
4 . . ., having been struck by the beauty of its buildings on a previous visit.
5 Bearing in mind the fact that he has never done anything wrong before, . . .
6 When seen in this light, . . .

7 . . ., having decided that he had little chance of winning the competition.

8 . . ., creating fear and terror among the population.

9 I haven't yet . . . raised in your last letter. (Past participle related to the object)

10 Convinced that his luck must eventually turn if he persisted long enough, . . .

11 . . ., fully intending to pay it back the following Friday, when I received my week's wages.

12 Generally speaking, . . . (Unrelated participle)

149 Complete the sentences, using clause (a) as a participial clause, and clause (b) as a gerundial clause (i.e. a non-finite noun clause), subject of the sentence.

    a. Deciding not to go any further that day, . . .
    b. Deciding on where to spend one's holidays . . .
    a. Deciding not to go any further that day, we put up at the nearest hotel. (*Deciding* is related to the subject *we*)
    b. Deciding on where to spend one's holidays can be a difficult matter. (*Deciding* is the subject of *can be*)

Note that the participial clause is immediately followed by the subject of the sentence, and is separated from it by a comma. The gerundial clause is itself the subject of the sentence, and is immediately followed by a verb.

1a Looking hard at the prisoner, . . .
  b Looking at pictures in art-galleries . . .
2a Reading between the lines, . . .
  b Reading aloud . . .
3a Trying desperately to reach the chalet before nightfall, . . .
  b Trying to teach backward children . . .
4a Swimming strongly and confidently, . . .
  b Swimming in the sea . . .
5a While digging the foundations of the house, . . .
  b Digging in the garden in hot weather . . .
6a Driving round the difficult Le Mans circuit with superb skill, . . .
  b Driving at night . . .
7a While doing his homework, . . .
  b His always doing things in a hurry . . .

8*a* Finding himself short of petrol, . . .

  b Finding the best way of doing things . . .

9*a* While tuning up his violin, . . .

  b Tuning pianos . . .

10*a* Calling on a friend late one night, . . .

  b Your calling on us just at this time . . .

General review: gerunds, infinitives, and participles

150 Rewrite the sentences, using the verbs in brackets in the gerund, participle, or infinitive form. Note where alternatives are possible.

1 After (get) (know) him better, I regretted (judge) him unfairly.
2 The man the police found (act) suspiciously in the shop doorway was charged with (loiter) with intent.
3 I can't bear the thought of (you, go) home without someone (accompany) you.
4 'A job worth (do) is worth (do) well.'
5 I should prefer (go) to the cinema rather than (sit) here (listen) to the radio.
6 Don't stand there (do) nothing.
7 He tried (speak) German but found that he couldn't. His attempts at (speak) Spanish were equally unsuccessful.
8 I tried (cook) eggs and bacon together, and found that this was a much quicker way of (prepare) a meal.
9 Surely you recollect (he, say) that he would agree to (I, borrow) his car if I didn't mind (pay) for the petrol?
10 You know I hate (disappoint) you, but much as I would like (go) out this evening, I have to finish (decorate) this room.
11 I would advise (you, wait) before (decide) (accept) his offer.
12 At present the new child is very shy of (join) in with the others, but very soon I expect (have) (he, show) more confidence.

151 Instructions as above

1 If I catch (you, cheat) again, I shall make you (stay) in after school (do) some extra work.
2 It's no use (blame) him really. You know he had no choice but (do) as he was told.
3 She can't bear (be left) alone in the dark, (be) accustomed as a child to (have) a light on all night.

183

4 He does nothing but (complain) when he is asked (do) anything that means (put) himself out.

5 Keats never became hardened to (have) his poetry unfavourably reviewed by critics, and some people would go as far as (say) that this caused him (die) prematurely.

6 Surely you remember (lend) him the money? I hope, at least, that *he* won't forget (pay) you back, for he has a habit of (forget) things he doesn't want (remember).

7 The fire needs (make up). Would you mind (attend) to it?

8 I can well understand (you, be) unwilling (rely) on him after (he, let) you down on a previous occasion.

9 Some children wish people wouldn't keep on (point out) how, years ago, children were made (show) far more respect to their elders.

10 Like many other people, I dislike (have) someone (look) over my shoulder (read) my newspaper. I find it difficult (prevent) myself from (say) something sarcastic.

11 Mothers may sometimes be horrified at the idea of a young (girl, live) alone or (go) on a holiday without a friend (accompany) her, but don't always realize that these are just two examples of (women, become) emancipated.

12 Excuse (I, ask), but what effect does your (husband, be) a teacher have on your children? Do you find them more inclined to (study) or less? Do you have any difficulty in (persuade) them (do) their homework, or do they seem (want) (emulate) their father?

The position of adverbs

An adverb, or an adverbial phrase or clause, may in some cases be taken out of its normal position and placed at the beginning of a sentence or clause for emphasis. If this construction is used with negative adverbs or adverbs of degree, the subject and verb of the sentence or clause to which the adverb relates must be inverted (using *do* if necessary):

a. He had *hardly* finished eating his breakfast when he asked what they would be having for lunch. (Normal)
Hardly had he finished eating his breakfast when he asked what they would be having for lunch. (Emphatic)

b. Most people would agree that a doctor should hide the truth from his patient *only in exceptional circumstances*. (Normal)
Most people would agree that *only in exceptional circumstances should a doctor* hide the truth from a patient. (Emphatic)

Naturally, there can be no inversion when an adverb of this type is one of a group of words qualifying the subject:

Not only the professionals but also the amateurs will benefit from the new training facilities.

This may be compared with:

The professionals *not only demanded* new training facilities; they also proposed a revision of membership fees.

In this sentence, *not only* modifies the verb, and the sentence may be reconstructed:

Not only *did* the professionals *demand* new training facilities; they also proposed a revision of membership fees.

152 Rewrite the sentences, placing the adverbs or adverbial phrases in italics at the beginning of their sentence or clause, and making the necessary inversions.

1 He had *no sooner* put down the receiver with a great sigh of relief than the telephone rang again.
2 The thieves *little* realized that the police had already thrown a cordon round the bank, and that all means of escape had been cut off.
3 The doctor told his patient that he should *on no account* return to work until he had made a complete recovery.
4 I would*n't* doubt his integrity *for one moment*. ('Not for . . .')
5 The whole truth did*n't* become known *until many years later*. ('Not until . . .')
6 The smoke was *so dense* that even breathing-apparatus proved ineffective against it.
7 His fear of failing the examination was *such* that he resorted to cheating.
8 We have *rarely* seen such public interest as is being shown in the appeal for funds to save the cathedral.

9 The Member for Oxbridge tried *in vain* to rally popular support for his proposal.

10 Their hopes had been raised *to such a pitch* that they were almost bound to be disappointed.

11 You will find a greater concentration of financial skills *nowhere else in the City* than in a merchant bank.

12 Such a situation should *never again* be allowed to arise.

13 The pilot agreed to land the plane *only when the hijackers threatened to shoot some of the passengers.*

14 Contributions to computer technology are *no longer* confined to any one country. This is *nowhere* more true than in Europe.

15 A lasting peace will be established in the area *only if both sides accept the agreement.*

Some negative adverbs, or adverbial phrases and clauses, may be introduced by *It is* or *It was* and still retain their emphatic force when placed at the beginning of their sentence. In this case, however, no inversion of subject and verb is necessary. We thus find that there are two possible ways of reconstructing a sentence like the following, the alternative *b* being the emphatic form commonly found in the spoken language:

> I did*n't* realize how ill he was *until I visited him.* (Normal)
> a. *Not until I visited him did I* realize how ill he was. (Emphatic)
> b. *It was* not until I visited him *that I realized* how ill he was. (Emphatic)

153 Rewrite the sentences, placing the adverbs or adverbial phrases in italics at the beginning of their sentence or clause, and making inversions in those sentences that require it.

1 The back of this radio should *under no circumstances* be removed unless the set has first been disconnected at the mains.

2 We have seen such security measures as are being taken for the President's visit *on only one previous occasion.*

3 He has, *no doubt*, good reason for thinking as he does.[1]

4 Such a major operation has proved completely successful *in very few cases.*[2]

---

[1] *No doubt* is a sentence adverb, i.e. it modifies the sentence as a whole, and does not relate to a particular verb.

[2] *Few* carries a negative implication; *a few* is positive.

5 It has been found that, *in a few cases*, people can have this disease and not be aware of it.

6 He mentioned it to me *only yesterday*. ('It was . . .')

7 He wouldn't answer the questions of the reporters, *and* he would*n't* pose for a photograph. ('. . . the reporters, nor . . .')

8 We have*n't* had the opportunity of hearing this fine pianist in action *for some time now*. ('Not . . .')

9 Wild duck have, *on one or two occasions*, been seen flying over central London.

10 The police admitted that they had *seldom* had to deal with such a baffling case.

11 The Minister claimed that help from the Government had been forthcoming *on each occasion* to deal with emergencies, and that such emergencies had continued for longer than one day *in not one single case*.

12 The Bill was given a sympathetic hearing *in neither the Commons nor the Lords*.

13 The two countries first began talks about signing a treaty *as long as four years ago*. ('It was . . .')

14 The talks did*n't* appear to have much chance of success *until quite recently, however*.

15 There is now substantial agreement *on all but a few issues*.

154 Complete the sentence-openings, using inversions where necessary.

1 To such an extent . . .

2 The teacher explained the point a second time, but not even then . . .

3 So complicated . . . that . . .

4 Only three men . . .

5 The customer complained that no sooner . . . than . . .

6 Neither the driver nor his passengers . . .

7 Neither on this occasion nor on the previous one . . .

8 Only after a great deal of discussion . . .

9 It was only after a great deal of discussion . . .

10 In answer to his critics, the Prime Minister said that at no time . . .

155 In each of the sentences, there are at least two possible positions for the adverbs given. Write each sentence twice, placing the adverbs so as to suggest two distinctly different meanings. Show the difference between your two versions by explaining each one or by paraphrase, e.g.

Differential rates of pay cause friction among workers. (generally)

a. Differential rates of pay generally cause friction among workers.
= Differential rates of pay do, in most cases where applied, cause friction among workers.

b. Differential rates of pay cause friction among workers generally.
= Differential rates of pay cause friction among workers as a whole.

1 He expressed his thanks. (naturally)
2 The teacher thought the student was not intelligent. (obviously)
3 There were a few passengers on the bus on weekdays. (only)
4 The speaker had not argued his case at all. (clearly)
5 Some club members were horrified at the suggestion of small changes. (even)
6 I remember his being able to play football. (well)
7 The rescue party managed to take ten of the crew off the ship before it sank. (just)
8 I don't want to put myself under an obligation to him by asking a favour. (particularly)
9 I think he will find he has been rash in investing his money in those shares. (rather)
10 Frank has decided to spend a few days in Austria on his way to Switzerland. (also)

156 Instructions as above

1 When I mentioned the money involved, he undertook to do the work. (promptly)
2 He appreciated that my idea was a good one, but he still wasn't willing to lend me his support. (quite)
3 Do you think you'll have enough money at the end of the month to take a short holiday? (still)
4 I should ask him what he meant by his statement. (personally)
5 Have you made up your mind about what you want to do when you leave school? (really)

6 He had the grace to admit that he was partly in the wrong. (at least)

7 He will explain quite clearly what he intends to do. (in future)

8 The student overheard the teacher saying that his last piece of homework was better. (distinctly)

9 A spokesman for the bus company pointed out that buses couldn't run on Sundays because of the unwillingness of the staff to work overtime. (normally)

10 As the solicitor said, the money had been divided among the brothers and sisters of the dead man, who had no children. (rightly)

Reported speech[1]

Exercises in 'translating' passages of direct speech into reported speech should not be treated as mere practice in mental gymnastics. Exercises of this type are really essays in comprehension and flexibility of expression. The following observations are offered as having particular relevance to the exercises that follow:

1. There are many verbs besides *say* and *tell* that can be used in reported speech and that are often more expressive and precise than these two rather neutral verbs. Practice with various other verbs in both direct and reported speech will be found in Exercises 157, 158, 159, and 162.

2. *a* Some verbs used in direct speech cannot be used in reported speech, and have to be expressed with *said* and an appropriate adverb manner indicating the *way* in which something was said. Practice with these verbs in both direct and reported speech will be found in Exercises 159 and 160.

   b Sometimes the tone of the original can be preserved in the reported version only by the use of *said*, again with an appropriate adverb of manner. Practice in using adverbs with *said* in direct speech will be found in Exercise 161, and in reported speech in Exercise 162.

3. Tenses are not always changed mechanically when speech is reported. It is especially important to remember this when dealing

---

[1] See also the following exercises: *11* (can, could, may, might), *19* (shall), *26* (must, mustn't, have to), *28* (needn't, not need to, not have to), *66* (Present Perfect), *71* (Past perfect), *89, 90* (conditionals), *134* (VP. S × V × O × infinitive)

with conditionals (see page 104). Practice with conditionals will be found in Exercise 163.

4. In longer passages particularly, it is most important to preserve the *spirit* of the original, and this consideration should be put before a strict adherence to the form. Students must, therefore, not only understand the content but also appreciate the style and tone of the original if their own version is not to sound flat or unnatural by comparison.

157 Replace the word *said* in the sentences by one of the words at the head of the exercise. Use each word once only.

suggested	agreed	muttered	exclaimed
insisted	whispered	boasted	admitted
shouted	claimed	objected	protested

1 'I can speak six languages fluently,' he said.
2 'Let's go to the cinema this evening,' he said.
3 'Stop that noise in the classroom,' said the teacher.
4 'That car you are driving is my property,' the man said.
5 'Yes, I broke the windows with my catapult,' the boy said.
6 'You can't take me to prison. I know my rights,' the man said.
7 'I shall always love you,' said his fiancée.
8 'We don't have enough money to carry out the plan,' said the treasurer.
9 'This teacher doesn't know what he's talking about,' said the student.
10 'Well, it is a surprise to meet you here today!' she said.
11 'Well, yes; if the weather is bad, we can't go,' he said.
12 'If you can't come today, you simply must come tomorrow,' she said.

158 When you have checked your answers to the last exercise, rewrite the sentences in reported speech.

159 Write a statement consistent with the verbs given.

1 '. . .,' he complained.   2 '. . .,' he sneered.
3 '. . .,' he stammered.   4 '. . .,' he snapped.
5 '. . .,' he announced.   6 '. . .,' he explained.
7 '. . .,' he retorted.   8 '. . .,' he declared.
9 '. . .,' he promised.   10 '. . .,' he groaned.
11 '. . .,' he conceded.   12 '. . .,' he gasped.

160 When you have checked your answers to the last exercise, re-write your sentences in reported speech. If necessary, use *said* with an appropriate adverb of manner in place of the original verb.

161 Write a statement consistent with the adverbs given.

1 '. . .,' he said angrily.
2 '. . .,' he said pompously.
3 '. . .,' he said passionately.
4 '. . .,' he answered sharply.
5 '. . .,' he said brutally.
6 '. . .,' he said accusingly.
7 '. . .,' he said callously.
8 '. . .,' he said defiantly.
9 '. . .,' he commented derisively.
10 '. . .,' he whispered shyly.
11 '. . .,' he observed sarcastically.
12 '. . .,' he said sympathetically.
13 '. . .,' he said patiently.
14 '. . .,' he said agreeably.
15 '. . .,' he said complacently.
16 '. . .,' he said fiercely.

162 Write the sentences in reported speech, using the most suitable reporting verb for each sentence, or using *said* with an adverb of manner.

1 'Do as you wish, but don't come and ask me for help if you get into difficulties.'
2 '*I'm* not worried about losing *my* job. I'm too valuable to my employers.'
3 'For Heaven's sake stop asking me stupid questions!'
4 'Surely you don't think your friend is serious?'
5 'Do as you're told, and stop arguing!'
6 'What a fool I was not to accept the job! Still, it can't be helped now.'
7 'Here's to the bride and bridegroom.'
8 '*Please* don't say anything to him, for *my* sake.'
9 'Who asked *you* to say anything? What do *you* know about the business anyway? You've only been working here two months.'

10 'I've had just about enough of your insolence. One more word out of you and you'll go to the headmaster.'

11 'Do you mean to say that you've lost the money on horse-racing?'

12 'If you're so clever, why don't you try doing it yourself?'

13 'Of course, I could have won the race easily if I had really tried.'

14 'Go away! Can't you see I'm busy?'

15 'Give me the keys to the safe or you'll regret it.'

163 Rewrite the sentences in reported speech.

1 'Shall I post this letter for you?'

2 'Will you post this letter for me?'

3 'Shall I be able to come to the party?'

4 'If I am free I shall go there next Tuesday.'

5 'You must never do that again.'

6 'If I were you, I would say nothing about it.'

7 'I'm just going out, so I can't stop to speak to you now.'

8 'I was just going out, but since you've come such a long way to see me, I suppose I'd better put off my shopping till tomorrow.'

9 'If I were free next week, I would visit you.'

10 'Are you free tomorrow?'

11 'This machine underwent exhaustive trials before it was placed on the market.'

12 'Not until later did I understand the full significance of his words.'

13 'As I was leaving the house it started to rain.'

14 'If anyone is at fault, it is you yourself.'

164 Rewrite the sentences in direct speech. Note that in most of the examples there is an implied dialogue, and that the reported version is, in some cases, very much a paraphrase of the original. Students should reconstruct the sentences in their most likely original form, e.g.

Tony accepted without reservation my suggestion that we should try to get local support for the new theatre company.

'I would suggest, Tony, that we try to get local support for the new theatre company.'

'Yes, I thoroughly agree with you.'

1 The playwright agreed to do as the producer asked—to modify one or two passages of his play before its first night the following Monday.

2 My friend told me he had heard the previous week that the local Music Society was thinking of putting on an opera if enough support could be found.

3 When questioned by the master about the disappearance of a bicycle from the school cycle sheds two days before, the boy flatly denied having had anything to do with it.

4 Peter's request to his employer to have the next day off met with a blunt refusal.

5 He asked me to lend him five pounds, which I agreed to do, somewhat reluctantly, on condition that he paid me back the following week.

6 Michael rang up Jean at the last moment, apologizing profusely for being unable to go to dinner with her that evening. Despite his apology, Jean was very put out, and said that he might have let her know earlier; she wouldn't have needed to make such elaborate preparations.

7 I was taken completely by surprise, and in fact could hardly believe Margaret was serious when she told me she was going to leave England early the following year to take up a job abroad.

8 The Chancellor said that if the nation were to work harder and increase output, wage increases would be fully justified. He emphasized, however, that until this came about, it would be economic suicide to allow inflation to develop once again.

9 When the lady protested at being told to open her suitcase for inspection, the Customs Official firmly but politely pointed out that she must do as she was asked.

10 The customer called the waiter and complained that the soup was cold, adding that it ought to have been served in a hot dish, and that the waiter should have known better than to have served it like that.

11 Alan's objection to Graham's suggestion that they should spend the Easter holiday in Austria was that they wouldn't be able to see much of the country in such a short time, and that, in any case, such a short holiday hardly justified the expense of travelling so far.

12 After the accident, the bus driver accused the motorist of not looking where he was going, to which the latter retorted that if the

other hadn't been driving so fast, he himself would have had a chance of stopping in time.

165 Rewrite the passage in reported speech

'Have you been here long?' inquired the newcomer of another person in the hotel lounge.

'No, just over a week; that's all.'

'You don't know the place very well, then?'

'I'm a stranger in these parts. But of course even a stranger learns a few things in a week.'

'Would you mind telling me if anybody's been here called Penlark?'

'Penlark?' said the middle-aged man. 'It's odd you should mention that name. I remember the man well: a big tall fellow, with a dark moustache. He went off this morning.'

'Do you know where he went?' asked the newcomer.

'Well, he said he was going to London.'

(From the Cambridge Lower Certificate Oral Examination, December 1956.)

166 Instructions as above

'Would you like to bathe, or to go out in one of the boats?' Nora asked.

'You'll think I'm a coward,' answered Jack, 'but I can see how cold the water is without going into it. I'd rather go out in a punt or in the rowing-boats.'

'All right,' said Nora. 'I think we'll go in the punt. It's safer because you can't tip it over.'

'No,' replied Jack, 'but you can stick the pole too hard in the mud. Then the punt slides away from you, and all you can do is to hang miserably on to the punt pole. It may keep steady for a moment, but when it begins to tilt you go very slowly into the water and have to swim ashore, with all your friends laughing at you.'

'I shouldn't laugh,' said Nora. 'I should run to the boat-house and fetch the little rowing-boat. Then I should row very fast to rescue you.'

'In that case,' said Jack, smiling, 'let's take the punt.'

(From the Cambridge Proficiency Certificate Oral Examination, December 1960.)

After breakfast, Charles followed his uncle into the study.

'Now young man,' his uncle began, 'I've always taken a keen interest in you and I want to help in any way I can. What sort of profession are you thinking of taking up?'

Charles had wondered about this several times, but had reached no decision.

'I think I'd rather not make up my mind just yet, Uncle,' he replied.

'You'll have to. You can't keep hanging about the university all your life.'

This was just what Charles would have liked best, but he thought it would be unwise to say so.

'Now come along,' said his uncle. 'You must know what you're aiming for. Don't beat about the bush. What are you going to be?'

'A musician,' ventured Charles hopefully.

'Musician,' bellowed his uncle, becoming purple in the face. 'What sort of life do you think that will be? Running from one concert to another, always short of money; there's no future in it. Now, what would you say if I were to offer you a nice steady job in a bank?'

(From the Cambridge Lower Certificate Oral Examination, June 1958.)

Note: An alternative approach to the above exercise is to report the interview (i) as if you were Charles, and (ii) as if you were Charles's uncle.

168 Rewrite the passage in direct speech.

The man sitting opposite David asked him what time the train arrived at Barning Junction. David answered cheerfully that it arrived at three-fifteen if they were lucky, though the time-table said it was due in at three o'clock. The man asked David if he was sure of this: it seemed to him a very long time for such a short distance. Agreeing, David explained that the train stopped at every station. He knew this, as he had to make that journey once a week. The train suddenly stopped with a jerk. The man expressed concern at this, and wondered what was happening. He felt that at that rate they wouldn't get to Barning before midnight.

David told him not to worry, explaining with matter-of-fact calm that either a cow had wandered on to the line, or the guard had seen someone running down the hill to catch the train.

(Adapted from the Cambridge Proficiency Certificate Oral Examination, December 1958.)

169 Instructions as above

Joan and Peter were trying to decide what to send Aunt Harriet for a birthday present. Joan suggested that as their aunt was very fond of riding she would perhaps like a book about horses. Peter reminded her that they had sent their aunt a book the previous year, and thought that in any case she must be nearly too old for riding. He suggested they might send her a large box of chocolates. Joan pointed out that this wouldn't look very original as their aunt had sent them chocolates for a Christmas present. Just then, Peter's brother Andrew came into the room, and they both appealed to him for ideas. Andrew could only say, rather unhelpfully, that the trouble was that their aunt hadn't got enough interests; she spent most of her time sitting in that enormous house waiting for something to happen, and complaining when it did.

(Adapted from the Cambridge Lower Certificate Oral Examination, June 1959.)

170 Instructions as above

One evening, my friend Peter, who is a man of wild enthusiasms, came to see me, bursting with excitement. Without so much as a greeting, he announced decisively that what we needed to wake the town up was a music festival. I expressed amazement at the idea, and asked whether anyone would come to it. Peter emphatically affirmed that they would, saying that all we needed was a good orchestra and a few soloists, and people would come from miles around. I remained doubtful, asking how we were going to pay an orchestra, and what happened if there was bad weather, and nobody came. Peter brushed this objection aside, and went on to say that he had thought of a wonderful programme. All we needed, he said, was a few people to run the thing.

(Adapted from the Cambridge Lower Certificate Oral Examination, December 1959.)

171 Instructions as above

Mr Harding told the Archdeacon that he had informed Sir Abraham he would resign and that consequently he must do so. The Archdeacon couldn't agree that this was at all necessary, and pointed out that nothing Mr Harding said in such a way to his own counsel could be in any way binding on him. He had simply been there to ask his lawyer's advice. The Archdeacon felt sure that Sir Abraham had not advised any such step. Mr Harding agreed that he hadn't. The reverend cross-examiner went on to say that he was sure Sir Abraham had advised him against it, which, again, Mr Harding could not deny. Pressing home his advantage, the Archdeacon expressed his assurance that Sir Abraham must have advised Mr Harding to consult his friends. Mr Harding having been obliged to assent to this proposition also, the Archdeacon concluded by saying decisively that Mr Harding's threat of resignation therefore amounted to nothing and that they were just where they had been before.

(From *The Warden* by A. Trollope.)

172 Instructions as above

Joan worked in a shop selling gramophone records. One day a middle-aged woman came in, sat on a stool in front of the counter and beamed at Joan. Addressing Joan familiarly, she said she wanted a record—one she had heard on the radio that morning. Joan asked what the record was called. The woman shook her head, and said she didn't remember, though she would know it if she heard it. She suggested that Joan should play her some, and settled herself more comfortably on her stool. Joan pointed out that they had hundreds of records in stock, and that it would take a very long time to play her even a little of each. She asked the lady if she could hum it to her. The woman giggled, and replied that she couldn't sing 'God save the Queen' in tune. They would get into a worse muddle if she started humming. She looked very depressed, but suddenly her face brightened. She had just remembered something, she said; it came from a play in which there was a woman who spoke very badly, but who after a time learned to talk beautifully. Joan asked if it would be from *My Fair Lady*. The woman exclaimed that that was it. She wished

Joan had thought of it earlier instead of wasting time asking silly questions. She supposed Joan was new to the job.

(Adapted from the Cambridge Proficiency Certificate Oral Examination, December 1960.)

SECTION TWO

SENTENCE STRUCTURE AND SYNTHESIS[1]

Adjectival clauses[2]

173 Replace the finite clauses in italics (defining relative clauses) by non-finite clauses, using the present or past participle. Do not add any punctuation, since the *function* of the clauses will remain *defining* (see note on page 296 of the Appendix).

    a. The thieves took two mail bags *that contained registered letters.*
        The thieves took two mail bags *containing registered letters.*
    b. I couldn't understand the instructions *that were given in the manual.*
        I couldn't understand the instructions *given in the manual.*

1 Motorists *who intend to take their cars with them to the Continent* are advised to make early reservations.
2 I haven't yet had an opportunity to think over the proposals *that were made at the last meeting.*
3 Three armed men crossed the river *that marks the frontier.*
4 Any control of incomes *that is imposed by a government* and *that is not negotiated by unions and employers* is bound to create discontent.
5 Rising prices are the result of high living standards and high purchasing power *which have been created by full employment with high wages.*
6 Investors receive annually all the interest *that has been credited to their account during the year.*
7 Companies *that already use computers* have found that the number of staff *that is needed for stock-control* can be substantially reduced.
8 All aliens *who are already living in this country* have been asked to register with the police.

[1] For explanatory notes, see the Appendix.
[2] Students should have already completed Exercises 103–122 (on relative clauses) before starting these exercises.

9 The London Centre is an organization *which is designed to protect the young* by providing pleasant, low-cost accommodation.

10 We can deliver within three days any articles *that are ordered from stock*.

11 The school has now moved to new premises *which overlook the Thames*.

12 Reports *that are now reaching London* suggest that the number of casualties *that has been caused by the earthquake* may exceed two hundred.

174 Join the pairs of sentences in each of two ways: *a* change the second sentence into a non-defining clause with a *finite verb*, using *which* or *who*; and *b* change the second sentence into a non-defining clause with a *non-finite verb*, using the present or past participle.

1 The British Ambassador to Paris said that the destinies of France and Britain were indissolubly linked. He made his first public speech as ambassador yesterday.

a. The British Ambassador to Paris, *who made his first public speech as ambassador yesterday*, said that the destinies of France and Britain were indissolubly linked.

b. The British Ambassador to Paris, *making his first public speech as ambassador yesterday*, said that the destinies . . .

2 The Independent Television Authority has to ensure that the independent television companies maintain adequate standards. It was set up in 1954.

a. The Independent Television Authority, *which was set up in 1954*, has to ensure that the independent television companies maintain adequate standards.

b. The Independent Television Authority, *set up in 1954*, has to ensure that the independent television companies . . .

(Note that both the finite and non-finite clauses are non-defining in function, and so are enclosed by commas.)

1 The Earls Court Motor Show attracts increasing numbers of visitors. It is held every year in the autumn.

2 The present house stands on the site of a much earlier building. It still bears the same number.

3 The Prime Minister returned to 10 Downing Street yesterday after his summer holiday. He looked tanned and relaxed.

4 This new hostel will be opened next month. It accommodates 200 students.

5 The new freightliner trains carry forty-two containers. The trains are made up of twenty-one container wagons.

6 The invasion was completed within a matter of days. It was carefully planned and skilfully executed.

7 Our new houses should satisfy the most discriminating purchaser. They are built to the highest standards and range in price from £9,000–£18,000.

8 Typhoon 'Ida' left a trail of destruction in its wake. It swept the country from coast to coast.

9 Britain's building societies will soon be obliged to raise their rates of interest to investors and borrowers. They are at present struggling hard to attract more money.

10 The *Queen Elizabeth II* sailed from Southampton to New York last night. She was making her maiden voyage.

175 Replace the finite clauses in italics by non-finite clauses, using the infinitive. Do not change the punctuation, e.g.

> This is a point *which we should bear in mind*.
> This is a point *to bear in mind*.

1 Measures *that will restrain home demand* have already been considered by the Chancellor.

2 There are more than fifty proposals *that will be discussed at the conference*.

3 The changeover to the metric system has given manufacturers plenty *that they must think about*.

4 The Government has been considering means *that would bring about a redistribution of wealth*.

5 There are many difficulties *that must be surmounted* before any agreement can be reached.

6 Britain has little *that she can be proud of* in the latest set of trade figures.

7 Our company builds houses *that suit many different types of* purchasers.

8 Before our cars leave the factory, there is an exhaustive series of tests *that must be passed*.

9 There is still a long way *that we must go* before we reach our sales targets.

10 Before a person can get legal aid, there are certain procedures *that must be followed.*

11 British trains have communication cords, *which may be operated only in an emergency.*

12 The chemist gave her the tablets, *which were to be taken three times daily.*

13 The Consumers' Association has set up a new body *which will check on price rises in household goods.*

14 The Government hopes that these new driving regulations, *which will come into operation from the first of next month,* will result in improved road safety.

15 Many people have written to *The Times* about the new inland postage rates *which will be introduced shortly.*

16 A significant point *that has emerged from the Government's survey* is that large numbers of people living in Council houses would like the opportunity to become house owners.

176 Complete the sentences with an adjectival clause, using the punctuation given. State whether your clauses are finite or non-finite in structure. (*Note:* Ensure that your clauses are not co-ordinating in function—see under *Relative Clauses*, page 139, and paragraph 2.4. of the Appendix.)

1 The house . . . has at last been sold.
2 We spent our holiday in the town . . .
3 The housing problem, . . ., is now almost solved.
4 He recalled the time when . . .
5 I wanted to buy a car . . .
6 Do you remember the name of the place . . .?
7 What did he do with the money . . .?
8 He is the sort of man . . .
9 This letter is from my brother, . . .
10 English scenery has a beauty . . .
11 He did his medical training at a hospital . . .
12 I am prepared to agree to anything . . .
13 Something . . . quite startled me.
14 I remembered the reason . . .
15 Perhaps you could tell me the name of the shop . . .
16 That's the first time . . .
17 These rare books, . . ., were sold for a record price.

18 Perhaps you didn't know that it was my son . . .
19 I can't really believe his story, . . .
20 We returned by the same train . . .
21 I am sure there is no one here but . . .[1]
22 Beethoven is one of the greatest composers . . .
23 His father, . . ., said he intended to retire shortly.
24 We were advised to buy the larger dictionary, . . .
25 In 1953, a British expedition succeeded in climbing Everest, . . .

Co-ordinate relative clauses

177 Complete the sentences with co-ordinate clauses, using *which, who, whom, when,* or *where.* (*Note:* relative pronouns and relative adverbs with a co-ordinating function are not descriptive, but continuative, i.e. they may be replaced by *and this, and he, and there, and then,* etc.)

1 That evening we went to the cinema, . . .
2 He had intended to buy the goods before seeing them, . . .
3 I had almost given up expecting him, . . .
4 The Queen was, after all, unable to attend the charity concert, . . .
5 The father left his business to his son, . . .
6 The campers moved on without extinguishing their fire, . . .
7 The man dived fully clothed into the river to save the boy, . . .
8 We were beginning to think that our view from the mountain-side would be obscured by cloud, . . .
9 Last year we spent our holiday in Austria, . . .
10 I gave the message to Peter, . . .
11 In some cinemas, smoking is prohibited, . . .
12 Last night we went to the opera at Covent Garden, . . .
13 The letter I received was in fact intended for John, to . . .
14 The contractors have now sent a satisfactory estimate for building the school, on the basis of . . .
15 He missed a lot of work through his absence from school, to make up for . . .

[1] Used as a relative pronoun, *but* is equivalent to *that . . . not,* e.g. There wasn't one boy in the class *but knew* (= that didn't know) exactly what the teacher was referring to.

Adverbial clauses[1]

Below is a list of the principal conjunctions used to introduce the different types of adverbial clauses, but one important fact must be remembered: some conjunctions have multiple uses, and the type of clause they introduce can be determined only by an examination of the *function* of the clause. A look at the chameleon-like properties of the conjunction *as* will give ample illustration of this point:

1 He did his work *as his employer had instructed*. (Adverbial clause of manner)
2 He can't speak English as well *as he writes it*. (Adverbial clause of comparison)
3 He decided to spend his holiday in Austria, *as he had never been there before*. (Adverbial clause of reason)
4 *As he was posting the letter*, he suddenly realized that he hadn't put a stamp on the envelope. (Adverbial clause of time)
5 You've made the same mistake *as you made before*. (Adjectival clause)
6 A welfare state does not necessarily make everyone happier, *as some people are now beginning to realize*. (Co-ordinate clause)

Conjunctions used to introduce adverbial clauses

TIME	when, whenever, while, as, since, after, before, until, as soon as, once, now (that)
PLACE	where, wherever
MANNER	as, as if
COMPARISON	as, then, the × comparative
REASON or CAUSE	because, as, since
PURPOSE	so that, in order that, for fear that, lest, (in order to, so as to: non-finite clauses)
RESULT	so that, so × adjective × that (result clauses associated with degree), such . . . that

[1] See also *Conditional Sentences*, page 88, *Participles and Gerunds*, page 175, and Exercises 23 (clauses of purpose with *should*), 43 and 65 (tenses in time clauses), and 70 (non-finite/finite clauses of time and reason).

CONDITION	if, unless, whether, provided that, supposing, on condition that, as (or so) long as
CONCESSION	although, though, even though, even if, while, whatever, wherever, whenever, no matter

Note: Many of the sentences in these exercises could be completed equally well with an adverbial phrase or, in some cases, a single adverb. Students should remember that the group of words they add must contain a verb in order to constitute a clause. Here is a sentence completed in four possible ways, (c) or (d) being of the type required in these exercises:

Apparently, he tried to telephone me . . . (Time)

a. Apparently, he tried to telephone me *yesterday*. (Adverb of time)

b. Apparently, he tried to telephone me *the evening before last*. (Adverbial *phrase* of time)

c. Apparently, he tried to telephone me *as soon as he RECEIVED my letter*. (Finite adverbial *clause* of time)

d. Apparently, he tried to telephone me *after RECEIVING my letter*. (Non-finite adverbial *clause* of time)

178 Complete the sentences with finite or non-finite adverbial clauses of the type indicated. State whether your clauses are finite or non-finite.

1 He speaks English much better . . . (Comparison)
2 They decided to climb the mountain . . . (Time)
3 We left the car . . . (Place)
4 The United Nations Organization was formed . . . (Purpose)
5 The book was so boring . . . (Result)
6 We went swimming . . . (Concession)
7 I should be delighted . . . (Condition)
8 . . ., I didn't have time to come. (Reason)
9 He arranged to come early . . . (Purpose)
10 (a) As . . ., that won't be necessary. (Reason)
   (b) As . . ., I met someone I hadn't seen for years. (Time)
   (c) He did the job as . . . (Comparison)
11 I wrote to you . . . (Time)
12 He was so angry . . . (Result)

179 Instructions as above

1 You should meet me . . . (Place)
2 . . ., they live very simply. (Concession)
3 We arranged to hire a coach . . . (Purpose)
4 We booked rooms at the hotel lest . . . (Purpose)
5 The men were told that they would be dismissed . . . (Condition)
6 Examination candidates are known by a number, and not by name, . . . (Purpose)
7 . . ., I shall expect to see you more often. (Time)
8 . . ., I have now changed my mind. (Concession)
9 . . ., the more I like him. (Comparison)
10 Provided that . . ., you will be allowed to join the Society. (Condition)
11 As long as . . ., we were safe. (Time/Condition)
12 I decided to invite some friends to my house while . . . (Time)

180 Instructions as above

1 Such was his anxiety . . . (Result)
2 Whatever . . ., it's best to take his advice. (Concession)
3 We lit a fire before . . . so that . . . when . . . (Time, Purpose, Time)
4 However . . ., he shouldn't have been so rude to his host (Concession)
5 The English have to pay taxes to the Government, whether . . . (Concession)
6 'Patrons arriving late at the opera house will not be admitted . . .' (Time)
7 The meeting became so disorderly . . . (Result)
8 I am learning English . . . when . . . (Purpose, Time)
9 Much as . . ., I couldn't lend him the money because . . . (Concession, Reason)
10 . . ., the sooner you will be able to relax. (Comparison)
11 No matter . . ., I couldn't persuade him to change his mind. (Concession)
12 So enthusiastic were the audience that not until . . . would they . . . (Time, Result)

181 Replace the sentences or co-ordinate clauses in italics by subordinate adverbial clauses of reason or concession, as appropriate, using the conjunctions *because, as, since, although, even though,* or *while,* and making any necessary omissions.

> *a. He didn't understand,* so he asked the teacher to explain.
> *As he didn't understand,* he asked the teacher to explain.
> *b. It was raining hard.* Nevertheless, the two captains decided that the pitch was playable.
> *Although it was raining hard,* the two captains decided that the pitch was playable.

1 *The colour didn't suit her,* so my wife decided not to buy the dress.
2 *He had overslept.* As a result, he was late for work.
3 *I didn't have any stamps.* Therefore I couldn't post the letter.
4 *The course cost a lot of money.* Even so, I decided to take it.
5 *We left rather late.* We arrived on time, however.
6 *She likes England very much.* She's looking forward to going home, nevertheless.
7 *I agreed to follow his advice,* but I did so with some misgivings.
8 *I had promised to visit him* so I felt obliged to go.
9 *His doctor had given him strict instructions to stay in bed.* Despite this, he went in to work.
10 *He won't listen to me,* so you'd better try talking to him yourself.

182 Complete the sentences with adverbial clauses, using in turn each of the conjunctions given. State the function of the clause(s) you have added, and say whether your clauses are finite or non-finite.

We decided to take our raincoats with us so that . . .
        because . . .
        after . . .
        in case . . .
        although
        if . . .

183 Instructions as above

As . . ., everyone taking part in the play had to be word perfect.

Although . . .,
If . . .,
Before . . .,
When . . .,
As soon as . . .,

184 Instructions as above

They intended to visit the Scottish Highlands while . . .
even if . . .
before . . .
after . . .
however . . .
unless . . .

185 Instructions as above

Whatever . . ., please don't tell him what I said.

If . . .,
Since . . .,
Much as . . .,
Although . . .,
Whether . . .,
Lest . . .,

186 Instructions as above

You had better repeat your instructions carefully so that . . .
in case . . .
if . . .
unless . . .
before . . .
while . . .

187 Instructions as above

Even though . . ., you ought to have
given him some advice when . . .
As . . .,   before . . .
When . . .,   in case . . .
Whether . . .,   so that . . .

Noun clauses[1]

188 Join the sentences, using noun clauses, and giving alternative constructions where indicated, e.g.

[1] See also *Verb Patterns with -Ing Forms, Infinitives, and 'that' Clauses*, page 145, *Reported Speech*, page 189, and Exercises 22, 24 (noun clauses with *should*), 121, and 122 (*what* in noun clauses).

He was taking a risk. He fully realized this.
He fully realized that he was taking a risk.

1 The sun sometimes shines in England. He seems surprised to discover this.

2 Old-age pensions were still miserably low. The Opposition deplored this fact.

3 He hadn't telephoned his girl friend. His girl friend later understood why.

4 Your bank manager won't lend you money without security. Don't run away with the idea that he will.

5 The law student was destined for a brilliant career at the bar. This was clear to everyone. (*a* It was . . .; *b* That . . .)

6 He didn't even apologize. This made me really angry. (*a* The fact . . .; *b* What . . .)

7 The boy should be sent to a boarding school. This was the parents' view. (*a* It . . .; *b* The parents' view . . .)

8 Children nowadays get too much pocket money. This is my opinion. (*a* It . . .; *b* My opinion . . .)

9 He says one thing in private. He does another thing in public. The two things are inconsistent with each other. (What . . .)

10 He manages to reconcile the two things. I just don't know how he does it. (*a* I . . .; *b* How . . .)

189 Rewrite the sentences, substituting a finite noun clause for the non-finite clauses in italics, e.g.

> *His now knowing the secret* creates a rather difficult situation.
> The fact *that he now knows* the secret creates a rather difficult situation.

1 The teacher insisted *on the students' arriving* punctually for their lessons.

2 *Being ignorant of the law* is not accepted as an excuse for breaking the law.

3 I am surprised *at your thinking London* a dull place to live in.

4 A conceited man often cannot understand *the reasons for people disliking him.*

5 *Your having accepted this job* means *your having to travel* much further to work.

6 I refused to believe *his having told me the truth.*

7 The child's criminal tendencies were put down to the fact *of his coming from a broken home.*

8 Did *his father's being a professor* help him in his career?
9 He insisted *on my checking again* to see that the train left at 5.30, despite *my having already assured him* that it did.
10 Before buying this painting, you should make sure *of its being genuine*.
11 On entering the hotel, we immediately realized *the reason for its being so popular* with tourists.
12 The fact *of his having learned French in France* doesn't imply *his being able to speak the language perfectly*.

190 Rewrite the sentences, substituting a non-finite clause for the finite noun clauses in italics, using the infinitive, e.g.

> The whole family made the decision *that they would emigrate*.
> The whole family made the decision *to emigrate*.

1 The chairman put forward a plan *that they should take over other companies* engaged in complementary activities.
2 Several insurance companies have now reluctantly made the decision *that they should withdraw from the American market*.
3 I now regret having made a promise *that I would join in the scheme*.
4 The Council have agreed to a proposal *that they should build a new ring road*.
5 A suggestion *that they should postpone further discussion* pending investigations was accepted by a majority of three to one.
6 Six companies have signed an agreement *that they should share the costs of research and development*.
7 What our team seems to lack at the moment is the determination *that it will win*.
8 How often have I made a resolution *that I will give up smoking*!
9 The employers have at last expressed a desire *that they should re-open talks with the unions*.
10 The Ministry's inspector rejected the scheme *that the road should be made part of a one-way system*.

191 Reconstruct the sentences so that the finite or non-finite noun clauses come at the beginning, starting with the words in italics.

1 It soon became obvious *that* the conversation was upsetting him.
2 It was due to luck rather than judgement *that* the driver succeeded in avoiding an accident.

3 It remains a mystery *what* the thieves did with all the money.

4 It wasn't at all easy for the audience to follow *what* the speaker said.

5 It wasn't at all easy for the audience *to follow* what the speaker said.

6 It wasn't at all easy *for* the audience to follow what the speaker said.

7 It's easy, with the benefit of hindsight, *to see* how things went wrong.

8 It makes me feel guilty, *watching* you working so hard.

9 It's very inconsiderate of them *to have asked* you to give up your one free evening.

10 It's a little difficult to judge *whether* he really meant what he said.

11 It wasn't made clear at the time *why* we were to meet again so soon.

12 It was a matter of disagreement *how* the Company should promote the new product.

13 It isn't yet known *where* the pilot finally managed to land.

14 It hasn't yet been discovered *precisely* who originated the plan.

15 It is difficult to estimate at this stage *how* much the scheme would cost.

In the next three exercises, special care should be taken with appositional noun clauses, which are always introduced by *that*, following the noun to which the clause stands in apposition (see paragraphs 3.3 and 3.4 of the Appendix). Appositional noun clauses are very often found with the noun *fact*:

> The fact *that he didn't turn up* shows that he was never really serious about coming.

But appositional noun clauses may be used with a wide range of nouns, as these exercises will show, and students should be clear about the distinction between adjectival clauses introduced by *that* and noun clauses in apposition:

a. He hotly denied the rumour *that* (or *which*) *was then being circulated*.

b. He hotly denied the rumour *that he had been visited by the police in connection with the recent crime*.

The 'that' clause in sentence *a* defines which rumour he denied, though it does not tell us what the rumour was. It is an adjectival clause, and could equally well be introduced by the alternative relative pronoun, *which*. The 'that' clause in sentence *b* tells us what the rumour was; it *is* the rumour, expressed in other words. In this case, it is impossible to replace *that* with *which*, since *that* is functioning as a conjunction, and not as a relative pronoun.

192 Complete the sentences with a finite or non-finite noun clause, and state the function of the clause you have added.

1 He said that he . . .
2 The fact . . . is now generally known.
3 What . . . is of direct concern to the country.
4 He rarely succeeds in achieving what . . .
5 I wanted to discover how . . .
6 The man told the police where . . .
7 What . . . is less important than what you do.
8 I asked the waiter if . . .
9 The writer deplored the fact . . .
10 It is clear that . . .
11 It was generally agreed that . . .
12 If that is what . . ., why don't you ask him?

193 Instructions as above

1 Deciding on . . . can be very difficult.
2 We were all shocked by . . .
3 His argument is that . . .
4 That . . . was clear from his subsequent remarks.
5 May I infer, from what . . ., that . . .? (two noun clauses)
6 Your idea that . . . will probably prove very unpopular.
7 Shareholders left the meeting with the feeling that . . .
8 No one seemed to know when . . .
9 A view widely held by experts was that . . .
10 I was of the opinion that . . .
11 It is a common failing to put off doing . . .
12 Is it true that . . .?

194 Instructions as above

1 Having learned that . . ., he left the country.
2 Don't run away with the idea that . . .

3 I was under the impression that . . .

4 It seems that . . .

5 I now remember why . . .

6 Repeating . . ., the accused maintained his alibi that . . . (two noun clauses)

7 He put forward the startling proposal that . . .

8 That . . . is almost inconceivable.

9 What was even more surprising was the fact . . .

10 Exactly how . . . will never be known.

11 The experts couldn't agree as to which . . .

12 Pointing out that . . ., the manufacturers said they could give no assurance that . . . (two noun clauses)

Non-finite clauses

195 Replace the finite clauses in italics with non-finite clauses, using the non-finite forms suggested, and making any other necessary changes. (NB. *-ing* = present participle or gerund, *-ed* = past participle, *inf.* = infinitive.)

1 Would anyone *who wishes* to attend the meeting please notify the Secretary? (-ing)

2 We left the meeting, *since there was obviously no point* in staying. (-ing)

3 *If the situation is looked at in this way,* it doesn't seem so desperate. (-ed)

4 We left early *so that we should arrive in good time.* (inf.)

5 Children under the age of fourteen are not allowed into the cinema *unless they are accompanied by an adult.* (-ed)

6 I remember *that he once offered* to help us if ever we were in trouble. (-ing)

7 Until the disaster, everyone had believed *that the ship was unsinkable.* (inf.)

8 We had to leave quietly *so that we shouldn't disturb other people.* (inf.)

9 *Since we didn't have any time to spare,* we couldn't visit all the places we would have liked to. (-ing)

10 *As we had never been to the city before,* we bought a guidebook at the first stationer's we came to. (-ing)

213

11 There are still many difficulties *that must be surmounted*. (inf.)

12 The public official *who had been involved in the scandal* agreed *that he should offer his resignation*. (2 clauses: -ed/inf.)

13 *Whether it was restored in the nineteenth century or not*, the painting was unanimously attributed to Tiepolo. (-ed)

14 We're very disappointed *now that we hear* that you can't come. (inf.)

15 The Chancellor has now decided *that he will introduce measures that will stimulate the economy*. (2 clauses: inf./inf.)

16 The instructions were written in such bad English *that they were positively misleading*. (inf.)

Synthesis

It is inadvisable for students to embark on these exercises until they have completed the exercises on sentence structure (Exercises 173–195). Earlier practice in techniques relevant to synthesis will be found in Section One, Exercises 105–119 (using relative clauses) and Exercises 145–148 (using participial constructions).

(196) Combine each group of sentences to form one complex sentence. Students may make any necessary changes in the disposition of material and in the wording, but must not change the sense of the original. Skeleton structures have been suggested for many of the sentences to indicate possible approaches to the synthesis, but students should feel free to adopt their own approach.

1 No one was watching. The thief first made sure of this. He climbed up a drainpipe. He climbed up to a window on the first floor. He succeeded in entering the house through the window. He was not observed.

Having first . . ., the thief . . . to a first-floor . . ., through which . . . unobserved.

2 I had the opportunity of spending my holiday at sea. I had no experience of sailing. Nevertheless, I decided to take the opportunity. Some friends of mine invited me to join them. They were very keen yachtsmen. They wanted to sail round the British Isles.

Despite . . ., I decided . . . when some friends. . ., who . . . and who . . ., invited . . .

3 A man may be pronounced guilty only by twelve of his fellow citizens. They must be left free to make their decision. They must be left to do so without influence from the judge. He may, however, direct them as to points of law. This is the jury system. It is an outstanding characteristic of British judicial procedure.

An outstanding . . . is . . ., under which a man . . .

4 The M.1 is the first of a new network of roads. ('M' stands for 'Motorway'.) The roads are comparable to those found in some European countries. The roads are being built. They are to provide Britain with a first-class system of motorways. The motorways are between principal centres of population.

The M.1 ('M' . . .) is the first of . . .

197 Instructions as above

1 The English queue up for public transport. They do so in an orderly way. Visitors from the Continent are surprised at this. They innocently join the front of the queue. They do this when they first arrive in England. Angry glares are given them. They cannot understand this.

Visitors . . . at the . . . in which . . ., and they . . . when, on first . . ., they innocently . . .

2 Television has power to influence minds. It can influence them for good or ill. Independent Television was introduced in 1954. A controlling body was set up in the same year. It was called the the I.T.A. It was to ensure that adequate standards were maintained.

Since . . . ill, a controlling body . . . 1954, when . . ., to ensure . . .

3 The bubonic plague raged in England during the Middle Ages. The name given to it was 'The Black Death'. It carried off thousands of the population. In some cases, it exterminated whole towns and villages.

'The Black Death' . . ., carrying . . . and . . . exterminating . . .

1 Fleet Street was once famous for its coffee houses. Men used to meet there. They were prominent in the literary world. It is now synonymous with journalism and English national newspapers. It takes its name from the Fleet Stream. This used to run from Hampstead. It ran down into the Thames at Blackfriars.

Fleet Street, once . . . where men . . . and now . . ., takes . . .

2 Guy Fawkes was the leader of a band of conspirators. They intended to blow up the Houses of Parliament. They intended to do this while the King and his Ministers were in session. Guy Fawkes's memory is perpetuated. There are firework displays. These are held on November 5th each year.

Guy Fawkes, whose memory . . . each year, was . . .

3 I returned to the city. I had been born there. I had been absent for many years. Many of its narrow streets had been demolished. So had their picturesque houses. They had made way for shop-lined thoroughfares. These were modern but undistinguished. I was dismayed to find this.

When . . ., I was dismayed to . . .

1 The Pilgrim Fathers were a group of English Puritans. They first spent some years in exile in Holland. They did this to escape religious persecution. They later sailed to America in the *Mayflower*. They established a colony at Plymouth in Massachusetts.

2 A great financial crash occurred in Britain in 1720. 'The South Sea Bubble' was the name given to it. It followed a wave of national speculation. The dimensions of this speculation have since been repeated only once. This was before the great crash on Wall Street, New York. This was in 1929.

3 Sir Christopher Wren (1632–1723) had already attained distinction as an astronomer. He was only sixteen then. Nevertheless, later, he seriously took up the study of architecture. This was not till he was nearly thirty. The most precious fruit of this study was St Paul's Cathedral.

Although . . ., it was not till . . . that . . .

200 Combine each group of sentences so as to form not more than *two* complex sentences. Students may make any necessary changes in the disposition of material and in the wording, but must not change the sense of the original.

1 There is a present-day demand for equality of opportunity. Comprehensive schools have been established in response to this. There are three types of Secondary school. These are Grammar, Technical, and Modern. They are combined under one roof in the Comprehensive school. This makes easier a transfer of pupils from one type of school to another. This is done in cases where the child's real ability becomes clear only later in his education. This is the purpose of the Comprehensive school.

2 British Railways came into being in 1948. This happened on the nationalization of rail transport. The Labour Government did this. Previously, railways in Britain were run privately. They were run in four main networks. There was the London, Midland, and Scottish Railway. Another was the Southern Railway. The Great Western Railway was a third. Last, there was the London and North-Eastern Railway.

3 The Beauchamp Tower is semicircular in plan. It projects eighteen feet beyond the face of the wall. It was originally built for defensive purposes. But it was very soon used as a prison. One of the first unwilling guests in it was the third earl of Warwick. His family name thus became associated with this part of the Tower of London.

201 Instructions as above

1 What the English call 'Public Schools' are in fact private or independent schools. Foreigners are frequently surprised to learn this. These schools cater, in the main, for fee-paying pupils. These pupils come from middle and upper-class families. Many of these families have to make great financial sacrifices. They do this in order to send their children to the school of their choice.

2 The jury system has disadvantages. This is the opinion of many people. Nevertheless, the disappearance of this system is unthinkable. In the same way, in principle there is a very great deal to be said for making magistrates out of certain persons. These

persons are prominent local citizens. This is their chief qualification.

3 The headmaster spoke on the dangers of playing on railway tracks.
He spoke at length. Even experienced railwaymen could not
always hear the approach of an express diesel locomotive. He
pointed this out. The headmaster then warned the boys. They
would not only be severely punished. They would also risk
expulsion from the school. This would be done if any of them
persisted in playing near the railway.

202 Instructions as above

1 Money or plate may be found hidden anywhere in Britain. It may
have no owner. It is then called 'Treasure-Trove'. It is legally
the property of the Crown. The finder must hand over his 'trove'
to the authorities. He is, however, in practice, given its full value
in return.

2 The South Choir Aisle of Peterborough Cathedral contains some
very fine marble effigies of former abbots of the monastery. The
South Choir aisle is also the site of the tomb of Mary, Queen of
Scots. Her body rested beneath the Choir for twenty-five years.
In 1612 it was removed to Westminster by order of her son,
James the First.

3 Very little armour has survived from a time earlier than the
fifteenth century. This is a sad fact. Mail was particularly liable
to destruction. It was even cut up for other uses. Fortunately,
much of the enriched armour of the sixteenth century has been
preserved. It owes its preservation to its artistic quality and
personal associations.

203 Instructions as above

1 Miss Green was untrained for office work. Bearing this in mind,
one thing was surprising. She coped most efficiently with all her
duties as personal secretary to the chairman. This had been
her position in the firm since 1950. She came to London in that
year. Her intention in coming to London was to become a fashion
model.

2 The English football season culminates in May each year. The
Football Association Cup Final marks the culmination. Two
teams play each other at Wembley Stadium. These teams have

survived a knock-out competition. This competition began in September the previous year. They now play to see who will win the F.A. Cup.

3 Queens' College was the second royal foundation at Cambridge. King's College was the first. The former is distinguished from the college of the same name at Oxford in a certain respect. It owes its foundation to two Queens. One was Margaret. She was the wife of Henry the Sixth. The other was Elizabeth. She was the wife of Edward the Fourth. This is why the apostrophe comes after the 's'.

Distinguishing between similar sentences

204 Show the difference in meaning between the sentences in pairs, either by explaining each sentence or by rewriting the sentences in your own words.

a. The mother said her son was seeing the doctor in the afternoon.
b. The mother said her son was to see the doctor in the afternoon.

Explanation

a implies that the mother is telling someone what her son is going to do in the afternoon; *b* implies that the mother is telling someone what has been arranged for her son to do in the afternoon.

Paraphrase

a The mother said her son was going (or intended) to see the doctor in the afternoon. *b* The mother said it had been arranged that her son should see the doctor in the afternoon.

If students choose the latter method of distinguishing between the sentences, they should ensure that their rewritten versions are not *simply* paraphrases: they must make clear the difference between the original sentences.

1*a* Only the chairman objected to the proposal to build more houses.
b The chairman objected only to the proposal to build more houses.

2a Clearly, the man didn't understand the legal document at all.
 b The man didn't understand the legal document at all clearly.
3a He didn't promise to attend the meeting.
 b He promised not to attend the meeting.
4a He said he would like to go to the theatre, but he didn't have enough money.
 b He said he liked going to the theatre, but he didn't have enough money to.
5a I remember telling him that there was no bus on Sundays.
 b I remembered to tell him that there was no bus on Sundays.
6a You won't have much money to spend on your holiday.
 b You won't have to spend much money on your holiday.
7a I haven't seen him this morning. Have you?
 b I didn't see him this morning. Did you?
8a I was very busy last week.
 b I have been very busy for the last week.

205 Instructions as above

1a Even he admitted that the tax was unfair.
 b He even admitted that the tax was unfair.
2a He admitted that even the tax was unfair.
 b He admitted that the tax was even unfair.
3a The mechanic didn't pretend to know what had gone wrong.
 b The mechanic pretended not to know what had gone wrong.
4a He couldn't stop saying thank you for all his friend had done.
 b He couldn't stop to say thank you for all his friend had done.
5a Although I said that I was engaged on the Sunday, he went on asking me to see him that day.
 b Although I had said that I was engaged on the Sunday, he went on to ask me to see him that day.
6a He recovered from his cold so quickly that he didn't need to visit a doctor.
 b He recovered from his cold so quickly that he needn't have visited a doctor.
7a Perhaps you can tell me when you see me again?
 b Perhaps you could tell me when you will see me again?
8a They looked admiringly at a portrait of Holbein.
 b They looked admiringly at a portrait of Holbein's.

1a He said finally that he hoped to bring the negotiations to a satisfactory conclusion.
 b He said that he hoped finally to bring the negotiations to a satisfactory conclusion.
2a The committee as a whole felt that the financial situation had
   improved.
 b The committee felt that the financial situation as a whole had
   improved.
3a He was used to getting up early.
 b He used to get up early.
4a Why don't you try to hire a television set?
 b Why don't you try hiring a television set?
5a He must have had a new lock put on the door.
 b He must have put a new lock on the door.
6a The shop will let me know when the goods are in stock.
 b The shop will let me know when the goods will be in stock.
7a She spends a lot of money on clothes.
 b She's spending a lot of money on clothes.
8a He asked the manager if he would go ahead with the project.
 b He asked the manager if he should go ahead with the project.

207 Instructions as above

1a I don't particularly want to see him now.
 b I particularly don't want to see him now.
2a In vain did he try to prevent the work from being done.
 b He tried to prevent the work from being done in vain.
3a I regret to say that you'll be held responsible.
 b I regret saying that you'd be held responsible.
4a Did you say nothing because you were afraid to make him angry?
 b Did you say nothing because you were afraid of making him
   angry?
5a The manager was told he should have more workers trained on
   the job.
 b The manager was told he should have more trained workers on
   the job.
 c The manager was told he should have trained more workers on
   the job.

6*a* I always meet her at the station.

  b I am always meeting her at the station.

7*a* It's raining hard now.

  b It's hardly raining now.

8*a* I will send you the goods direct.

  b I will send you the goods directly.

208 Instructions as above

1*a* The orator made himself generally unpopular with the crowd.

  b The orator generally made himself unpopular with the crowd.

2*a* Naturally, one doesn't expect oranges to grow in England.

  b One doesn't expect oranges to grow naturally in England.

3*a* The design of the building was not obviously attractive.

  b The design of the building was obviously not attractive.

4*a* The chairman has resigned to make way for a younger man.

  b The chairman is resigned to making way for a younger man.

5*a* The Home Secretary said that the powers of the police in the case of peaceful demonstrations should be limited to prevent public disturbance.

  b The Home Secretary said that the powers of the police in the case of peaceful demonstrations should be limited to preventing public disturbances.

6*a* He's sure to be offered the job.

  b He's sure he'll be offered the job.

7*a* The President, in one of his rare long speeches, told the people that the country was facing a crisis.

  b The President, in one of his rare, long speeches, told the people that the country was facing a crisis.

8*a* I enjoy living in London, although I have made few friends here.

  b I enjoy living in London, because I have made a few friends here.

209 Instructions as above

1*a* As we had anticipated, the scheme didn't work out in practice.

  b The scheme didn't work out in practice as we had anticipated.

2*a* Approaching the bank, he noticed two suspicious-looking men.

  b He noticed two suspicious-looking men approaching the bank.

3*a* I haven't seen him recently. Has he gone on holiday?

b I haven't seen him recently. Has he been on holiday?

4*a* You are now speaking like a teacher.

b You are now speaking as a teacher.

5*a* I have heard nothing of him for a very long time.

b I have heard nothing from him for a very long time.

6*a* The workers, who went on strike, were dismissed.

b The workers who went on strike were dismissed.

7*a* He said he had been waiting a long time and wasn't at all pleased.

b He said he had been waiting a long time, and he wasn't at all pleased.

8*a* The rescue party said there was slight chance of there being any survivors.

b The rescue party said there was a slight chance of there being some survivors.

210 Instructions as above

1*a* She went to the shop only to discover how expensive the dress was.

b She went to the shop, only to discover that the dress was very expensive.

2*a* She drinks tea with breakfast, as is customary in England.

b She drinks tea with breakfast, as it is customary in England.

3*a* The builders can't proceed with the work unless he gives permission.

b The builders can't proceed with the work until he gives permission.

4*a* I'll pay you at the end of the month.

b I'll pay you by the end of the month.

5*a* There was no reason for him to think such a thing.

b There was, for him, no reason for thinking such a thing.

6*a* Isn't he definitely staying in London?

b Is he staying in London indefinitely?

7*a* He wasn't a writer originally.

b He wasn't an original writer.

8*a* I've found myself unable to appreciate a few of the modern paintings I've seen.

b I've found myself unable to appreciate the few modern paintings I've seen.

1*a* When he comes, please tell him where I am.

 b If he comes, please tell him where I am.

2*a* If you told a lie, it was very foolish of you.

 b If you told a lie, it would be very foolish of you.

3*a* He won't come to the cinema even if he has nothing else to do.

 b He won't come to the cinema, even though he has nothing else to do.

4*a* On checking through the accounts you may discover discrepancies.

 b By checking through the accounts you may discover discrepancies.

5*a* He gave a brilliant illustrated lecture.

 b He gave a brilliantly illustrated lecture.

6*a* Did you see him yesterday?

 b Didn't you see him yesterday?

7*a* Is there someone in that room?

 b Is there anyone in that room?

8*a* There were no fewer than 10,000 people at the meeting.

 b There were not fewer than 10,000 people at the meeting.

212 Each of the sentences may, without any changes in word order or punctuation, be interpreted in two different ways. Explain the two possible meanings. (NB. In some cases, the different meanings would be expressed in spoken English by means of stress or intonation.)

1 The work should be completed by the end of the month.

2 She burned his last letter, in which he had proposed to her, so that no one could ever discover the truth.

3 He might have realized that you were pulling his leg.

4 She left me to get on with her work.

5 After the marathon race the runners were very tired, if not exhausted.

6 Will you call on him and tell him?

7 We felt sure they would arrive in time.

8 It was not well received by the public because it was a play of ideas.

213 Instructions as above

1 The Queen is expected to arrive on time for the celebrations.
2 We have found her a good daily help.
3 The ambassador did not leave London to take up an appointment in Africa.
4 The teacher insisted that his students always arrived early.
5 The tourists wanted to visit more interesting places.
6 Our visitors should have arrived at the airport by now.
7 No one liked the portrait he had painted.
8 He decided to retire when he reached the age of sixty.

214 Punctuate each of the sentences in two different ways, putting in the necessary capital letters, and explain the difference in meaning between your two versions.

1 the motorist said the bus driver was to blame for the accident
2 i wouldn't advise you to go there for his sake
3 the teacher left his students feeling very depressed
4 this type of education is very expensive indeed but it is well worth every penny spent on it
5 the headmaster said that the boys parents should exercise more control at home
6 leading british companies already well-known for their international outlook have begun setting up factories in europe

215 Instructions as above

1 the facts the prisoner admitted pointed to him as the guilty person but he protested he was innocent
2 once having lost our way in that remote part of scotland we had to spend the night camping by the road-side
3 the political demonstrators who felt strongly on the subject of racial discrimination were prepared to defy the police
4 cross-channel steamers unable to dock at dover because of gales had to go on to newhaven
5 he won't think he has any reason to thank you for all that you've done
6 i have just remembered something she said

SECTION THREE
VOCABULARY WORK

Note: For the work in this section of the book, students should use an English dictionary for foreign students, and *not* a translating dictionary. The dictionaries recommended are:

> The Advanced Learner's Dictionary of Current English or An English Reader's Dictionary.

For the majority of students, these dictionaries are more suitable than those intended for English people.

The use of words

216–218 Explain the difference in the meaning or use of the words in italics in the pairs or groups of sentences.

 216

1a I'll *teach* you to play tennis.
 b I'll *teach* you to steal my apples!
2a This book was *specially* written for foreign students.
 b This book is *especially* useful to foreign students.
3a Would you be *prepared* to help me in this way?
 b Would you please be *prepared* to leave the hotel at 8 a.m.?
4a His room *overlooked* the park.
 b He *overlooked* the error as it was my first day at work.
 c He *overlooked* the error, as he wasn't paying attention.
5a He said he wasn't *informed of* this matter.
 b He said he wasn't *informed in* these matters.
6a I think it wouldn't be wise to mention it to him *just now*.
 b I think it wouldn't be wise to mention it to him *just yet*.
7a He *enjoyed* a good education.
 b He *enjoyed* his lessons at school.
8a He said he had been *fairly* well treated by his captors.
 b He said he had been *fairly* treated by his captors.
9a After an *exhausting* search, they found the missing children.

b After an *exhaustive* search, they found the missing children.

10*a* *Undoubtedly*, that is the best method to adopt.

  b *No doubt*, that is the best method to adopt.

217

1*a* They left *at once*.

  b They were all talking *at once*.

  c The building was *at once* beautiful and functional in design.

2*a* They struck a *bargain* on how to share the market between them.

  b She bought a *bargain* in the January sales.

3*a* He *maintains* a large family.

  b He *maintains* that families should be large.

4*a* He *must* be out: no one has answered the door.

  b You *must* do as you are told.

5*a* On one *occasion* I remember, the meeting broke up in disorder.

  b I don't have *occasion* to visit London very frequently nowadays.

6*a* The teacher was driven almost to *distraction* by the misbehaviour of his pupils.

  b The child has so many *distractions* that he is disinclined to do his homework.

7*a* One should *take* full *advantage of* any opportunity to travel.

  b One shouldn't *take advantage of* the ignorance of others.

8*a* I hope he *appreciates* what this means.

  b I greatly *appreciate* what you did for me.

  c The value of the shares *appreciated* considerably in the course of a year.

9*a* He *certainly* doesn't believe in ghosts.

  b *Surely* he doesn't believe in ghosts?

10*a* She didn't buy the dress because it didn't *fit* her.

  b She didn't buy the dress because it didn't *suit* her.

218

1*a* They didn't *recognize* Mr Smith as the man they had known ten years before.

  b They didn't *recognize* Mr Smith as their leader.

2*a* Charles promised to *call for* me on his way to work.

  b Success in life generally *calls for* hard work.

3*a* People dislike him because he always *boasts* about his success.

  b The town *boasts* two cinemas, a theatre, and a swimming-pool.

4a One shouldn't be *jealous* of the good fortune of others.

 b The company is very *jealous* of its reputation for producing high-quality goods.

5a The Customs official didn't even *ask for* my passport.

 b Driving fast on any icy road is *asking for* trouble.

6a *Altogether*, it was a very enjoyable day's outing.

 b *Altogether*, there were thirty people on the outing.

7a The proposals should prove to be *in the interest of* the public.

 b The proposals should prove to be *of interest to* the public.

8a His friend *reproached* him *for* having disclosed the secret.

 b His friend *reproached* him *with* having disclosed the secret.

9a He *told* me he was leaving school.

 b He *told* me to leave the room.

10a The teacher *asked* the student to answer the question.

 b The teacher *asked* the student if he knew the answer.

Words confused or misused

219–238 Write sentences to show the difference in meaning or use between the words or phrases in pairs.

219

1	rob	steal
2	invaluable	valueless
3	passed	past
4	notorious	famous
5	principal	principle
6	sensible	sensitive

220

1	altogether	all together
2	at last	at least
3	loose	lose
4	beside	besides
5	presently	actually
6	channel	canal

221

1	fairly	rather
2	aloud	loudly
3	refuse	deny
4	overtake	overcome
5	all ready	already
6	experience (n)	experiences (n)

222

1	recount	re-count
2	specially	especially
3	imply	infer
4	hypocritical	hypercritical
5	affect	effect
6	worthless	priceless

223

1. combustible — inflammable
2. unable — incapable
3. no doubt — undoubtedly
4. presumption — assumption
5. alternate — alternative
6. new — novel

224

1. disused — misused
2. satisfying — satisfactory
3. dependent — dependant
4. sequence — consequence
5. industrial — industrious
6. incredible — incredulous

225

1. momentary — temporary
2. exceedingly — excessively
3. popular — populous
4. re-covered — recovered
5. regrettable — regretful
6. defective — deficient

226

1. impersonate — personify
2. historic — historical
3. precipitate — precipitous
4. irrational — unreasonable
5. say — tell
6. stationery — stationary

227

1. presently — at present
2. after — afterwards
3. intolerable — intolerant
4. unsatisfied — dissatisfied
5. adopt — adapt
6. exhausting — exhaustive

228

1. benefactor — beneficiary
2. conscious — conscientious
3. explicit — implicit
4. responsible to — responsible for
5. prize — price
6. adhesive — adherent

229

1. appreciable — appreciative
2. human — humane
3. disinterested — uninterested
4. comprise — consist
5. convince — persuade
6. hard — hardly

230

1. official — officious
2. remain — remind
3. confidently — confidentially
4. supplementary — complementary
5. everyone — every one
6. morale — moral

231

1 degenerate — deteriorate
2 eligible — illegible
3 prevent — avoid
4 continual — continuous
5 reception — receptacle
6 job — work

232

1 suit — suite
2 economic — economical
3 glance — glimpse
4 definite — definitive
5 accuse — convict
6 unmistak-able — infallible

233

1 stimulant — stimulus
2 agree — accept
3 advise — advice
4 ingenious — ingenuous
5 untouchable — intangible
6 treat — cure

234

1 eatable — edible
2 unanswer-able — irresponsible
3 credible — creditable
4 travel — journey
5 prophesy — prophecy
6 devise — device

235

1 chance — possibility
2 license — licence
3 interfere — interrupt
4 distinct — distinctive
5 discover — invent
6 co-operate — collaborate

236

1 evade — avoid
2 unexcep-tional — unexception-able
3 insist — persist
4 incidental — accidental
5 predominant — pre-eminent
6 right — rightly

237

1 comprehen-sive — understand-able
2 artful — tasteful
3 precise — concise
4 until — unless
5 reform — re-form
6 frequent (v) — attend

238

1 efficient — effective
2 pretence — pretension
3 raise — rise
4 borrow — lend
5 impassable — impossible
6 contemp-tible — contemp-tuous

Comparisons and contrasts

239–244 Explain the similarities and differences between the words in each pair. Students should answer in complete sentences, and should vary the construction of their answers. The following forms may be found useful:

(a) Both . . . , but while the first . . . , the second . . .
(b) While the second . . . , the first . . .
(c) Both . . . , the first, however, being . . . and the second . . .
(d) —— describes . . . , while —— describes . . .
(e) —— is something that . . . , and —— is something that . . .
(f) Whereas —— . . . , —— . . .
(g) Although both . . . , the first . . . and the second . . .

239

1 barrister	solicitor
2 audience	spectators
3 physician	surgeon
4 booklet	leaflet
5 index	appendix
6 shore	bank

240

1 friend	acquaintance
2 hotel	hostel
3 newspaper	magazine
4 prejudice	superstition
5 salary	fees
6 supervisor	surveyor

241

1 teacher	professor
2 weariness	drowsiness
3 orator	speaker
4 copy	facsimile
5 error	fault
6 aroma	odour

242

1 hedge	fence
2 education	upbringing
3 instinct	intuition
4 abnormal	unusual
5 dismay	disappointment
6 compensation	reward

243

1 frankness	sincerity
2 criminal	prisoner
3 thanks	gratitude
4 providence	fate
5 liability	responsibility
6 guardian	warden

244

1 intelligence	cunning
2 attendant	assistant
3 eye-witness	onlooker
4 review	survey
5 verdict	sentence
6 mob	crowd

Words and their associations

The following five exercises give practice in using words that express broadly related ideas. They have been included in order to focus attention on an important aspect of learning and using new words: their meaning and use should be learned, as far as possible, from their connotations or associations. For example, 'stride' and 'strut' are, broadly speaking, both ways of walking, but each has its particular associations and must be used in an appropriate context. At the end of most sentences in Exercises 245, 247, and 248, a clue is given to the appropriate associations of the word needed, in some cases by a repetition of words from the sentence.

245 Complete the sentences, using the words given at the head of the exercise. Use each word *once* only.

stagger	plod	march	pace
loiter	stride	stray	strut
ramble	lurk	creep	wander

1 The victorious army . . . through the conquered city. (soldiers)
2 Not wishing to be discovered, the small boy . . . downstairs. (fear of making a noise)
3 The thieves . . . in the shadows for their unsuspecting victim. (waiting with evil intentions)
4 The turkey . . . up and down the farmyard. (arrogance)
5 The drunkard . . . from the public house and clung to a lamp-post. (unsteady movement)
6 We reached the village after a very long walk, and . . . wearily to our hotel. (wearily)
7 The manager . . . into the office and asked who was responsible for the error. (purposeful)
8 The mother told her son to do the errand quickly, and not to . . . on the way. (necessity for speed)
9 The dog had . . . from its home, and was now completely lost. (lose the way)
10 As last Sunday was a fine day, we decided to . . . around the countryside. (walking for pleasure, and without aim)
11 The man whose wife was expecting a child . . . nervously up and down the hospital waiting-room. (nervously up and down)
12 On my first visit to the city, I . . . from place to place without any sense of direction. (no sense of direction)

246 Write sentences illustrating the use of each of the words given.

1 stroll	2 rush	3 scramble	4 crawl	5 limp
6 stumble	7 trudge	8 step	9 lurch	10 prowl

247 Complete the sentences, using the words given at the head of the exercise. Use each word *once* only.

smile	sneer	grin	cheer	roar
jeer	giggle	laugh	titter	tease
snigger	chuckle	groan	mock	boo

1 The Queen . . . graciously as she passed through the . . . crowds. (graciously; crowds expressing approval)
2 The crowd . . . loudly when it appeared that the referee had given a wrong decision. (noisy expression of displeasure)
3 A nervous . . . was heard in the audience when the solo violinist broke a string in the middle of the performance. (nervousness, desire to suppress laughter)
4 The spectators . . . when the champion, who was lying third in the race, gave up, pretending to be suffering from cramp. (noisy expression of contempt)
5 Jokes are unpredictable in their effect. Sometimes they make the hearer . . . , sometimes they merely produce a . . . because the hearer has heard them before. (——; pretended pain)
6 At the end of the boxing match, the winner . . . broadly in response to the . . . of approval from the crowd. (broadly; loud expression of feelings)
7 An intellectual snob often . . . at the efforts of others to improve themselves. (contempt)
8 If you . . . me any longer, I shall get angry. (make fun of)
9 The school-children . . . when the headmaster tripped over his gown as he was mounting the school platform at morning assembly. (nervousness, school-children)
10 The boy . . . when shown a comic drawing of the teacher. (half-ashamed laughter)
11 The unwieldy package seemed to . . . at all my efforts to tie it securely. (defy contemptuously)
12 The reader, obviously finding the book very amusing, sat quietly . . . to himself. (to himself)

draw	drag	jerk	pull	lug
tug	wrench	haul	tow	

1 The thieves, unable to open the safe, had . . . it from its fixtures and taken it away. (pull violently)
2 My car broke down and had to be . . . to a garage. (broke down)
3 The bus braked sharply and stopped with a . . . , throwing several passengers to the floor. (sudden stopping)
4 The trawlermen had taken such a huge catch that they had difficulty in . . . the nets aboard. (raising a heavy load)
5 The load of hay was being . . . by two horses.
6 The piece of furniture was so heavy that it had to be . . . along the floor. (pull without lifting)
7 My friend arrived at the station . . . a heavy suitcase. (pull or carry something cumbersome)
8 The cross-Channel swimmer had to be . . . out of the water exhausted.
9 He . . . so hard at the window sash that it broke, and the window came crashing down. (pull sharply)

249 Write sentences illustrating the use of each of the words given.

1 hold 2 grasp 3 clutch 4 seize 5 snatch 6 grip
7 clasp 8 capture 9 pluck 10 clench

Substituting adverbs for adverbial phrases

250 Replace each group of words in italics by one of the adverbs given at the head of the exercise, making any necessary changes in punctuation and word order. For each of the four remaining adverbs, write a sentence illustrating its use.

conceivably	stealthily	outspokenly	interminably
imaginatively	reluctantly	concurrently	radically
indifferently	clandestinely	explicitly	conclusively
substantially	superficially	querulously	indiscriminately

1 *Although unwilling to do so,* he came to the conclusion that no better scheme was practicable.
2 The party leader's speech seemed to go on *and on without end.*
3 The electorate viewed *with lack of interest* the prospect of a Communist government coming to power.
4 Until the new method had proved its worth, the management agreed that the old and the new should be used *together at the same time.*
5 The Secretary General said that the new plan the Russians had proposed was, *in most respects,* the same as the one that had been rejected earlier.
6 Having been officially banned, the political party was obliged to meet and operate *in secret.*
7 This course of action could, *it may be imagined,* lead to ruin.
8 A member of the Opposition voiced his objections *without any reticence or reserve.*
9 The sick man asked *in a complaining manner* why no one ever visited him.
10 The chairman of the company said that new techniques had, *in a very fundamental way,* changed their production methods.
11 The fingerprints proved *beyond all doubt* that Mr X was the murderer.
12 An avid reader, he reads all books *without regard to differences in quality or theme.*

251 Instructions as above

judiciously	conscientiously	wilfully	inadvertently
tremulously	inopportunely	adroitly	conversely
hysterically	tirelessly	lavishly	vicariously
prematurely	emotionally	slavishly	blindly

1 The lost child gave its name *with a nervous and shaking voice.*
2 He did his work *with great care and thoroughness.*
3 Knowing that the weather might quickly change for the worse, the climbers *very wisely* took extra equipment with them.
4 The woman trapped in the blazing house was screaming *with uncontrollable emotion and fear.*
5 Everyone agreed that Mr Hammarskjöld was a man who had worked for peace *with unremitting effort.*

6 More exports means, *looking at the question from the opposite point of view*, fewer goods for the home market.

7 Many people enjoy the thrills of climbing *indirectly by reading of the experience of others*.

8 This book, illustrated *regardless of expense*, is offered at only £2·00.

9 Having no mind of his own, the critic adopted *with complete lack of originality* the opinion of others.

10 The patient was, *through an oversight*, given the wrong prescription by the doctor.

11 The man in court was charged with obstructing the police *with intention and determination*.

12 The death of the Finance Minister occurred *at a very inconvenient time* in an economic crisis.

252 Instructions as above

severely	temperamentally	synthetically	tentatively
wistfully	apprehensively	triumphantly	arbitrarily
briskly	characteristically	aggressively	persuasively
leniently	surreptitiously	scrupulously	earnestly

1 Men are now able to produce more and more raw materials *by artificial means*.

2 The winners of the football championship ran off the field carrying the silver cup *and expressing their pride in victory*.

3 I suggested *in a hesitating way* that what my friend was doing was wrong.

4 Heavy rain hampered rescue operations *in an extreme way*.

5 Intending aircrew undergo searching tests to discover whether they are *by disposition and character* suitable for the work.

6 The thief took the goods *in a way that no one would notice* and left the shop.

7 A judge must always be *perfectly and in every way* fair.

8 The children pressed their noses against the shop window and looked *with unsatisfied longing* at the goods inside.

9 The drunkard spoke *in a quarrelsome way* when asked by the police to accompany them to the police station.

10 We walked *actively and with energy* along the cliffs and soon became warm despite the cold wind.

11 The workers complained that their wage claim had been rejected *without impartial consideration* by their employers.

12 The wife of the first man in space sat at home waiting *with anxious fear* for his return to earth.

253 Replace the words in italics by a single adverb of equivalent meaning, making any necessary changes in punctuation and word order.

1 The young students were discussing the subject *in a lively manner*.

2 They managed to settle the dispute *in a friendly way*.

3 I have almost finished my work, and I shall be with you *very soon*.

4 He expressed his point of view *in very few words*.

5 Church organs, which used to be pumped *by hand,* are now pumped *by machine*.

6 In the accident that occurred last night, two men were *so badly* injured *that they died*.

7 His novel ideas are *time and again* getting him into trouble with his more conservative colleagues.

8 This machine is out of order *for the time being*.

9 When asked why he had been absent from school, the boy replied, *in a manner lacking all respect,* that he had gone fishing instead.

10 England is *by reputation* a land of everlasting rain and fog.

11 He undertook the work *of his own free will*.

12 The motion was carried *with the agreement of all*.

254 Instructions as above

1 The room has been furnished *in a manner showing good taste*.

2 The Music Festival was held *every year*.

3 He won the first prize three years *one after another*.

4 The politician realized that by supporting a pacifist policy he would, *beyond all hope of recall,* forfeit his chances of becoming the party leader.

5 He could see, *looking back over the past,* where he had gone wrong.

6 The farmer found that his crops were, *in comparison with those of other farmers,* undamaged by the heavy rainstorm.

7 He said that they had, *it was to be regretted,* been obliged to give up the scheme through lack of support.

8 He felt angry, *as he had every reason to be*, at the way he had been treated.

9 The new building was at once functional and pleasing *in its appeal to one's sense of beauty*.

10 The man was found to have married *again while still legally married to his first wife*.

11 Investigators agreed that passengers on the airliner that had crashed must have died *at the very moment of the crash*.

12 A thousand pounds was given to the Cancer Research Fund *without the name of the donor being made known*.

Adjectives ending in -ible, -able, and -uble

255 Replace the words in italics by an adjective ending in -ible or -able, making any necessary changes in word order.

1 Many people are *easily influenced by* flattery. (. . . to)

2 Adolescents often go through a phase when they are completely *lacking in any sense of responsibility*.

3 He argued so cogently that his critics found *they could not answer* him.

4 Despite several setbacks, the climbers went on with their plans for an assault on Eiger with enthusiasm *that could not be repressed*.

5 A good ear for nuances is *absolutely necessary* if one wishes to speak a foreign language perfectly.

6 Being impatient is *opposed in nature or character* with being a good teacher.

7 The police admitted to having made a mistake *that was very much to be regretted* in accusing an innocent man.

8 Your attitude in this matter is *such as cannot be defended*.

9 The value of Elgar's contribution to the reputation of British music is *too great to be estimated*.

10 Negotiations between the employers and the workers broke down because both sides were too *determined not to be turned aside from, or to modify, their purpose*.

11 Although the two vessels collided with a sharp impact, the damage was found, on inspection, to be *of little or no significance*.

12 Most people like to think they are so efficient at their job that they would be *impossible to replace*.

1 Humidity is so intense in some parts of the tropics that Europeans find *they are unable to endure* it.

2 He found he *could not be chosen* for the job because he hadn't the necessary qualifications. (was . . .)

3 The two views are *such as cannot be reconciled to one another.*

4 All men are *liable to make mistakes.*

5 He spoke so quickly *that no one could understand him.* (as to be . . .)

6 In Wales there is a village whose name is, for English people, *impossible to pronounce.*

7 The number 12 *can be divided* by 2, 3, 4, and 6. (is . . .)

8 We had the greatest difficulty *one could imagine* in persuading the authorities that we had come to England only to study.

9 Froebel believed that unless children were trained properly from a very early age they would develop faults of character that would later become *fixed so firmly that they couldn't be rooted out.*

10 The quality that makes a picture a masterpiece is often *impossible to define or explain.*

11 It's useless to go ahead with a plan if you think it may prove *impossible to put into practice.*

12 After he had followed a course in elocution, his speech was *quite without faults.*

257 Complete the sentences with adjectives ending in -able, -ible, or -uble, derived from the verbs given in brackets. Note that in some cases the negative form of the adjective is required if the sentence is to make good sense.

1 England is linked by such (dissolve) ties to America that any permanent quarrel between the two countries is (conceive).

2 Employers claimed that yet another strike would do (repair) harm to the public image of Trade Unions.

3 Most people would agree that the greatest of poets are (translate).

4 Only a limited number of types of fungi are (eat).

5 My first sight of mountains made an (delete) impression on my memory.

6 You won't persuade him to change his mind. His decision is (revoke).

7 His moods are very (change).

8 I've never met such a man. His energy seems (exhaust).

9 Mozart's style has been found to be (imitate).
10 He is in the (envy) position of being completely independent.
11 Though once friends, they are now the most (placate) of enemies.
12 Floods having carried away the bridge, the river was (pass).

258 Instructions as above

1 Many fabrics are specially treated so as to be (shrink).
2 Men may die, but their words are (destroy).
3 Unfortunately, the problem of recurring inflation appears to be (solve).
4 Extra police were called in when it appeared that the crowd might become (control).
5 It was a (remember) day when peace was declared.
6 Britain has many miles of (navigate) waterways.
7 Cheques are generally (negotiate).
8 Day changes to night by almost (perceive) stages.
9 He returned to his university after twenty years' absence to find that (number) changes had taken place.
10 The residents complained of the (object) smell produced by the tanning factory.
11 The engineers engaged on tunnel construction had to blast away tons of (penetrate) rock.
12 Many currencies are now freely (convert).

259 Instructions as above

1 In the poorer parts of underdeveloped countries many people live in a (pity) state.
2 Airmen are supplied with (inflate) rubber dinghies, to be used if they bale out over the sea.
3 We spent a very (enjoy) evening talking about old times.
4 Even as late as the nineteenth century, sheep-stealing was (punish) by death.
5 The goods were so badly damaged in transit that they were found to be (sell).
6 The problem of slum clearance is (separate) from the problem of building new houses.
7 When shown the music of Tschaikowski's violin concerto, the violinist for whom it was written declared it to be (play).

8 Since his bad habits were never broken when he was a child, they are now (correct).
9 The English now regard free education as an (alienate) right.
10 Children's minds are very (impress).
11 How a nail came to be in the meat pie was quite (explain).
12 The English butler is generally assumed to be (perturb).

Adjectives ending in -ive

260 Replace each group of words in italics by one of the adjectives given at the head of the exercise, making any necessary changes in word order. For each of the four remaining adjectives, write a sentence illustrating its use.

abortive	defective	excessive	lucrative	submissive
abusive	defensive	formative	pervasive	successive
acquisitive	discursive	indicative	plaintive	
deceptive	evasive	intensive	repulsive	

1 Present-day English society is often labelled '*wanting to gain things for itself*'.
2 Would you prefer to be thought obedient or *merely humble and meekly unassertive*?
3 The measures the Government has already taken are *some sign* of the seriousness with which it views the present crisis.
4 The child had come under bad influences during the years of his life *that were decisive in shaping his character*.
5 The police charged the man with using language *that was meant to be insulting*.
6 Picasso has exerted an influence *that has had a widespread effect* on the art of this century.
7 We had almost given up hope of finding our cat, when we heard a *mournful and sorrowful* miaow from the branch of a near-by tree.
8 The Company's profits have increased by 5 per cent in *each of the last* three years.
9 The machine *that didn't work properly* had to be returned to the makers.
10 Efforts to put the scheme into practice proved *such that they ended in failure*.

11 When we asked the boy who knocked on the door what the money he was collecting was for, he gave us an answer *that was intended to avoid being a direct reply.*

12 He does a trade *that brings in a lot of money* by selling vegetables grown in his back garden.

13 Most students found the lecture useless because it was too *prone to wander from one point to another without plan.*

14 'Appearances can often be *liable to mislead.*'

261 Replace the words in italics by a single adjective ending in *-ive*, making any necessary changes in word order.

1 One side of a postage stamp is *covered with a sticky substance.*

2 A man *who is apt to be moved by sudden impulse* acts first and thinks afterwards.

3 Children are very *apt to ask questions* and often have memories more *able to remember facts* than adults.

4 A passage of writing *whose purpose is to describe* can be very difficult to summarize.

5 *A great deal of* damage was caused by the fire before it could be brought under control.

6. The Eastern Counties have a soil *that produces crops of a very high yield.*

7 In a debate, it is always good to have at least one speaker whose arguments are *intentionally irritating or designed to produce a strong reaction.*

8 It is a platitude that wealth is not always *likely to lead* to happiness.

9 Parliament recognized the formidable difficulties involved in making the law *apply to the past.*

10 The public needs to be assured that the Stock Exchange does not offer too many opportunities to the investor *who is merely concerned with financial operations of a risky but potentially highly profitable nature.*

Adjectives ending in -ous

262 Replace each group of words in italics by one of the adjectives given at the head of the exercise, making any necessary changes in word order. For each of the four remaining adjectives, write a sentence illustrating its use.

boisterous	homogeneous	miscellaneous	presumptuous
capricious	ingenious	momentous	specious
extraneous	ingenuous	obnoxious	strenuous
fallacious	ludicrous	precocious	supercilious
fastidious	malicious		

1 Most teachers prefer a class that is fairly *consistent in having pupils of the same level*.

2 The hotel porter gave me a *contemptuous and haughty* stare as I alighted from the bus with a rucksack and approached the entrance.

3 Mountain-climbing can often be dangerous in winter because of the *unpredictable and ever-changing* weather.

4 Nobody could agree with the speaker because all his arguments and ideas sprang from assumptions that were *based on error*.

5 What a pity it is that some cheeses have such a *thoroughly unpleasant* smell that people are deterred from eating them!

6 Children *who develop faculties at an unusually early age* do not always fulfil their promise later in life.

7 This writer keeps strictly to his subject, and is careful not to introduce any matter *that is not directly relevant to the subject*.

8 Only a person who can't think for himself will be taken in by arguments *that seem right or true but are not really so*.

9 In a speech *of great importance and gravity*, the Prime Minister announced that Britain would join a politically united Europe.

10 The man's fellow workers felt he had been *taking an unwarranted liberty* in putting himself forward as their spokesman.

11 When questioned by the master about a theft from a cloakroom, the boy, with an *open and innocent* expression on his face, pretended to know nothing about it.

12 The newspaper was sued for having made remarks *motivated by ill will and spite* about the famous singer.

13 At certain ages, many children are *very difficult to please or very particular* about the food they eat and the clothes they wear.

14 Fifty years ago, the idea of flying to the moon appeared *absurd or ridiculous*.

263 Replace the words in italics by a single adjective ending in -ous, -ious, -uous, or -eous, making any necessary changes in word order.

1 Comedians must depend to some extent on the fact that laughter is *likely to spread to or influence others*.

2 They chose the village hall for the party as it was *roomy* and had, at the same time, a homely atmosphere.

3 The audience at the circus broke into *natural and unforced* applause as the acrobat completed his most daring turn.

4 Trees *that shed their leaves each year* look very bare in winter.

5 In some of his experiments with dogs, Pavlov had to keep them from food until they were *almost fierce from lack of food* in order to induce the desired response to stimuli.

6 Contrary to expectations, the House was far from *being all of the same mind* on the question of building new universities.

7 Comparatively few people are *able to use either hand with equal facility*.

8 Until the nineteenth century, governments tended to view the problem of the aged and the poor with *hard and insensitive* indifference.

9 Shop assistants must sometimes find it difficult to remain *polite and showing good manners* when faced with an unpleasant or rude customer.

10 In Elizabethan times, censorship of the drama was used mainly to prevent the presentation of plays that contained ideas *that were* either *intended to make the people disobey the Government* or *that spoke about God in a disrespectful or wicked way*.

264 Complete the sentences with an adjective ending in *-ous*, *-ious*, *-uous*, or *-eous*, according to the definitions given in brackets.

1 Perhaps he was simply trying to make an impression, but I found him rather . . . (full of self-importance)

2 The houses were clearly subsiding. Several . . . cracks had appeared in the walls. (having a threatening or unfavourable aspect)

3 In some parts of England, river pollution is now reaching a level where it could be . . . to health. (likely to cause harm or injury)

4 His eldest daughter was growing up into a . . . young lady. (lively, high-spirited)

5 London was once . . . for its smog, but things have improved since the introduction of smokeless zones. (well known for a bad reason)

6 The lawyer advised the publishers to withdraw from the book

several passages that might be considered ... (likely to damage the character or reputation of someone)

7 Our short cut proved to be a very hilly and ... road. (full of twists and bends)

8 Some students took ... notes during the lecture. (plentiful, in abundance)

9 In the Hebrides, off the coast of Scotland, there has been a revival in ... crafts such as weaving. (native, belonging naturally to the area)

10 The sentence he had written was ... (capable of more than one interpretation)

11 It seemed to me that the taxi driver was taking a most ... route. Perhaps he just didn't know the way. (roundabout or indirect)

12 An older generation often regards the behaviour of the young as ... (shocking; beyond all reasonable limits)

265 Form adjectives ending in *-ous*, *-ious*, *-uous*, or *-eous*, according to the definitions given, and write sentences illustrating their use.

1 taking care not to make mistakes or get into danger (c . . .)
2 offering service that is not wanted; intrusive (o . . .)
3 flourishing, successful, thriving
4 difficult, requiring the use of much energy (a . . .)
5 careful to act according to what one's conscience tells one is right; showing a strong sense of duty
6 full of a strong desire to do or be something, or for success, fame, or honour
7 untrustworthy or disloyal; not to be depended on (tr . . .)
8 happening or done at the same time
9 costly or luxurious (s . . .)
10 merry or gay, usually in a rather noisy way (b . . .)
11 delighting in the infliction of injury (v . . .)
12 showing or influenced by unreasonable belief in the supernatural, in magic or in witchcraft

Adjectives and verbs ending in -ate[1]

266 Form adjectives ending in *-ate* according to the definitions given, and write sentences illustrating their use.

[1] See also Exercises 283–285.

1 thoughtless of others
2 avoiding extremes
3 permitted by law
4 unable to read or write
5 in proper proportion with (com . . .)
6 having little or no hope
7 inborn or natural
8 stubborn or inflexible of will
9 occurring, done, at once; coming nearest
10 sufficient
11 loving, showing love or fondness
12 dominated by, or easily giving way to, strong feelings (p . . .)
13 pure, faultless, right in every detail (im . . .)
14 fine, soft or tender (d . . .)

267 Replace the words in italics by a suitable form of a verb ending in -*ate*, making any necessary changes in word order.

1 The two authors *worked together* on the book.
2 While he was a prisoner of war, his captors attempted to *instil their own beliefs into* him.
3 Investors have seen the value of their shares *go down* considerably during the last six months.
4 Far from improving matters, what you have done has only *made* the problem *worse*.
5 The fact that the management is trying to reach agreement with five separate unions has tended to *make* the negotiations *more difficult and complex*.
6 It is now clear that members of the Conservative Party were not *trying to make the situation seem more serious than it was* when they claimed that the country was still facing enormous problems.
7 The cross-examining lawyer was soon able to show that the witness had simply *invented* the story from beginning to end.
8 The new methods will *make easier* the speedy handling of goods in the docks.
9 The two thieves gained access to the house by *pretending to be* policemen.
10 The whole consignment of tinned food was condemned as being *impure and likely to cause disease*.

11 Next year, we shall *prepare* a much larger area of ground for growing crops.
12 The Government has been forced to abandon its incomes policy in order to *pacify* the unions.

268 Form verbs ending in -*ate* according to the definitions given, and write sentences illustrating their use.

1 pull up by the roots, get rid of (e . . .)
2 utterly destroy (a . . .)
3 take part in
4 make inquiries into
5 soak thoroughly (s . . .)
6 restore to good condition (ren . . .)
7 fill with holes (p . . .)
8 estimate too highly
9 propose for election (n . . .)
10 make very angry (inf . . .)
11 turn into vapour
12 subject to questioning

269 Instructions as above

1 have commanding influence and position (d . . .)
2 supply land with water
3 preserve in memory by celebration (com . . .)
4 try to do as well as or better than (e . . .)
5 pierce, enter into
6 look forward to a thing before it comes
7 buy or sell where there is a great risk of loss and a great chance of gain; form opinion (without having complete knowledge)
8 go round, revolve
9 go through the main points of again (re . . .)
10 place apart or alone (i . . .)
11 look at or think about seriously
12 use movements of the hands and arms to express ideas or feelings

Verbs ending in -fy

270 Complete the sentences with a suitable tense or form of a verb ending in -*fy*, according to the definitions given in brackets.

1 He was so enraged that nothing I could say or do would . . . him. (calm or quieten down)
2 This new motor policy . . . the holder against all risks. (give safeguard or protection by means of insurance)
3 The rescued climbers said they had drunk hot chocolate to . . . themselves against the cold. (support or strengthen)
4 After months of negotiations, the two sides have now . . . the new agreement. (confirm or formally accept)
5 In our tour of the factory, we saw the molten metal being poured into moulds, where it quickly . . . (become hard or firm)
6 The witness . . . that he had seen the accused leaving the house at around midnight. (give evidence)
7 Even some experts are . . . as to how the Government arrived at the latest set of trade figures. (puzzle, bewilder)
8 In his budget speech, the Chancellor of the Exchequer went to great lengths to . . . his decision to raise income tax. (show to be right, reasonable, or proper)
9 Independent auditors were called in to . . . the figures given in the Company's annual accounts. (check the truth and accuracy of)
10 In England, one must follow a three years' course of training to . . . as a teacher. (become entitled to work)
11 The effect of the latest round of wage increases is to . . . the attempts of the Government to keep wages and prices under control. (make useless, make null and void)
12 The speaker was invited to . . . some of his earlier remarks, which had caused quite a stir among the audience. (make larger or fuller, give more details relating to)

271 Form verbs ending in -*fy* according to the definitions given, and write sentences illustrating their use. (NB. Except in No. 12, the verb is directly related to one of the words in the definition.)

1 make pure
2 make or become clear
3 fill with terror
4 put right

5 give notice of, report
6 make false or incorrect
7 make or become liquid
8 arrange in classes or groups
9 make or become more intense
10 illustrate by example; be an example of
11 form into one, unite
12 be a symbol of; be representative of (t . . .)

Verbs ending in -ize

272 Form verbs ending in -*ize* according to the definitions given, and write sentences illustrating their use.

1 make (soil) productive
2 make of one size, shape, quality, etc., according to fixed standards
3 prepare for movement or action
4 practise terrorism upon
5 reduce to a minimum
6 use sparingly
7 speak in general terms
8 give authority to
9 subject to penalty
10 establish a colony
11 put in danger (j . . .)
12 make permissible by law

273 Instructions as above

1 understand, be fully conscious of, see clearly (r . . .)
2 arouse horror and indignation in a person (sc . . .)
3 compose or produce something without preparation (im . . .)
4 act as deputy
5 bring up to date, make suitable for present-day needs
6 say that one is sorry for doing wrong
7 support by means of a subsidy
8 be or become a specialist
9 become fact (m . . .)
10 represent, be a symbol of
11 make a victim of
12 go through carefully and correct where necessary

Words with variable stress and pronunciation

274–282 Each of the following words can function as a verb, and can also function as either a noun or an adjective. The grammatical function of the words is reflected in the stress pattern employed. If they function as verbs, the stress falls on the second syllable, whereas if they function as nouns or adjectives, the stress falls on the first syllable (in many cases, the vowel sounds also change):

> He refused to believe what I said. (verb = /ri'fju:zd/)
> The streets were littered with refuse. (noun = /'refju:s/)

Write sentences using the words either (*a*) as verbs, or (*b*) as nouns or adjectives, and state on which syllable the stress falls in the words as you have used them.

274

1 accent
2 contest
3 object
4 rebel
5 project
6 abstract

275

1 transfer
2 compound
3 convict
4 export
5 suspect
6 imprint

276

1 perfect
2 extract
3 exploit
4 discount
5 attribute
6 transport

277

1 torment
2 absent
3 compress
4 escort
5 essay
6 contrast

278

1 frequent
2 convert
3 present
4 conflict
5 increase
6 progress
7 refill

279

1 conduct
2 record
3 contract
4 desert
5 incense
6 subject
7 fragment

280

1 converse
2 redress
3 content
4 protest
5 prospect
6 combine
7 incline

281

1 insult
3 permit
3 confine
4 compact
5 decrease
6 dictate
7 reject

282

1 upset
5 digest

2 produce
6 overflow

3 entrance
7 survey

4 addict
8 reprint

¹ See also page 273.

283–285 Each of the following words[1] can function as a verb, and can also function as either a noun or an adjective. The grammatical function of the words is reflected in the pronunciation of the syllable *-ate*. If they function as verbs, *-ate* is pronounced /eit/, whereas if they function as nouns or adjectives, *-ate* is pronounced /it/:

> He graduated at Yale University. (verb = /'graedjueitid/)
> He is a graduate of Yale University. (noun = /'graedjuit/)

Write sentences using the words either (*a*) as verbs, or (*b*) as nouns or adjectives, and state the pronunciation of the syllable *-ate* in the words as you have used them.

283	284	285
1 appropriate	1 degenerate	1 precipitate
2 estimate	2 delegate	2 animate
3 intimate	3 desolate	3 advocate
4 deliberate	4 separate	4 approximate
5 elaborate	5 articulate	5 predicate
6 moderate	6 co-ordinate	6 regenerate
7 duplicate	7 alternate	7 subordinate
8 associate	8 repatriate	8 initiate

Prefixes and suffixes

286–293 Explain the force of the prefixes in the words given. Give at least two other words formed with each prefix, and write sentences illustrating their use.

286	287	288	289
1 *omni*bus	1 *non*sense	1 *anti*pathy	1 *ambi*dextrous
2 *peri*meter	2 *counter*part	2 *co*herent	2 *auto*matic
3 *for*go	3 *post*pone	3 *homo*phone	3 *inter*fere
4 *fore*cast	4 *pre*mature	4 *bi*cycle	4 *circum*ference
5 *deci*pher	5 *semi*circle	5 *multi*ply	5 *ante*cedent

---

[1] See also Exercises 266–269.

290	291	292	293
1 *mono*tony	1 *syndi*cate	1 *ob*trusive	1 *bene*factor
2 *over*charge	2 *trans*form	2 *con*nect	2 *sub*tract
3 *super*intend	3 *sur*plus	3 *mis*lead	3 *pseudo*-Gothic
4 *retro*active	4 *uni*form	4 *e*vict	4 *hyper*bole
5 *mal*treat	5 *out*class	5 *pro*ceed	5 *contra*vene

294–296 Make as many verbs as you can from the stems given by adding different prefixes. Write sentences illustrating the use of each verb, or of a noun or adjective derived from it.

294	295	296
1 -tract	1 -tain	1 -pose
2 -pel	2 -mit	2 -scribe
3 -fer	3 -press	3 -sist
4 -vert	4 -nounce	4 -tend
5 -cur	5 -pound	5 -claim
6 -duce	6 -plete	6 -sent
7 -sume	7 -voke	7 -volve

297–299 Explain the force of the suffixes in the words given. Give at least two other words formed with each suffix, and write sentences illustrating their use.

297	298	299
1 trouble*some*	1 nomin*ee*	1 speed*ometer*
2 note*worthy*	2 wait*ress*	2 fruit*less*
3 old*ish*	3 leaf*let*	3 phil*ology*
4 headmaster*ship*	4 strength*en*	4 photo*graphy*
5 parent*hood*	5 mountain*eer*	5 dormit*ory*

Compound words

300–304 Make compound words (with hyphens if necessary) according to the definitions, using the word given as the first part of the compound. Write sentences illustrating the use of each word.

300

1 fool   (*a*) taking unnecessary risks
        (*b*) made in such a way that even a fool can understand or use safely

2 heart (*a*) sincere, deeply felt
        (*b*) causing deep grief or distress
        (*c*) suffering deeply from grief

3 stop   (*a*) a temporary substitute
        (*b*) late news printed in a special column in a newspaper
        (*c*) an instrument used for recording the time taken for a race

4 head   (*a*) forward motion, progress
        (*b*) self-willed, obstinate
        (*c*) words printed in large or heavy type giving information about the subject-matter of a newspaper article
        (*d*) place from which (e.g. police or army) operations are controlled

5 foot   (*a*) a safe place for the foot, especially when climbing
        (*b*) a row of lights along the front of a stage
        (*c*) sound of footsteps

301

1 over   (*a*) covered with clouds
        (*b*) sum of money drawn or borrowed from a bank in excess of one's deposit
        (*c*) failure to notice something

2 by   (*a*) a road that enables the traveller to avoid going through the centre of a town
        (*b*) regulation made by a local authority
        (*c*) substance made or obtained during the manufacture of some other substance

3 long   (*a*) tediously long
        (*b*) patient and uncomplaining in spite of trouble, pain, or insults
        (*c*) dating from long ago, not recent

4 book   (*a*) person who keeps accounts (e.g. of a business)
        (*b*) person devoted to reading

(c) supports to keep books upright when they are not kept on a shelf

5 shop (a) made dirty or faded by being shown or handled in a shop

(b) one who steals goods while pretending to be a customer

(c) one elected by his fellow workmen to act as their spokesman on conditions of work

302

1 hand (a) pair of metal rings joined by a short chain for securing a prisoner's hands

(b) printed notice circulated by hand

(c) not made by machine

2 light (a) cheerful, free from care

(b) clever at stealing

(c) giddy; thoughtless or forgetful

3 stand (a) unfriendly, distant in manner

(b) stoppage

(c) thing or person to be used or called on if necessary

4 play (a) someone who often goes to the theatre

(b) dramatist

(c) piece of land for children to play on

5 mouth (a) one who speaks for others or puts forward the views of others

(b) small musical instrument with metal reeds played by blowing into small openings

303

1 up (a) tumult, violent disturbance

(b) outcome, result

(c) padding and covering of chairs and sofas

2 self (a) selfish, never thinking of the interests of others

(b) obviously true, needing no proof

(c) convinced of one's own goodness

3 lay (a) person who is not an expert with regard to a profession, science or art

(b) manner in which something is arranged or disposed

    (*c*) piece of surfaced land at the side of a road where cars may park

4 show (*a*) place where goods are displayed

    (*b*) a full declaration of facts, intentions, or strength

    (*c*) something produced mainly for show or to attract attention

5 oil (*a*) waterproof cloth

    (*b*) container for oil

    (*c*) place where oil is found

304

1 fire (*a*) made of material that will not burn

    (*b*) gun, rifle, or revolver

    (*c*) company or group of men that put out fires

2 wind (*a*) something built or planted to give protection from the wind

    (*b*) the front window of a motor-car

    (*c*) unexpected and lucky receipt of money, or source of money

3 quick (*a*) mentally alert

    (*b*) easily made angry

    (*c*) expanse of soil that will not support any weight, but sucks down anyone who tries to walk on it

4 back (*a*) accumulation of work or business not yet attended to

    (*b*) principal piece of scenery on the stage, often left visible even though other parts of the scenery are changed

    (*c*) speaking evil of a person

5 eye (*a*) circumstance that brings enlightenment and surprise

    (*b*) an ugly or unpleasant thing to look at

    (*c*) one who has himself seen something happen

Word formation

305–313 Give an adjective and noun related to each verb, and write sentences illustrating the use of each word.

 e.g. receive (verb) receptive (adjective) reception (noun)

                  or receipt

                  or receptacle

a. He should have *received* the money by now. (verb)

b. I enjoy teaching that class because the children's minds are so *receptive*. (adjective)

c. A *reception* was held in the village hall after the wedding. (noun) *or* I should keep the *receipt* for the money for the time being. *or* 'Please place your cigarette ends in the *receptacles* provided.'

305

1 persist
2 abstain
3 complete
4 retain
5 proceed
6 deepen

306

1 deceive
2 vary
3 grieve
4 authorize
5 compare
6 explore

307

1 defy
2 explain
3 explode
4 irritate
5 imitate
6 observe

308

1 depend
2 conceive
3 attend
4 fail
5 hasten
6 fertilize

309

1 migrate
2 sympathize
3 repeat
4 presume
5 analyse
6 defraud

310

1 simplify
2 defend
3 conclude
4 heal
5 invigorate
6 apologize

311

1 appear
2 distinguish
3 repel
4 remember
5 interpret
6 encumber

312

1 reveal
2 avenge
3 broadcast
4 em-
   phasize
5 exceed
6 resolve

313

1 continue
2 exemplify
3 foresee
4 submit
5 inform
6 prosper

Homonyms

314–323 Each of the words given has at least two distinct meanings. Write two sentences for each word illustrating its different uses. The words given may be used as verbs in any tense or form, as nouns in the singular or the plural, or as adjectives, e.g. *stage*:

a. At this *stage*, it would be better to confine the discussions to general matters. (noun)

b. The local dramatic society will *stage* a production of *Pygmalion* in the autumn. (verb)

314 **315** **316** **317** **318**

314	315	316	317	318
1 book	1 strike	1 fine	1 leaf	1 post
2 bear	2 measure	2 party	2 just	2 stick
3 bank	3 rifle	3 case	3 chest	3 slight
4 mark	4 side	4 well	4 box	4 saw
5 bill	5 leave	5 type	5 bark	5 train
6 table	6 mean	6 right	6 sentence	6 sound
7 pore	7 wing	7 nail	7 file	7 row
8 blow	8 hide	8 grave	8 express	8 execute

319 **320** **321** **322** **323**

319	320	321	322	323
1 record	1 address	1 curious	1 mould	1 just
2 tear	2 note	2 mine	2 fair	2 park
3 state	3 tender	3 fray	3 dock	3 found
4 grate	4 might	4 can	4 drill	4 pen
5 rear	5 hamper	5 jar	5 limp	5 brief
6 swallow	6 rent	6 shed	6 sole	6 tap
7 lean	7 matter	7 utter	7 yard	7 lead
8 board	8 bore	8 firm	8 pitch	8 temper

Homophones

324–329 Each of the words below is one of a pair or group of words that have *exactly* the *same pronunciation*, but a different spelling and a different meaning. Supply one other such word in each case, and write a sentence illustrating its use, e.g.

find (/faind/)   *fined* (/faind/)

The driver was *fined* for causing an obstruction with his car.

324

1 allowed
2 blue
3 berry
4 cereal
5 days
6 road
7 higher
8 key
9 nose
10 male

325

1 horse
2 miner *minor*
3 pier *pear*
4 principle *principal*
5 gilt *guild*
6 saw
7 through *thro*
8 way
9 wear *where*
10 board *bored*

326

1 caught
2 cue
3 die
4 guest
5 least
6 morning
7 praise
8 stare
9 tax
10 whether

327

1 bowled
2 ceiling
3 frays
4 hole
5 heard
6 one
7 pair
8 paste
9 rain
10 sent

328

1 bear
2 course
3 fair
4 feet
5 hall
6 pore
7 passed
8 raise
9 sell
10 tire

329

1 crews
2 flower
3 idle
4 piece
5 sight
6 sweet
7 sort
8 war
9 sauce
10 steak

Related word groups

330–335 Arrange the words in four groups of six. Three group should each contain only words that are related, and the fourth group should contain six unrelated words.

330

locomotive   palace   sleepers   reins
chain   court   impudence   handlebars
trial   rails   mudguard   carriage
eraser   saddle   counsel   sentence
tender   plaintiff   fine   pedals
inner tube   offer   attempt   compartment

259

331

gramophone	suit	chest	exchange
pin	caller	catalogue	record
needle	suite	directory	convict
receiver	visitor	amplifier	sofa
armchair	loudspeaker	dial	office
slot	bureau	turntable	divan

332

session	account	cabinet	navigator
cheque	truce	loan	draughtsman
speaker	fuselage	debate	safe
hangar	poster	stewardess	parliament
extension	overdraft	kerb	bankrupt
propeller	constituency	cockpit	decrease

333

warehouse	bough	eiderdown	bedstead
platform	dock	branch	trunk
twig	mattress	blanket	concrete
port	bark	mist	sheets
sherry	dog	log	barge
bolster	quay	cargo	subsidiary

334

clutch	windscreen	tiles	indicator
grasp	drainpipe	wallet	calendar
chimney	socket	flex	dashboard
engine	seed	shoes	gutter
switch	bulb	loft	shade
mortar	boot	lamp	shadow

335

ladder	eyewitnesses	banisters	grip
congregation	rung	audience	funnel
leak	port-hole	retreat	stairs
tunnel	ornament	cabin	onlookers
flight	sightseers	hold	deck
bridge	landing	spectators	boycott

Phrasal and prepositional verbs[1]

1 The terms *phrasal verb* and *prepositional verb* are employed here
to denote verbs used with an adverbial or prepositional particle
to form a group whose meaning is, in many cases, independent
of the separate elements that constitute it. Exercises in the use
of such semi-compounds have been included not only because
of the problem of word order raised specifically by phrasal
verbs (verb + adverbial particle), but also because of the larger
and more inherent problem of the meaning of phrasal and prepositional verbs in general.[2]

The elements that make up phrasal and prepositional verbs
can be deceptively simple: students will know the meaning of
put and *up*, or *take* and *after*, but the two words used in combination have quite independent idiomatic meanings, *give
lodging to* and *resemble*, respectively:

> If you've nowhere to stay, we could easily *put* you *up*.
> John obviously *takes after* his father.

2 Compare these sentences:

1*a* He *looked* / up the chimney.
  b He *looked up* / the meaning of the word.
2*a* He *came* / across the road.
  b He *came across* / an interesting book.

In a comparison of these pairs of sentences, two observations
may be made:

i In sentences *a*, the words *up* and *across* are both prepositions
whose function is to express the relationship between a verb and
a noun, and in each case, the preposition is more strongly attracted
to the noun following it than to the verb before it.

---

[1] See also Exercises 94–96 (The Passive).
[2] Students will find that the meaning of phrasal verbs consisting of verbs of
movement + an adverbial particle is often clear from the separate elements:

> Please *bring* the book *back* when you've finished reading it.
> Surely you *haven't thrown* the letter *away*?

For this reason, such phrasal verbs have been excluded from the examples
used in this introduction.

ii In each of the sentences *b*, it is clear that the particle is more strongly attracted to the verb than to the noun, and that one could make a pause only after the verb + particle group. In the case of *1a*, moreover, we could form the question 'Where did he look?' (= 'up the chimney'), whereas in the case of *1b*, we could not ask, similarly, 'Where did he look?' (= *'up the meaning of the word'). It is also clear that the groups *looked up* and *came across* as used in sentences *b* have idiomatic meanings independent of their separate elements.

To look up is a phrasal verb (verb + adverbial particle), and *to come across* is a prepositional verb (verb + prepositional particle), and each has different characteristics with regard to word order.

3 Word order after *phrasal verbs*[1] shows a clearly defined pattern:

i With phrasal verbs used transitively, the position of the adverbial particle is determined by the nature of the object:

a. If the object is a pronoun, the particle comes after it:

> You can *count* me *out*. (= exclude)
> The customer *turned* it *down*. (= rejected)

b. If the object is a noun, the particle may come before or after it:

> They managed to *put out* the fire. (= extinguish)
> *or* They managed to *put* the fire *out*.

c. If the object is a long noun phrase, a noun with a qualifying clause, or a noun clause, the particle comes immediately after the verb, so as to avoid too great a separation of the verb and its particle:

> They *turned down* lots of perfectly good suggestions. (= rejected)
> They're bound to *turn down* any suggestions I make.
> You should *think over* what I've just suggested. (= consider further)

ii With intransitive phrasal verbs, the particle comes immediately after the verb:

> He *broke off* as I came into the room. (= stopped talking)

[1] The adverbial particles most commonly used to form part of a phrasal verb are: up, down, in, out, on, off, away, back.

4 *Prepositional verbs* raise no such problems, the prepositional particle never being placed anywhere but immediately after the verb:

John obviously *takes after* his father. (= resembles)

The same is true of verb groups consisting of a verb + *two* particles (one adverbial and one prepositional), sometimes called *prepositional phrasal verbs*:

I refused to *put up with* his rudeness any longer. (= tolerate)
The plan *came in for* a lot of criticism. (= met)

These differences in word order after phrasal and prepositional verbs help us to distinguish the two types of semi-compound, and are the most helpful feature for a student to learn to recognize initially. Other differentiating tests, such as stress or the absence of stress on the particle, are more difficult for a student to apply. Students may refer to *Exercises in English Patterns and Usage, Book 3*, by Ronald Mackin (Oxford University Press) for practice material on the identification of phrasal verbs. Teachers may refer to the books by F. R. Palmer and B. M. H. Strang, listed on pages xvii and xviii).

It is with phrasal and prepositional verbs whose meanings can least easily be understood from their separate elements that the following exercises are mainly concerned. Students can learn their meanings only by a steady process of assimilation, as with all new vocabulary, and no attempt should be made to work through the exercises systematically day after day.

336 Replace the words in italics by a suitable pronoun, making any necessary changes in word order.

a. The applicant filled in *the form*.
  The applicant filled *it* in. (Phrasal verb)
b. John takes after *his father*.
  John takes after *him*. (Prepositional verb)

1 Companies do a great deal of research in order to find out *exactly what their customers want*.
2 The motorist ruled out *one particular route* because the road had a poor surface.
3 Who's looking after *your house* while you're away?

4 Employees working in research departments are forbidden to give away *confidential information*.

5 We might have known he would blurt out *the news* to everybody!

6 I looked at *the problem* quite differently.

7 His publishers will soon be bringing out *his latest collection of essays*.

8 The Company has put forward *several new proposals*.

9 You should put away *the medicine* where the children can't get at *the medicine*.

10 The Council has decided to try out *new defensive barriers* along the centre of the motorway.

11 Accountants seem to develop a remarkable facility for adding up *a long column of figures*.

12 If the dog isn't kept chained up, he goes for *everyone who enters the garden*.

13 Don't come here stirring up *trouble*!

14 I took to *your friend* as soon as I met him.

337 Replace the pronouns in italics by the words at the end of the sentences, making any necessary changes in word order. If you think there are two possibilities, state both.

    a. The applicant filled *it* in. (the form)
        The applicant filled *the form* in.
        or The applicant filled in *the form*.

    b. The applicant filled *it* in. (the long and complicated application form)
        The applicant filled in *the long and complicated application form*.

1 The Minister brushed *them* aside. (all objections)

2 The Minister brushed *them* aside. (objections made by members of the Opposition)

3 The Embassy refused to hand *him* over. (the man who sought political asylum)

4 It is not yet clear who will take *it* on. (the job)

5 It is not yet clear who will take *it* on. (the captaincy of the English touring team)

6 He always wraps *them* up in a cloud of obscurity. (his arguments)

7 The State should not interfere in matters where it cannot bring *it* about. (an improvement)

8 Insurance companies expect clients shortly to be putting *them* in after the recent floods. (some very heavy claims)

9 To become competitive in world markets, British manufacturers must keep *them* down to the absolute minimum. (their production costs)

10 The industrial spy handed *them* over. (the confidential papers he had obtained)

11 They are trying *them* out in America. (many new synthetic products)

12 No one brought *it* up. (the question)

13 No one brought *them* up. (the questions everyone most wanted to hear asked)

14 I read *it* quickly through. (the letter I had just received)

338–344 Replace the words in italics, using the verbs indicated at the head of the exercises together with an adverbial or prepositional particle, and making any necessary changes in word order. (NB. In some cases, two particles are required.)

338 TURN

1 The manager *refused* his request for a day off.
2 I waited half an hour for my friend, but he didn't *come*.
3 It's about time we *went to bed*.
4 Would you *lower* the gas when the kettle boils?
5 His landlady *evicted* him for not paying his rent.
6 The police told the suspected thief to *empty* his pockets.
7 Crowds of people had to be *refused admission to* the theatre.
8 This popular sports car is now being *produced* at the rate of a thousand a week.
9 Our visit *proved* to be a waste of time because fog reduced visibility.
10 After being hit by a huge wave, the rowing-boat *capsized*.
11 Although the dog appeared to be friendly, it would *attack* anyone who tried to fondle it.

339 GET

1 We wondered how he was *progressing* in his new job.
2 I don't think I shall *complete* all this work this afternoon.

3 She is so upset at her husband's death that I don't think she will ever *recover from* the shock.

4 She put the book in a place where the child couldn't *reach* it.

5 As it's got to be done, we may as well *have done with* it.

6 The prisoner *escaped* from the prison by climbing a ten-foot wall.

7 He says that his lack of success is beginning to *depress* him.

8 You must really *apply yourself* to some serious work.

9 I see no way of *avoiding* the problem.

10 Their business partnership flourished despite the fact that they didn't *agree* well personally.

11 It must be *nearly* ten o'clock!

340 TAKE

1 The teacher said I ought to *start learning* French.

2 He *resembles* his father in many ways.

3 The son *assumed control of* the business on the retirement of his father.

4 The man looked so respectable and honest that I was completely *deceived*.

5 He *undertook* so much work that he couldn't really do it efficiently.

6 The secretary *wrote* the letter in shorthand as the manager dictated it to her.

7 When he discovered the truth, he *retracted* all he had previously said.

8 That teacher has a way with children: they seem to *like* her immediately.

9 I don't wish to *occupy* too much of your time.

10 The shopkeeper agreed to *deduct* 5 per cent from the bill.

341 PUT

1 I had to *postpone* my visit because of the weather.

2 He refused to *tolerate* laziness on the part of his pupils.

3 They were very *annoyed* when they learned that the train had been cancelled without notice.

4 The rebellion was *suppressed* by the army.

5 He had managed to *save* quite a lot of money over the years.

6 He *advanced* the theory that those who had money always made money.

7 His aggressiveness was *attributed* to the fact that he had had an overbearing father.

8 How many hours do you have to *work* each week?

9 Don't let the fact that I didn't enjoy the play *deter* you *from* seeing it.

10 The workers have *made* a claim for higher wages.

11 When the teacher asked who had broken the window, all the boys *assumed* an air of innocence.

12 If I visit you at the week-end, will you be able to *give* me *lodging* for one night?

342 STAND

1 What does this abbreviation *mean*?

2 Many people dislike Communism and all that it *represents*.

3 I must make it clear that I refuse to *tolerate* such behaviour.

4 He hoped that when the time came I would *keep* my promise.

5 One man particularly *was conspicuous* at the meeting.

6 When he realized that his nomination would mean competing with his closest friend, he decided to *withdraw*.

7 Troops were ordered to *be in a state of readiness* for action.

8 The understudy had to *take the part of* the leading actor, who had fallen ill.

9 The employers in this case were obliged to *take no part* in the dispute, which was purely the result of inter-union rivalry.

10 The machine soon went wrong: it was never intended to *withstand* the rough treatment it was given.

343 COME

1 While looking through the books he *found* an old and valuable map.

2 Although he was unconscious when we found him, he soon *recovered consciousness*.

3 When his father died he *received* a lot of money under his father's will.

4 We never discovered how the accident *occurred*.

5 Although it seemed a good idea in theory, in practice it didn't *succeed*.

6 His new book will *be published* next week.

7 The whole truth *became known* at the trial.

8 The film didn't *equal* our expectations.

9 No one thought that any good could *result from* discussing the question further.

10 The problem of finance *is* always *raised* on such occasions.

344 GIVE

1 He *resigned from* his job in the Foreign Office when the truth about his past became known.

2 Because of difficulties in getting a visa, we had to *relinquish* the idea of visiting Russia.

3 Although he agreed with me on most points, there was one on which he was unwilling to *yield*.

4 He *returned* the money to the man who had lost it.

5 The bad cheese *emitted* a very unpleasant smell.

6 The men crossing the Sahara found to their horror that their supplies would *come to an end* before they reached safety.

7 The English like coal fires even though these don't always *produce* much heat.

8 Every time cigarettes go up in price, many people try to *stop* smoking.

9 The escaped prisoner had tried to disguise his appearance, but a scar on his cheek *betrayed* him.

345-346 Replace the words in italics by a verb in the appropriate tense.

345

1 I'm afraid I have to *go back on* my promise to lend you the money.

2 Your speech *went down* very well at last night's dinner. (passive)

3 Do you ever *go in* for any of the newspaper competitions?

4 Despite the noise, he *went on* working as if nothing were happening.

5 We haven't got time to *go into* that question now.

6 As it's most important that nothing should go wrong, let's *go over* the details of the plan again.

7 The index of industrial production *went up* by 4 per cent last month.

8 Many new buildings have *gone up* in London during the last year. (Passive)

9 I think you are most ungrateful, considering all the trouble I *went to*.

10 The fuse had been inserted wrongly, and the bomb failed to *go off*.

11 I think we should *go back* before it gets dark.

12 He simply *went off* without saying a word of apology.

1 Please *look* me *up* if ever you come to London.

2 We went to *look over* the house, but it wasn't suitable.

3 The police decided that they must *look* further *into* the matter.

4 A leader must be one whom the people can *look up to*.

5 He *looks down on* people with less knowledge than himself.

6 The teacher *looked on* the student's absence as a serious matter.

7 I should be grateful if you would *look in* at the library to see if a book has arrived for me.

8 Please *look through* the agreement before you sign it.

9 He *looked for* a reward when he returned the valuable ring to its owner.

10 Although it had been a bad year, the chairman thought that business was now *looking up*.

347 Complete the sentences with a phrasal verb opposite in meaning to those in italics, e.g.

> When they had finished playing, the children were made to
> ... ... all the toys they had *taken out*.
> When they had finished playing, the children were made to
> *put away* (*or* back) all the toys they had taken out.

1 *Go away*, and don't ... ... till you're in a better frame of mind!

2 It's getting rather late. Perhaps we should *go back* rather than ... ...

3 No one likes the buildings they're *putting up* in place of the ones that were ... ...

4 If you want to help with the cooking, you'd better ... ... your jacket and *put on* this apron.

5 This picture keeps *falling down*. How can I make it ... ... ?

6 Let's *go out* somewhere. I'm tired of ... ... every evening.

7 Prices always seem to be ... ... It's about time they started *coming down*.

8 Having *picked up* several articles as if he intended to buy them, the customer ... them all ... again.

9 The plane *took off* from London at 09.00 and ... ... in Geneva at 10.30.

10 The racing cars ... ... at the corners and *speeded up* along the straights.

348 Instructions as above

1 My suitcase wasn't big enough. I *put in* everything I could, but I had to ... ... several things I would have liked to take.

2 It's nearly midnight. You can *stay up* if you like, but I'm ... ...

3 That's the wrong map. *Fold* it *up* and ... ... the other one.

4 The children who had finished their work were *let out* on time, but the others were ... ... for another twenty minutes.

5 Who's *taken down* the notice I ... ... ?

6 This page is loose. Whoever *tore* it *out* ought to have ... it back ...

7 The firm *took on* a lot of extra staff before Christmas, but ... them ... in January when business was slack.

8 The phone has gone dead. I told the man to *hold on* while I fetched you, but he must have ... ...

9 He was obviously hoping they would *take up* his suggestion, but for some reason they ... it ...

10 He *looks up to* people with money and ... ... everyone else.

349–351 Answer the questions with complete sentences, using the verbs indicated together with an adverbial or a prepositional particle.

349

1 What must you do if you find you are living beyond your means? (cut)

2 How do we express the fact that someone learns things quickly? (pick)

3 What would be done if it were found that a search was proving useless? (call)

4 What would two men do before entering into a partnership? (draw)

5 What would you say if you couldn't get rid of a cold? (shake)

6 What might a parent ask a child who had a guilty look on his face? (be)

7 How would you ask someone to confirm the truth of what you had said? (bear)

8 What are we expected to do when a friend shows a group photograph in which he appears? (pick)

9 How do we express the fact that there isn't enough for everyone? (go)

10 How would you describe a plan that had been carefully considered in every detail? (think)

11 What must a motorist do if the traffic lights show red? (pull)

12 What might you promise to do if someone made you an unusual proposal? (think) (Do not use 'about')

13 Before you bought a second-hand car, what would you want to do? (try)

14 How do we express the fact that a mine has been exhausted of its deposit? (work)

350

1 What might a crowd have to do if fire hoses were turned on it? (fall)

2 What would we say of a friend who had failed us in some way? (let)

3 How do we express the fact that a school term has ended? (break)

4 What do we say if we cannot read or understand what someone has written? (make)

5 When do you use a dictionary? (look) (Do not use 'for')

6 What does one do in order not to be late for an appointment? (set)

7 What would most parents like to think of their children? (bring)

8 What may happen when friends disagree and quarrel? (fall)

9 What do we fear may happen if a few people leave a party early? (break)

10 What might a magistrate agree to do with a first offender? (let)

11 What might happen to a plan if a majority of people withdrew their support? (fall)

12 How do we express the fact that one thing enhances the appearance of another? (set)

1 If a new way of doing things proves impracticable, what must you do? (fall)
2 If a student made a mistake, what would he expect the teacher to do? (point)
3 What might you say if someone were taking a very long time to reach a decision? (make)
4 How do we express the fact that bad weather seems likely to continue for some time? (set)
5 What would annoy you if you were going somewhere in a hurry by car? (break)
6 If a hunted man saw a policeman following him, what would he do? (make)
7 If someone fainted what would you try to do? (bring)
8 How would you describe a decrease in the circulation of a newspaper? (fall)
9 If the Government wished to investigate a matter of national importance what could it do? (set)
10 What would you do if you were criticizing someone in his absence and he suddenly entered the room? (break)
11 What do we say if there is a possibility that cannot be excluded? (rule)
12 What must we do if we have been delayed and wish nevertheless not to be late? (make)

Compound words derived from phrasal verbs

Besides being able to create phrasal verbs by adding different particles to commonly-used verbs (*take over*, *take in*, etc.), we can often also use in other combinations the elements of the phrasal verbs themselves (take over—overtake).

There are two different ways in which the elements of phrasal verbs may be combined. The verb and particle may be placed in reverse order to form a compound verb or noun: take over—overtake (verb), put out—output (noun):

> The Kenyan runner soon *overtook* the other competitors.
> *Output* at the factory has now risen considerably.

or the verb and particle may simply be joined, sometimes with a hyphen, to form a compound noun: break down—breakdown, make up—make-up:

Our car had a *breakdown*.
His girl friend uses a lot of *make-up*.

In some cases, both types of compound may be made from the same phrasal verb: take over—overtake—take-over.

As in words with variable stress,[1] the grammatical function of the compounds formed in this way is reflected in the stress pattern of the syllables or elements. If the compound is a verb, the main stress falls on the second element: overtake (ˌouvəˈteik); and if it is a noun, the stress falls on the first element: take-over (ˈteik-ouvə):

Couldn't we overtake that car in front?
The Company has changed considerably since the take-over.

Compounds formed from phrasal verbs are not necessarily related in meaning to the original verb:

A new manager *took over* last week. (= assumed control)
The Kenyan runner soon *overtook* the other competitors. (= caught up with and passed)

In some cases, two different compounds may be formed, corresponding to two different meanings of the original verb:

War *broke out* in 1914. (verb = began)
He was born at the *outbreak* of the war. (noun = beginning)
Three criminals *broke out* of the prison. (verb = escape)
There was a *break-out* at the prison. (noun = escape of prisoners)

English people make full use of this facility for forming new compounds, and the following exercises can give only a small selection of those in current use.

352 Complete the sentences with one of the compound nouns from the list at the beginning, using plural forms where necessary. Use each word once only.

break-out	lay-off	outbreak	set-back
bypass	look-over	outcry	upkeep
intake	offshoot	outlook	uptake

[1] See Exercises 274–282.

1 British hopes of a gold medal in the Olympic Games suffered a sharp . . . yesterday, when Smith failed to qualify during the preliminary heats.

2 The Royal Commission on Public Schools strongly favoured a broader social . . . to these schools.

3 The British company is a(n) . . . of a much larger American concern.

4 There was a public . . . when the Post Office proposed higher charges for postal services.

5 Many men have already been made idle by the stoppage, and further . . . will be inevitable unless agreement is reached soon.

6 The National Trust will accept suitable properties, provided sufficient funds are made available for their . . .

7 There was a sudden . . . of violence among students, following a period of relative calm.

8 Only one prisoner remains at large, following yesterday's . . . by six men from Dartmoor prison.

9 You can avoid going through the town centre by taking the . . .

10 We had time to give the property only a quick . . .

11 Some people have a very curious . . . on life.

12 I dropped several broad hints, but he seemed to be very slow on the . . .

353 Complete the sentences with a noun formed by a suitable combination of the words in brackets, using plural forms where necessary, e.g.

Many observers are pessimistic about the possibility of a successful . . . to the present round of talks. (come out)
Answer: *outcome*

1 The lower level of industrial activity is likely to lead to a considerable . . . in capital investment. (cut back)

2 As the . . . of answers to the questionnaire shows, there was rarely a full response to every question. (break down)

3 After a(n) . . . of over £10m. on new machinery during the last year, the factory is now among the most modern in Europe. At the same time, the . . . of the assembly lines has been radically changed. (lay out)

4 If the two companies merge, we can expect a great . . . in the electrical industry as a whole. (shake up)

5 Since last March, there has been an encouraging . . . in the volume of our exports. (turn up)

6 There has been a great . . . in industrial activity since the beginning of the year. (surge up)

7 Over-ambitiousness finally brought about his . . . (fall down)

8 Our company's . . . of this chain of stores will increase the number of our retail . . . to 250. (take over, let out)

9 The discovery of this latest drug marks a . . . in the treatment of the common cold. (break through)

10 In making the . . . to decimal coinage, Britain has drawn on the recent experience of other countries. (change over)

11 The company's . . . increased by 25 per cent last year. (turn over)

12 After being out of favour with investors for several years, the shares are now staging a . . . (come back)

354 Complete the sentences with a noun formed by a suitable combination of the verbs in brackets with one of the following particles: *back, by, down, off, out, up*. Use plural forms if necessary, e.g.

There has been a marked increase in industrial . . . during the past nine months. (put) Answer: *output*

1 There seems likely to be a . . . between the Government and the unions over the question of the new legislation to control wages and prices. (show)

2 We always keep a spare gallon of petrol in the car as a . . . (stand)

3 One of the cars involved in the accident was a complete . . . (write)

4 Despite its many . . . , the plan has much to commend it. (draw)

5 . . . for the moon is 06.00 tomorrow, and . . . in the Pacific will be at 15.30 on Friday. (blast, splash)

6 Two men thought to have been involved in the armed . . . of the bank are now helping the police with their inquiries. (hold)

7 Managerial staff made redundant by mergers often feel it is quite a . . . when they have to take a job at half their previous salary. (come)

8 There was yet another . . . yesterday at the factory over the question of tea-breaks. (walk)

9 The police will be keeping a sharp . . . for drug-peddlers at the pop festival. (look)

10 No one can yet predict what the . . . of the talks is likely to be. (come)

11 It's difficult to understand the exact nature of the . . . between the two firms. (tie)

12 The speaker's outrageous remarks were met by a(n) . . . of anger among the audience. (burst)

Irregular plurals

355 Rewrite the sentences, making the words in brackets plural.

1 The Leader of the Opposition recalled the (crisis) of the past year.

2 The ships were unloading their (cargo) on to the (wharf).

3 Many people think that (parent-in-law) are potentially a nuisance.

4 Poisonous (gas) were being discharged from the exhaust pipes of the (bus).

5 He arranged that his books should contain detailed (index).

6 The eyes are sometimes (index) of character.

7 Shakespearian (hero) are generally the victims of circumstance.

8 (A mouse) can sometimes take the cheese without being caught in the (mousetrap).

9 Highly-coloured (fungus) were growing near the base of the tree.

10 He wished to place certain (memorandum) before the committee.

11 He agreed that these were strange (phenomenon).

12 We cannot proceed on such unlikely (hypothesis).

13 Servicemen found guilty of desertion of duty are tried by (court martial).

14 The new (syllabus) will be drawn up according to different (criterion).

15 Television and newspapers are the mass (medium) of advertising.

16 The (thief) broke into the shop without attracting the attention of (passer-by).

17 Piano (solo) will be played by John Smith.

18 The police called for (eyewitness) to come forward and give evidence.

19 The accused men had carefully prepared what appeared to be good (alibi).

Idioms and proverbs

356–357 Each of the sentences contains one or more idioms (in italics). These common idioms are found particularly in newspapers, and they can easily pass unobserved or be misunderstood. Explain their meaning or use in the following contexts.

356

1 The modernization of British Railways *is* now *well under way*.
2 The pilot said that with one engine of the aeroplane out of action, it had been *touch and go* over the Channel.
3 The strike is to continue because of a last-minute *hitch* in the negotiations.
4 The Bolshoi Ballet Company *has taken* London *by storm*.
5 The Prime Minister has now to gain the support of *the rank and file*.
6 Nationalization is a *bone of contention* among members of the Labour Party.
7 British cars have *pride of place* at this year's International Motor Show.
8 The Chancellor said that the country's economy was *in better shape* than it had previously been, but that we were not yet *out of the wood*.
9 The Opposition cannot afford to *sit on the fence* in such an important matter.
10 Before criticizing the Government, the Opposition should *set its own house in order*.
11 Furniture manufacturers are now *feeling the pinch* of the latest hire purchase restrictions.
12 As to the Government's future plans, the Prime Minister is *playing his cards very close to his chest*.
13 Matters *came to a head* yesterday in the dock strike, when the Government threatened to call in troops.

357

1 The country cannot afford to *live from hand to mouth*, as it has been doing for the past few years; reserves must be built up to a satisfactory level.
2 Desirable as this plan is, many of its provisions will have *to be watered down* before it is generally acceptable.

3 Some Trade Unions look on a National Wages Council as *the thin end of the wedge*.

4 Unit Trusts have enabled the small investor *to have a stake in* industry.

5 New laws will be enacted in an attempt to close *the loopholes* in the present tax system.

6 Although the latest Russian proposal on a nuclear-test ban looks very much like an earlier one, the Western Powers think it would be unwise to reject it *out of hand*.

7 The Foreign Minister was *rapped* severely *over the knuckles* for *taking* what appeared to be *an independent line*.

8 The worker was *sent to Coventry* by his fellow workmen for refusing to join the Trade Union.

9 It is believed that Civil Servants *will be given short shrift* by the Chancellor when they submit their latest pay claim.

10 His latest book has received *a good press*.

11 In view of the present economic situation, the Government has had to *shelve its plans* for lowering personal taxation.

12 There will have to be some fast talking if the employers are to meet the *deadline* fixed by the unions for settling the dispute.

13 Mr Smith has resigned from the Cabinet. It is, of course, *common knowledge* that he was often frustrated at having to *toe the line* with his Cabinet colleagues.

358 Paraphrase the sentences.

1 'This plan falls between two stools.'
2 'He's just making a virtue of necessity.'
3 'Everything was at sixes and sevens.'
4 'She can't make ends meet.'
5 'I take everything he says with a pinch of salt.'
6 'He's a square peg in a round hole.'
7 'They are hand in glove with one another.'
8 'He hasn't a leg to stand on.'
9 'They beat us to it.'
10 'You've hit the nail on the head.'
11 'You should take the bull by the horns.'
12 'We're all in the same boat.'
13 'Even if he doesn't get this job, he has other irons in the fire.'
14 'I called his bluff.'
15 'Let's put all our cards on the table.'

359 Outline the situations in which the proverbs might serve as comments.

1 'Once bitten, twice shy.'
2 'One swallow doesn't make a summer.'
3 'Actions speak louder than words.'
4 'One good turn deserves another.'
5 'Don't count your chickens before they're hatched.'
6 'It never rains but it pours.'
7 'Make hay while the sun shines.'
8 'A stitch in time saves nine.'
9 'Necessity is the mother of invention.'
10 'Never look a gift horse in the mouth.'
11 'Blood is thicker than water.'
12 'Prevention is better than cure.'
13 'Nothing venture, nothing gain.'
14 'Rome wasn't built in a day.'
15 'A bird in the hand . . . '

Colloquial phrases and responses

The following represent a small selection of phrases and responses frequently heard in conversations. Students will not be thoroughly at home with the language unless they can both understand and use these colloquialisms, and it is more important that students should know the context in which they might be used than that they should be able to explain their meanings.

360–361 Write short dialogues of two or three sentences, incorporating these phrases and responses, e.g. 'Never mind!':

'I'm sorry; I forgot to post your letter.'
'Never mind! I'll post it myself when I go out.'

360

1 'Not on your life!'
2 'Rather!'
3 'Right you are!'
4 'Don't mind me!' (ironic)

5 'Well, I never!'
6 'I don't get it.'
7 'It can't be helped.'
8 'I like that!' (ironic)
9 'Not at all!'
10 'Honestly?'
11 'Here you are!'
12 'Well, really!'
13 'It's hardly worth it.'
14 'Yes, thanks to you!' (ironic)

1 'I could do with one!'
2 'Let me see . . . '
3 'Nothing doing.'
4 'Have it your own way!'
5 'What's up?'
6 'Just my luck!'
7 'Very well!'
8 'I beg your pardon!'
9 'I beg your pardon?'
10 'I'll see to it.'
11 'What are you getting at?'
12 'I'd rather not.'
13 'Yes, you'd better.'

Newspaper headlines

362–363 Explain in complete sentences what each of the headlines is about. Do not give any information not suggested by the headline.

1 FORTNIGHT'S HOLIDAY ON A SHOESTRING
2 BY-PASS CRASH: MOTORIST CHARGED
3 POOLS PROBE: PROMOTER'S COMMENT

4 VICE SQUAD SWOOP. TWO MEN HELD

5 COMMUNIST WITCH-HUNT. UNION CHIEF BLAMES PRESS

6 GOYA FOR THE NATION

7 BIGGER GRANTS FOR REPERTORIES

8 BUDGET LEAK. COMMONS ROW

9 MANCHESTER BLACKOUT IN POWER CUT

10 CITY SCANDAL. FRAUD SQUAD CALLED IN

11 P.M.'S PLANE—RISK WAS NEGLIGIBLE

12 H.P. RESTRICTIONS HIT INDUSTRY. 300 MEN LAID OFF

363

1 FOOTBALL FIXTURES HIT—PITCHES FROZEN

2 POSTMISTRESS FOILS ARMED ATTACKER

3 GOLD RESERVES REACH NEW PEAK

4 COLD SPELL WILL CONTINUE. ROADS TREACHEROUS SAYS A.A.

5 CHRISTMAS ROAD TOLL WORST EVER

6 GALLUP POLL GIVES TORIES LEAD

7 BOOM IN EXPORTS. SUCCESS OF RECENT DRIVE

8 ELECTRIC KETTLE FAULT WARNING

9 SMUGGLING CHARGES: TWO MEN CLEARED

10 MINERS BAN OVERTIME

11 NEW FLYOVER SPEEDS TRAFFIC FLOW

12 MURDER RIDDLE STILL UNSOLVED—YARD BAFFLED

General knowledge

The material in these exercises includes a variety of terms, phrases and words, of practical use to a student having to cope with everyday life in England, and, more generally, to any student who reads newspapers or listens to the radio. For students in England, the exercises may be used as a test of the degree of their awareness of what is going on around them, while for students abroad, the exercises may be used to prompt something more than an academic interest in the language. In the latter case, students should be asked to do some private research before any particular exercise is used in class, if it is thought that the material will be unfamiliar to them.

364–373 Say what the following are, or explain what they mean.

364

The electorate	A session
A constituency	To divide the House
To stand for Parliament	To dissolve Parliament
Polling day	A Tory
A three-cornered contest	A Life Peer
A marginal seat	The Budget
A by-election	A Private Member's Bill
The Speaker	A Civil Servant
The Opposition	A Town Council
The Shadow Cabinet	An alderman

365

A Premium Bond	The Stock Exchange
Hire Purchase	Gilt-edged securities
An overdraft	A take-over bid
A current account	A Board
A crossed cheque	Shareholders
Purchase tax	A stockbroker
A subsidy	Unearned income
Income tax	A jobber

366

An Employment Exchange	A demarcation dispute
A Trade Union	Picketing
A shop steward	Arbitration
'White-collar' workers	Piece-work
An unofficial strike	Shift-work
A 'blackleg'	A Co-operative Society
Overtime	'Working to rule'

367

A flyover
Lighting-up time
A roundabout
A by-pass
A layby
A ring road
A traffic jam
A 'bottleneck'
A toll-gate

Point duty
'Diversion'
A trunk road
A parking meter
'Dual carriageway'
A 'T' junction
A zebra crossing
A season ticket
A 'day-return'

368

Scotland Yard
To release on bail
To remand in custody
Jurors
The plaintiff
A Probation Officer

Penal reform
An open prison
A 'gaolbird'
A by-law
A shop-walker
A shop-lifter

369

Press comment
An editorial
A newsagent
A mass-circulation daily
A 'small ad.'
A hoarding

A 'scoop'
A poster
Paperbacks
A book token
A 'blurb'
A book review

370

Royal Shakespeare Theatre
The dress circle
A seat in 'the gods'
The orchestra pit
The footlights
A dress rehearsal
An usherette
A 'Prom' concert
A continuous performance

Viewers
'On the air'
Radio Three
Studio performance
An understudy
The *Radio Times*
The Listener
Credit titles
A Repertory theatre

371

The Cup Final
A Test Match
Derby Day
The Pools
A sweepstake
A bookmaker
A betting shop

A raffle
A teetotaller
A public convenience
The 'local'
A deck-chair
A Bank Holiday

372

The Union Jack
Grace and favour residences
A Chelsea Pensioner
The Royal Mint
Big Ben
The National Trust
The British Council
Kew Gardens
A Building Society

Dr Barnado's Homes
A Public school
A Comprehensive school
The 'eleven plus'
An Approved School
'Old Boys'
A blazer
A Youth Hostel
An Estate Agent

373

A Chain store

A launderette
'L.V.'s accepted'
'No hawkers'
A commuter
The green belt

A compulsory purchase
    order
'Red Tape'
Copyright
A Girl Guide
The 'Top Ten'
'Highbrow'

Abbreviations

374–375 Say what the following abbreviations stand for and, where necessary, explain what they are:

374

O.H.M.S.	PS.
Y.M.C.A.	IOU
R.S.P.C.A.	I.T.A.
G.M.T.	B.B.C.
G.P.O.	T.U.C.
H.P.	P.T.O.
c/o	C.I.D.
Lib.	M.A.
e.g.	f.o.b.

375

C.O.D.	H.R.H.
R.S.V.P.	G.P.
NO.	V.I.P.
B.O.A.C.	oz.
F.R.S.	Cantab.
A.A.	G.C.E.
Lab.	B.Sc.
c.i.f.	Cons.
fig.	i.e.

SECTION FOUR
COMPOSITION WORK

Preliminary composition work

Write one descriptive or explanatory paragraph (75–100 words) for each of the following, using each sentence as the *first* sentence of your paragraph, and taking care to ensure that in each paragraph your use of tenses is consistent.

1 Yesterday, I met an old man.
2 A Customs official has to be a good judge of character.
3 Hans had found life difficult during the first week of his stay in England.
4 The wedding reception is to be on a grand scale.
5 The day of the examination had come; he not only knew it, but felt it.
6 A week from now, I shall be on holiday on the Mediterranean coast.
7 Although the car cost more than they could really afford, they felt they simply had to buy it.
8 What a lot of patience nurses must have!

Write one descriptive or explanatory paragraph (75–100 words) for each of the following, using each sentence as the *last* sentence of your paragraph, and taking care to ensure that in each paragraph your use of tenses is consistent.

1 I left the manager's office, relieved that the interview was over.
2 For this reason at least, it seems unlikely that ships will ever be completely superseded by aircraft as a means of passenger transport.
3 He began to wish he had never come to the party.
4 I decided that this should be my excuse for not turning up, but would anyone believe me?
5 There is only one doubt in my mind: when I *do* reach retiring age, shall I still feel like doing any of these things?
6 Only then did he begin to wish that he had worked harder at school.

Write two or three paragraphs (100–150 words) on the following subjects:

1 The ideal kitchen.
2 Men's fashions.
3 Living on one's own.
4 Keeping pets.
5 Window-shopping.
6 How to break the ice (socially).
7 What annoys me most about the opposite sex.
8 How to make a good impression at an interview.
9 Buying presents.
10 Modern furniture.

Arguments 'for' and 'against'

These exercises may be used as an introduction to both composition and discussion work. Students are asked to write down *two* arguments against and two arguments in favour of each proposition. A class will, between them, probably produce four or five arguments for and against. These arguments may then be discussed, and students should write a short essay (150–200 words), using any notes they may have taken during the discussion.

1 A boarding-school education.
2 Self-service stores.
3 Working mothers.
4 Censorship.
5 School uniforms.
6 Having the vote at the age of eighteen.
7 Pocket-money for children.
8 Conducted holiday tours.
9 Beards.
10 Marrying young.
11 Living in a foreign country.
12 Divorce.
13 Mass production of goods.
14 Travelling by car.
15 Being an only child.

16 Compulsory school sports.
17 The use of cosmetics.
18 Advertising.
19 Co-educational schools.
20 Living in the country.

Students should develop the technique they have used in this exercise when preparing their compositions on the subjects given on the following pages.

Composition subjects

(250–300 words)

1 When are parents most useful and when are they most annoying?
2 To what extent have your ideas about England and the English been modified since you came to this country?
3 My favourite month.
4 A dialogue between a landlady and a tenant, one of them complaining to the other.
5 The country I would choose to live in other than my own.
6 The world as it will be a hundred years from now.
7 What qualities I expect to find in a teacher.
8 'How glad we were to be back!' Using this as the last sentence of your essay, describe what events came before.
9 Books, television, radio—if you had to do without one of these, which would you rather give up?
10 Write a newspaper review of any film or play you have seen recently.
11 A dialogue between a traffic policeman and a woman driver wishing to park her car in an unauthorized place.
12 My first week in England.
13 A day in the life of a telephone operator or a bus conductor.
14 My greatest disappointment in life.
15 Visiting relatives.
16 Everyone lives by selling something.
17 The most significant events in my life.
18 The week-end.
19 A day in the life of a pound note.

20 Neighbours.
21 What I like about winter.
22 Public transport in England.
23 An incident in a restaurant.
24 My bad habits.
25 A dialogue between a hairdresser and a client whose hair has accidentally been dyed the wrong colour.
26 My first day at school as a child, and my last day at school before going out to work.
27 Grandparents.
28 If I were Prime Minister . . .
29 The ideal house.
30 English newspapers.

Composition subjects

(350–500 words)

1 'Spare the rod and spoil the child.'
2 National characteristics.
3 The telephone.
4 University education for women is largely a waste of effort and Government money.
5 A politically united Europe.
6 What may account for the present-day increase in juvenile delinquency?
7 England's scenery.
8 All men are not born equal.
9 The uses and abuses of television.
10 The best form of government.
11 Modern scientific discoveries—curse or blessing?
12 The essence of a holiday is change.
13 What makes for a cultured man.
14 The purpose of prisons.
15 The tradition of service is dying.
16 Superstitions.
17 The effect of labour-saving devices on the modern housewife.
18 Everyone is a snob at heart.
19 The English Channel.

20 Money isn't everything.
21 The Trade Unions.
22 Everything is becoming bigger and better.
23 The effects of newspaper reviews.
24 Hypocrisy is a social virtue.
25 The morals of advertising.
26 Nature or Nurture—which has the more influence on the formation of character?
27 Can war bring with it good as well as evil?
28 Prejudices.
29 Old age as a social problem.
30 What are the deadly sins of our age?

Subjects for letters

(90–120 words)

1 You have found a flat in London. Write to a friend, describing the flat and inviting him (or her) to share it with you.

2 Write to the Principal of a school, asking for details of a course you would like to attend.

3 Write to your parents giving your first impressions of England.

4 Write a letter to your local Council, complaining about a parking meter that has been placed outside your house.

5 Write a letter of thanks to a relative for a Christmas present that you didn't want and didn't like.

6 Write a letter of application to an English company for a post as secretary.

7 Write to the editor of a newspaper, pointing out some errors of fact that appeared in an article on foreigners in England.

8 Write a letter to your bank to arrange credit facilities in London during your stay in England.

9 Write to a friend, inviting him (or her) to spend a holiday with you in some part of Britain outside London. Explain your plans and say why you think the holiday will be interesting and enjoyable.

10 Write a letter to a hotel at which you wish to stay for a holiday, asking for information.

11 You have left your handbag (or wallet) on a train. Write to the Lost Property Department reporting your loss, and describe the handbag (or wallet) and its contents.

12 Write a letter of congratulation to a friend on the birth of her first child.

13 Write to an Estate Agent, asking for details of properties that are for sale. State your requirements clearly.

14 Write to a tourist agency, complaining about an unsatisfactory coach tour.

15 Write a letter to your host at a party, apologizing for having been rude to him and for having made an embarrassing scene.

16 Write to a prospective employer, asking for the time of an interview to be changed.

17 Write to the manager of a restaurant to arrange the catering for a dinner and party for fifty guests.

18 Reply to the invitation in Letter 9 above, saying that you would prefer to visit another part of the country.

19 Write to the headmaster of your former school, asking him to write you a testimonial.

20 Write to an interior decorator, asking him to prepare an estimate for redecorating your house, and giving him all the necessary details.

APPENDIX

Notes on clauses

1 Introductory

1.1 Compare these sentences:

1a We bought a *large* house.
1b We bought a house *that would be large enough for conversion into flats*.

The group of words in italics in *1b* has the same function as *large* in *1a*. It is doing the work of an ADJECTIVE, qualifying the noun *house*.

2a *Your speech* gave everyone great pleasure.
2b *What you said* gave everyone great pleasure.

The group of words in italics in *2b* has the same function as *your speech* in *2a*. It is doing the work of a NOUN, as subject of the verb gave.

3a I shall see you *tomorrow*.
3b I shall see you *when I return from my holiday*.

The group of words in italics in *3b* has the same function as *tomorrow* in *3a*. It is doing the work of an ADVERB, modifying the verb *see*.

From these three pairs of sentences, we can see that the work of an ADJECTIVE, a NOUN, or an ADVERB may be done either by a single word or by a group of words.

1.2 Look at these groups of words from sentences *b* above:

that *would be* large enough for conversion into flats
what you *said*
when I *return* from my holiday

Each group contains a *finite verb* (a verb that has number, person, and tense). A group of words containing a finite verb is called a FINITE CLAUSE, and the groups of words in italics in *1b*, *2b*, and *3b* above are finite clauses; respectively, an ADJECTIVAL clause, a NOUN clause, and an ADVERBIAL clause.

All these clauses in italics have an auxiliary function in relation to the remainder of each sentence, and they are called SUBORDINATE (or DEPENDENT) clauses. The remainder of each sentence (which also contains a finite verb) is called the MAIN (or PRINCIPAL) clause.

1.3 The following parts of the verb are *non-finite*, and the clauses in which they operate are called NON-FINITE clauses:

Infinitive

I have something *to tell you*. (non-finite adjectival clause, qualifying *something* in the main clause)

To give up at this stage would be a great pity. (non-finite noun clause, subject of *would be* in the main clause)

To speed up the delivery of letters, the Post Office introduced automatic sorting. (non-finite adverbial clause of purpose, modifying *introduced* in the main clause)

Gerund

Closing the factory would mean unemployment for many of the town's work force. (non-finite noun clause, subject of *would mean* in the main clause)

Present participle

The thieves took two mail-bags *containing registered letters*. (non-finite adjectival clause, qualifying *mail-bags* in the main clause)

He was taken ill *while travelling by air from New York to London*. (non-finite adverbial clause of time, modifying *was taken* in the main clause)

Past participle

I couldn't understand the instructions *given in the manual*. (non-finite adjectival clause, qualifying *instructions* in the main clause)

Given time, he'll make a first-class tennis player. (non-finite adverbial clause of condition, modifying *'ll make* in the main clause)

Perfect participle

Having received their final medical check, the astronauts boarded their spacecraft. (non-finite adverbial clause of time, modifying *boarded* in the main clause)

1.4 If a sentence contains two or more main clauses, these clauses are called CO-ORDINATE (of equal rank, analytically speaking):

> The station-master waved his green flag and the train started moving.

This sentence may be divided into two clauses, each of equal rank:

> *A* The station-master waved his green flag (Main clause, co-ordinate with *B*)
> *B* (and) the train started moving (Main clause, co-ordinate with *A*)

If a sentence contains subordinate clauses, we can determine the function of these in relation to the main clause or to another subordinate clause by asking:

> Does it qualify a noun in the main clause or in another subordinate clause? (Is it an ADJECTIVAL clause?)
> Does it provide the main clause or another subordinate clause with a subject, object or complement? (Is it a NOUN clause?)
> Does it modify the verb in the main clause or in another subordinate clause? (Is it an ADVERBIAL clause?)

2 Adjectival clauses[1]

2.1 The picture *that hangs over the fireplace* is a family heirloom.

Analysis

> *A* The picture is a family heirloom (main)
> *a1* that hangs over the fireplace (Subordinate)

Clause *a1* qualifies the noun *picture* in clause *A*, and is therefore an Adjectival clause.

In some defining relative clauses, the relative pronoun is not expressed:

> The shoes *you're wearing* are identical to the pair *I bought yesterday*.

[1] See also *Relative Clauses*, page 120.

    A The shoes are identical to the pair (Main)

    a1 you're wearing (Subordinate Adjectival clause qualifying *shoes* in *A*)

    a2 I bought yesterday (Subordinate Adjectival clause qualifying *pair* in *A*)

2.2 Examples of non-finite adjectival clauses:

> The thieves took two mail-bags *containing registered letters.*
> (Compare: 'that contained registered letters')
>
> I couldn't understand the instructions *given in the manual.*
> (Compare: 'that were given in the manual')
>
> There are many factors *to be taken into consideration.*
> (Compare: 'that must be taken into consideration')

Note: the term 'non-finite' should not be confused with the terms 'defining' and 'non-defining', employed in the section on relative clauses (pages 120–145). The term 'non-finite' relates to the type of verb structure employed, and can be applied to any type of clause (adjectival, noun, or adverbial) that employs a non-finite verb form (see examples on page 294).

The terms *defining* and *non-defining* are used for two types of relative clause, and both defining and non-defining relative clauses can be finite or non-finite in structure:

> The picture *that hangs over the fireplace* is a family heirloom.
> (Adjectival clause—defining relative clause—finite in structure)
>
> The picture *hanging over the fireplace* is a family heirloom.
> (Adjectival clause—equivalent to a defining relative clause —non-finite in structure)
>
> The Victoria Line, *which runs from Victoria to Walthamstow*, was opened in March 1969. (Adjectival clause—non-defining relative clause—finite in structure)
>
> The Victoria Line, *running from Victoria to Walthamstow*, was opened in March 1969. (Adjectival clause—equivalent to a non-defining relative clause—non-finite in structure)

2.3 Not every clause introduced by a relative pronoun is an adjectival clause. Non-defining clauses sometimes have an explanatory function: they may suggest an adverbial idea, implying the reason or cause of the facts presented in the main clause:

The manufacturers soon stopped marketing the drug, *which was found to have serious side-effects.* (i.e. *because* it was found to have serious side-effects)

2.4 Not every clause introduced by a relative pronoun is a Sub-ordinate clause. *Which* may introduce a Co-ordinate clause:

He's not on the telephone, *which makes it very difficult to get in touch with him.*

Analysis

A He's not on the telephone
B which makes it very difficult to get in touch with him

Clause B does not qualify any single word in Clause A (in other words, it hasn't an auxiliary function as adjective or adverb in relation to clause A). It introduces a further idea or additional comment 'and this makes it very difficult to get in touch with him'. Clause B is, then, a Main clause, co-ordinate with clause A.[1]

In a similar way, *who* may introduce a Co-ordinate clause:

He told his wife, *who then passed on the information to a neighbour.*

Analysis

A He told his wife
B who then passed on the information to a neighbour

Clause B does not describe *wife* in clause A (i.e. it is not doing the work of an adjective). It introduces a further idea 'and she passed on the information'; it is, therefore, a Main clause, co-ordinate with clause A. The difference between such co-ordinate clauses and adjectival clauses introduced by *who* may be seen more clearly if the above sentence is compared with:

He told the story to his wife, *who is a great lover of gossip.*

[1] Students who feel that the first clause is more important than the second, and that these clauses cannot therefore be co-ordinate, should remember that clauses may be *Independent* (in the case of *one* Main clause in the sentence), *Subordinate* (serving another clause as an adjective, noun, or adverb), or *Co-ordinate* (where there are two or more Main clauses in the sentence). Since Clause B in this example is not subordinate according to the definition given, it must be Co-ordinate, analytically speaking, with the first, Clause A.

In this sentence, *who* introduces a clause describing *wife* in the Main clause (i.e. it introduces an Adjectival clause).

2.5 Do not be misled by the word that introduces a Subordinate clause. We can determine the function of a subordinate clause by asking: is it doing the work of an adjective, a noun, or an adverb? An Adjectival clause may, for example, be introduced by *when* or *where*, as in the following sentences:

1 He spoke of the time *when he was a boy*.

Analysis

A He spoke of the time (Main clause)
a1 when he was a boy (Subordinate Adjectival clause, qualifying *time* in *A*)

2 Do you remember the place *where we first met?*

Analysis

A Do you remember the place (Main clause)
a1 where we first met (Subordinate Adjectival clause, qualifying *place* in *A*)

3 Noun Clauses[1]

3.1 AS SUBJECT   Compare these two sentences:

1 *Your talk* was very interesting.
2 *What you said* was very interesting.

In sentence *1*, there is only one verb (*was*), and its subject is *your talk*. In sentence *2*, there are two finite verbs, and two clauses:

a1 What you said (Subordinate)
A was very interesting (main)

Clause *a1* is clearly the subject of *was* in Clause *A*, just as *your talk* is the subject of *was* in sentence *1* above. It should be noted that the Main clause cannot stand alone without the subordinate noun clause.

[1] See also *Verb Patterns with -Ing Forms, Infinitives and 'that' Clauses*, page 145.

298

Examples of *non-finite* clauses as subject:

> *To give up at this stage* would be a great pity.
> *Closing the factory* would mean unemployment for many of the town's work force.

3.2 AS OBJECT   Compare these two sentences:

> *1*   They now know *the facts*.
> *2*   They now know *that the scheme is impracticable*.

In *1*, there is only one verb (*know*), and its object is *the facts*. In *2*, there are two finite verbs and two clauses:

> *A* They now know (Main)
> *a1* that the scheme is impracticable (Subordinate)

Clause *a1* is the object of *know* in Clause *A*, just as *the facts* is the object of *know* in sentence *1*.

Examples of *non-finite* clauses as object:

> He claims *to be an expert on the subject*.
> I hate *putting you to any trouble*.

3.3 IN APPOSITION TO THE SUBJECT

> *i* The fact *that you haven't enough time* is no excuse.

Analysis

> *A* The fact is no excuse (Main)
> *a1* that you haven't enough time (Subordinate)

Clause *A* is complete: it contains subject, verb, and complement. Clause *a1* is not, however, an adjectival clause: it does not describe *fact* in Clause *A*; it *is* the fact, expressed in other words. In this case we call it a Noun clause in apposition to the subject. If in doubt as to the function of *that* (is it a conjunction or a relative pronoun?), try substituting *which*:

> *The fact which you haven't enough time is no excuse.

This is clearly impossible, and *that* in the sentence above is functioning as a conjunction, not as a relative pronoun.

> *ii* It seems unlikely *that he would do such a thing*.

Analysis

  A   It seems unlikely (Main)
  a1 that he would do such a thing (Subordinate)

Clause *a1* is represented by the word *it* in the Main clause, and could replace *it*. Clause *a1* is a Noun clause in apposition to the subject. It is possible to begin such sentences with the noun clause:

  That he would do such a thing seems unlikely.

This alternative construction is quite frequently found in written English, but is not commonly used in the spoken language.
  Examples of non-finite clauses in apposition to the subject:

  The proposal *to increase taxes* met with fierce opposition.
  It would be tactless *to mention the subject*.
  It's boring *sitting here doing nothing*.

3.4 IN APPOSITION TO THE OBJECT

  He resented the suggestion *that he didn't work conscientiously*.

Analysis

  A   He resented the suggestion (Main)
  a1 that he didn't work conscientiously (Subordinate)

As in 3.3 *i* above, Clause *A* is complete, having subject, verb, and object. Clause *a1* does not describe *suggestion* in *A*, it *is* the suggestion, expressed in other words. It is a Noun clause in apposition to the object.

Example of a non-finite clause in apposition to the object:

  The Government has now made a decision *to increase old-age pensions*.

3.5 AS COMPLEMENT   Compare these sentences:

  1   The news was *a shock to us all*.
  2   The news was *that the police had arrested a suspect*.

In *1*, there is only one verb (*was*), and the complement of the verb is *a shock to us all*. In *2*, there are two finite verbs, and two clauses:

> *A* The news was (Main)
> *a1* that the police had arrested a suspect (Subordinate)

Clause *a1* completes the predicate of *was* in the Main clause, just as *a shock to us all* does in Sentence *1*. Clause *a1* is, therefore, a Noun clause, complement of the verb *was* (never 'object' of the verb *to be*).

Examples of non-finite clauses as complement:

> His intention was *to say nothing about it*.
> Our main problem was *finding time to do the work*.

3.6 AS OBJECT OF A PREPOSITION   Compare these sentences:

> *1* They were engrossed in *his speech*.
> *2* They were engrossed in *what he was saying*.

In *1*, *his speech* is the object of the preposition *in*. In *2*, there are two clauses:

> *A* They were engrossed in (Main)
> *a1* what he was saying (Subordinate)

Clause *a1* is the object of the preposition *in*, just as *his speech* is in sentence *1*.

Example of a non-finite clause as object of a preposition:

> He insisted on *seeing you personally*.

3.7 SUMMARY

Noun clauses may function:

> *1a* as the subject of a verb
> *b* in apposition to the subject
> *2a* as the object of a verb
> *b* in apposition to the object
> *3* as complement of a verb (e.g. *to be*)
> *4* as the object of a preposition

4 Adverbial clauses[1]

4.1 TIME

> I shall speak to you *when I come back*.

Analysis

> *A* I shall speak to you (Main)
> *a1* when I come back (Subordinate)

Clause *a1* modifies the verb *shall speak* in Clause *A*, telling us *when* 'I' shall speak. It is an Adverbial clause of Time. Clauses of time may also come at the beginning of a sentence:[2]

> *When I come back*, I shall tell you what happened.

Example of a non-finite clause of time:

> *Having received their final medical check*, the astronauts boarded their spacecraft.

Note

a. *When* may introduce an Adjectival clause:

> He spoke of the time *when he was a boy*. (See under Adjectival clauses, page 298).

b. *When*, like *which*, may also introduce a Co-ordinate clause:

> They had given up hope of finding their way, *when a guide arrived*.

Analysis

> *A* They had given up hope of finding their way
> *B* when a guide arrived.

---

[1] See also *Participles and Gerunds*, page 175.
[2] This is simply an observation of what is grammatically possible, and is not intended to suggest that the choice of one position or the other is purely arbitrary. Quite often (but depending on intonation), the first of two clauses in a sentence comprising a main clause and an adverbial clause represents information that is familiar, taken for granted, or secondary in importance to the information carried by the second clause.

In the sentence 'I shall speak to you *when I come back*', attention is focused on *when* I shall speak to you, rather than on *what* I shall do at the time referred to; whereas in the sentence 'When I come back *I shall tell you what happened*', attention is focused on *what* I shall do rather than on *when* I shall do it. Stylistic considerations also have to be taken into account.

The possibility of making such distinctions arises, of course, only when the two clauses are reversible.

Clause *B* does not tell us *when* they had given up hope. It introduces a further idea *and then a guide arrived*. It is a Main clause, co-ordinate with Clause *A*. (Note, also, that the two clauses are not reversible in this case.)

c. When may also introduce a Noun clause.[1] Compare these sentences:

1 Please tell me *the time of your arrival*.
2 Please tell me *when you will arrive*.

In *1*, there is one finite verb (*tell*), and its object is *the time of your arrival*. In *2*, there are two finite verbs and two clauses:

A Please tell me (*me* is an indirect object) (Main)
a1 when you will arrive (Subordinate)

Clause *a1* provides *tell* in Clause *A* with an object, just as *the time of your arrival* is the object of *tell* in sentence *1*, and is therefore a Noun clause. (Again, the clauses are not reversible.)

4.2 PLACE

I am always meeting him *where I least expect*.

Analysis

A I am always meeting him (Main)
a1 where I least expect (Subordinate)

Clause *a1* modifies the verb *am meeting* in Clause *A*, telling us *where* I meet him, and is an Adverbial clause of Place.

Note

a. Where may introduce an Adjectival clause:

Do you remember the place *where we first met*? (See under Adjectival clauses, page 298).

b. Where, like *when* and *which*, may also introduce a Co-ordinate clause:

He was taken to the police station, *where he proceeded to make a full confession*.

[1] See also note (i) on page 53.

Analysis

> A He was taken to the police station
> B where he proceeded to make a full confession

Clause *B* does not describe *police station* in Clause *A*. It introduces a further idea *and there he proceeded to make a full confession*. Clause *B* is the main clause, co-ordinate with clause *A*.

c. *Where* may introduce a Noun clause. Compare these sentences:

> 1 Perhaps you could show me *the place*.
> 2 Perhaps you could show me *where you put it*.

In sentence *1*, there is only one verb (*could show*), and its object is *place*. In *2*, there are two clauses:

> A Perhaps you could show me (*me* is an indirect object) (Main)
> a1 where you put it (Subordinate)

Clause *a1* supplies *show* in Clause *A* with an object, just as *place* is the object of *show* in sentence *1*, and is therefore a Noun clause.

4.3 MANNER

> He solved the problem *as one might have expected*.

Analysis

> A He solved the problem (Main
> a1 as one might have expected (Subordinate)

Clause *a1* tells us *how* he solved the problem, and is an Adverbial clause of Manner.

Note

The insertion of a comma after *problem* would change the function of the second clause and create a difference in meaning:

> He solved the problem, *as one might have expected*.

Analysis

> A He solved the problem,
> B as one might have expected

304

Clause *B*, after the comma, does *not tell us how* he solved the problem. It introduces a further idea *and one might have expected this*. It is, therefore, a Main clause, co-ordinate with Clause *A*. In this case, the clauses are reversible:

As one might have expected, he solved the problem.[1]

4.4 COMPARISON

i He writes as incoherently *as he speaks*.

Analysis

A He writes as incoherently (Main)
a1 as he speaks (Subordinate)

Clause *a1* tells us how (comparatively) incoherently he speaks, and is an Adverbial clause of Comparison, modifying the adverb *incoherently* in Clause *A*.

ii His stepfather treated him more kindly *than any real father would have done*.

Analysis

A His stepfather treated him more kindly (Main)
a1 than any real father would have done (Subordinate)

Clause *a1* tells us how (comparatively) kindly his stepfather treated him, and is an Adverbial clause of Comparison, modifying the adverb *kindly* in Clause *A*.

4.5 REASON OR CAUSE

He stole the money *because he was out of work*.

Analysis

A He stole the money (Main)
a1 because he was out of work (Subordinate)

Clause *a1* explains *why* he stole the money, and is an Adverbial clause of Reason or Cause. Clauses of reason or cause can also come at the beginning of a sentence:

[1] We could, of course, insert an adverb of manner, indicating *how* he solved the problem:
    He solved the problem *easily*, as one might have expected.
or   As one might have expected, he solved the problem *easily*.

> *Since we haven't heard from him,* we must assume he isn't coming.

Example of a non-finite clause of reason or cause:

> *Having heard nothing further from him,* we assumed he wasn't coming.

or We assumed he wasn't coming, *having heard nothing further from him.*

4.6 PURPOSE

> He spent most of his time studying *so that he might later get a better job.*

Analysis

> *A* He spent most of his time studying (Main)
> *a1* so that he might later get a better job (Subordinate)

Clause *a1* explains his *aim* in spending his time studying, and is an Adverbial clause of Purpose. Clauses of purpose can also come at the beginning of a sentence:

> *So that you should know exactly* how things stand, I have put everything in writing.

Example of a non-finite clause of purpose:

> *To speed up the delivery of letters,* the Post Office introduced automatic sorting.

or The Post Office introduced automatic sorting *to speed up the delivery of letters.*

4.7 RESULT

> The boy was so exhausted *that he fell asleep on the bus.*

Analysis

> *A* The boy was so exhausted (Main)
> *a1* that he fell asleep on the bus. (Subordinate)

Clause *a1* tells us the result of the boy being so exhausted, and is an Adverbial clause of Result.

Example of a non-finite clause of result:

> Drug-taking is now increasing so much *as to constitute a* major national problem. (= . . . so much *that it constitutes* a major . . .)

Note

A clause introduced by *so that* may also be an Adverbial clause of Purpose. Compare these sentences:

1. The doctor explained the nature of my illness in medical terms, *so that I didn't understand fully.*
2. The doctor explained the nature of my illness in medical terms *so that I shouldn't understand fully.*

In *1*, where the *so that* clause is introduced by a comma, we have an Adverbial clause of Result; but in *2*, where the comma is omitted, we have instead an Adverbial clause of Purpose. A difference may also be observed in the sequence of tenses in the two sentences above, and students should note that the clauses in *2* are reversible:

> *So that I shouldn't understand fully,* the doctor explained the nature of my illness in medical terms.

4.8 CONDITION

> *If I were rich,* I would go on a world cruise.

Analysis

> A I would go on a world cruise (Main)
> *a1* if I were rich

Clause *a1* tells us what condition would have to be fulfilled in order to make my going on a world cruise possible, and is an Adverbial clause of Condition. Clauses of condition can also come after the main clause:

> I would go on a world cruise *if I were rich.*

Examples of non-finite clauses of condition:

> *Given time,* he'll make a first-class tennis player.
> *or* He'll make a first-class tennis player, *given time.*
> *All being well,* we should arrive just after lunch.
> *or* We should arrive just after lunch, *all being well.*

4.9 CONCESSION

Although he is over eighty, he's still very active.

Analysis

A He's still very active (Main)
a1 although he is over eighty

Clause *a1* makes the admission (i.e. concedes) that *he is over eighty*, and modifies the verb *is* in Clause *A* (in spite of this fact, he's still very active). Clause *a1* is an Adverbial clause of Concession. Clauses of concession can also follow the main clause:

He's still very active, *although he's over eighty*.

Example of a non-finite clause of concession:

Although approving the plan in general, the committee expressed several serious reservations on individual points.

or The committee expressed several serious reservations on individual points in the plan, *although approving it in general*.

Clauses of concession may also be introduced by an adjective, adverb, or verb followed by *as*:

Tired as they were, the rescuers continued searching among the ruins for survivors. (= Although they were very tired)

Hard as he tried,
However hard he tried, he couldn't force the door open.
Try as he might,

(= Although he tried very hard *or* No matter how hard he tried)

Key to exercises

Note: Answers to exercises marked with an asterisk (*) are suggestions only, and are provided for the guidance of students working independently of a teacher. This applies mainly to exercises in 'free completion'. It should not be assumed, however, that in all other cases the answers in the key are offered as the only acceptable ones. Alternatives are suggested where appropriate, but these may not exhaust all the possibilities. Students working with a teacher can, of course, discuss their own suggestions in class. The abbreviation *ALDCE* is used throughout the key for *The Advanced Learner's Dictionary of Current English*.

1 1 have been trying/have you been; 2 have met/saw/were not; 3 looks/has been burning/have forgotten to switch/went; 4 to have kept you waiting; 5 was going to buy *or* would have bought/heard/changed; 6 have been waiting/have known/would be; 7 has been working/returns/shall not have seen; 8 see/will be struck/has improved/went; 9 had told/had already bought/wouldn't have given/is; 10 shall ring/hasn't answered/have gone/wouldn't have bothered to come/had known; 11 brought *or* have brought/hadn't/would have been *or* would be; 12 have remembered to tell/had/would have arrived.

2 1 arrived *or* had arrived/was/was/had given/have stood/saving; 2 had told/were coming *or* would be coming/had known/wouldn't have had to; 3 didn't you tell/could/needn't have borrowed *or* wouldn't have needed to borrow; 4 couldn't understand/had broken down/had undergone/being; 5 were going *or* went/don't leave/shall miss; 6 were/was talking/were/have gone; 7 is talking/will be free to see/would you like to take; 8 to have written/have been/haven't had/writing/would have telephoned/had forgotten *or* have forgotten; 9 saw/was living/told/was thinking *or* had been thinking of emigrating/well have done; 10 am/going ski-ing/will be/have tried; *or* was/going ski-ing/would be/had tried; ski-ing/making; 11 had let me know/wouldn't be able *or* weren't able/would certainly not have gone/had known; 12 didn't want to see *or* wouldn't want to see/had heard/was/had suggested *or* suggested.

3 1 didn't come/have never seen/would have been; 2 complete *or* have completed/shall have been living *or* shall have lived/don't think/shall stay; 3 should mention *or* mention/was just thinking/(was) wondering/had become *or* became; 4 wouldn't call/were/will have got *or* has got; 5 wished/had been able to see/left/would have liked to say/hoped/would accept; 6 are/is/could have sworn *or* could swear/talking; 7 hasn't worked/are/have got/rang/certainly wouldn't have come/hadn't asked; 8 arrived *or* had arrived/

did we discover/was/had wasted *or* were wasting/calling; 9 hasn't taken *or* didn't take/to get/needn't have taken/have saved/spent/had; 10 made/choosing/don't decide/will never settle down; 11 didn't realize/had been informed/had been asked to go on talking/was being traced *or* was traced; 12 will hardly believe/is/has telephoned/(has) apologized/getting/rings/shall not answer.

4 1 could drive . . . when he was eighteen; 2 could understand/could speak it when I first arrived in England; 3 could have let . . . money yesterday; 4 could have persuaded . . . come last week/could; 5 could play . . . beautifully at one time; 6 could see . . . was bored to death at the party last night; 7 couldn't get . . . because I had forgotten my key; 8 could overhear . . . said in the hotel we stayed at; 9 could have seen you yesterday; 10 When they asked my advice, I could suggest; 11 could well understand/felt . . . at the time; 12 couldn't get/could have got it done by the following morning.

5 1 we shan't be able to get; 2 we shall be able to give; 3 we were able to take; 4 was able to escape; 5 were able to find; 6 I've been unable *or* I haven't been able; 7 to be able to show; 8 to be able to speak; 9 they'd been unable to get *or* they hadn't been able to get; 10 had been able to get.

6*1 . . ., we could all make notes about the lesson. 2 . . ., we could go much faster. 3 . . ., we could visit you more often. 4 I could give you more help myself if . . . 5 . . ., you could have kept to the main roads. 6 I could have done something about it if . . . 7 . . ., we could stay and have coffee with you. 8 We could have stayed and had coffee with them if . . . 9 . . ., we could fix it straight away. 10 We could have fixed it there and then if . . .

7*1 . . ., we'd all be able to make notes about the lesson. 2 . . ., we'd be able to go much faster. 3 . . ., we'd be able to visit you more often. 4 I'd be able to give you more help myself if . . . 5 . . ., you'd have been able to keep to the main roads. 6 I'd have been able to do something about it if . . . 7 . . ., we'd be able to stay and have coffee with you. 8 We'd have been able to stay and have coffee with them if . . . 9 . . ., we'd be able to fix it straight away. 10 We'd have been able to fix it there and then if . . .

8 1 She can be quite forgetful. 2 Holidays abroad can be quite cheap. 3 Racial harmony can be difficult to achieve. 4 . . ., discipline could be very strict. 5 He could occasionally be quite gay. 6 September can be a wonderful month . . . 7 Students . . . can be very critical . . . 8 The English method . . . can be very confusing . . . 9 She can look quite pretty at times. 10 English cooking can, in fact, be excellent.

9 1 You may find; 2 We might (*or* could) get; 3 He might (*or* could) change; 4 trains may be; 5 Parents may find; 6 we may find; 7 He may (*or* might) be able; 8 He may (*or* might) not turn up; 9 The Government's policy might (*or* could) prove; 10 Getting . . . may (*or* might) not be.

10*1 We may have missed the bus. 2 He might not have wanted to see us. 3 They might have gone out for the evening. 4 He could have broken a window. 5 He may not have known the answer. 6 They could have guessed what we intended to do. 7 He may already have known about it. 8 They may have lost their way. 9 They may have gone away for a time. 10 She could have forgotten your address. 11 He may not have had the time. 12 He might have changed his mind about it.

11 1 The manager told me I might leave . . . if I wanted to. 2 His interviewer told him he could put off . . . 3 The Customs officer asked if he could see . . . 4 The teacher asked the student if he might ask him . . . 5 I told my friend he could . . . provided he took . . . 6 The police inspector asked his colleague if he might see . . . he was holding. 7 The notice stated that cars might be parked . . . 8 The chairman asked the speaker politely if he might interrupt him . . . 9 He asked his friend if he might join him. 10 The regulations stated that the travel allowance might not be used . . .

12 1 The restaurant may be expensive, but . . . 2 The method may be crude, but . . . 3 He may be badly paid, but . . . 4 The book may be long, but . . . 5 He may be old, but . . . 6 The climb may have been exhausting, but . . . 7 I may have been rude to him, but . . . 8 He may have acted unwisely, but . . . 9 His work may have improved, but . . . 10 Old-age pensions may have risen considerably, but . . .

13 1 You might let me know . . . 2 He might be . . . 3 You might perhaps ask him . . . 4 You might post this letter . . . 5 You might have warned me . . . 6 You might have apologized . . . 7 He might have tried . . . 8 She might keep . . .

14 1 The Conservatives should win . . . 2 There should be a lot . . . 3 . . . says it should be fine . . . 4 Our visitors should have arrived . . . 5 It shouldn't be too difficult . . . 6 The meeting ought to have finished . . . 7 The Cabinet should be meeting . . . 8 It shouldn't have taken us so long . . . 9 . . . regulations shouldn't affect . . . 10 We should be able to move . . .

15*1 . . . be very much in love with him. 2 . . . left it in my other jacket. 3 . . . be rolling in money. 4 . . . been taken in by his charming manner. 5 . . . read it very carefully. 6 . . . be crazy. 7

... received it. 8 ... be getting any better. 9 ... had a quarrel about something or other. 10 ... forgotten all about it. 11 ... be much later ... 12 ... got to know him very well.

16 1 This will be what ... 2 That will be the postman ... 3 You will appreciate that ... 4 As you will no doubt have heard, he's ... 5 You won't (*or* wouldn't) have seen ... 6 He would have been the manager's ... 7 You won't know my name ... 8 You wouldn't have seen my ... 9 The family won't have finished ... 10 ..., he won't have understood properly.

17 1 They will sit ... 2 He will often buy things and then leave ... 3 My wife *will* leave things ... 4 ..., the water pipes would freeze ..., and we would have to call in ... 5 ... he would interrupt ... 6 ... he would insist ... 7 Why *will* you be so difficult? 8 ..., everyone would listen ... 9 You *will* go out ... 10 ..., people would go to church ...

18 1 will do; 2 will hold; 3 won't work; 4 won't fit; 5 will seat; 6 will reach; 7 will suit; 8 will bear.

19 1 'I can manage ..., but I shall need ...' 2 'When ... comes into force, we shall be obliged to raise ...' 3 'I shall have more to say about this problem later.' 4 'I shall be writing to you ... to let you know ...' 5 'I shall be working ... this evening.' 6 'Do you think we shall need to take ...?' 7 'I shan't be sorry to see ...' 8 'I assume I shall be given ...' 9 'We shall never get there, at the rate we're going.' 10 'We shall be making ... tomorrow morning, ...'

20 1 belief; 2 characteristic behaviour; 3 request; 4 agreement; 5 prediction/inherent capacity; 6 command/instruction; 7 prediction; 8 characteristic behaviour; 9 prediction; 10 promise; 11 belief; 12 inherent capacity.

21* 1 He should cut down on bread and potatoes. 2 You should get up earlier. 3 We'd better take our seats. 4 He shouldn't have been driving so fast. 5 I'd better inform the police. 6 We'd better get a builder to look at it tomorrow. 7 You ought to have stayed in a hotel. 8 She shouldn't have lain in the sun so long. 9 You'd better start learning some Spanish. 10 You'd better think about buying a new one. 11 You ought to see a doctor. 12 We should have bought more in the first place. 13 He ought to change his job instead of complaining. 14 You should have taken umbrellas with you. 15 We'd better ask someone the way.

22 1 The Government recommended that the housing programme should be speeded up. 2 The judge ordered that the court should adjourn for lunch. 3 The Speaker ruled that the MP should withdraw his remark. 4 The Colonel decided that his troops should attack at dawn. 5 The chairman proposed that the minutes should be taken as read. 6 Teachers advocated that more nursery schools should be set up. 7 The magistrate directed that the man should be released. 8 The police gave instructions that members of the public should not approach the two men but should report to the nearest police station. 9 Shareholders demanded that the Board should give more detailed information about profits. 10 The employers urged that the men should return to work so that negotiations could begin.

23 1 . . . table so that I should be sure . . . 2 . . . undertones so that the teacher shouldn't overhear . . . 3 . . . warning in order that the public should be . . . 4 . . . umbrella in case it should rain. 5 . . . bank lest the house should be burgled. 6 Lest you should think I'm . . . truth, I have brought . . . 7 . . . university so that he should have . . . 8 . . . here so that you should have . . . 9 . . . hall so that everyone should have . . . 10 . . . number in case you should want . . .

24 1 It's natural that you should be upset . . . 2 It's incredible that we should have been living . . . 3 It's a pity that you should have missed . . . 4 It's curious that he should have asked . . . 5 It's typical of him that he should expect . . . 6 It's odd that they should be getting married, . . . 7 It's crazy that you should have to . . . 8 It is essential that you should look over . . . 9 It is important that you should read . . . 10 It's splendid that you should be coming . . . 11 It's interesting that you should have bought . . . 12 It is vital that emergency supplies should reach . . .

25 1 must; 2 must; 3 must; 4 have to; 5 had to; 6 must; 7 must; 8 must; 9 have to; 10 have to; 11 must; 12 having to *or* to have to; 13 will probably have to; 14 must/must; 15 must *or* has to/must *or* has to; 16 mustn't/have to; 17 have had to; 18 mustn't; 19 had to; 20 must; 21 have to.

26 1 . . . we must hurry, or we'd be late. 2 . . . application forms must be returned to the office . . . 3 . . . he must visit us . . . 4 . . . he could never remember . . . He always had to . . . 5 . . . the car had broken down, and we had to have it . . . 6 . . . the situation had now become intolerable, and that something must be done . . . 7 . . . I realized how difficult . . . was, but he must try . . . get him down. 8 . . . visas . . . must be obtained . . . 9 . . . I was sorry to have to tell him that, but he left me . . . 10 . . . it wasn't fair. He always had to do . . . 11 . . . I really must try . . . 12 . . . no one liked having (*or* to have) to work . . . 13 . . . whichever party . . . would probably have to reintroduce . . . 14 . . . candidates must write . . . and must write . . . 15 the verdict . . . must (*or* has to *or* had to) be unanimous: if . . ., the case must (*or* has to *or* had to) be retried . . . 16 . . . they had made . . . but they mustn't forget . . .

problems still had to be cleared up before they could say that
agreement was in sight. 17 ... the crowd had dispersed peaceably.
If ... hadn't, the police might have had to ... 18 ... we mustn't
make ... or he wouldn't take ... 19 ... had suddenly taken ...,
and she had had to call ... 20 ... problem cropped up again, he
must report ... 21 ... it was ... to have to make.

27 1 We needn't (*or* don't need to) leave; 2 You don't have to come;
3 we need (*or* need to) take; 4 you don't have to pay; 5 you needn't
(*or* don't need to) decide; 6 you don't have to go; 7 you don't have
to take; 8 we shan't have to rush; 9 I wouldn't need to keep;
10 he's never had to earn; 11 you don't have to do/do you; 12 I
need hardly say; 13 You needn't have told; 14 this needn't make;
15 he had never had to deal; 16 we didn't need to do; 17 he didn't
even have to have; 18 you needn't have made; 19 he need never
discover; 20 you needn't (*or* don't need to) be alarmed; 21 I need
have gone.

28 1 we needn't (*or* didn't need to) leave/didn't start; 2 didn't have to
go ... to please him; 3 need (*or* needed to) take; 4 didn't have to
pay; 5 I needn't (*or* didn't need to) decide/I could let him know
the following day; 6 it was ... the next day/I didn't have to go;
7 didn't have to take/He could go ... himself. 8 we got ... then,
we wouldn't have to rush; 9 he listened/he wouldn't need to keep
... for his benefit; 10 he didn't know/was. He had never had to
earn; 11 he didn't have to do/he told him; 12 need hardly say/he
was/I'd done; 13 I needn't have told/It was none; 14 I wouldn't
be able ... the following day, but that this needn't make ... to
their plans. 15 he was completely/he had never had to deal; 16 the
house had just been decorated, so they didn't need (*or* hadn't
needed) to do; 17 had offered/didn't even have to have *or* hadn't
even had to have; 18 had been/I needn't have made; 19 I chose
... myself/he need never discover; 20 he needn't (or didn't need
to) be alarmed; 21 had come up/He didn't think he need have
gone.

29 1 rises in the/sets in the; 2 sells; 3 flows through; 4 lies on (*or* at)
the; 5 stands on; 6 doesn't exist on the; 7 make a; 8 generates;
9 treat the; 10 indicates a; 11 work at; 12 floats on; 13 doesn't
believe in.

30 buy a ticket/show it/sucks it in/scans/records/releases a barrier/
leave a station/takes your ticket/lets you out/is a season.

31 faces a higher tax rate/faces the sharpest rise/pays a marginal rate/
moves from £10,000/faces a tax burden/is far heavier/illustrate
the point/is left with about £1,100/are left with more than £3,000/
reaches £20,000/have two important/receives a relatively small
reward/apply at about £10,000/makes perfectly sound/is little
financial incentive.

32* 1 I generally get up at seven. 2 I often spend the morning in bed. 3 I occasionally go abroad. 4 I never listen to light comedy. 5 I always walk. 6 I hardly ever read thrillers. 7 I nearly always enjoy documentaries. 8 One usually finds a full stop. 9 They sometimes ask me to tidy up my room. 10 I usually keep some money and my driving licence in it. 11 I generally take aspirins. 12 I frequently meet my friends in a nearby coffee bar.

33* 1 My neighbour always catches the same train as me. 2 My father never drinks alcohol. 3 The manager generally goes for a drink after work. 4 My parents live in a bungalow. 5 My father plays golf nearly every week-end. 6 Our teacher never smokes cigarettes. 7 The neighbour usually takes the dog for a walk at about this time. 8 A friend of mine never walks anywhere if he can avoid it. 9 My secretary wears a different dress every day. 10 Most of the people in our town work in the local factory.

34 Free composition

35 Now here is a recipe for iced coffee mousse for six persons. We need three eggs, half a pint of strong black coffee, and half an ounce (or one level tablespoon) of powdered gelatine. We measure the coffee . . ., sprinkle in . . . and leave it to soak . . . Next we crack . . . Now we add . . . and then we place . . . and whisk until the mixture . . . That's ready now, so we remove the saucepan from the heat and gradually whisk in . . . We continue beating until the mixture has cooled . . . Next we beat . . . and then we beat . . . Now we use a metal spoon and fold the egg white . . . We pour the mixture into . . . and chill it until it has set firm.

36 1 MP DEMANDS; 2 INJURIES HIT; 3 BOOM CONTINUES; 4 BRITISH RAILWAYS FORECAST(S); 5 PLANE CRASHES; 6 AMERICA LAUNCHES; 7 BOYS FIND; 8 WINDOWS SURVIVE; 9 DOCTORS FEAR; 10 CHAMPION RETAINS.

37* 1 he meant; 2 I don't believe; 3 I think; 4 make(s) ten; 5 His tie doesn't match; 6 resembles his mother; 7 does this pen belong; 8 tank holds; 9 did he know; 10 deserved so much applause; 11 Do you see; 12 includes a section on this very problem; 13 tastes sour; 14 Does it suit; 15 He understands English; 16 does the mixture consist.

38 was S. Johnson's pupil/accompanied him/left Lichfield/appeared as an actor/made his reputation/proved his versatility/joined Lacy/produced a large number/made his last appearance.

39* 1 I spent my holiday in France. 2 I chose France, because I'd never been there. 3 I went there in September. 4 I travelled by plane. 5 I went alone. 6 I took a suitcase and a hold-all. 7 I lived in a hotel. 8 I paid in cash. 9 I met several interesting people— a reporter from England, a teacher from America and several students from Japan. 10 I spent most of the time sightseeing, swimming, and reading. 11 I ate typical French food. 12 I usually drank the local wine, which was very good. 13 I had wonderful weather. 15 I generally slept about eight hours a night—more than usual in fact. 16 I generally woke up at about 7.30. 17 I didn't usually get up till about eight o'clock. 17 I sent postcards to several of my friends. 18 I didn't bring home any souvenirs. 19 The whole holiday cost me £70. 20 I felt I needed another holiday before I went back to work.

40–41 Free composition

42 1 The exhibition closes . . . 2 Clearance . . . hall begins . . . 3 My plane leaves . . . 4 The new regulations come into force . . . 5 What time does the concert end . . .? 6 The Commonwealth games open . . . 7 The ship makes . . . 8 . . ., the winter term finishes . . ., and the spring term starts . . . 9 When do you take up . . .? 10 The new motorway opens . . .

43 1 will have/takes; 2 will start/return; 3 will have/expires; 4 will he do/leaves; 5 is/will renew; 6 sets/will be; 7 will be/ opens; 8 don't leave/will be/get; 9 wait/make/will be; 10 comes/will take; 11 will supersonic travel become/comes; 12 will interrupt/have; 13 don't tell/will simply keep on/do; 14 hear/will let/will be.

44 1 I'm trying; 2 The kettle's nearly boiling. 3 I'm still reading it. 4 are killing; 5 I'm dying; 6 I'm just brushing; 7 I'm driving; 8 I'm going/my car's giving; 9 Peter's acting; 10 earth's happening; 11 How are you getting on; 11 I'm beginning/he's not coming; 13 Aren't you rather jumping; 14 why aren't you taking; 15 you're being.

45 1 Industry is gradually changing over to . . . 2 The present credit squeeze is severely reducing the ability . . . 3 The Company's activities abroad are expanding. 4 Living standards are rising significantly in . . . 5 The police are investigating the crime. 6 The strike at London Airport is resulting in heavy . . . 7 Passenger services on suburban lines are steadily improving. 8 Domestic appliance manufacturers are fighting to maintain . . . 9 In many factories, old-style canteens are now being replaced by . . . The new methods are steadily gaining in favour among workers. 10 The re-equipment programmes of . . . industry are creating a tremendous . . . 11 One big motor manufacturer is extending the use . . . 12 British exporters are also recognizing the efficiency of . . . goods, and a new race of . . . is emerging. The European transport scene is, in fact, constantly changing.

46 1 were talking/passed; 2 was sleeping/was awakened/went/was happening/knew/was barking; 3 didn't take/thought/was joking; 4 broke/were approaching/took/restarted/stopped; 5 were drinking/broke out/soon came/called/was just beginning/arrived/took/were getting/made/succeeded/were still looking; 6 burst/taxied *or* was taxi-ing/was injured; 7 was going on/called/rang/didn't answer/was coming/thought/be having; 8 was looking *or* looked/were you sitting; 9 left/were still talking/seemed to be having; 10 was just wondering/didn't ask/was living.

47 reported; told/looks/are venting/is; Mission control asked/is it coming/do you see; Spacecraft: is coming/is giving/I'm suspecting *or* I suspect/is/is/is spinning; was working/came/I'm transmitting/don't have/is/is; were kept/reported/was falling/ordered; reported/looks/is; confirm/confirms; Does it look/it is still going down; It's slowly going down/are starting; is/we're thinking.

48 1 appears/be gaining; 2 are you sitting/watching/know/be getting; 3 be getting on *or* get on/I'm waiting; 4 think/hear/talking; 5 leave/be waiting; 6 call/be having; 7 says/knows/do/wonder/be thinking; 8 be sitting/doing; 9 seems/be improving/has; 10 smell/burning; 11 be travelling/are overtaking; 12 accept/says/be telling.

49 1 Union leaders are meeting ... 2 I'm taking ... 3 Are you visiting ...? 4 ... because I'm going out. 5 Some friends of ours are coming ... We are meeting them ... 6 ... because I was seeing him ... 7 ... said he was holding ... 8 When is Sviatoslav Richter coming ...? 9 The chairman ... said that they were opening three ... 10 They are taking the show ...

50 1 be coming/meet; 2 be entertaining; 3 be doing; 4 like/be repeating; 5 be seeing/mention; 6 be working/get; 7 disappoint/be expecting; 8 be waiting/go; 9 make/be moving; 10 be waiting/recognize/be wearing.

51 1 I've been waiting; 2 has been learning; 3 had been asking; 4 I've been working; 5 haven't been listening/I've been saying; 6 have been pointing out; 7 had been expecting; 8 had been looking; 9 had been giving; 10 had been flying; 11 you've been seeing; 12 has been operating.

52* 1 It weighs —— 2 It measures —— by —— 3 It costs —— 4 I have —— copies. 5 It contains —— exercises. 6 It feels —— 7 It looks —— 8 They come on page —— 9 I like —— best. 10 It lacks ——

53 1 think/already know; 2 I'm thinking; 3 I'm just smelling/don't they smell; 4 I'm gradually forgetting; 5 see/you're not looking/is pointing; 6 don't hear/you're just imagining; 7 is hearing; 8 I'm just tasting/does it taste; 9 think/is seeing/don't approve; 10 don't think/really knows/he's saying.

54 1 We have unanimously agreed; 2 the man had already died; 3 programme will have been completed; 4 meeting will already have started; 5 flights had been cancelled; 6 he will have reached; 7 parents had already gone to bed; 8 he will have left hospital; 9 plans have changed; 10 I've forgotten the name of the book. 11 it had already taken off; 12 They have got married.

55 1 I've never met him; 2 I haven't tried eating it; 3 He had never studied it before; 4 had been feeling ill; 5 will all have died; 6 hadn't slept very well; 7 It's all been used up; 8 haven't spoken to; 9 had obviously broken in and ransacked the house; 10 haven't read it yet; 11 I hadn't been told anything about it; 12 I'd forgotten your number; 13 It's already been sent; 14 I've just found them.

56* 1 I've been cleaning the car. 2 I've been looking through it. 3 We've been clearing out the cupboard. 4 I haven't had time to look at them yet. 5 It's been raining for the last twenty minutes. 6 Someone has been taken ill. 7 I've been given a day off. 8 I've just come back from a holiday cruise. 9 I thought it had been cancelled. 10 I've been offered a very good job at a much higher salary.

57 has continued/have led/have left/has been resumed/have grown/ has risen/has not been.

58 has made/has been/has been maintained/have improved/has progressed.

59 1 is writing/have already been published; 2 is now going ahead/ have already been completed; 3 are rapidly approaching/has already been reached; 4 are at present taking/has already been scrapped; 5 am saying/has often been said; 6 is currently trying/ have been acquired; 7 is constantly receiving/have on occasion been; 8 is pushing ahead/have been opened; 9 is (or are) apparently managing/have been sanctioned; 10 are still having to/has now quietened down.

60 Free composition

61 1 have taken/was raised; 2 has shown/was first announced; 3 introduced/have taken; 4 made/has been/has now been established/has been; 5 was first published/have changed; 6 were introduced/has been reduced; 7 has gone down/was instituted; 8 have been/were nationalized; 9 has had/took over; 10 rose/has remained.

62 1 I haven't been to the dentist for two months. 2 He hasn't spoken to me about his plans for a year. 3 I haven't met him since he was 15 years old. 4 He hasn't written to me since I was in America. 5 It hasn't rained for three weeks. 6 The side hasn't won a home game for two months. 7 I haven't had a cold since last winter. 8 I haven't set eyes on him since he borrowed some money from me. 9 The Company hasn't made a profit since 1968. 10 I haven't been on holiday for six moths. 11 We haven't seen a batsman of his calibre since the days of Bradman. 12 I haven't mentioned it to him since we met a month a go.

63 1 It's two months since I went . . . 2 It's a year since he spoke . . . 3 It's three weeks since it rained. 4 It's two months since the side won . . . 5 It's six months since I went . . . 6 It's four days since I smoked . . . 7 It's ten days since they wrote saying . . . 8 It's a long time since we were all living . . . 9 It's such a long time since I read the book that . . . 10 It seems ages since he visited us.

64 1 I've written; 2 he's been writing; 3 have you been doing/I've been sitting; 4 we've always lived; 5 have you been keeping; 6 What has happened? 7 He's been drinking; 8 I've already drunk; 9 It's been cooking; 10 Haven't you finished/You've been reading; 11 has forgotten/I've been expecting; 12 Have you been waiting; 13 have you known/I've only just found out/I've been finding out *or* I've found out; 14 he's asked/he's asked.

65 1 I'll let/I've finished; 2 Do not start/have completed; 3 Don't make up/you've had; 4 shall be/I've finished; 5 will man go/has conquered; 6 you'll get/you've worked/you've got/you'll find; 7 will start/have been approved; 8 He'll make/he's had; 9 have thrashed out/shall be able; 10 do not smoke/has taken off.

66 1 let him know/I had finished; 2 to start/they had completed; 3 to make up his mind/he had had; 4 he would be/he had finished; 5 man would go/he had conquered; 6 he would get used to their methods/he had worked there/he had got used to their methods/he would find; 7 would start/had been approved; 8 would make/had had; 9 we would be able/we had thrashed out; 10 to smoke/had taken off.

67 1 got down/had been introduced; 2 died/had reigned; 3 had settled/circulated; 4 was moved/had taken; 5 refused/had been cleared up; 6 realized/had had; 7 returned/had been broken into; 8 understood/had managed; 9 wrote/hadn't yet arrived/replied/had already been sent; 10 called/discovered/had just missed/had gone out; 11 set out/had left/had still not returned; 12 had/had been strengthened; 13 saw/had occupied; 14 won/had not previously been beaten; 15 decided/had stood.

68 1 were/had expected; 2 happened/had feared; 3 arrived/had envisaged; 4 agreed/had not anticipated; 5 were already/had made/had ever dared; 6 seemed/had been made; 7 said/had broken/had succeeded/had previously been thought; 8 began/had ever set; 9 discovered/had not taken; 10 found/had earlier rejected.

69 had been opened/had started/had been invited/had been fixed/had been published.

70 1 . . . since he had already failed . . . 2 When they had made quite sure . . . 3 . . . since they had come no nearer . . . 4 . . . after he had spent . . . 5 . . . since I had always assumed . . . 6 . . . since he had failed . . . 7 . . . he had represented . . . 8 . . . since my old one had expired. 9 . . . since its circulation had dropped . . . 10 . . . as only a small number had ever been put . . .

71 It raises/I can give; British shipbuilders booked/which was; figures were/represented/amounted; This is; This pressure has meant/British yards have been taking/than seemed possible; which amounted/reached; It was never intended/scheme should mean/was there any belief/would guarantee; The board is taking/that is not limited; They have formed/who are examining; They have promised or made/applications are coming up; The *Q.E.2* is/industry is engaged; The Government has not in any way intervened; The ship is/ experts are able; I have discussed; I have also consulted/who has been looking; has been widely reported/there is/I can add.

72* 1 If flowers don't get any water, they die. 2 If the traffic lights are at red, a motorist must pull up. 3 If you want to write a letter, you need pen and paper. 4 If I'm very thirsty, I like to drink lager. 5 If businessmen want to borrow money, they go to see their bank manager. 6 If I make a mistake, I expect the teacher to correct it. 7 If one wants to visit a foreign country, one must have a valid passport. 8 If people feel ill, they go to see a doctor. 9 If there is a power failure, all electrical appliances stop working. 10 If people work in an office, they wear a suit.

73* 1 If those shoes in the window fit me, I shall buy them. 2 If you drop that vase, my wife will murder you! 3 If it's fine tomorrow, we can have a picnic somewhere. 4 If I change my job, I'll try to get something more interesting. 5 If we're late for the theatre, we may not be able to get seats. 6 If you lose my library book, I shall have to pay for it. 7 If you meet some friends of mine in London, introduce yourself to them. 8 If he passes his exam, he'll go on to university. 9 If it's a boy, they'll call it John. 10 If I get a rise next year, we'll think of buying a house.

74 1 If your car should need . . . 2 If I should be . . . 3 If the baby should wake up, give . . . 4 If the talks should break down, . . . 5 If he should dare to show . . . 6 If he will accept . . . 7 If you will take . . . 8 If you will wait . . . 9 If my father will give . . . 10 . . . if he won't give . . .?

75* 1 . . . we leave immediately. 2 . . ., I'll tell him what you said. 3 . . . you will support it with evidence. 4 . . . you'll be in really serious trouble. 5 . . ., I shall buy a new car next month. 6 . . . they can't reach an agreement? 7 . . ., you can assume I'm not coming. 8 . . ., we can expect further industrial unrest. 9 . . ., you will be ready to take the examination next term. 10 I will let you into the secret . . . 11 . . . it is really impossible for you to work it out yourself. 12 . . . he ever discovers the truth? 13 . . . we can give up the idea completely. 14 . . . and I'll find a solution.

76* 1 . . ., he would be able to advise you much better than I can. 2 . . . would take a different view, . . . 3 . . ., you'd probably earn a lot more money elsewhere. 4 . . ., he'd soon tell you whether it was serious or not. 5 . . ., we'd certainly need to buy ourselves a car. 6 . . ., we'd show them round. 7 . . . if we agreed to pay him a bit more. 8 . . ., they would change them for you. 9 . . ., you'd begin to appreciate what the writer is trying to say. 10 . . ., we'd have enough money to rent a comfortable flat.

77 1 If I went to America, I'd visit —— 2 If I could live my life over again, I'd —— 3 If someone called me a fool, I'd —— 4 If I were able to change my first name, I'd —— 5 If I had the chance, I'd —— 6 If I decided to live abroad, I'd —— 7 If I had the money, I'd —— 8 If I saw a house on fire, I'd —— 9 If I had something stolen, I'd —— 10 If I went to live on a desert island, I'd ——

78 1 If she loved him, she would marry him. 2 If our teacher didn't explain things clearly, we wouldn't understand his lessons. 3 If I had a watch, I could tell you the time. 4 If Britain exported enough, she wouldn't have a constant balance of payments problem. 5 If I didn't know the meaning of the word, I'd have to look it up. 6 If this exercise were difficult (*or* weren't easy), not everyone would get the correct answers. 7 If I didn't know the answer, I couldn't tell you. 8 If we had some matches, we could light the fire.

79 1 I wish I could speak . . . Why? Because if I could, —— 2 I wish I had a car. Why? Because if I did, —— 3 She wishes her parents approved . . . Why? Because if they did, —— 4 I wish I were . . . Why? Because if I were, —— 5 I wish you liked . . . Why? Because if you did, ——

80* 1 What would you do about the problem . . .? 2 If I were earning a good salary, . . . 3 . . ., I would tell him to mind his own business. 4 . . . a stranger asked you how old you were? 5 . . ., you'd understand what the writer is trying to say. 6 . . ., your English would probably show a noticeable improvement. 7 . . . I didn't have to? 8 . . . I could afford it. 9 . . . we asked yet another person's opinion. 10 . . ., what could he do about it? 11 . . ., his friends might be more sympathetic. 12 . . . said exactly what you think.

81 1 If he had given . . ., I could have telephoned . . . 2 If the sun hadn't been . . ., the photographs wouldn't have come out . . . 3 If the shop had packed . . ., they wouldn't have got damaged. 4 If the Government hadn't raised . . ., they wouldn't have been . . . 5 If he had been able . . ., he would have passed . . .

82* 1 If he had passed . . ., he would have gone to university. 2 If we had got there . . ., we wouldn't have found the doors locked in our faces. 3 If she had read . . ., she would have understood what I meant. 4 If we hadn't understood . . ., we would have asked him to explain again. 5 If the rocket had gone . . ., it would have marked a step forward in space research.

83* 1 He would have passed . . . if he had taken a little more care. 2 We would have got there . . . if we had left just fifteen minutes earlier. 3 She would have read . . . if she had been able to get a copy. 4 We wouldn't have understood . . . if he hadn't explained in laymen's terms. 5 The rocket would have gone . . . if the third stage had fired successfully.

84 1 If he hadn't failed . . ., he wouldn't be taking . . . 2 If the Government hadn't made . . ., it would win . . . 3 If we hadn't missed . . ., we wouldn't be waiting . . . 4 If there hadn't been . . ., we wouldn't be able . . . 5 If you had taken . . ., you wouldn't be . . .

85* 1 . . . there hadn't been quite such a crowd of people there. 2 It would have been a wonderful day for sailing . . . 3 . . . I had asked you last week? 4 . . ., you wouldn't have got into such difficulties. 5 . . ., I'd have thought it over much more carefully. 6 . . ., he would never have got the job. 7 . . ., it might have avoided a lot of unpleasantness. 8 . . . you had known how desperately he needed it? 9 . . . we had followed your plan rather than mine? 10 . . ., the damage wouldn't have been nearly so extensive. 11 . . . she had known him better. 12 If they hadn't arrived just at that moment, . . .

86 1 Should you need . . . 2 . . . should the need arise. 3 Should you be late . . . 4 Were it not . . . 5 Were such a merger ever to be proposed . . . 6 Were it not . . . 7 Had it not been . . . 8 Had he taken . . . 9 Had the attempted assassination succeeded, . . . 10 Had purchase tax on cars been raised . . .

87* 1 If only you had acted sensibly, . . . 2 If my bank manager calls, . . . 3 . . . he expects us to believe him, . . . 4 . . ., you must take a much greater interest in your work. 5 So long as you watch out for small boats, . . . 6 . . . he'd be willing to help you. 7 . . . you're not feeling very well? 8 How on earth did you find me, . . .? 9 . . ., tell him I'll phone him back later this afternoon. 10 . . . the rival parties are each given an opportunity to explain their policies. 11 If anything goes wrong tomorrow, . . . 12 . . ., why didn't you write it down? 13 . . . I cleaned and oiled it before giving it back. 14 . . ., please say so now. 15 When would we be likely to arrive . . .? 16 . . ., I would never have forgiven them. 17 . . . I didn't have to get up and go to work this morning! 18 . . ., the Prime Minister will be compelled to offer his resignation. 19 If you want to back out from the scheme at this stage, . . . 20 . . . were able to write your letters in English.

88 Free composition

89* 1 . . . we would just manage . . . if we left . . . 2 . . . if I saw him . . ., I would tell . . . you had said. 3 . . . I would accept his explanation only if he would support . . . 4 . . . tell me the truth or he would be . . . 5 . . . my bank manager would lend . . ., I would buy . . . the following month. 6 . . . would happen if they couldn't reach . . . 7 . . . didn't hear from him by the following Friday, I could assume . . . 8 . . . the Government continued . . . in that way, we could expect . . . 9 . . . his work continued . . ., he would be ready . . . the following term. 10 . . . would let me . . . only if I would promise . . . 11 . . . look up . . . only if it was . . . for them . . . themselves. 12 . . . he would say if he ever discovered . . . 13 . . . the worst came to the worst, we could give up . . . 14 . . . give me time and I would find . . .

90* 1 . . . explained . . . to my solicitor, he would be able . . . me . . . than *he* could. 2 . . . would take . . . if I spoke . . . him myself. 3 . . . changed my job, I'd probably earn . . . 4 . . . went . . . he'd soon tell me . . . 5 . . . bought . . ., we'd certainly need . . . 6 . . . came . . ., we'd show . . . 7 . . . would take . . . if we agreed . . . 8 . . . took . . ., they would change . . . me. 9 . . . he read . . ., he'd begin . . . was trying . . . 10 . . . we all pooled . . ., we'd have . . .

91 1 This fact is very well known. 2 The theatre was opened only last month. 3 It will soon be forgotten. 4 The answers must be written in ink. 5 Two of my books have been taken. 6 The vacancy has already been filled. 7 What should be done in such cases? 8 Was anything interesting said? 9 Was it never made clear how the machine was operated? 10 New lawns should be sown in September. 11 I don't think it can be done. 12 He would undoubtedly have been sent to prison if he had been found guilty. 13 The work must be finished by seven o'clock. 14 This type of transistor radio is now being manufactured in Japan. 15 The secret could not possibly have been known. 16 Have all the necessary arrangements been made? 17 Fortunately, nothing had been said about it. 18 All orders will be promptly executed (*or* executed promptly). 19 The man was kept in custody. 20 Are all the rooms regularly cleaned (*or* cleaned regularly)?

92 1 was destroyed; 2 had been bitten; 3 be respected; 4 are being demolished; 5 have been instructed; 6 was saved; 7 is expected to be declared; 8 has been done; 9 was being victimized; 10 was evicted; 11 had been thought; 12 will have been built; 13 be discontinued; 14 being cross-examined; 15 Having been threatened; 16 being treated; 17 to have been informed/had been withdrawn; 18 are asked/have been given/be rectified; 19 not being offered; 20 having been found.

93 1 will be added to; 2 was sent to/(was) distributed among; 3 were made at *or* during *or* before *or* after; 4 has been arranged between *or* for *or* by; 5 had been built since *or* after; 6 to be left in; 7 have been consulted on; 8 be kept out; 9 was discovered towards *or* before *or* at *or* by; 10 will not be felt till (until) *or* before/will have been exhausted. 11 have now been converted into; 12 will be equipped with; 13 will not be known for; 14 be defeated by; 15 to be closed for *or* during; 16 is being investigated by; 17 be switched off at *or* by *or* before *or* after; 18 has been heard of *or* from; 19 have been handled with; 20 will be met at.

94 1 It must be pulled out. 2 It has to be washed up. 3 They should be pointed out. 4 I might be (*or* get) knocked down. 5 It would be blown out. 6 He may be let off. 7 They are often broken off. 8 It is held up. 9 They are laid off. 10 It is taken down (and may be used in court). 11 It must be given up. 12 It must have been taken down (*or* away). 13 It could have been picked up. 14 The meeting could be put off till a later date.

95 1 The search was given up . . . 2 That ought to have been pointed out to me . . . 3 That question wasn't brought up . . . 4 The matter should be looked into. 5 . . . that the child had been well brought up. 6 Our visit had to be put off . . . 7 . . . that your house had been broken into. 8 I was given to understand that my services would be called on if (they were) needed. 9 Don't speak until you're spoken to. 10 He will stop showing off if no notice is taken of him (*or* if he's taken no notice of). 11 His request . . . was turned down by . . . 12 Many new buildings are being put up . . . 13 Every penny you spent must be accounted for. 14 It was pointed out that the matter couldn't be dealt with until all the facts were known. 15 This stamp hasn't been stuck on . . . 16 The meeting had to be broken up by . . . 17 The truth of what I'm saying will be borne out by events. 18 We were held up at the Customs for . . . 19 How can the desired result be brought about? 20 He hates being made fun of.

96 1 are *or* are being *or* were *or* were being *or* will be turned out; 2 had been *or* would be provided for; 3 is being done up; 4 being taken on; 5 is always being told off; 6 be looked up; 7 was still being run in; 8 be drawn up; 9 will be broken off; 10 would be looked into; 11 had been badly let down; 12 having been blotted out.

97 1 The oldest councillor was given the freedom . . . 2 Access to the . . . was denied to . . . 3 The child was shown how . . . 4 He was declared 'persona non grata' and was allowed . . . 5 He was given . . . 6 Why wasn't he offered the job? 7 Weren't you promised a rise . . .? 8 He was left a legacy . . . 9 . . . stamps, he found he had been sold forgeries. 10 What were you paid for . . .? 11 He should be told never . . . 12 You were asked to meet . . . 13 Shall I be sent the details? 14 The goods will be sent to you . . . 15 That boy must be taught a lesson! 16 Slum-clearance must be given priority over . . .

98* 1 He should be given a sedative. 2 He is paid a salary. 3 A witness is asked questions by a lawyer (who is acting for the opposite side). 4 He must be shown a (valid) passport. 5 Friends and relatives are sent gifts or Christmas cards. 6 I might be sent a prospectus. 7 He is given an anaesthetic. 8 I would most resent being told that I was a fool. 9 I would like to be offered the opportunity of visiting Moscow. 10 In England, an MP is paid £3,250 p.a. 11 They might be left a legacy. 12 The people are denied freedom of speech. 13 I would need to be lent some money. 14 I was taught French.

99 1 He is said to be . . . 2 This surgeon is considered to be . . . 3 Some redundancy in the Midlands is now thought to be . . . 4 The statements he had made were proved to be . . . 5 Mr Smith was understood to be willing . . . 6 The Chancellor is believed to be thinking . . . 7 The electricity supply industry is expected to be running . . . 8 Several . . . manufacturers are reported to be planning . . . 9 The brewers are expected to raise . . . 10 The drug was claimed to produce . . . 11 The police are said to have acted . . . 12 The Prime Minister was alleged to have misled . . . 13 The Government is believed to have had . . . 14 The explosion was believed to have been caused . . . 15 The . . . equipment is presumed to have been put . . . 16 The information was later admitted to have been obtained . . .

100 1 The fact that such a storm . . . was raised by the new scheme means that it can't have been properly explained to . . . 2 He was warned by . . . not to let himself be led astray by . . . 3 . . . that too much time was being taken up in . . . 4 The boy's rudeness was put down to his having been spoiled by . . . 5 Fascism isn't accepted by . . ., any more than Communism is. 6 Couldn't someone be asked to do . . . without it(s) being known? 7 Not until later was it discovered that the picture had been stolen. 8 Never before had anyone been sent to prison for . . . 9 Only in this way could the law be made . . . 10 On very few occasions was this question fully debated in . . .

101 1 It was said that no agreement could be reached on . . . 2 The rebellion was put down by . . . and martial law was declared. 3 He wanted the information to be treated as confidential. 4 His property will be disposed of and the proceeds (will be) shared among . . . 5 Had I been told that the subject . . . was to be brought up at . . . 6 He dislikes being thought a fool by . . . 7 After having been ignored by . . ., 8 Should it be proved beyond doubt that the fire was caused by an accident, the man who is at present being held (by the police) on suspicion of arson will, naturally, be released. 9 On being informed that he was wanted by the police, the man realized that he had been betrayed by . . . 10 When the stolen car was finally discovered by the police, it was found that it had been stripped of . . ., and that the air had been let out of . . .

102 1 The Prime Minister was to have made . . ., but had to cancel it at the last minute because . . . 2 The fire brigade finally got the fire under control, but not before it had caused extensive damage. 3 The police arrested the car thief after chasing him . . . 4 Don't let your failure depress you. 5 In view of the widespread concern (that) the community feels at the plan to build . . . village, the local Council has decided to hold a . . . 6 We (*or* the management) respectfully inform(s) patrons that we (*or* it) reserve(s) the right to refuse admission to anyone, without giving any reason. 7 Thieves had broken into the house and (had) stolen two . . . 8 Only after the scientists had subjected the new . . . tests did the Company put it on the market. 9 Macaulay stated that the British public had hounded Byron . . . 10 The leader hadn't thought out the plan at all well. 11 The Board ought to have made it quite clear to the shareholders, before they held . . . meeting, that they would not allow them to vote for . . . 12 You should have obtained your . . . before you made any decision to take . . . 13 The army authorities needn't have caused him . . . distress by telling him that . . . action, as they later discovered that they had made a mistake as to . . . 14 The reporter withheld information about the source from which he had obtained . . . 15 The Minneapolis Symphony Orchestra gave a . . .

103* An atheist is a person who believes that there is no God. An actor . . . who acts on the stage or for cinema films. A journalist . . . who writes for a newspaper. A barber . . . who cuts men's hair. A newsagent . . . who sells newspapers. An MP . . . who represents electors in the House of Commons. A spokesman . . . who speaks on behalf of a group. An eyewitness . . . who can bear witness from what he has himself seen. A solicitor . . . who prepares legal documents. A stockbroker . . . who buys and sells shares, often on behalf of others. A greengrocer . . . who sells fruit and vegetables. A teetotaller . . . who never drinks alcoholic liquor.

104 A person who steals things is called a thief. . . . beer is called a brewer. . . . clothes is called a tailor. . . . plans and drawings . . . draftsman (*or* draughtsman). . . . examinations . . . examiner. . . . shares in a company . . . shareholder. . . . foreign languages . . . linguist. . . . theatre regularly . . . theatre-goer. . . . public house . . . publican. . . . bicycle . . . cyclist. . . . office or position . . . nominee. . . . hospital . . . patient. . . . plays . . . playwright. . . . House of Lords . . . peer. . . . concerts, etc., . . . reviewer.

105 1 The pipeline that (*or* which) carries the town's water supplies has been severed. 2 The exhibition my friend took me to see was not . . . 3 . . . things a computer can do is to save . . . 4 . . . one major problem the Government has yet to tackle. 5 . . . an issue which (*or* that) raises strong emotions. 6 . . . deal of work that (*or* which) has to be done before . . . 7 . . . in the sale which (*or* that) took place . . . 8 . . . that many men who (*or* that) went on strike were in fact willing . . . 9 . . . a system which, he said, had won . . . 10 The gales which (*or* that) swept . . . last night caused widespread damage. 11 . . . prices which (*or* that) compare . . . 12 Is the offer you made last week still open? 13 . . . of people who will be travelling . . . 1980's will place a heavy strain . . . 14 . . . for the goods we buy from abroad. 15 . . . wreck which (*or* that) had lain . . . 16 . . . at a price young couples can afford to pay. 17 . . . very person who will do the job quickly. 18 . . . closely knit community life which (*or* that) gives older towns . . . 19 . . . of many people who might otherwise still be living . . . 20 . . . is a fact of life people have grown accustomed to facing.

106* 1 . . . man that/who commits such crimes should . . . 2 The suit you're wearing is identical . . . 3 . . . Englishman that/who works in the City carries . . . 4 Laws that/which have outlived their usefulness should . . . 5 The yacht that/which started last arrived first. 6 The house that/which stood in the path of the new motorway has . . . 7 The car that/which won the race was . . . 8 . . . the photographs we took in Austria? 9 . . . man I've ever spoken to. 10 . . . anything you ask him to. 11 The man you saw talking to her was . . . 12 . . . call she has received this evening. 13 Nothing I do is . . . 14 . . . anyone that/who will listen attentively. 15 . . . someone that/who speaks his mind.

107* 1 . . . a teacher that/who understands their problems. 2 . . . students who/that have a sense of humour. 3 . . . people who are sure to pay him back. 4 . . . work you've done? 5 . . . food one gets in England is not . . . 6 . . . uncles who/that give them presents. 7 . . . women who/that chatter incessantly. 8 . . . men who/that are in love with their cars. 9 The excuse the student gave was . . . 10 . . . water that/which separates England and France is called . . . 11 . . . the damage I did. 12 . . . anyone among the audience here tonight that/who puts any faith in the promises of the present Government. 13 . . . a man that/who believes in the value of self-discipline. 14 . . . people that/who criticize others behind their backs. 15 . . . country that/which has long been popular as a tourist centre.

108* 1 . . . are wearing look rather expensive. 2 . . . made aroused fierce opposition. 3 I returned the book you lent me. 4 . . . writes is full of spelling mistakes. 5 . . . took last year was much too short. 6 . . . have listened to put no expression into their performances. 7 . . . complained about was very inexperienced. 8 . . . cooks is delicious. 9 . . . have just bought was surprisingly cheap. 10 What do you think of the clothes the English wear? 11 The audience clearly disagreed with every word the speaker said. 12 . . . must deal with quickly is the housing shortage. 13 I hope you took the medicine the doctor prescribed for you. 14 . . . are now building are getting more and more complex. 15 Could you understand the information the policeman gave you?

109* 1 He was expelled from every school he attended. 2 . . . asked puzzled the teacher. 3 . . . finds itself in is an unenviable one. 4 Did you follow the advice your lawyer gave you? 5 . . . left was given away to charity. 6 . . . ever gave was under Koussevitzki in Paris. 7 . . . wish to interview are all aged between 22–25. 8 . . . gives are extremely tedious. 9 . . . received were of very uneven quality. 10 Is there anything I can do to help? 11 Nobody liked the plans the architect had drawn up. 12 Is he the Mr Smith you were telling me about? 13 I haven't yet met the girl my brother intends to marry. 14 . . . had so carefully made had to be abandoned. 15 The London you describe is very different from the London I remember.

110 1 . . . dispute, which disrupted . . . lasted, has now been settled. 2 . . . the Cabinet, which now . . . members, will be reduced . . . 3 . . . policemen, who are . . . helpfulness, were sent . . . 4 . . . estate, which is situated . . . 5 . . . Exchequer, who had . . . reporters, later issued . . . 6 . . . *Don Giovanni*, which opened . . . night, looks like . . . 7 . . . London, which will . . . week, contains . . . 8 . . . first speech, which was broadcast, was . . . second, which he gave before . . . 9 . . . weather, which they often associate with fog and rain and which sometimes makes . . . England, is not so bad . . . 10 . . . Egbert, who united . . . 11 . . . Parliament, which cost . . . build, were begun . . . 12 . . . Corporation, which had begun . . . 1922 as the British Broadcasting Company, launched . . . *or* . . . Corporation, which, as the British Broadcasting Company, had begun . . . 1922, launched . . . 13 . . . Authority, which was . . . 1954, provides . . . 14 . . . figure, which was artificially inflated . . .

111 1 . . . speaker, who spoke . . . 2 . . . job, which would be . . . 3 . . . projectors, which are . . . 4 . . . type, which have been . . . 5 . . . Oxbridge, who had failed . . . occasion, was expelled . . . 6 . . . garage, which gives . . . 7 . . . manner, which to our way of thinking was . . . 8 . . . new car, which seats . . . luggage, will be very popular . . . 9 . . . microfilm, which is one . . . 10 . . . goods, which were . . .

112* 1 . . . book, which was published last week, is about . . . 2 . . . Company, which specializes in Shakespearian productions, is . . . 3 . . . car, which has an aerodynamic design, should . . . 4 His father, who set up in business ten years ago, has . . . 5 . . . asbestos, which is fireproof, will . . . 6 . . . code, which has been thoroughly revised in the light of new standards, should . . . 7 . . . talk, which was given on television, was . . . 8 . . . bicycle, which could yield some important clues, has . . . 9 . . . application, which he had sent off as soon as the advertisement appeared. 10 . . . Race, which is generally televised, takes . . . 11 . . . Gas, which is available in enormous quantities, is now . . . 12 . . . meeting, which was attended by two rival groups, broke up . . . 13 . . . lighting, which will make for much greater safety on the roads. 14 Trams, which disappeared from Britain many years ago, are still . . . 15 . . . flowers, which grow in a variety of wonderful colours, are . . .

113* 1 . . . scheme, which we shall introduce in the new year. 2 . . . Dover, which can be seen from France on a clear day, are . . . 3 . . . horse, which was ridden by a young and unknown jockey, was . . . 4 . . . grandfather, who is now in his eighties, was . . . 5 . . . Conrad, who was Polish by birth, wrote . . . 6 . . . Railways, which have been running at a loss for many years, are . . . 7 . . . Cambridge, which traces its beginnings to the twelfth and thirteenth centuries, comprises . . . 8 . . . lawyer, who spoke with great conviction, made . . . 9 . . . water, which is essential to life, does not . . . 10 . . . Shaw, who wrote many controversial plays, died . . . 11 . . . Street, which is the centre of the newspaper world in Britain, is . . . 12 . . . Music, which attracts visitors from all over the world. 13 . . . tides, which were abnormally high, . . . 14 . . . breakfast, which is often quite a substantial meal. 15 . . . harvest, which promised to be a very good one till the rain came, has . . .

114 1 ... Richter, whose virtuosity ... 2 ... Minister, whose support ... declined, may ... 3 ... Russell, whose philosophical ... world, died ... 4 ... Bill, whose provisions ... controversy, will be ... 5 ... President, whose administration ... months, is unlikely ... 6 ... lecture, the subject of which was ... 7 ... driver, on whose shoulders rested ... accident, was sent ... 8 ... Nelson, in whose memory a column ... Square, was famous ... 9 ... the man without whose generosity your Society ... 10 ... Smith, whose letter ... yesterday, should check ... 11 ... hospital, many of whose patients are ... 12 ... this car, whose exterior dimensions ... unchanged, gives ... 13 ... Company, whose results ... forecast, and whose long-term recovery ... 14 ... men whose contracts had been ... 15 ... Government, over some of whose policies they have ...

115 (*Note:* Although the prepositions could come at the beginning of the relative clauses in every case, the answers suggest the most likely position.) 1 ... the person I'm sharing a flat with a very congenial ... 2 ... address you should write to. 3 ... man you can absolutely depend on. 4 ... the person I gave the money to. 5 ... job you can take your time over, because ... 6 ... the pupils he was responsible for had suddenly ... *or* ... the pupils for whom he was responsible had suddenly ... 7 ... businessmen I spoke to recently thought ... 8 ... a medium through which ideas ... 9 ... space during which both men and management ... 10 ... chassis around which the car is built gives ... 11 ... a basis on which talks ... 12 ... structure under which the men ... 13 ... model on which reliable tests ... 14 ... disease in which high sugar consumption ... 15 ... places in which everybody lives ...

116* 1 Which is the cupboard the wine glasses are kept in? 2 I don't like the material the curtains are made of. 3 Have you read the book this quotation comes from? 4 I can't find the cup this saucer belongs to. 5 What's the name of the programme we're listening to? 6 Trigonometry is a subject I don't get on with. 7 ... asked for. 8 ... can speak to? 9 She bought the house her daughter now lives in. 10 What's the name of the school you went to? 11 The thieves couldn't open the safe the money was kept in. 12 ... we had got into was ...

117 1 ... passengers, four of whom were British, all ... 2 ... stations, all of which are ... 3 ... questions, the answers to which proved ... 4 ... force, the composition and power of which would be ... 5 ... by-pass, by means of which heavy congestion ... relieved, have now ... 6 ... maintenance, on which Mr Heath ... reputation, was ... 7 ... project, to which the Government ... support, could earn ... 8 ... proposals, the most far-reaching of which are ... 9 ... staff, without whose unremitting support it would not ... 10 ... taxation, the study of whose provisions will be ... 11 ... tankers, ten of which it already has ... *or* ... tankers, of which is already has ten ... 12 ... Europe, two of which are ... 13 ... beans, of which we are ... 14 ... supporters, among whom was Bertrand Russell, ... 15 ... constituencies, each of which returns ...

118 1 ... course, which was ... 2 ... heating, which should make ... 3 ... bed, which explains ... 4 ... diversity, which they could do ... 5 ... years, which is ... 6 ... everything, which I thought ... 7 ... secretary, who was supposed ... 8 ... meeting, which was ... 9 ... repair, which means ... 10 ... solicitor, who advised ... 11 ... decade, which is ... 12 ... enough, which may well prove ... 13 ... thoroughly, which was ... 14 ... resignation, which was ...

119 1 ... safe, the door of which he then carefully locked before ... 2 ... houses, in addition to which they would look ... 3 ... attitude, having said which she burst ... 4 ... apologized, (to do) which required ... 5 ... cuttings, in the subsequent planting of which the greatest ... 6 ... encore, at which the audience burst ... 7 ... paddock, which (fact) must be borne ... 8 ... tournament, despite which, however, he managed ... 9 ... next year, some allowance for which must be made ... 10 ... food, well over half which was ... 11 ... towns, the unfortunate neglect of which in the past has been ... 12 ... later, by which time, however, the thieves ...

120 1 The days when you could travel ... 2 ... America, where he advocated ... 3 ... times when everyone ... 4 ... a situation where you know ... 5 ... past when he had experienced ... 6 ... 1586, where, some time later, he became ... 7 ... reason why you should take ... 8 ... roads, where it was possible ... 9 ... a policy where premiums are related ... 10 ... country where there is ... 11 ... 1975, when Britain begins ... 12 ... raised, when it was ... 13 ... (as may well be the case) ... 14 ..., and such friends as he has ... 15 ... enough, as has been ... 16 You have the same problem ... car as we had ... 17 ... situation, as we later discovered.

121 1 What the speaker said ... 2 ... explain what you have ... 3 ... remembered what they had learned. 4 What you're asking ... 5 He's what's known as ... 6 ... just what I didn't want ... 7 What amazes me is ... 8 ... be what you're ... 9 Mind what you say ... 10 ... marked out what seemed ...

122* 1 ... what he was talking about. 2 ... what eventually happened? 3 ... what he had paid for it. 4 ... what we have just discussed? 5 ... what you did? 6 ... what he intended to do. 7 ... what I have just suggested? 8 What I can't understand is

... 9 ... what other people think about this problem. 10 What most surprised her teachers was ...

123* 1 lifting restrictions in the near future; 2 following such a course of action; 3 doing the same thing day after day; 4 bullying younger boys. 5 walking unaccompanied in the park at night; 6 bringing up his children. 7 pointing out other people's faults; 8 disobeying the orders of a superior officer; 9 taking matches into the mines; 10 locking the building at night? 11 using factory-built units to a far greater extent; 12 saving money, instead of hoping to win it on football pools; 13 satisfying the demands of the local residents; 14 going to the Arctic for a holiday; 15 doing as they had originally planned; 16 being short-sighted, this agreement will help in making future disputes unlikely.

124* 1 eating starchy foods; 2 going abroad; 3 making school furniture; 4 smoking in restaurants; 5 being so late; 6 giving the jury clear directions; 7 always being well dressed; 8 putting everything back in its place; 9 travelling on a slow train; 10 introducing the new topic immediately; 11 entering my house; 12 deciding whether to take legal action; 13 swimming in that particular part of the sea/being carried away by dangerous currents; 14 putting the assistant to a great deal of trouble/buying anything; 15 having to contend with rough seas/crossing the Channel in record time; 16 taking fewer subjects/getting a good result in the examination.

125* 1 meeting; 2 eating; 3 having seen; 4 lending; 5 speaking; 6 staying; 7 smoking; 8 increasing; 9 having made; 10 travelling; 11 following; 12 restraining.

126 1 trying/answer; 2 building; 3 increasing; 4 becoming; 5 trying/make; 6 having; 7 dislike/living; 8 winning; 9 try/discuss/speaking; 10 teaching; 11 increasing; 12 travelling.

127* 1 losing; 2 redecorating; 3 telling; 4 making; 5 lending; 6 laughing; 7 waiting; 8 speaking; 9 listening; 10 reading; 11 being sent; 12 supporting; 13 crying; 14 travelling; 15 arriving; 16 taking.

128 1 receiving *or* having received; 2 seeing *or* having seen; 3 receiving *or* having received; 4 my trying; 5 actually promising; 6 the Government setting up; 7 there being; 8 being; 9 his being; 10 him *or* his ever agreeing.

129* 1 people begging in the streets; 2 telling me to mind my own business; 3 making a decision; 4 inviting him to the party/meeting lots of strangers; 5 my getting drunk last night/reminding him of a few of his own past lapses; 6 mentioning it/having friends of your own nationality; 7 meeting you; 8 being away from home a lot? 9 buying your things there/waiting in queues? 10 getting married; 11 coming forward to give evidence; 12 going to Scotland/visiting Wales; 13 making a decision/taking a step which he might afterwards regret; 14 discussing the question with him; 15 paying a whole month's rent in advance; 16 agreeing to co-operate?

130 1 to solve; 2 to meet; 3 to have; 4 to close down; 5 to be; 6 not to understand; 7 to resign; 8 to do; 9 never to follow; 10 to know; 11 to look into; 12 to meet.

131* 1 to do the work unpaid; 2 to have the operation performed? 3 to bring out the trapped miners; 4 to raise production by 5 per cent/to increase it still further; 5 to leave their homes; 6 to call at the shop/to pick up the goods myself; 7 to visit it again; 8 to ask him for help; 9 to snow quite a lot; 10 to see my driving licence; 11 to know; 12 to be.

132* 1 We can't afford to waste time discussing the matter. 2 The students appeared to understand most of the lecture. 3 The men have decided not to work overtime in future; 4 The contractors paid a heavy penalty for failing to complete the building on time. 5 The shop assistant hastened to apologize for appearing rude. 6 By his great presence of mind, the driver managed to avoid a serious accident. 7 Do you think the firm will offer to repair the damage caused by one of their employees? 8 I'm sure he won't refuse to listen to what I have to say. 9 Having been asked to say a few words on the subject, the man proceeded to make a long speech about something entirely different. 10 The shipyard undertook to finish the job within 6 months.

133* 1 to make; 2 to exercise; 3 to state; 4 to rejoin; 5 to do; 6 to have; 7 to investigate; 8 to strike; 9 to build; 10 to postpone.

134 1 The letter summoned me to appear . . . 2 The notice warned the public not to bathe . . . was flying. 3 . . . a note reminding him to lock . . . 4 A notice . . . terminal instructed passengers to check in . . . 5 My old friend pressed me to have . . . I went. 6 The teacher told the student to pay . . . he was doing. 7 She implored her friend not to tell her husband. 8 The speaker challenged his opponent to state . . . if he dare(d). 9 I invited the new member to join . . . 10 My friend encouraged me to take . . . matter. 11 The letter directed him to make his way . . . and (to) wait . . .

135* 1 to make such a cutting remark? 2 to investigate and report on the role of the Public Schools; 3 to increase their sales efforts abroad; 4 to speak English? 5 to stop smoking; 6 to take him to the nearest police station; 7 to abandon our cherished plan; 8 to take up a life of crime; 9 to spend the night at the airport; 10 to do the clearing up; 11 to check the pressure of the tyres; 12 to take a holiday myself; 13 to support many deserving causes; 14 to give up hope completely.

136* 1 The manager has chosen Smith to lead ... America. 2 I didn't mean you to tell anyone. 3 I didn't expect the Robinsons to invite us to dinner. 4 Will you help me (to) finish the work? 5 He expects everyone to be punctual. 6 The firm will probably ask him to resign. 7 I want you to give me some information. 8 The police wish to interview two men. 9 The man elected to go to prison. 10 He didn't mean to make you unhappy. 11 Your parents have been begging us to go and visit them. 12 He didn't dare (to) inform the police that he was being blackmailed.

137 (*Note:* the alternatives given in brackets are acceptable, but are less likely than the first suggestion) 1 to keep; 2 convincing (*or* to be convinced); 3 to come; 4 causing (*or* having caused); 5 to take *or* taking; 6 smoking; 7 him *or* his saying (*or* having said); 8 you to see; 9 to be; 10 you to consult (*or* your consulting); 11 you to go; 12 the holder to cash (*or* the holder's cashing); 13 to swim (*or* swimming); 14 learning *or* to learn; 15 to watch; 16 to speak; 17 driving; 18 their members to think/deciding to strike; 19 to pass/to mention (*or* mentioning); 20 to answer.

138 1 me to say; 2 him to think; 3 locking (*or* having locked); 4 his listeners to give; 5 causing *or* having caused; 6 all cars to be regularly tested; 7 him to drop *or* his dropping; 8 him to try.

139* 1 mentioning it to him; 2 to keep your appointment last night; 3 to revise much of our work *or* telling how important the examination was; 4 completely overhauling *or* to be completely overhauled; 5 to discuss your private affairs; 6 travelling by ship to travelling by plane; 7 pay all those bills soon; 8 stay out late; 9 getting involved in anything dishonest; 10 to cross swords with him; 11 to deal briefly with the remainder; 12 doing the same job/working in an office; 13 doing it the way I suggested; 14 to do something constructive.

140* 1 enter *or* entering the building; 2 making those disparaging remarks about him; 3 fight *or* fighting the blaze; 4 beating on our necks; 5 feeling better; 6 come in; 7 taking *or* to take the man's wallet; 8 making their way slowly towards the summit; 9 hidden under a pile of papers; 10 reading her diary; 11 put right; 12 leave *or* leaving the building; 13 to be broken; 14 hanging with my coat; 15 walking towards the ticket barrier; 16 waiting a very long time; 17 scorching; 18 talking for ever; 19 sitting on a makeshift raft; 20 approaching.

141* 1 tell us; 2 go; 3 get him down; 4 come back and put things right; 5 cycle to school; 6 take a breathalyser test; 7 deter us; 8 get out of control; 9 follow the instructions of the official leadership; 10 change their (*or* its) tactics.

142* 1 I was made to say my prayers. 2 I was made to get dressed. 3 I was made to wash my hands. 4 I was made to clean my teeth. 5 I was made to go to church. 6 I was made to apologize. 7 I was made to write a 'thank you' letter. 8 I was made to tidy it up. 9 I was made to go to the doctor. 10 I was made to work harder.

143 1 that their informant was; 2 that the situation is; 3 that it was; 4 that it was; 5 that what he said was; 6 that it was; 7 that his long-term optimism was; 8 suspects that his party has; 9 that the ascent had taken; 10 that his evidence had been; 11 that earlier theories were; 12 that the gain in reserves was (*or* has been); 13 that they had been stolen; 14 that their candidate was; 15 that the cost of the scheme was/that its implementation was.

144 1 declared the book to be; 2 found the overhead projector to be; 3 thought the film to be; 4 considered the speaker to have over-stated; 5 showed the man's alibi to be; 6 assumed the construction of such a building to be/believed it to be; 7 revealed himself to be; 8 knew him to be; 9 discovered £20,000 worth of precious stones to be; 10 thought it to be.

145 1 Having witnessed the crime; 2 Learning (*or* Having learned); 3 saying; 4 protesting violently; 5 When visiting a strange city; 6 Although receiving general support from the House; 7 intending to take their cars with them to the Continent; 8 He strikes me as being an intelligent man. 9 Having (now) heard your side of the question; 10 Having been warned; 11 Judging by what the critics say; 12 Spring having (now) come.

146 1 Being away at the time . . . floods, I could do nothing to help . . . 2 I found . . . sale, the best bargains having already been snapped up . . . 3 Deciding that it would be . . . persisted, the rescue party put off . . . 4 Having been brought up in the belief . . . sinful, he now leads . . . 5 The children . . . holiday, the school having been closed because of . . . 6 Even allowing for the fact that . . . under-rehearsed, last night's concert . . . 7 He was very angry . . . down, having had it serviced . . . 8 No one was surprised . . . Bank Rate, it having already been confidently expected . . . 9 The man . . . work, having been passed over in favour . . . 10 We decided . . . Oxford, it being then the time . . . vacation and there being few students . . . (*or* . . . vacation and few students being in residence). 11 He had to . . . house, the Bank being unable to lend . . . 12 The police . . . boy wandering about the docks, (and) apparently looking . . .

147* 1 . . ., still firmly maintaining that he was innocent. 2 Having had some experience in these matters, . . . 3 . . . hidden in a disused cellar. 4 While digging the foundations of a new office block, . . . 5 . . . driving on icy roads. 6 Having been told what English food is like, . . . 7 . . . going towards the river bank. 8 . . . having been erected on three sides of it. 9 . . . stating that their earlier reports were quite wrong. 10 . . . shooting pheasants out of season. 11 Having promised to give him every assistance, . . . 12 . . . waving goodbye to friends and relatives.

148* 1 . . ., they decided to stay at home. 2 . . ., he was even more anxious to get hold of a copy. 3 . . ., he gets very ill-tempered. 4 They decided to re-visit Edinburgh, . . . 5 . . ., I think he should be let off with a caution. 6 . . ., the matter doesn't seem quite so serious. 7 The champion decided to withdraw from the tennis tournament, . . . 8 A lion escaped from the zoo, . . . 9 I haven't yet considered the questions . . . 10 . . ., the gambler tried to borrow money from his friends at the casino. 11 I borrowed a few pounds from a friend, . . . 12 . . ., the English are less insular than they used to be.

149* 1a the judge sentenced him to six years' hard labour; b is a popular Sunday activity in London; 2a I would say that the Government are more worried than they will admit; b is a very difficult art; 3a the climbers took several risks during their hasty descent; b requires great patience and understanding; 4a the cross-Channel swimmer approached Cap Griz Nez four hours after leaving the English coast. b is for some people more enjoyable than going to a swimming-pool. 5a the workmen unearthed a hoard of Roman coins; b is not my idea of fun; 6a the champion soon left his challengers behind; b demands more concentration than daytime driving; 7a John was interrupted several times; b generally results in mistakes in his work; 8a the motorist drew up at the next filling station; b often means making several preliminary attempts; 9a the soloist broke a string; b requires a good ear; 10a I noticed a suspicious character loitering near the house; b was most unexpected.

150 1 getting/to know/judging or having judged; 2 acting/loitering; 3 you or your going/to accompany or accompanying; 4 doing/doing; 5 to go/sit or to sit/listening; 6 doing; 7 to speak/speaking; 8 cooking/preparing; 9 him or his saying/my borrowing/paying; 10 disappointing or to disappoint/to go/decorating; 11 you to wait/deciding/to accept; 12 joining/to have/him showing.

151 1 you cheating/stay/to do; 2 blaming/to do; 3 being left or to be left/having been accustomed/having; 4 complain/to do/putting; 5 having/to say/to die; 6 lending/to pay/forgetting/to remember; 7 making up/attending; 8 your or you being/to rely/his letting;

336

9 pointing/to show; 10 having/looking/to read *or* reading/to prevent/saying; 11 girl living/going/to accompany *or* accompanying/women having become; 12 my *or* me asking/husband's being/study/persuading/to do/to want/to emulate.

152 1 No sooner had he put down; 2 Little did the thieves realize; 3 The doctor ... that on no account should he return; 4 Not for one moment would I doubt; 5 Not until many years later did the whole truth; 6 So dense was the smoke that; 7 Such was his fear; 8 Rarely have we seen; 9 In vain did the Member for Oxbridge try; 10 To such a pitch had their hopes been raised that; 11 Nowhere else in the City will you find ... skills than in a; 12 Never again should such a situation be allowed; 13 Only when ... passengers did the pilot agree; 14 No longer are contributions ...technology confined/Nowhere is this more true; 15 Only if ... agreement will a lasting peace be established.

153 1 Under no circumstances should the back of this radio be removed; 2 On only one previous occasion have we seen; 3 No doubt he has good reason; 4 In very few cases has such a major operation proved; 5 In a few cases, it has been found that; 6 It was only yesterday that he mentioned; 7 nor would he pose for a photograph; 8 Not for some time now have we had; 9 On one or two occasions, wild duck have been seen; 10 The police admitted that seldom had they had to deal; 11 The Minister ... that on each occasion help from the Government had been forthcoming, and that in not one single case had such emergencies continued; 12 In neither the Commons ... Lords was the Bill given; 13 It was as long as four years ago that the two countries first began; 14 Not until quite recently, however, did the talks appear; 15 On all but a few issues there is now.

154* 1 To such an extent had the situation deteriorated that troops had to be called in. 2 ..., but not even then did everyone understand. 3 So complicated was the machine that only a skilled operator could use it. 4 Only three men know the true facts of the situation. 5 ... that no sooner had he tried to use the machine than it stopped working. 6 Neither the driver nor his passengers realized what danger they had been in. 7 ... nor on the previous one did anyone raise this particular problem. 8 ... of discussion did the delegates finally reach agreement. 9 ... of discussion that the delegates finally reached agreement. 10 ..., the Prime Minister said that at no time had he promised to reduce the level of taxation.

155 1 *a*He expressed his thanks*b*. (naturally): *a* Of course, he expressed his thanks; *b* He expressed his thanks in a natural manner. 2 *a*The teacher*a* thought the student was*b* not*c* intelligent. (obviously): *a* It is clear that the teacher thought the student was not intelligent; *b* In the teacher's opinion, the student's lack of intelligence was obvious; c The student was intelligent, but his intelligence wasn't immediately apparent. 3 There were[a] a few passengers[a,b] on the bus[c] on week-days[c]. (only): *a only* emphasizes the fewness of the passengers; b implies *but not on* other forms of transport; c implies *but not at week-ends.* 4 [a]The speaker had not argued his case at all[b]. (clearly): a It was clear that the speaker had not in any way supported his case with arguments; b The speaker had argued his case, but his arguments weren't very clear. 5 [a]Some club members were[b] horrified at[c] the suggestion of[d] small changes. (even): a Other people were horrified, but also, and rather surprisingly, some club members; b Club members had other feelings, but also went to the extreme of being horrified; c The suggestion alone was enough to horrify some club members, not to mention the changes themselves; d One might have expected some club members to be horrified at the suggestion of big changes, but, rather surprisingly, small changes were enough to horrify them. 6 I[a] remember his being able to play football[b]. (well): a I remember this clearly; b He was a good footballer. 7 The rescue party[a] managed to take[b] ten of the crew off the ship[c] before it sank. (just): a They managed with difficulty (they nearly didn't succeed); b They took ten of the crew and no more; c They rescued the crew immediately before the ship sank. 8 I[a] don't[b] want to put myself under an obligation to him[c] by asking a favour. (particularly): a I am very anxious not to put myself under an obligation; b I would rather not do so if it can be avoided; c I don't want to put myself under an obligation to him in any way, and least of all by asking a favour. 9 I[a] think he will find he has been[b] rash in investing his money in those shares. (rather): a I am inclined to think this; b He will find he was not positively rash, but more rash than was wise. 10 Frank[a] has [a,b] decided [b,c] to spend a few days in Austria on his way to Switzerland. (also): a In addition to other people Frank, too, has decided this; b Frank has already made other decisions, this being an additional one; c Apart from spending time elsewhere, he will spend some time in Austria too.

156 1 When I mentioned the money involved, he[a] undertook to do the work[b]. (promptly): a He immediately said he would do the work; b He promised that there would be no delay in doing the work. 2 He[a] appreciated that my idea was[b] a good one, but he still wasn't [c]willing to lend me his support. (quite): a He completely understood or agreed; b My idea was good to a certain extent; c He wasn't completely willing. 3 Do you[a] think you'll[b] have enough money at the end of the month to take a short holiday? (still): a Do you continue to think what you previously thought; b You have enough money now, but will this situation remain unchanged at the end of the month? 4 [a]I should ask him[b] what he meant by his statement. (personally): a If I were you, I . . .; b You need to see him in person, rather than to write or telephone. 5 Have you^a made up your mind about what you^b want to do when you leave school? (really): *a* Have you taken a firm decision? *b* Have you decided what would most interest you? 6 ^aHe had^a the grace^b to admit that he was^c partly in the wrong. (at least): *a* Perhaps he could have done more by way of apology, but he *did* do something; *b* He went so far as to *admit* that he was wrong, though he could perhaps have gone further than this; *c* He wouldn't admit that his conduct was completely wrong, but he went so far as to admit he was partly wrong. 7 ^aHe will explain quite clearly^a what he intends to do^b. (in future): *a* In *future* tells us when he will explain; *b* In *future* tells us when he will do what he intends. 8 The student^a overheard the teacher saying^b that his last piece of homework was^c better. (distinctly); *a* The student heard quite clearly; *b* The teacher spoke very clearly; *c* The improvement in his work could be clearly seen. 9 A spokesman for the bus company pointed out that^a buses couldn't^a run^b on Sundays^a because of the unwillingness of staff to work overtime. (normally): *a* Generally speaking, buses couldn't run on Sundays; *b* Buses could run on Sundays, but not according to their usual timetable. 10 As the solicitor^a said, the money had^b been divided among the brothers and sisters of the dead man, who had no children. (rightly): *a* The solicitor was quite correct in saying this; *b* The money had been divided in accordance with the law or the dead man's will.

157 1 boasted; 2 suggested; 3 shouted; 4 claimed; 5 admitted; 6 protested; 7 whispered; 8 objected; 9 muttered; 10 exclaimed; 11 agreed; 12 insisted.

158 1 He boasted that he could speak . . . 2 He suggested that they (should) go . . . that evening. 3 The teacher shouted at the students to stop the noise . . . 4 The man claimed that the car I was driving was his property. 5 The boy admitted that he had broken . . . his catapult. 6 The man protested that they couldn't take . . . : he knew his rights. 7 His fianceé whispered that she would . . . him. 8 The treasurer objected that they didn't . . . 9 The student muttered that the teacher didn't know . . . was talking about. 10 She exclaimed what a surprise it was . . . him there that day. 11 He agreed that if the weather was bad they couldn't go. 12 She insisted that we come (*or* came) the next day if we couldn't come that same day.

159* 1 'No one ever takes my advice.' 2 'You don't call *that* thing a car, do you?' 3 'I—I didn't mean to be rude.' 4 'You might try minding your own business.' 5 'The meeting will begin at 7.30.' 6 'You have to push this button first, and then the machine will work.' 7 'If you don't like my way of doing things, you can get on with the job yourself.' 8 'I've never seen anything like it.' 9 'You shall have the money back by the end of the week.'

10 'That's the fifth time I've heard that joke.' 11 'I see that you were right, after all.' 12 'I've just seen a murder committed.'

160* 1 He complained that no one . . . took his . . . 2 He made a sneering comment about my car. 3 He stammered that he hadn't meant . . . 4 He told me snappishly that I might try . . . my own . . . 5 He announced that the meeting would . . . 6 He explained that you had to push this button . . . would work. 7 He retorted that if I didn't like his . . ., I could get on . . . myself. 8 He declared that he'd never seen . . . 9 He promised that I should have . . . 10 He said with a groan that it was . . . he'd heard that joke. 11 He conceded that I'd been right . . . 12 He gasped out that he'd just seen . . .

161* 1 'Don't keep asking such silly questions.' 2 'You should treat your elders with more respect.' 3 'I shall always love you.' 4 'Mind your own business.' 5 'No one cares whether you live or die.' 6 'I thought you said you were ill yesterday.' 7 'That's *your* problem, not mine.' 8 'You can go to the devil!' 9 'You could try reading it up the right way.' 10 'Tell me what to say to her.' 11 'You think you're a genius, don't you?' 12 'I quite understand how you feel.' 13 'Let's try again, shall we? It *is* rather difficult.' 14 'I think it's been a very pleasant evening.' 15 'I've made very good progress.' 16 'That's what I intend to do, and no one's going to stop me.'

162* 1 He told me to do as I wished, but warned me not to go and ask him for help if I got into difficulties. 2 He had the complacency to say that *he* wasn't worried about losing *his* job. He was too valuable to his employers! 3 The mother snapped at her daughter, telling her to stop . . . 4 I was surprised at the idea that he should think his friend was serious. 5 The teacher told the boy sharply to do as he was told and (to) stop arguing. 6 He exclaimed that he had been a fool not to accept the job, but then added resignedly that it couldn't be helped now. 7 The wedding guests proposed a toast to the bride . . . 8 The girl begged her father not to say anything to her boy friend, for her sake. 9 He made it quite clear that he resented my giving any opinion. He asked scornfully what I knew . . . anyway, since I had only been working there . . . 10 The master said angrily that he had had just about enough of the boy's insolence. One more word from the boy, he threatened, and he would be sent to . . . 11 She asked her husband indignantly if he really had lost . . . 12 He suggested sarcastically that I should try . . . myself if I was . . . 13 With cool assurance, he said he could have won . . . if he had . . . 14 He shouted angrily at me to . . ., and asked irritably if I couldn't see he was busy. 15 The thief, threatening the cashier, ordered him to give him the keys of the safe.

163* 1 He asked if he should post the letter for me. 2 He asked if I would post . . . him. 3 She wondered if she would be able . . . 4 He announced that he would go . . . the following Tuesday if he was free. 5 I was told I must never do that again. 6 My advice to him was to say nothing . . . 7 He said he was just going out and so couldn't stop to speak to me then. 8 She said she *had* been going, but since I'd come . . . to see her, she thought she'd better put off . . . next day. 9 I assured her that if I had been . . . following week I would have visited her. 10 He wondered if I was free the next day. 11 It was stated that the machine had undergone . . . before being . . . 12 He admitted that it was not until later that he had understood . . . of your words. 13 She told her friend that it (had) started to rain as she was leaving . . . 14 He stated quite firmly that if anyone was at fault, it was me myself.

164* 'Would you change one or two passages in your play before the first night next Monday?' the producer asked. 'Yes, I'll do what I can,' answered the playwright. 2 'I heard last week that the local Music Society is thinking of putting on an opera if they find support for the idea,' my friend told me. 3 'Are you sure you had nothing to do with the disappearance of a bicycle from the school cycle sheds two days ago?' the master asked. 'Quite sure,' answered the boy. 'I had nothing to do with it.' 4 'Could I possibly have the day off tomorrow?' Peter asked his employer. 'Most certainly not,' answered his employer. 5 'Would you lend me five pounds?' he asked. 'Well, yes, provided you pay me back next week,' I said. 6 'Hello! Jean? Look, I'm terribly sorry to ring up at the last minute like this, but I can't come to dinner with you this evening. Will it put you out terribly?' Michael asked. 'Yes, it will,' Jean replied angrily. 'You might have let me know earlier, and I wouldn't have needed to make such elaborate preparations.' 7 'I'm going to leave England early next year to take up a job abroad,' Margaret said. 'Good heavens! Are you really serious?' I asked. 8 'If the nation were to work harder and increase output, wage increases would be fully justified,' said the Chancellor. 'I must emphasize, however, that until this comes about, it would be economic suicide to allow inflation to develop once again.' 9 'Would you please open your suitcase, Madam?' The Customs officer said. 'Well, really! Is that necessary?' said the woman. 'Yes, Madam. I'm afraid it is. Would you please open it?' 10 'Waiter! This soup's cold. It should've been served in a hot dish. You should've known better than to serve it like that.' 11 'Let's spend the Easter holiday in Austria, shall we?' Graham suggested. 'Well,' said Alan, 'we have such a short holiday that we wouldn't be able to see much of the country, and it wouldn't be worth the expense of travelling so far.' 12 'Why don't you look where you're going,' said the bus driver to the motorist. 'What do you mean?' said the motorist. 'If you hadn't been driving so fast, I'd have had a chance of stopping in time.'

165* The newcomer asked another person in the hotel lounge if he had been there long. The other man said he hadn't—he'd been there just over a week, that was all. The newcomer assumed that he didn't know the place very well in that case. The man replied that he was a stranger in those parts, but added that even a stranger learnt a few things in a week. The newcomer then asked if he would mind telling him if anybody had been there called Penlark. The middle-aged man repeated the name with a note of surprise in his voice, and said it was odd the newcomer should mention that name. He remembered the man well—a tall big fellow . . . moustache. He had gone off that morning. When asked if he knew where he had gone, the man could only repeat what Penlark himself had said—that he was going to London.

166* Nora asked Jack whether he would like to bathe, or to go out . . . boats. He answered that she would think he was a coward, but he could see . . . was . . . it. He'd rather go out . . . rowing-boat. This was all right with Nora, who decided they'd go . . . punt. It was safer because you couldn't . . . over, she said. Jack agreed that you couldn't, but pointed out that you could stick . . . mud. Then the punt slid . . . you, and all you could do was to . . . pole. It might . . . for a moment, he explained, but when it began to tilt, you went . . . and had to . . . with all your friends laughing at you. Nora said she wouldn't laugh. She would run . . . rowing-boat. Then she would row . . . rescue him. Jack agreed, smiling, that in that case they should take the punt.

167* After breakfast, Charles . . . study. His uncle went straight to the point. He said he'd always taken a . . . in Charles and wanted to help in any way he could. He asked Charles what . . . he was thinking of taking up. Charles had wondered . . . times, but . . . no decision. He replied tentatively that he'd rather not make up his mind just yet. His uncle said firmly that he'd have to. He couldn't keep . . . all his life. This was . . . best, but he thought . . . say so. When Charles said nothing, his uncle began to lose patience, and told him not to beat about the bush. He must surely know what he was aiming for. What was he going to be? Charles ventured to say, hopefully, that he was going to be . . . His uncle was so staggered, he became purple in the face and repeated the word with a bellow. He asked Charles what sort of life he thought that would be—running . . . another, always . . . money. There was no future in it. Adopting a more reasonable tone, he then asked what Charles would say if he were to offer him . . . bank.

168* 'What time does this train arrive . . . Junction?' asked the man . . . David. 'At three-fifteen if we're lucky,' answered David cheerfully, 'though the timetable says it's due in at . . . o'clock.' 'Are you sure? It seems a very long time for . . . distance.' 'Yes, but this train stops at every station. I know. I have to make this journey . . . week.' The train . . . jerk. 'Oh dear, what is happening now?' said the man. 'At this rate we shan't get . . . midnight.' 'Don't worry,' said David. 'Either a cow has wandered . . . line, or the guard has seen someone . . . the train.'

169* Joan and Peter were trying . . . present. 'She's very fond of riding,' said Joan, 'so perhaps she'd like . . . horses.' 'We sent her a book last year,' replied Peter, 'and in any case she must be . . . riding. What about a . . . chocolates?' 'She sent us chocolates . . . present, so it wouldn't look . . . original.' Just then, Peter's brother . . . ideas. 'The trouble is,' said Andrew, 'that she hasn't got . . . interests. She spends . . . her time sitting . . . that enormous house waiting . . . happen, and complaining . . . it does.'

170* One evening . . . excitement. 'A music festival,' he said. 'That's what we need to wake the town up.' 'What, here?' I asked in amazement. 'Would anyone come to it?' 'Of course they would. All we need is . . . orchestra . . . soloists, and people will come . . . around.' 'How are we going to pay an orchestra?' I persisted. 'What happens if there's bad weather, and nobody comes?' Peter brushed . . . aside. 'I've thought of a wonderful programme,' he went on, 'and all we need is a few . . . thing.'

171* 'I told Sir Abraham that I would resign; and of course I must do so,' Mr Harding said to the archdeacon. 'Not at all,' said the archdeacon. 'Nothing that you say in such a way to your own counsel can be in any way binding on you; you were simply there to ask his advice. I'm sure Sir Abraham did not advise any such step.' 'No, he didn't.' 'I am sure he advised you against it,' continued the reverend cross-examiner. 'Yes, he did.' 'I'm sure Sir Abraham must have advised you to consult your friends.' 'Yes.' 'Then your threat of resignation amounts to nothing and we are just where we were before.'

172* Joan worked . . . records. One day . . . at Joan. 'I want a record, dear. One I heard on the radio this morning,' she began. 'What was the record called?' Joan asked. The woman shook her head. 'I don't remember. I should know it if I heard it, though. Perhaps you'll just play me some.' She settled . . . stool. 'We have hundreds of records in stock,' Joan pointed out. 'It would take . . . to play you . . . each. Could you hum it to me?' The woman giggled. 'I can't sing . . . tune. We should get into a worse muddle if I started humming.' She looked . . . brightened. 'I've just remembered something,' she said. 'It comes from a play. There's a woman who speaks . . . but after a time she learns to talk beautifully.' 'Would it be from *My Fair Lady*?' Joan asked. 'That's it, dear. I wish you'd thought . . . sooner, instead of . . . questions. I suppose you are new to the job.'

173 1 Motorists intending to take . . . Continent; 2 proposals made . . . meeting; 3 river marking the frontier; 4 incomes imposed . . . government and not negotiated . . . employers; 5 power created by . . . wages; 6 interest credited . . . year; 7 companies already using/staff needed for stock-control; 8 aliens already living . . . country; 9 organization designed . . . young; 10 articles ordered from stock; 11 premises overlooking the Thames; 12 Reports now reaching London/casualties caused . . . earthquake.

174 1 *a* Show, which is held . . . autumn, attracts; *b* Show, held . . . autumn, attracts; 2*a* house, which still bears . . . number, stands; *b* house, still bearing . . . number, stands; 3*a* Minister, who looked . . . relaxed, returned; *b* Minister, looking . . . relaxed, returned; 4 *a* hostel, which accommodates 200 students, will be; *b* hostel, accommodating 200 students, will be; 5*a* trains, which are made up . . . wagons, carry; *b* trains, made up . . . wagons, carry; 6*a* invasion, which was . . . executed, was completed; *b* invasion, carefully planned . . . executed, was completed; 7*a* houses, which are built . . . and which range . . . £18,000, should satisfy; *b* houses, built . . . and ranging . . . £18,000, should satisfy; 8*a* 'Ida', which swept . . . coast, left; *b* 'Ida', sweeping . . . coast, left; 9*a* societies, which are . . . money, will soon; *b* societies, at present struggling . . . money, will soon; 10*a* The Q.E.2, which was making . . . voyage, sailed; *b* The Q.E.2, making . . . voyage, sailed.

175 1 Measures to restrain; 2 proposals to be discussed; 3 plenty to think about; 4 means to bring about; 5 difficulties to be surmounted; 6 little to be proud of; 7 houses to suit; 8 tests to be passed; 9 way to go; 10 procedures to be followed; 11 cords, to be operated; 12 tablets, to be taken; 13 body to check; 14 regulations, to come . . . month, will result; 15 rates to be introduced; 16 point to have emerged.

176* (*Note:* all the suggestions are *finite* clauses.) 1 that has stood empty for so long; 2 which had suffered such disastrous floods the previous year; 3 which the local Council started to tackle fifteen years ago; 4 beer was only sixpence a pint; 5 that would be economical to run; 6 where we stayed two years ago; 7 he inherited; 8 who'll go out of his way to help people; 9 who is now working as a mining engineer in Australia; 10 that few countries can equal; 11 that specializes in heart surgery; 12 you might like to suggest; 13 he came out with; 14 he had given for not coming; 15 which might stock this particular model; 16 he's mentioned the problem to me; 17 which haven't been on the market for over twenty-five years; 18 whom you spoke to on the telephone; 19 which is full of inconsistencies; 20 as we had taken on the outward journey; 21 agrees with what I'm saying; 22 the eighteenth century produced; 23 who was already over sixty; 24 which cost nearly twice as much as the smaller one; 25 which till then had remained unconquered.

177* 1 where we met a group of friends; 2 which would have been advisable under the circumstances; 3 when he suddenly turned up; 4 which was a great disappointment to the organizers; 5 who immediately began planning a major reorganization; 6 which was an act of almost criminal negligence; 7 for which he later received a commendation for bravery; 8 when the sun unexpectedly broke through; 9 which was a new departure for us; 10 who was supposed to pass it on to you; 11 which has been welcomed by anti-smoking campaigners; 12 where we saw the much-publicized new production of *The Trojans*; 13 whom I sent it on; 14 which the School governors have now authorized work to begin; 14 which his parents engaged a private tutor.

178* (*Note*: all the suggestions are *finite* clauses.) 1 than he writes it; 2 as soon as the weather improved; 3 where we generally leave it; 4 so that countries could discuss world problems together; 5 that I gave up reading it half way through; 6 although the water was still rather cold; 7 if they could come with us; 8 Since I had so much work to do at home; 9 so that we should have time for a talk before dinner; 10 *a* As the car has already been repaired; *b* As I got off the bus; *c* as quickly as he could; 11 When I reached my destination; 12 that he left the room without saying a word.

179* 1 where I told you to; 2 Although they're very well off; 3 so that we could all travel together more easily; 4 we should find no vacancies on our arrival; 5 if they didn't return to work the following day; 6 so that no one should be able to accuse the examiners of prejudice or favouritism; 7 When you live a little nearer us; 8 Although I agreed to in the first place; 9 The more I see of him; 10 you agree to abide by the rules; 11 we didn't get separated from the guide; 12 They were staying in the district.

180* 1 that he couldn't stop trembling; 2 your own private feelings may be; 3 we left/the house should be warm/we returned; 4 drunk he was; 5 they like it or not; 6 until a suitable interval occurs; 7 that the speaker had to shout into the microphone; 8 so that I shall be able to get a more interesting job/I finish my studies; 9 I would have liked to/I simply didn't have that much spare cash; 10 The quicker we get there; 11 how much I argued with him; 12 the singer had given another encore/leave the concert hall.

181 1 Since the colour . . . her, my wife decided . . . 2 Because he had overslept, he was . . . 3 As I didn't . . . stamps, I couldn't . . . 4 Even though the course cost . . . money, I decided . . . 5 Although we left . . . late, we arrived on time. 6 While she likes . . .

much, she's looking forward . . . home. 7 Although I agreed . . .
advice, I did so . . . 8 Since I had . . . him, I felt obliged . . .
9 Although his doctor . . . bed, he went in to work. 10 Since he
won't . . . me, you'd better try . . .

182★ (*Note:* all the suggestions are *finite* clauses.) so that we shouldn't
get wet if it rained (purpose, condition); because the weather
looked unsettled (reason); after we saw heavy black clouds
approaching (time *or* reason); in case it rained (purpose);
although it was fine when we left (concession, time); if it looked
like rain (condition).

183★ (*Note:* all the suggestions are *finite* clauses.) As it was the dress
rehearsal (reason); although it was only a preliminary rehearsal
(concession); if the playwright was to be satisfied (condition);
before they gave their first performance (time); when the casting
had finally been decided (time); as soon as the rehearsals started
in earnest (time).

184★ (*Note:* all the suggestions are *finite* clauses.) while they were in
that area (time); even if it meant making a detour (concession *or*
condition); before they left Scotland (time); after they had seen
Edinburgh (time); however little time they had to spare (concession); unless the weather got worse (condition).

185★ (*Note:* all the suggestions are *finite* clauses.) Whatever pressure
he puts on you (concession); If he starts asking questions (condition); Since it would only make matters worse (reason); Much
as I dislike not being open with him (concession); Although the
information might be useful to him (concession); Whether he
brings up the subject or not (condition); Lest he should mis-
understand (purpose).

186★ (*Note:* all the suggestions are *finite* clauses.) so that no one
makes a mistake (purpose); in case a few people aren't clear
about what to do (purpose); if anyone appears to be in doubt
(condition); unless you have written them down (condition);
before the group disperses (time); while you have everyone
assembled (time).

187★ (*Note:* all the suggestions are *finite* clauses.) Even though you
dislike him (concession)/when he was in difficulties (time);
As he respects your opinion (reason)/before he took such a decisive
step (time); When he mentioned the project to you (time)/it might
be useful (purpose); Whether or not he was likely to accept it
(concession)/so that he couldn't blame you if things went wrong
later (purpose, condition).

188 1 He seems . . . discover that the sun . . . 2 The Opposition deplored the fact that old-age pensions . . . 3 His girl friend later understood why he . . . her. 4 Don't run away . . . idea that your bank manager . . . 5a It was clear . . . that the law student was . . . b That the law student was . . . bar was clear . . . 6a The fact that he didn't even apologize made me . . . b What made me . . . angry was the fact that he didn't . . . 7a It was the parents' view that the boy . . . b The parents' view was that the boy . . . 8a It is my opinion that children . . . b My opinion is that children . . . 9 What he says in private is inconsistent with what he does in public. 10a I just don't know how he manages . . . b How he manages . . . things I just don't know.

189 1 insisted that the students should arrive; 2 The fact that one is ignorant of the law; 3 that you (should) think; 4 why people dislike him; 5 The fact that you have accepted this job/that you will have to travel; 6 that he had told me the truth; 7 that he came from a broken home; 8 the fact that his father is (*or* was) a professor; 9 that I (should) check again/the fact that I had already assured him; 10 that it is genuine; 11 why it was (*or* is) so popular; 12 that he (has) learned French in France/that he is able to speak.

190 1 to take over other companies; 2 to withdraw from the American market; 3 to join in the scheme; 4 to build a new ring road; 5 to postpone further discussion; 6 to share the costs; 7 to win; 8 to give up smoking; 9 to re-open talks; 10 for the road to be made part of a one-way system.

191 1 That the conversation . . . him soon became obvious; 2 That the driver . . . an accident was due to luck . . . 3 What the thieves . . . money remains a mystery. 4 What the speaker said wasn't at all easy . . . to follow. 5 To follow what . . . said wasn't at all easy . . . audience. 6 For the audience to follow what . . . said wasn't at all easy. 7 To see how . . . wrong is easy, with the benefit . . . 8 Watching you . . . hard makes me . . . 9 To have asked you to give . . . evening is very inconsiderate . . 10 Whether he really . . . said is a little . . . judge 11 Why we were . . . soon wasn't made clear . . . time. 12 How the Company . . . product was a matter . . . 13 Where the pilot . . . land isn't yet known. 14 Precisely who originated the plan hasn't yet . . 15 How much . . . cost is difficult to . . . stage.

192* (*Note:* all the suggestions are *finite* clauses) 1 that he didn't like my attitude (object of *said*); 2 that the Prime Minister was seriously ill at the time of the crisis (in apposition to subject *fact*); 3 What is being discussed at this conference (subject of *is*); 4 what he sets out to do (object of *achieving*); 5 how the trick was performed (object of *discover*); 6 where he had hidden the body (object of *told*); 7 What you say (subject of *is*); 8 if there was any fish on the menu (object of *asked*); 9 that moral standards were declining (in app. to object *fact*); 10 that the unions should take stronger measures to control their members (in app. to subject *it*); 11 that the two parties had reached a reasonable compromise (in app. to subject *it*); 12 what you want to know (complement of *is*).

193* (*Note:* all the suggestions are *finite* clauses) 1 what should be done in an emergency (object of preposition *on*); 2 what had happened to him (object of preposition *by*); 3 that it would be better to leave things as they are (complement of *is*); 4 That he was very dissatisfied with the outcome (subject of *was*); 5 what you have just said (object of prep. *from*)/that you intend to offer your resignation (object of *infer*); 6 that we should raise membership fees (in app. to subject *idea*); 7 that the Company needed a new management (in app. to object *feeling*); 8 when the train was due to arrive (object of *know*); 9 that a tunnel would prove cheaper in the long run than a bridge (complement of *was*); 10 that we had been overcharged considerably (in app. to object *opinion*); 11 what needn't be done immediately (object of *doing*); 12 that they're getting married (in app. to subject *it*).

194* (*Note:* all the suggestions are *finite* clauses) 1 that the police were closing in (object of *having learned*); 2 that all Englishmen are the same (in app. to object *idea*); 3 he just didn't care (in app. to object *impression*); 4 that we're going to be late again (complement of *seems*); 5 why he disappeared so suddenly (object of *remember*); 6 what he had already told the court (object of *repeating*)/that he was at home at the time referred to (in app. to object *alibi*); 7 that euthanasia should become common practice (in app. to object *proposal*); 8 That there may be life on another planet (subject of *is*); 9 that no one foresaw the disaster (in app. to complement *fact*); 10 how the climbers met their deaths (subject of *will be*); 11 which of the two paintings was the original (object of prep. *to*); 12 that production costs had risen considerably (object of *pointing out*)/that prices wouldn't rise again in the near future (in app. to object *assurance*).

195 1 wishing; 2 there obviously being no point: 3 Looked at in this way, the situation doesn't seem; 4 to arrive *or* in order to arrive *or* so as to arrive; 5 unless accompanied; 6 him *or* his once offering; 7 the ship to be unsinkable; 8 not to disturb *or* in order not to disturb *or* so as not to disturb; 9 Not having any time to spare; 10 Never having been . . . before; 11 to be surmounted; 12 involved . . . scandal/to offer . . . resignation; 13 (Whether) restored . . . or not; 14 to hear; 15 to introduce measures/to stimulate; 16 as to be positively misleading.

196* 1 Having first made sure . . . watching, the thief climbed up . . . to a first-floor window, through which he succeeded . . . the

house unobserved. 2 Despite the fact that I had no experience
. . ., I decided to take the opportunity of spending . . . sea when
some friends of mine, who were very keen . . ., and who wanted
to sail . . ., invited me . . . them. 3 An outstanding characteristic
. . . procedure is . . . system, under which a man may . . . citizens, who must be . . . decision without influence . . . judge,
although he may direct them as to . . . law. 4 The M.1 ('M'
stands . . .) is the first of . . . roads, comparable to . . . countries,
which are being built to provide . . . motorways between principal centres . . . population.

197* 1 Visitors . . . are surprised at the orderly way in which the
English . . . transport, and they cannot understand the angry
glares given them when, on first arriving in England, they
innocently . . . queue. 2 Since television has power . . . ill, a
controlling body called the I.T.A. was . . . 1954, when Independent . . . was introduced, to ensure that . . . maintained. 3 'The
Black Death' was the name given to the bubonic plague which
raged . . . Ages, carrying off . . . population, and in some cases
exterminating . . . villages.

198* 1 Fleet Street, once famous . . . houses where men prominent
. . . world used to meet, and now synonymous . . . newspapers,
takes its name . . . Stream, which used to run from Hampstead
down into . . . at Blackfriars. 2 Guy Fawkes, whose memory is
perpetuated by . . . displays held on . . . each year, was the
leader . . . conspirators who intended . . . Parliament while the
King . . . in session. 3 When I returned . . . city where . . . born,
I was dismayed to find that many of . . . streets and their . . .
houses had been demolished to make way for modern but undistinguished shop-lined thoroughfares.

199* 1 The Pilgrim Fathers were . . . Puritans who, having first
spent . . . Holland to escape . . . persecution, later sailed in the
Mayflower to America, where they established . . . Massachusetts. 2 'The South Sea Bubble' was the name given to a great
. . . crash which occurred . . . in 1720, following a wave . . .
speculation, the dimensions of which have since been repeated
only once, before . . . Wall Street, New York, in 1929. 3 Although
Sir . . . had already attained . . . astronomer when he was only
sixteen, it was not till he was . . . thirty that he seriously took up
. . . architecture, the most precious fruit of which was . . .
Cathedral.

200* 1 In response to . . . equality of opportunity, Comprehensive
schools have been established, combining under one roof the
three types . . . school, Grammar, Technical, and Modern. The
purpose of . . . school is to make easier a transfer . . . from . . . to
another in cases where the child's real ability becomes clear . . .

education. 2 British Railways came into being in 1948 on the nationalization . . . by the Labour Government. Previously, railways in Britain were run privately in four main networks: the London, Midland, and . . . railway, the Southern . . ., the Great . . ., and the London . . . railway. 3 Although the Beauchamp Tower, semicircular in plan and projecting . . . wall, was originally built . . . purposes, it was very soon . . . prison, one of its first unwilling guests being . . . Warwick, whose family name thus . . . Tower of London.

201★ 1 Foreigners are frequently surprised to learn that what the English call 'Public Schools' are in fact . . . schools, catering in the main for fee-paying pupils from . . . families. Many of these families have to make great . . . sacrifices to send . . . choice. 2 Although in the opinion . . . people the jury . . . has disadvantages, the disappearance . . . unthinkable. In the same way, there is in principle a very great deal to be said for making magistrates out of persons whose chief qualification is that of being prominent local citizens. 3 Having spoken at length on . . . tracks, pointing out that even experienced . . . locomotive, the headmaster warned the boys that if any of them persisted . . . railway, they would not only be . . . punished, but would also risk . . . school.

202★ 1 If money or plate is found hidden . . . Britain and has no owner, it is called 'Treasure-Trove' and is . . . Crown. Although the finder must hand over . . . authorities, he is, in practice, given . . . return. 2 Besides containing some very fine . . . monastery, the South . . . Cathedral is also the site . . . Scots, whose body rested . . . years before being removed to Westminster in 1612 by order . . . First. 3 It is a sad fact that very little . . . century, mail being particularly . . . destruction and even being cut up . . . use. Fortunately, much . . . preserved, owing to its artistic quality . . . associations.

203★ 1 Bearing in mind the fact that Miss Green was . . . work, it was surprising that she coped . . . chairman. This had been . . . 1950, when she came to London intending to become . . . model. 2 The English . . . culminates . . . year in the Football . . . Final, when two teams who have survived . . . competition beginning in September the previous year play each other at Wembley Stadium to see who will . . . Cup. 3 Queens' College was the second . . . Cambridge (King's College being the first) and is distinguished from . . . Oxford in that it owes its . . . Queens, Margaret, wife of Henry the Sixth, and Elizabeth, wife of Edward the Fourth. This is why . . .'s'.

204 1a The chairman was the only person who objected; b The proposal was the only thing he objected to. 2a It was quite obvious

350

that the man didn't understand in any way; *b* The man had only a vague understanding of the document. 3*a* He made no promises about attending; *b* He made a promise that he wouldn't attend. 4*a* He wanted to go on that particular occasion, but couldn't afford to; *b* Theatre-going was one of his pleasures, but one that he couldn't afford to indulge. 5*a* I now remember that I told him at some earlier time; *b* First I remembered and then I told him. 6*a* You won't have much money which you can spend; *b* You won't be obliged to spend much money. 7*a* The question is asked in the morning (thus, the morning is still part of present time); *b* The question is asked during the afternoon or evening (thus, the morning is regarded as past time). 8*a* *last week* = the period ending last Saturday (past time); *b the last week* = the period of seven days up to the day of speaking (which includes present time).

205 1*a* Other people made the admission, but also, and perhaps surprisingly, he did; *b* He not only perhaps thought or felt this, but went so far as to admit it. 2*a* He admitted the unfairness of other things, but also, and perhaps surprisingly, that of the tax; *b* Apart from admitting other characteristics of the tax, he went so far as to admit its unfairness. 3*a* He didn't claim that he knew; *b* He tried to give the impression that he didn't know. 4*a* His expressions of gratitude were unending; *b* He didn't say thank you because he didn't have time. 5*a* He persisted in asking what he had already asked before; *b* Although he knew what the answer must be, the next thing he did was to ask the question. 6*a* We assume he didn't go to the doctor; *b* He visited the doctor, but this later proved to have been unnecessary. 7*a* You can tell me *then* (viz. when you see me again); *b* could you tell me *this* (viz. when you will see me again). 8*a* The subject of the portrait was Holbein; *b* The painter of the portrait was Holbein.

206 1*a* This was the last thing he said; *b* He hoped that a satisfactory conclusion would be the end result. 2*a* This was the general opinion of the committee; *b* the financial situation in general had improved. 3*a* He got up early so regularly that it wasn't a difficulty or a hardship for him; *b* At some past time, he habitually got up early (but we are not told his feelings or attitude towards this). 4*a* See whether it's possible to hire a set; *b* Hire a set; you might, for example, find this cheaper or more convenient than buying one. 5*a* He must have arranged for someone to do this; *b* He must himself have done this. 6*a* They will let me know *then* (viz. when the goods are in stock); *b* They will let me know *this* (viz. when the goods will be in stock). 7*a* This is a general observation on how she spends her money; *b* This is a comment on what is regarded as a temporary phenomenon. 8*a* He asked 'Will you go ahead?'; *b* He asked 'Shall I go ahead?' *or* 'Should you go ahead?'

207 1*a* I would rather not see him if it can be avoided; *b* I am very anxious not to see him. 2*a* His attempt was futile: the work was done anyway; *b* His concern was to see that the work had some useful result. 3*a* I am sorry that I must now tell you this; *b* I apologize for having said this earlier. 4*a* Did you lack the necessary courage? *b* Were you reluctant to upset him in this way ('your' courage isn't in question). 5*a* He should arrange for the workers to receive training while they are working; *b* He should be employing more workers who already possess the necessary skills; *c* he should himself have organized and carried out the training before now. 6*a* Whenever I meet her, I meet her at the station (though we are not told how often this occurs); *b* This happens extremely frequently nowadays. 7*a* The rain is coming down heavily; *b* The rain has nearly stopped. 8*a* *direct* = not via an agent or some other intermediary; *b* *directly* = at once.

208 1*a* He was unpopular with the crowd as a whole; *b* More often than not he was unpopular. 2*a* Of course, one doesn't expect this; *b* Oranges can't grow under natural conditions. 3*a* The design was attractive, but not obviously so; *b* It's unattractiveness was obvious. 4*a* The purpose of his resignation is to make way for a younger man; *b* He has now accepted the fact (though perhaps reluctantly) that he must make way for a younger man. 5*a* (in order) *to prevent* expresses why police powers should be limited. *b* *to preventing* explains to what type of activity police powers should be limited; 6*a* The speaker is certain that the person will get the job; *b* The person himself feels confident of getting the job. 7*a* The President rarely made long speeches; *b* Speeches from the President were a rare occurrence, and were also long. 8*a* I enjoy . . ., despite the fact that I have made hardly any friends; *b* The reason for my enjoying living . . . is that I have made a small number of friends.

209 1*a* The fact that the scheme didn't work out in practice was something that we had foreseen; *b* The scheme worked out, but not in the way that we had foreseen. 2*a* He was approaching the bank when he noticed the men; *b* The men were approaching the bank when he noticed them. 3*a* The questioner asks if the man is now away on holiday; *b* The questioner asks if the man has been away and returned. 4*a* You are speaking just as if you were a teacher; *b* You are a teacher, and you are now speaking to me in that capacity (and not, e.g. as a friend). 5*a* No one has given me any information about him; *b* He hasn't communicated with me. 6*a* All the workers were dismissed because they went on strike; *b* The dismissals applied only to some of the workers, namely the strikers. 7*a* He said 'I've been waiting a long time, and I'm not at all pleased.' *b* He said 'I've been waiting a long time,' and he wasn't at all pleased. 8*a* The rescue party was pessimistic, holding out very little hope of there being any survivors; *b* The rescue party wasn't entirely without optimism—there might be a small number of survivors. (*NB.* the contrast between *any* and *some.*)

210 1*a* She went to the shop because she wanted this information. *b* She went to the shop (perhaps with the intention of buying the dress), but then found that the dress was very expensive. 2*a* She drinks tea with breakfast and so, incidentally, do most other people in England; *b* The reason for her drinking tea with breakfast is that it is the custom in England. 3*a* i.e. but we don't know whether or not he will give permission; *b* He is more or less expected to give permission; the builders simply have to wait for the time when he does. 4*a* I'll pay you when the end of the month comes; *b* I'll pay you at some time during the month, but in any case not later than the end of the month. 5*a* In the speaker's opinion, the person had no reason to think this; *b* He felt that he himself had no reason to think this. 6*a* Aren't his plans to stay in London fixed—I thought they were; *b* Does he propose to stay in London for an unlimited time? 7*a* Previously, he followed a different profession; *b* He didn't produce any new ideas or write in a new style. 8*a* I didn't like a small number of all the modern paintings I've seen; *b* I've seen hardly any modern paintings, and I haven't liked any of them.

211 1*a* His arrival is assumed; *b* We don't know whether he will arrive or not. 2*a* The speaker implies that perhaps 'you' *did* tell a lie on a past occasion (or 'you' may have admitted that you did); *b* The speaker refers to a hypothetical future possibility. 3*a even if* = even supposing he has nothing to do (we don't know whether he has or not); *even though* = despite the *fact* that he has nothing to do. 4*a On checking* = when you check; *b By checking* = by means of checking, by using this method. 5*a* His illustrated lecture was of exceptionally high quality; *b* His lecture was admirably illustrated. 6*a* The speaker simply asks for information—he has no idea as to the likely answer; *b* The speaker implies that he had expected 'you' to see the man, but now he has the impression that perhaps you didn't. 7*a* The speaker's impression is that there is someone in the room; *b* The speaker simply asks for information—he has no idea as to the likely answer. 8*a* There were 10,000 people at the meeting, which was a surprisingly large number; *b* There were at least 10,000 people at the meeting, and possibly more.

212 1*a* It is thought that this will happen. *b* The speaker is issuing instructions: 'These are my requirements.' 2*a so that* . . . expresses her purpose in burning the letter; *b so that* . . . expresses the result of her burning the letter. 3*a* It is possible that he realized; *b* He ought to have realized. 4*a* She left me so that she could get on with her work. *b* She left me in a situation where I had to get on with her work. 5*a* They were very tired, though perhaps not exhausted; *b* They were very tired, and perhaps even exhausted. 6*a* Is this what you intend to do? *b* Would you do this for me (please)? 7*a in time* = eventually, sooner or later; *b in time* = early enough. 8*a* Why didn't the public like it? Because it was play of ideas. *b* the public liked the play for some reason or other, but not for the reason mentioned.

213 1*a* It is thought likely that the Queen will arrive on time; *b* Punctuality is required of the Queen. 2*a* We have discovered that she is a good daily help; *b* We have obtained a good daily help for her. 3*a* He didn't leave London because he didn't take up the appointment. *b* He left London for some reason or other, but not in order to take up the appointment. 4*a* 'I insist that you arrive early,' the teacher told his students. *b* 'My students always arrive early,' the teacher insisted. 5*a* They wanted to visit an additional number of interesting places. *b* They wanted to visit places that were more interesting. 6*a* Perhaps they have arrived—this, at least, is what I expected. *b* They haven't arrived, which is contrary to what I expected. 7*a* No one liked the portrait which he himself had painted. *b* No one liked the portrait which he had commissioned to be painted. 8*a* When did he retire? At the age of sixty. *b* When did he make the decision? At the age of sixty.

214 1*a* 'The motorist,' said the bus driver, 'was to blame for the accident.' (The bus driver blamed the motorist.) *b* The motorist said, 'The bus driver was to blame for the accident.' (The motorist blamed the bus driver.) 2*a* I wouldn't advise you to go there for his sake. (Go there for some other reason if you like, but don't go just for his benefit.) *b* I wouldn't advise you to go there, for his sake. (Don't go there if you have his interests at heart.) 3*a* The teacher left his students feeling very depressed. (The students were in a state of depression when the teacher left them.) *b* The teacher left his students, feeling very depressed. (The teacher was feeling very depressed when he left the students.) 4*a* This type of education is very expensive indeed, but it is well worth . . . it. (It is exceedingly expensive, but . . .) *b* This type of education . . . expensive, indeed, but it is . . . spent on it. (It is very expensive, I agree, but . . .) 5*a* The headmaster said that the boy's parents . . . home. (The parents of the boy) *b* The head-master said that the boys' parents . . . home. (The parents of the boys) 6*a* Leading British companies, already well known . . . out-look, have begun . . . Europe. (All leading British companies are already well known for their international outlook, and they are all setting up factories in Europe.) *b* Leading British companies already well known . . . outlook have begun . . . Europe. (Not all leading British companies are setting up these factories, but only those that are well known for their international outlook.)

215 1*a* The facts the prisoner admitted pointed to him . . . person, but he protested he was innocent. (The prisoner admitted certain facts, and the speaker comments that although these facts indicated that the prisoner was guilty, the prisoner still protested his innocence.) *b* The facts, the prisoner admitted, pointed to him . . . person, but, he protested, he was innocent. ('The facts point to me as the guilty person, I admit, but I protest that I am innocent,' said the prisoner.) 2*a* Once having lost . . . Scotland, we had . . . road-side. (As soon as we had lost our way . . .) *b* Once, having lost . . . Scotland, we had . . . road-side. (On one occasion, when we had lost our way . . .) 3*a* The political demonstrators who felt strongly . . . discrimination were prepared . . . police. (Some of the political demonstrators were prepared to defy the police, namely those with strong feelings.) *b* The political demonstrators, who felt strongly . . . discrimination, were prepared . . . police. (All the demonstrators felt strongly, and all were prepared to defy the police.) 4*a* Cross-channel steamers unable to dock at Dover . . . gales had to . . . Newhaven. (Some cross-channel steamers had to go on to Newhaven, namely those that were prevented by gales from docking at Dover.) *b* Cross-channel steamers, unable to . . . gales, had to . . . Newhaven. (All the cross-channel steamers had to go on to Newhaven, because all were prevented from docking at Dover.) 5*a* He won't think he . . . thank you for all that you've done. (He won't think that what you have done justifies any thanks on his part.) *b* He won't think he . . . thank you, for all that you've done. (Despite all that you have done, he won't think . . . thank you.) 6*a* 'I have just remembered something she said.' (I said I had just remembered something which she had said.) *b* 'I have just remembered something,' she said. (She said that she had just remembered something.)

216 1*a* give instruction; *b* I'll punish you to deter you from stealing again. 2*a* written for this particular purpose; *b* more useful to foreign students than to anyone else. 3*a* willing; *b* physically ready. 4*a* had a view over; *b* chose to ignore; *c* failed to notice. 5*a* He hadn't been told; *b* He didn't have the specialized knowledge. 6*a* at this very moment; *b* neither now nor in the immediate future. 7*a* he had the benefit of; *b* got pleasure from. 8*a* His treatment had been quite good; *b* He had been treated justly. 9*a* that used up all their strength; *b* thorough. 10*a* certainly; *b* very probably.

217 1*a* immediately; *b* at the same time; *c* both. 2*a* concluded an agreement; *b* something that was very good value for money. 3*a* supports, provides for; *b* asserts; 4*a* I conclude that he is out; *b* are obliged to. 5*a* At one particular time; *b* reason to visit, or cause for visiting. 6*a* confusion of mind; *b* interesting and amusing things to do. 7*a* profit fully from; *b* profit unfairly from. 8*a* understands properly; *b* value and am grateful for; *c* rose in value. 9*a* I am certain of this; *b* I can hardly believe this. 10*a* it wasn't the right size; *b* it didn't look well on her.

218 1*a* know or identify again; *b* weren't willing to accept officially. 2*a* come and collect; *b* demands. 3*a* is full of self-praise; *b* is the proud possessor of. 4*a* feel unhappy at or feel ill-will because of; *b* anxious to maintain or protect. 5*a* demand to see; *b* inviting. 6*a* Taking everything into consideration; *b* In all. 7*a* for the public benefit; *b* that the public will take an interest in. 8*a* He had disclosed the secret, and his friend expressed regret that he done so. *b* His friend assumed that he had disclosed the secret, and blamed him for doing so. 9*a* informed; *b* instructed, ordered. 10*a* requested, instructed; *b* inquired, wanted to know.

219–238 Consult *ALDCE* for explanation and examples.

239–244 Consult *ALDCE* for explanations and examples.

245 1 marched; 2 crept; 3 lurked; 4 strutted; 5 staggered; 6 plodded; 7 strode; 8 loiter; 9 strayed; 10 ramble; 11 paced; 12 wandered.

246 Consult *ALDCE*.

247 1 smiled/cheering; 2 booed; 3 titter; 4 jeered; 5 laugh/groan; 6 grinned/roar(s); 7 sneers; 8 tease; 9 giggled; 10 sniggered; 11 mock; 12 chuckling.

248 1 wrenched; 2 towed; 3 jerk; 4 hauling; 5 drawn; 6 dragged; 7 lugging; 8 pulled; 9 tugged.

249 Consult *ALDCE*.

250 1 He reluctantly came; 2 to go on interminably; 3 viewed indifferently; 4 used concurrently; 5 was substantially the same; 6 operate clandestinely; 7 could conceivably lead; 8 objections outspokenly; 9 asked querulously; 10 had radically changed; 11 proved conclusively that; 12 books indiscriminately. (The Government has tried to approach this problem *imaginatively*. The big-game hunter *stealthily* approached the leopard. The book deals with the subject very *superficially*. The troops were told *explicitly* not to make a move until the enemy revealed their positions.)

251 1 tremulously gave *or* name tremulously; 2 work conscientiously; 3 judiciously took; 4 screaming hysterically; 5 worked tirelessly *or* peace tirelessly; 6 means, conversely, fewer goods; 7 climbing vicariously; 8 book, lavishly illustrated, is; 9 slavishly adopted; 10 was inadvertently given; 11 wilfully obstructing; 12 occurred inopportunely. (The child was born two months *prematurely*. The problem needs to be considered rationally rather than *emotionally*. Smith *adroitly* slipped the ball past a defender and scored a goal. Should we *blindly* follow where others lead?)

252 1 materials synthetically; 2 cup triumphantly; 3 I tentatively suggested; 4 rain severely hampered; 5 are temperamentally suitable; 6 goods surreptitiously; 7 scrupulously fair; 8 looked wistfully; 9 spoke aggressively; 10 walked briskly; 11 been arbitrarily rejected; 12 waiting apprehensively. (As it was the offender's first appearance in court, the magistrate dealt with him *leniently*. *Characteristically*, the writer keeps his readers in suspense until the last pages of the book. He argues so *persuasively* that it's difficult not to agree with him. Everyone *earnestly* begged him to reconsider his decision to resign.)

253 1 subject animatedly; 2 dispute amicably; 3 you presently (*or* shortly); 4 view concisely (*or* briefly); 5 pumped manually/ pumped mechanically; 6 were fatally injured; 7 are constantly getting (*or* repeatedly); 8 is temporarily out; 9 boy insolently replied (*or* impudently *or* disrespectfully); 10 is reputedly; 11 work voluntarily; 12 carried unanimously.

254 1 tastefully furnished; 2 held annually; 3 years successively; 4 would irrevocably forfeit; 5 Retrospectively, he could see; 6 were comparatively undamaged; 7 had regrettably been; 8 Naturally, he felt *or* He naturally felt; 9 aesthetically pleasing; 10 married bigamously; 11 died instantaneously; 12 given anonymously.

255 1 susceptible to; 2 irresponsible; 3 found him unanswerable; 4 irrepressible enthusiasm; 5 indispensable; 6 incompatible; 7 a regrettable mistake; 8 indefensible; 9 inestimable; 10 inflexible; 11 negligible; 12 irreplaceable.

256 1 unendurable *or* unbearable *or* intolerable; 2 he was ineligible; 3 irreconcilable; 4 fallible; 5 so quickly as to be incomprehensible; 6 unpronounceable; 7 12 is divisible by; 8 imaginable; 9 ineradicable; 10 indefinable; 11 impracticable; 12 impeccable.

257 1 indissoluble/inconceivable; 2 irreparable; 3 untranslatable; 4 edible; 5 indelible; 6 irrevocable; 7 changeable; 8 inexhaustible; 9 inimitable; 10 enviable; 11 implacable; 12 impassable.

258 1 unshrinkable; 2 indestructible; 3 insoluble; 4 uncontrollable; 5 memorable; 6 navigable; 7 negotiable; 8 imperceptible; 9 innumerable; 10 objectionable; 11 impenetrable; 12 convertible.

259 1 pitiable; 2 inflatable; 3 enjoyable; 4 punishable; 5 unsalable; 6 inseparable; 7 unplayable; 8 incorrigible; 9 inalienable; 10 impressionable; 11 inexplicable; 12 imperturbable.

260 1 'acquisitive'; 2 submissive; 3 indicative; 4 the formative years; 5 abusive language; 6 a pervasive influence; 7 plaintive; 8 three successive years; 9 The defective machine; 10 abortive; 11 an evasive answer; 12 a lucrative trade; 13 discursive; 14 deceptive. (Consult *ALDCE* for remaining four adjectives.)

261 1 adhesive; 2 An impulsive man; 3 inquisitive/have more retentive memories; 4 of descriptive writing; 5 Extensive; 6 productive soil; 7 provocative; 8 conducive; 9 retroactive; 10 the speculative investor.

262 1 homogeneous; 2 supercilious; 3 capricious; 4 fallacious; 5 an obnoxious; 6 Precocious children; 7 extraneous matter; 8 specious arguments; 9 momentous speech; 10 presumptuous; 11 ingenuous; 12 malicious remarks; 13 fastidious; 14 ludicrous. (Consult *ALDCE* for the remaining four adjectives.)

263 1 infectious; 2 spacious (*or* commodious); 3 spontaneous; 4 Deciduous trees; 5 ravenous; 6 unanimous; 7 ambidextrous; 8 callous; 9 courteous; 10 either seditious or blasphemous.

264 1 pompous; 2 ominous; 3 injurious; 4 vivacious; 5 notorious; 6 libellous; 7 tortuous; 8 copious; 9 indigenous; 10 ambiguous; 11 circuitous; 12 outrageous.

265 1 cautious; 2 officious; 3 prosperous; 4 arduous; 5 conscientious; 6 ambitious; 7 treacherous; 8 simultaneous; 9 sumptuous; 10 boisterous; 11 vicious; 12 superstitious. (Consult *ALDCE* for examples.)

266 (*Note:* the pronunciation of the final syllable is /it/, except in the case of No. 7, where it is /eit/.) 1 inconsiderate; 2 moderate *or* temperate; 3 legitimate; 4 illiterate; 5 commensurate; 6 desperate; 7 innate; 8 obstinate *or* obdurate; 9 immediate; 10 adequate; 11 affectionate; 12 passionate; 13 immaculate; 14 delicate. (Consult *ALDCE* for examples.)

267 (*Note:* the pronunciation of the syllable -*ate* is /eit/) 1 collaborated; 2 indoctrinate; 3 depreciate; 4 aggravated; 5 complicate; 6 exaggerating; 7 fabricated; 8 facilitate; 9 impersonating; 10 contaminated; 11 cultivate; 12 placate.

268 (*Note:* the pronunciation of the final syllable is /eit/) 1 eradicate; 2 annihilate; 3 participate; 4 investigate; 5 saturate; 6 renovate; 7 perforate; 8 overrate; 9 nominate; 10 infuriate; 11 evaporate; 12 interrogate. (Consult *ALDCE* for examples.)

269 (*Note:* the pronunciation of the final syllable is /eit/) 1 dominate; 2 irrigate; 3 commemorate; 4 emulate; 5 penetrate; 6 anticipate; 7 speculate; 8 rotate; 9 recapitulate; 10 isolate; 11 contemplate; 12 gesticulate. (Consult *ALDCE* for examples.)

270 1 pacify (*or* mollify); 2 indemnifies; 3 fortify; 4 ratified; 5 solidified; 6 testified; 7 mystified; 8 justify; 9 verify; 10 qualify; 11 nullify; 12 amplify.

271 1 purify; 2 clarify; 3 terrify; 4 rectify; 5 notify; 6 falsify; 7 liquefy; 8 classify; 9 intensify; 10 exemplify; 11 unify; 12 typify. (Consult *ALDCE* for examples.)

272 1 fertilize; 2 standardize; 3 mobilize; 4 terrorize; 5 minimize; 6 economize; 7 generalize; 8 authorize; 9 penalize; 10 colonize; 11 jeopardize; 12 legalize. (Consult *ALDCE* for examples.)

273 1 realize; 2 scandalize; 3 improvize; 4 deputize; 5 modernize; 6 apologize; 7 subsidize; 8 specialize; 9 materialize; 10 symbolize; 11 victimize; 12 scrutinize. (Consult *ALDCE* for examples.)

274–282 Consult *ALDCE* for explanations and examples.

283–285 Consult *ALDCE* for explanations and examples.

286–293 Consult *ALDCE* for parallel formations, and for explanations and examples.

294–296 Try the following prefixes, allowing for any necessary spelling changes in individual cases: ab-, ad-, com-, con-, de-, ex-, e-, im-, in-, ob-, per-, pre-, pro-, re-, sub-. Consult *ALDCE* for checking, and for explanations and examples.

297–299 Consult *ALDCE* for parallel formations, and for explanations and examples.

300 (NB. Hyphens are given as in *ALDCE*. In many cases, the two parts of the compound could be written as one word. See *ALDCE* for examples.) 1*a* foolhardy; *b* fool-proof. 2*a* heart-felt; *b* heart-rending; *c* heart-broken. 3*a* stopgap; *b* stop-press; *c* stop-watch. 4*a* headway; *b* headstrong; *c* headline; *d* headquarters. 5*a* foothold; *b* footlights; *c* footfalls.

301 (See note above.) 1*a* overcast (*or* overclouded); *b* overdraft; *c* oversight. 2*a* by-pass; *b* by-law; *c* by-product. 3*a* long-winded; *b* long-suffering; *c* long-standing. 4*a* book-keeper; *c* bookworm; *c* book-rests. 5*a* shop-soiled; *b* shop-lifter; *c* shop-steward.

302 (See note above.) 1*a* handcuffs; *b* handbill; *c* hand-made. 2*a* light-hearted; *b* light-fingered; *c* light-headed. 3*a* stand-offish; *b* standstill; *c* stand-by. 4*a* playgoer; *b* playwright; *c* playground. 5*a* mouthpiece; *b* mouth-organ.

303 (See note above.) 1*a* uproar; *b* upshot; *c* upholstery. 2*a* self-centred; *b* self-evident; *c* self-righteous. 3*a* layman; *b* lay-out; *c* lay-by. 4*a* show-room *or* show-case; *b* show-down; *c* showpiece. 5*a* oil-skin; *b* oil-can; *c* oil-field (*or* oil-well).

304 (See note above.) 1*a* fire-proof; *b* fire-arm; *c* fire-brigade. 2*a* wind-break; *b* wind-screen; *c* wind-fall. 3*a* quick-witted; *b* quick-tempered; *c* quicksand. 4*a* backlog; *b* back-cloth; *c* backbiting. 5*a* eye-opener; *b* eyesore; *c* eye-witness.

305 (NB. Adjectives are given first, then nouns. Consult *ALDCE* for explanations and examples. These lists are not necessarily exhaustive.) 1 persistent; persistence. 2 abstinent; abstinence, abstention, abstainer. 3 competitive; competition, competitor, competitiveness. 4 retentive; retention, retainer, retentiveness. 5 procedural; procedure, process. 6 deep; depth.

306 (See note above.) 1 deceptive, deceitful; deception, deceit. 2 various; variety, variation. 3 grievous; grief. 4 authoritative; authority, authorization. 5 comparative; comparison. 6 exploratory; exploration, explorer.

307 (See note above.) 1 defiant; defiance. 2 explanatory; explanation. 3 explosive; explosion, explosive. 4 irritable; irritation, irritability. 5 imitative; imitation, imitator. 6 observant; observer, observation, observatory.

308 (See note above.) dependent; dependence, dependant. 2 conceptual; conception, concept. 3 attentive, attendant; attendant, attendance, attention. 4 fallible; failure, failing. 5 hasty; haste. 6 fertile; fertility, fertilization, fertilizer.

309 (See note above.) 1 migratory; migration, migrant. 2 sympathetic; sympathy. 3 repetitive; repetition, repeat. 4 presumptuous; presumption. 5 analytical; analysis. 6 fraudulent; fraud.

310 (See note above.) 1 simple; simplification, simplicity. 2 defensive; defence, defendant, defender. 3 conclusive; conclusion. 4 healthy; health. 5 vigorous; vigour. 6 apologetic; apology.

311 (See note above.) 1 apparent; appearance, apparition. 2 distinctive, distinct; distinction. 3 repulsive, repellent; repulse, repulsion. 4 memorable; memory, memorial, remembrance. 5 interpretative; interpretation, interpreter. 6 cumbersome; encumbrance.

312 (See note above.) 1 revelatory; revelation. 2 vengeful; vengeance. 3 broadcast; broadcast. 4 emphatic; emphasis. 5 excessive; excess. 6 resolute; resolution, resolve.

313 (See note above.) 1 continuous, continual; continuation, continuity. 2 exemplificatory; example, exemplification. 3 foreseeable; foresight. 4 submissive; submission. 5 informative; information, informant. 6 prosperous; prosperity.

314–323 Consult *ALDCE* for explanations and examples.

324 1 aloud; 2 blew; 3 bury; 4 serial; 5 daze; 6 rode *or* rowed; 7 hire; 8 quay; 9 knows; 10 mail. (Consult *ALDCE* for explanations and examples.)

325 1 hoarse; 2 minor; 3 peer; 4 principal; 5 guilt; 6 sore *or* soar; 7 threw; 8 weigh; 9 ware *or* where; 10 bored. (Consult *ALDCE* for explanations and examples.)

326 1 court; 2 queue; 3 dye; 4 guessed; 5 leased; 6 mourning; 7 prays *or* preys; 8 stair; 9 tacks; 10 weather. (Consult *ALDCE* for explanations and examples.)

327 1 bold; 2 sealing; 3 phrase; 4 whole; 5 herd; 6 won; 7 pear *or* pare; 8 paced; 9 rein *or* reign; 10 scent *or* cent. (Consult *ALDCE* for explanations and examples.)

328 1 bare; 2 coarse; 3 fare; 4 feat; 5 haul; 6 pour; 7 past; 8 rays *or* raze; 9 cell; 10 tyre. (Consult *ALDCE* for explanations and examples.)

329 1 cruise; 2 flour; 3 idol; 4 peace; 5 site; 6 suite; 7 sought; 8 wore; 9 source; 10 stake. (Consult *ALDCE* for explanations and examples.)

330 locomotive, tender, rails, sleepers, carriage, compartment; chain, inner tube, saddle, mudguard, handlebars, pedals; trial, court, plaintiff, counsel, fine, sentence; (unrelated) eraser, palace, offer, impudence, attempt, reins.

331 gramophone, needle, loudspeaker, amplifier, turntable, record; receiver, slot, caller, directory, dial, exchange; armchair, suite, bureau, chest, sofa, divan; (unrelated) pin, suit, visitor, catalogue, convict, office.

332 session, speaker, constituency, cabinet, debate, parliament; cheque, account, overdraft, loan, safe, bankrupt; hangar, propeller, fuselage, stewardess, cockpit, navigator; (unrelated) extension, truce, poster, kerb, draughtsman, decrease.

333 warehouse, port, dock, quay, cargo, barge; bough, twig, bark, branch, log, trunk; eiderdown, bedstead, bolster, mattress, blanket, sheets; (unrelated) platform, sherry, dog, mist, concrete, subsidiary.

334 clutch, engine, windscreen, boot, indicator, dashboard; chimney, mortar, drainpipe, tiles, loft, gutter; switch, socket, bulb, flex, lamp, shade; (unrelated) grasp, seed, wallet, shoes, calendar, shadow.

335 ladder, flight, rung, landing, banisters, stairs; congregation, eye-witnesses, sightseers, audience, spectators, onlookers; bridge, port-hole, cabin, hold, funnel, deck; (unrelated) leak, tunnel, ornament, retreat, grip, boycott.

336 1 find it out; 2 ruled it out; 3 looking after it; 4 give it away; 5 blurt it out; 6 looked at it; 7 bringing it (*or* them) out; 8 put them forward; 9 put it away/get at it; 10 try them out; 11 adding it (*or* them) up; 12 goes for them; 13 stirring it up; 14 took to him.

337 (NB. alternatives in brackets are possible, but less likely on stylistic grounds.) 1 brushed aside all objections *or* brushed all objections aside; 2 brushed aside all objections made . . .; 3 hand over the man who . . .; 4 take the job on *or* take on the job; 5 take on the captaincy of . . .; 6 wraps up his arguments *or* wraps his arguments up; 7 bring about an improvement (*or* bring an improvement about); 8 putting in some very heavy claims *or* putting some very heavy claims in; 9 keep their production costs down *or* keep down their production costs; 10 handed over the confidential papers . . .; 11 trying out many new synthetic products (*or* trying many new synthetic products out); 12 brought the question up *or* brought up the question; 13 brought up the questions everyone . . .; 14 read quickly through the letter.

338 (NB. Particles marked with an asterisk are prepositions.) 1 turned down his request; 2 turn up; 3 turned in; 4 turn down the gas *or* turn the gas down; 5 turned him out; 6 turn out his pockets *or* turn his pockets out; 7 turned away from; 8 turned out; 9 turned out; 10 turned over; 11 turn on*.

339 (See note above.) 1 getting on; 2 get through*; 3 get over*; 4 get at*; 5 get it over; 6 got away; 7 get him down; 8 get down to*; 9 getting round*; 10 get on; 11 getting on for*.

340 (See note above.) 1 take up French; 2 takes after*; 3 took over the business (*or* took the business over); 4 taken in; 5 took on; 6 took down the letter *or* took the letter down); 7 took back all he . . .; 8 take to*; 9 take up too much . . .; 10 take off.

341 (See note above.) 1 put off my visit (*or* put my visit off); 2 put up with*; 3 put out; 4 put down; 5 put by quite a lot . . .; 6 put forward the theory; 7 put down; 8 put in; 9 put you off; 10 put in a claim . . .; 11 put on an air . . .; 12 put me up.

342 (See note above.) 1 stand for*; 2 stands for*; 3 stand for*; 4 stand by*; 5 stood out; 6 stand down; 7 stand by; 8 stand in for*; 9 stand aside; 10 stand up to*.

343 (See note above.) 1 came across*; 2 came round (*or* to); 3 came into*; 4 came about; 5 come off; 6 come out; 7 came out; 8 come up to*; 9 come out of*; 10 always comes up.

344 (See note above.) 1 gave up; 2 give up; 3 give in; 4 gave back the money *or* gave the money back; 5 gave off; 6 give out; 7 give out much heat (*or* give much heat out); 8 give up smoking (*or* give smoking up); 9 gave him away.

345 withdraw *or* break; 2 was very-well received; 3 enter; 4 continued; 5 discuss *or* examine; 6 study; 7 rose; 8 been built *or* been erected; 9 took; 10 explode; 11 return; 12 left *or* disappeared.

346 1 visit; 2 inspect *or* view; 3 investigate the matter further; 4 respect; 5 despises; 6 regarded; 7 call; 8 read *or* study; 9 expected; 10 improving.

347 1 come back; 2 go on *or* carry on; 3 pulled down; 4 take off; 5 stay up; 6 staying in; 7 going up; 8 put down; 9 touched down; 10 slowed down.

348 1 leave out; 2 turning in; 3 open out; 4 kept in; 5 put up; 6 stuck in; 7 laid off; 8 hung up *or* rung off; 9 turned down; 10 looks down on.

349* 1 You must cut down your expenses. 2 We say he picks things up quickly. 3 It would be called off. 4 They'd draw up an agreement. 5 I can't shake this cold off. 6 What have you been up to? 7 Would you bear me out on this? 8 We're expected to pick him out. 9 There isn't enough to go round. 10 It's a well thought out plan. 11 He must pull up; 12 I'll think it over. 13 I'd want to try it out; 12 The mine is worked out.

350* 1 It might have to fall back. 2 He has let us down. 3 The school has broken up (for the holidays). 4 I can't make this out. 5 When you want to look a word up. 6 One sets out in good time. 7 They would like to think they are well brought up. 8 They may fall out for a time. 9 The party may break up. 10 He might let him off. 11 The plan might fall through. 12 The one sets off the other.

351* 1 You must fall back on old or existing methods. 2 He would expect the teacher to point it out. 3 It's about time you made up your mind (*or* made your mind up). 4 The bad weather seems to have set in. 5 It would annoy me if the car broke down. 6 He would make off as quickly as possible. 7 I'd try to bring him round (*or* to). 8 The circulation has fallen off. 9 It could set up a Royal Commission or a Committee of Inquiry. 10 I'd immediately break off and talk about something else. 11 The possibility cannot be ruled out. 12 We must try to make up for lost time.

352 1 set-back; 2 intake; 3 offshoot; 4 outcry; 5 lay-offs; 6 upkeep; 7 outbreak; 8 break-out; 9 bypass; 10 look-over; 11 outlook; 12 uptake.

353 1 cut-back; 2 breakdown; 3 outlay/lay-out; 4 shake-up; 5 upturn; 6 upsurge; 7 downfall; 8 take-over/outlets; 9 break-through; 10 change-over; 11 turnover; 12 come-back.

354 1 show-down; 2 stand-by; 3 write-off; 4 drawbacks; 5 blast-off/splash-down; 6 hold-up; 7 come-down; 8 walk-out; 9 look-out; 10 outcome; 11 tie-up; 12 outburst.

355 1 crises ('kraisi:z); 2 cargoes/wharves; 3 parents-in-law; 4 gases/buses; 5 indexes; 6 indices; 7 heroes; 8 mice/mousetraps; 9 fungi *or* funguses; 10 memoranda; 11 phenomena; 12 hypotheses (hai'pɔθisi:z); 13 courts martial; 14 syllabuses (*or* syllabi) criteria; 15 media; 16 thieves/passers-by; 17 solos; 18 eyewitnesses; 19 alibis.

356 1 is making good progress; 2 a risky situation (there had been a narrow margin between safety and disaster); 3 stoppage caused by a problem; 4 the Company has been received with wild enthusiasm; 5 the ordinary members of his party who have no special responsibilities or position as members of the Government; 6 subject of dispute or disagreement; 7 the greatest prominence or admiration; 8 in better condition/free from troubles or difficulties; 9 remain neutral, not make up their minds; 10 puts its own affairs straight; 11 experiencing the painful consequences; 12 giving very little indication of his intentions; 13 reached a crisis.

357 1 spend money as soon as it is earned, save nothing; 2 weakened, made less drastic or less far-reaching; 3 a small innovation likely to lead to much larger (and undesirable) ones; 4 a share or financial interest; 5 opportunities for evasion; 6 at once, without giving it due consideration; 7 criticized or reproved/acting according to his own ideas or opinion; 8 ostracized; 9 will be given only brief attention or consideration; 10 good reviews in the newspapers; 11 postpone considering further or putting into operation; 12 time-limit; 13 known generally/accept and follow decisions taken collectively.

358 1 This plan fails through indecisiveness to meet the needs of either of two alternative situations. 2 He's pretending to act out of a sense of what is morally right, whereas in fact he is acting under compulsion. 3 Everything was in a muddle. 4 She can't live within her income. 5 I don't believe everything he says—he often exaggerates. 6 He's in a position (socially or at work) for which he is unsuited. 7 They are close partners (generally in some dubious or illegal enterprise). 8 He has nothing to support his opinion or claim. 9 They managed to do it (get there, find it, etc.) before we did. 10 You've drawn the right conclusion, or said exactly the right thing. 11 You should meet the difficulty decisively and with courage. 12 We're all in the same difficult situation. 13 He has already planned several other possibilities for employment. 14 I challenged him to do what he threatened to do (to test whether he really meant it). 15 Let's be quite open about our plans or intentions.

359 For comment or composition. Consult *ALDCE* for explanations, and the first book in *List A* (page xvii) for comment.

360–361 Composition exercises.

362–363 Comprehension and composition exercises.

364–373 Consult appropriate books in *List C* (page xviii).

374 *O.H.M.S.*, On Her (His) Majesty's Service; *Y.M.C.A.*, Young Men's Christian Association; *R.S.P.C.A.*, Royal Society for the Prevention of Cruelty to Animals; *G.M.T.*, Greenwich Mean Time; *G.P.O.*, General Post Office; *H.P.*, horse-power; hire purchase; *c/o*, (used in addressing letters to somebody in the) care of; *Lib.*, Liberal (in politics); *e.g.*, (Latin *exempli gratis*) for example; *PS.*, postscript; *IOU*, I owe you; *I.T.A.*, Independent Television Authority; *B.B.C.*, British Broadcasting Corporation; *T.U.C.*, Trades Union Congress; *P.T.O.*, please turn over; *C.I.D.*, Criminal Investigation Department; *M.A.*, Master of Arts; *f.o.b.*, (commercial use) free on board.

375 *C.O.D.*, cash (to be paid) on delivery; *R.S.V.P.*, (French *Répondez s'il vous plaît*) = Please reply; *No.*, number (plural *Nos.*); *B.O.A.C.*, British Overseas Airways Corporation; *F.R.S.*, Fellow of the Royal Society; *A.A.*, Automobile Association; *Lab.*, Labour (in politics); *c.i.f.*, (commercial use) cost, insurance, freight; *fig.*, figure, diagram; *H.R.H.*, Her (His) Royal Highness; *G.P.*, General Practitioner; *V.I.P.*, very important person; *oz.*, ounce; *Cantab.*, of Cambridge University; *G.C.E.*, General Certificate of Education; *B.Sc.*, Bachelor of Science; *Cons.*, Conservative (in politics); *i.e.*, (Latin *id est*) that is.